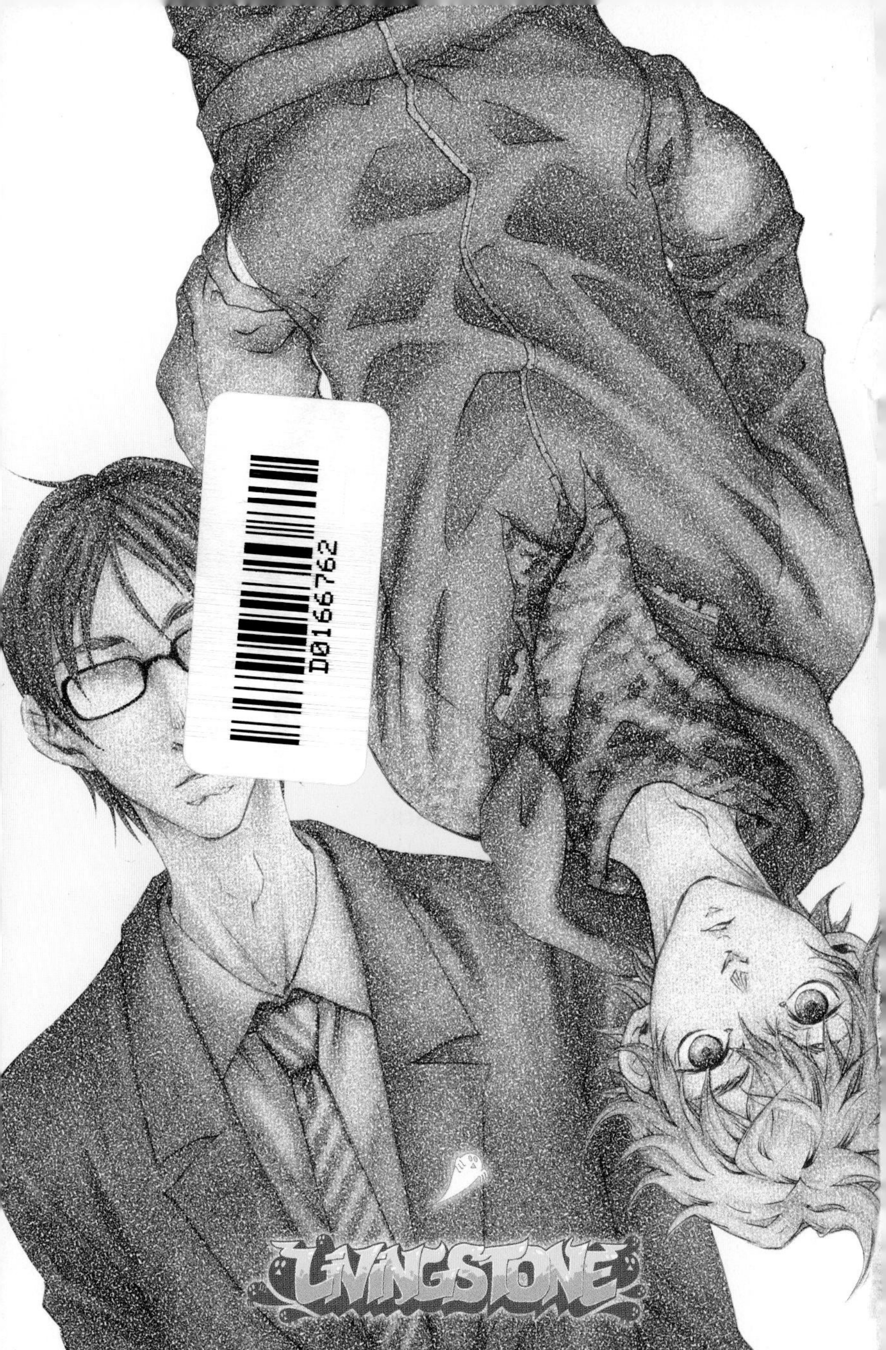

LIVINGSTONE

4

Story: Tomohiro Maekawa

Manga: Jinsei Kataoka

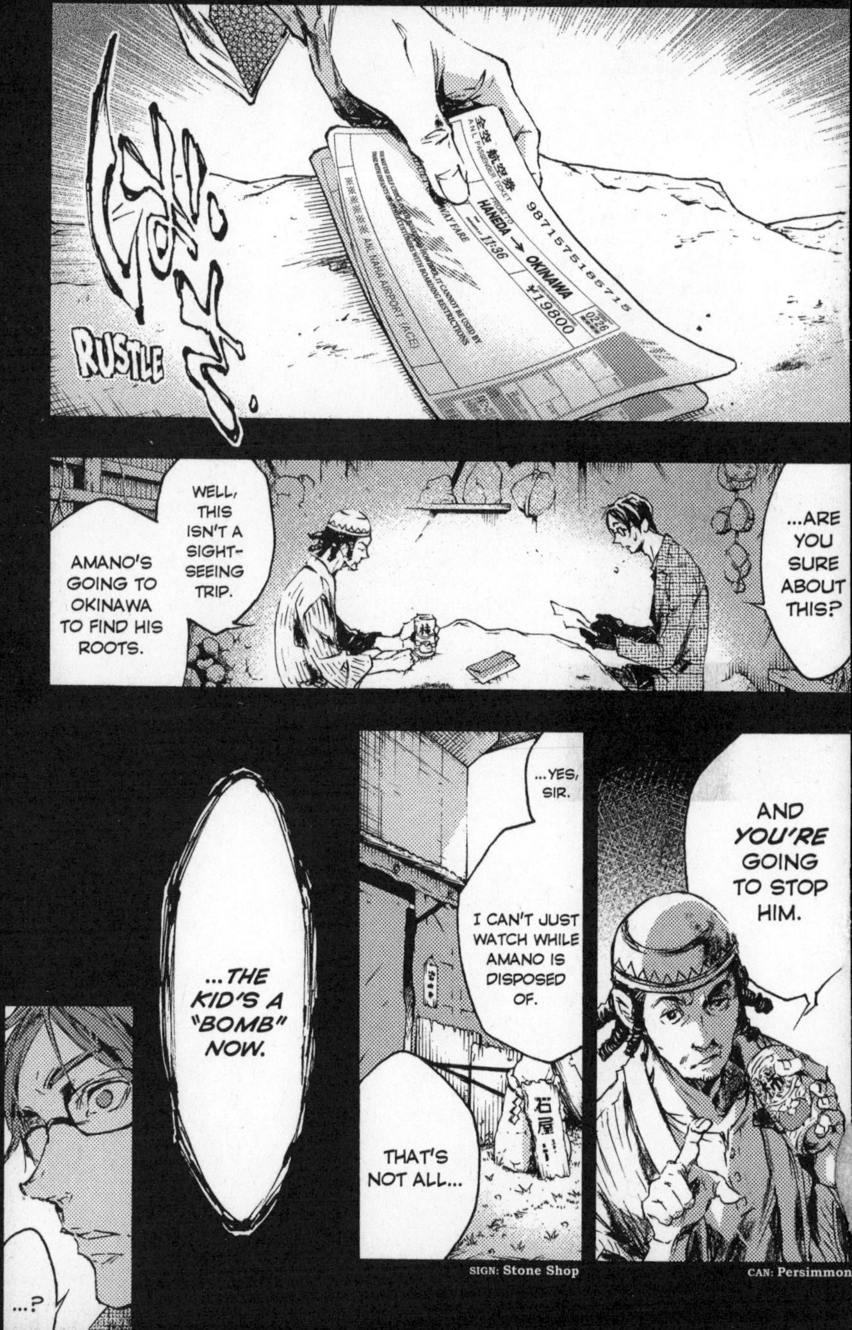
全空 航空券
ANL PASSENGER TICKET
9871575185715
HANEDA → OKINAWA
11:36
¥19800
RUSTLE
...ARE YOU SURE ABOUT THIS?
WELL, THIS ISN'T A SIGHT-SEEING TRIP.
AMANO'S GOING TO OKINAWA TO FIND HIS ROOTS.
AND *YOU'RE* GOING TO STOP HIM.
...YES, SIR.
I CAN'T JUST WATCH WHILE AMANO IS DISPOSED OF.
THAT'S NOT ALL...
石屋
...*THE KID'S A "BOMB" NOW.*
...?

SIGN: Stone Shop

CAN: Persimmon

Chapter 18 ✚ Time for Resolve

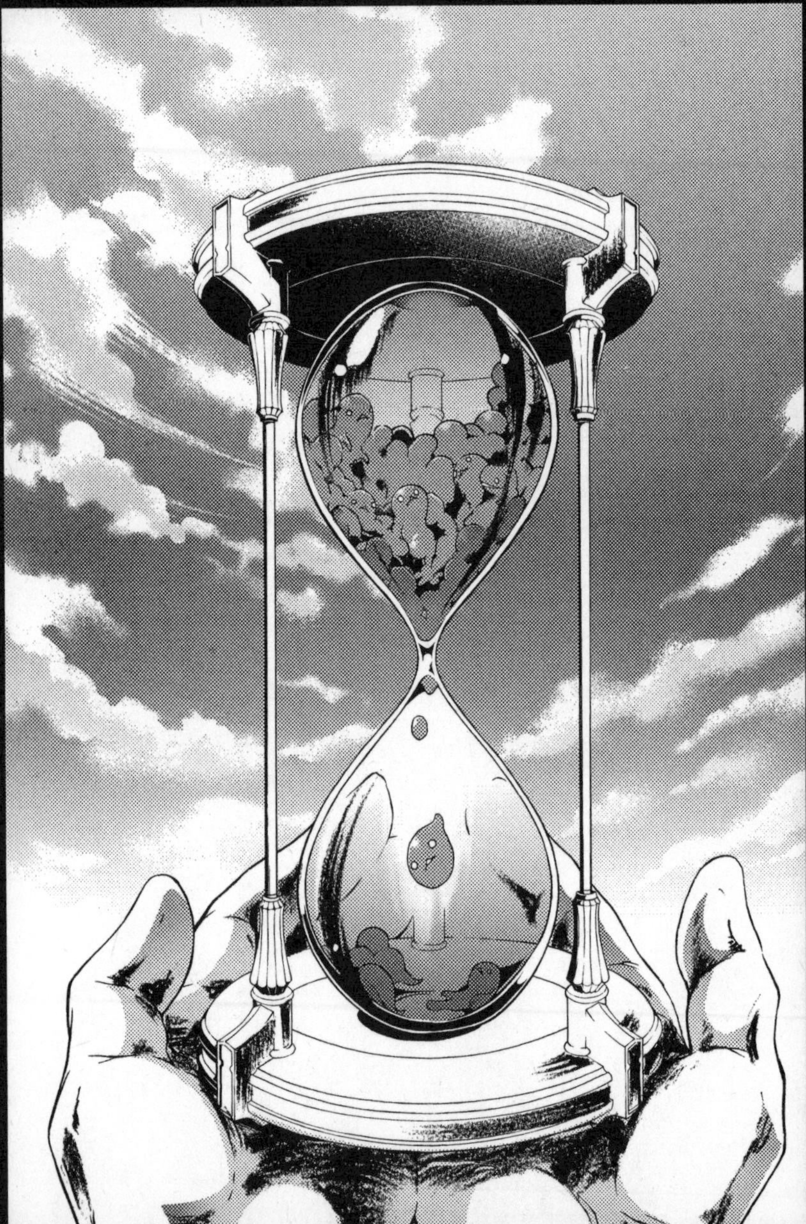

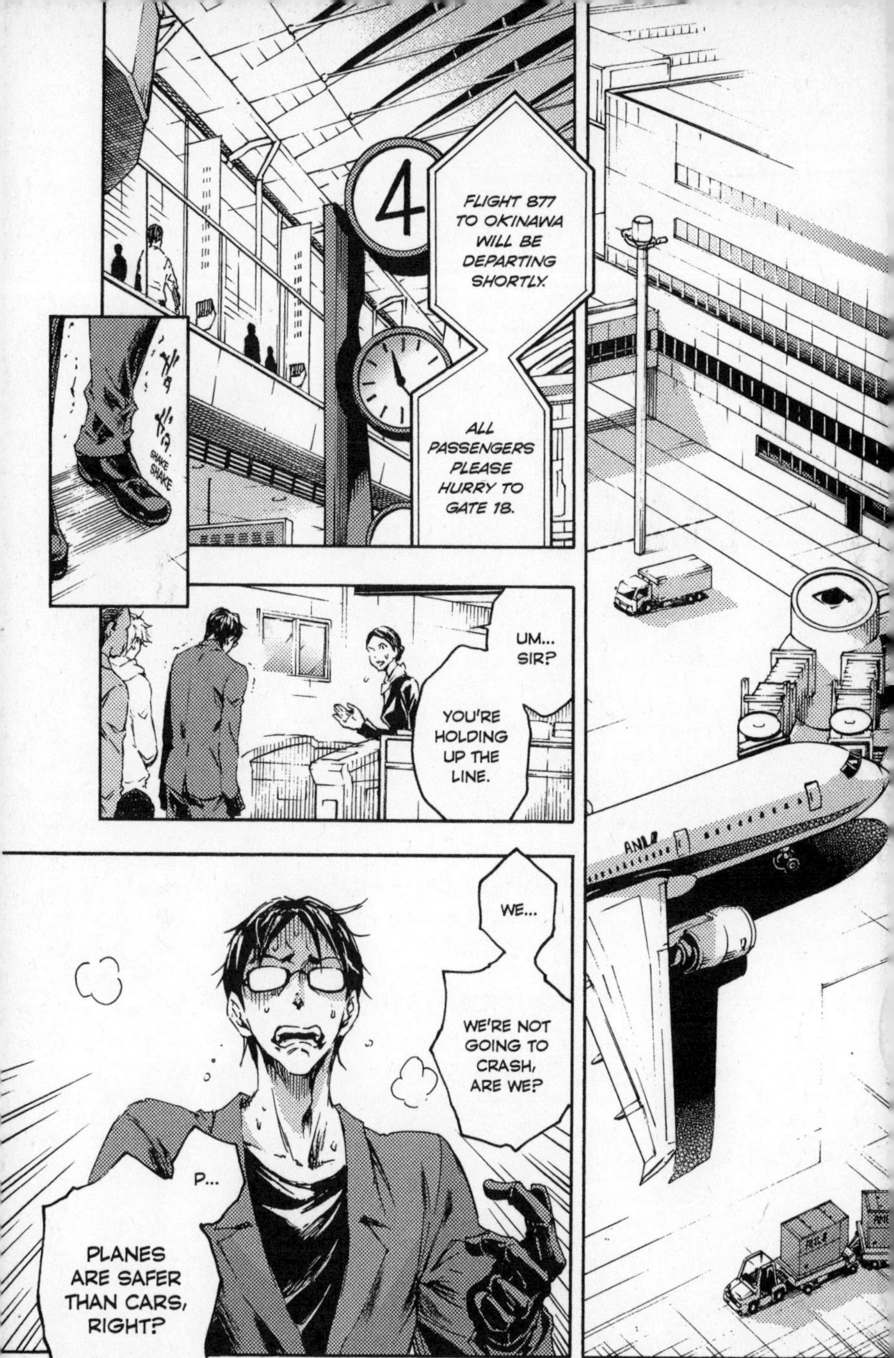
4
FLIGHT 877 TO OKINAWA WILL BE DEPARTING SHORTLY.
ALL PASSENGERS PLEASE HURRY TO GATE 18.
SHAKE SHAKE
UM... SIR?
YOU'RE HOLDING UP THE LINE.
WE...
WE'RE NOT GOING TO CRASH, ARE WE?
P...
PLANES ARE SAFER THAN CARS, RIGHT?

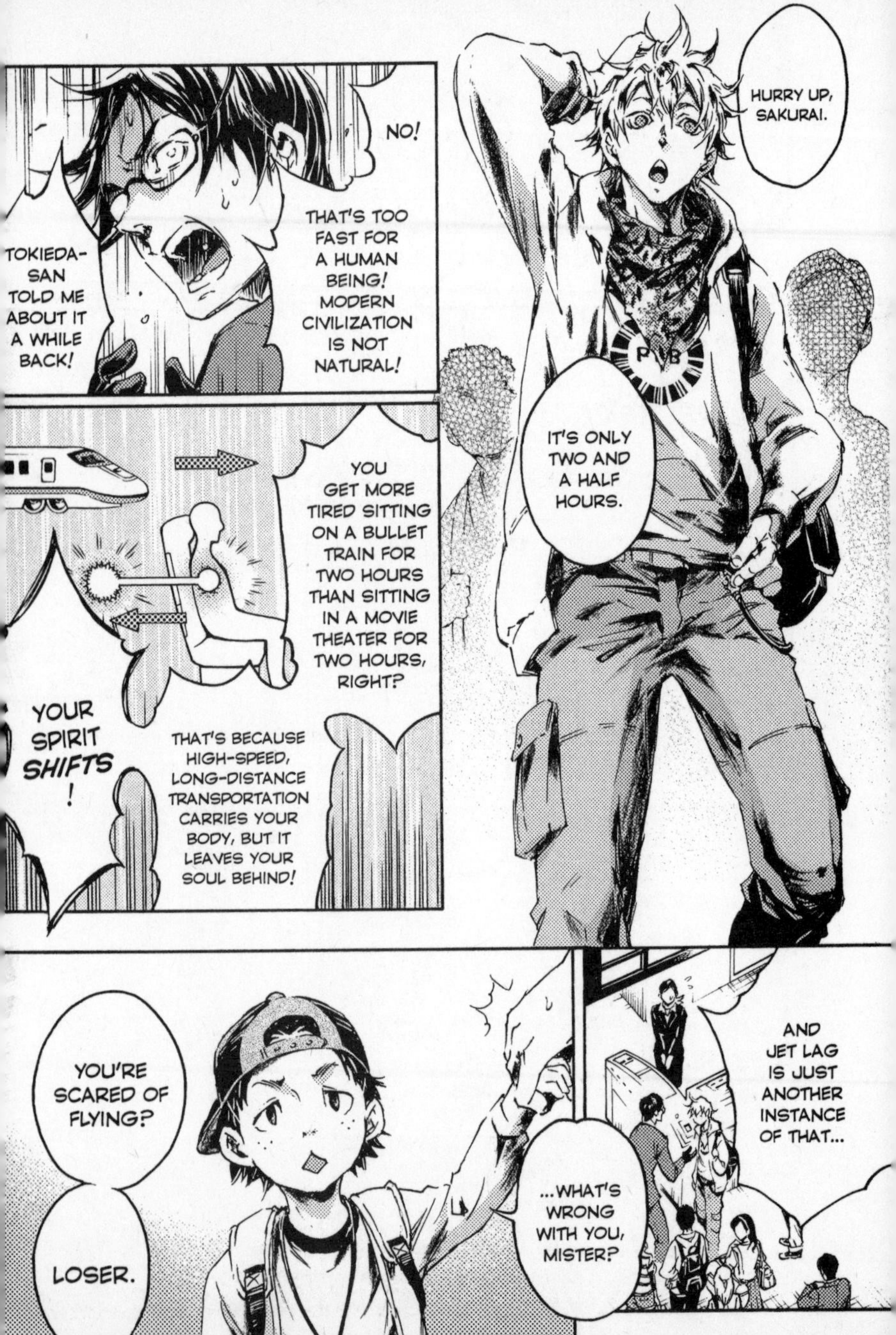
HURRY UP, SAKURAI.
IT'S ONLY TWO AND A HALF HOURS.
NO!
THAT'S TOO FAST FOR A HUMAN BEING! MODERN CIVILIZATION IS NOT NATURAL!
TOKIEDA-SAN TOLD ME ABOUT IT A WHILE BACK!
YOU GET MORE TIRED SITTING ON A BULLET TRAIN FOR TWO HOURS THAN SITTING IN A MOVIE THEATER FOR TWO HOURS, RIGHT?
THAT'S BECAUSE HIGH-SPEED, LONG-DISTANCE TRANSPORTATION CARRIES YOUR BODY, BUT IT LEAVES YOUR SOUL BEHIND!
YOUR SPIRIT *SHIFTS*!
AND JET LAG IS JUST ANOTHER INSTANCE OF THAT...
...WHAT'S WRONG WITH YOU, MISTER?
YOU'RE SCARED OF FLYING?
LOSER.

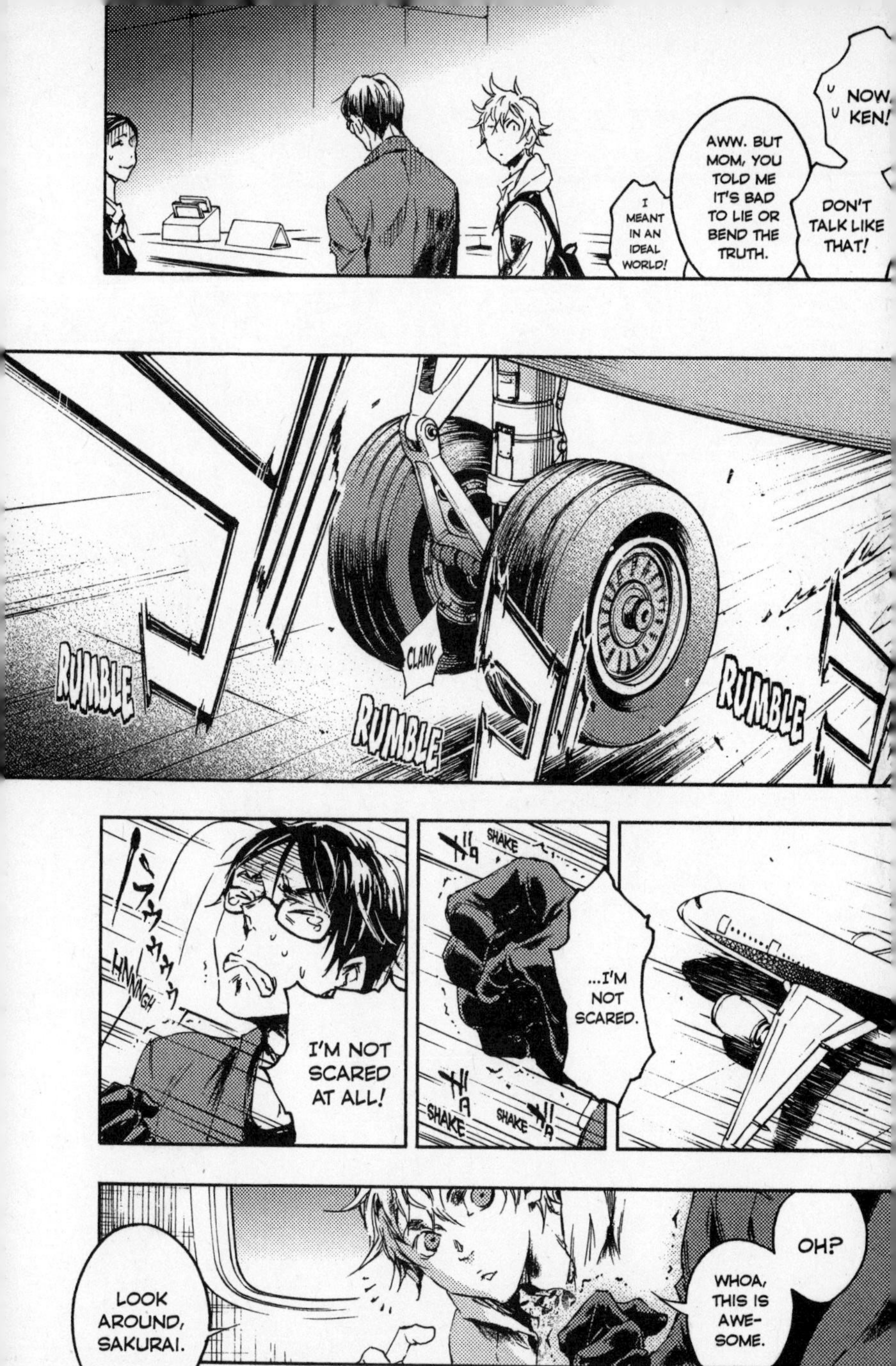
NOW, KEN!
DON'T TALK LIKE THAT!
AWW. BUT MOM, YOU TOLD ME IT'S BAD TO LIE OR BEND THE TRUTH.
I MEANT IN AN IDEAL WORLD!
RUMBLE
CLANK
RUMBLE
RUMBLE
SHAKE
...I'M NOT SCARED.
SHAKE
SHAKE
I'M NOT SCARED AT ALL!
HNNNNGH
OH?
WHOA, THIS IS AWE-SOME.
LOOK AROUND, SAKURAI.

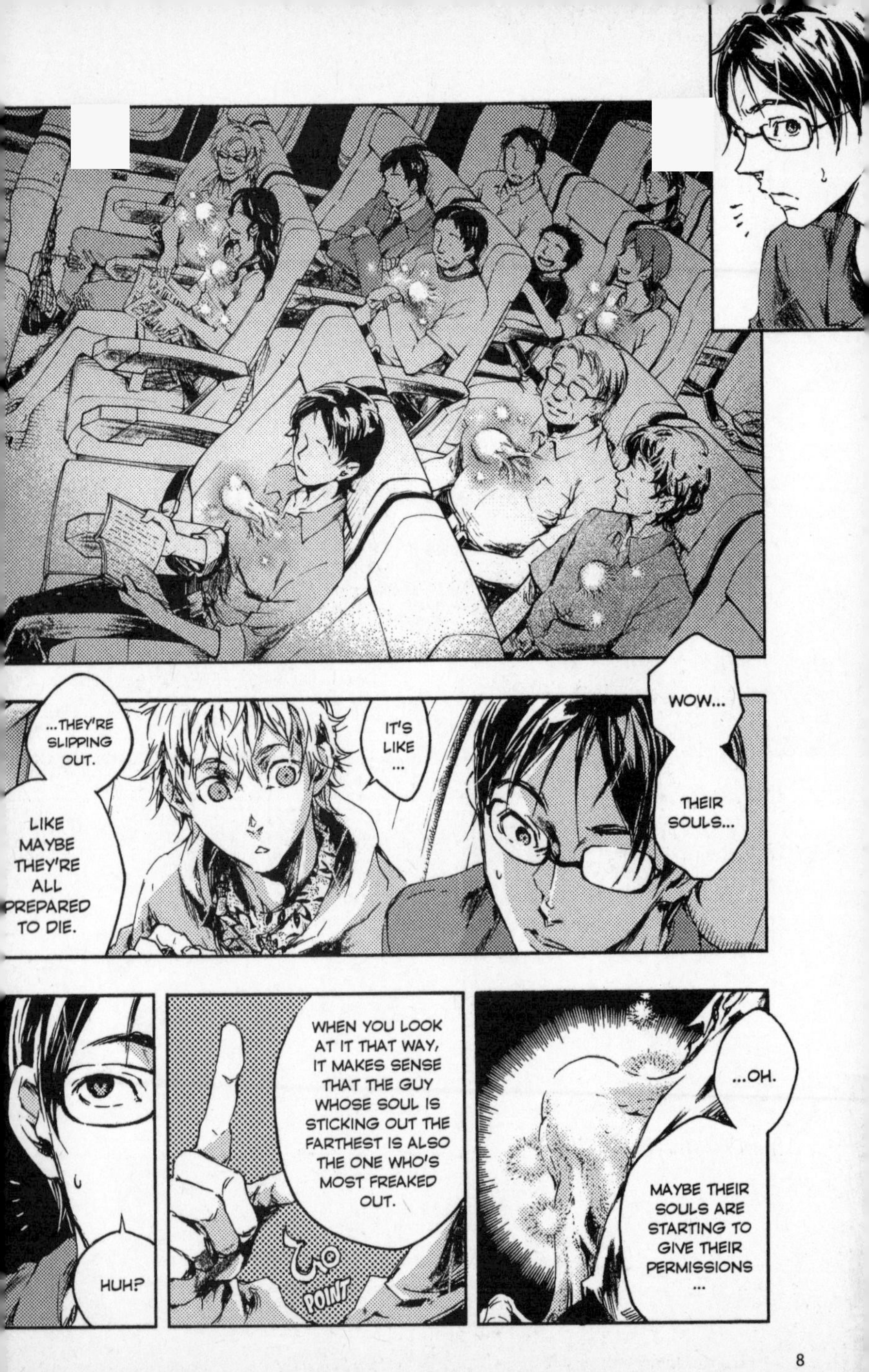
WOW...
THEIR SOULS...
IT'S LIKE ...
...THEY'RE SLIPPING OUT.
LIKE MAYBE THEY'RE ALL PREPARED TO DIE.
...OH.
MAYBE THEIR SOULS ARE STARTING TO GIVE THEIR PERMISSIONS ...
WHEN YOU LOOK AT IT THAT WAY, IT MAKES SENSE THAT THE GUY WHOSE SOUL IS STICKING OUT THE FARTHEST IS ALSO THE ONE WHO'S MOST FREAKED OUT.
POINT
HUH?

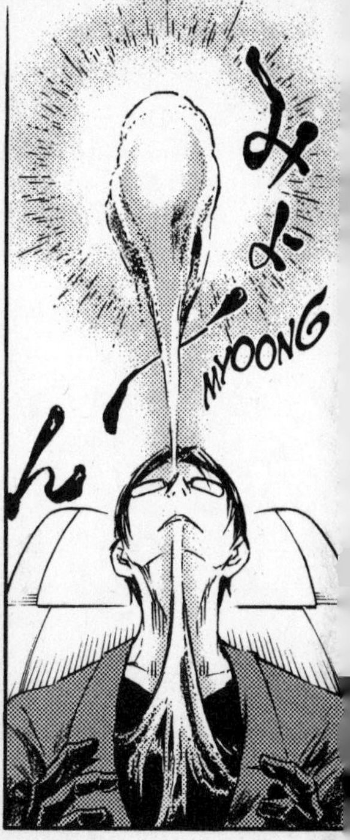
みょ〜ん
MYOONG
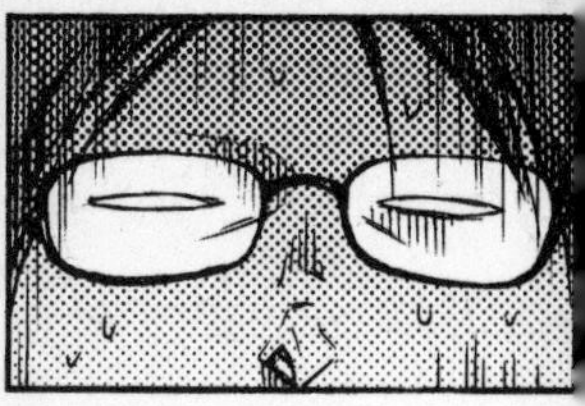
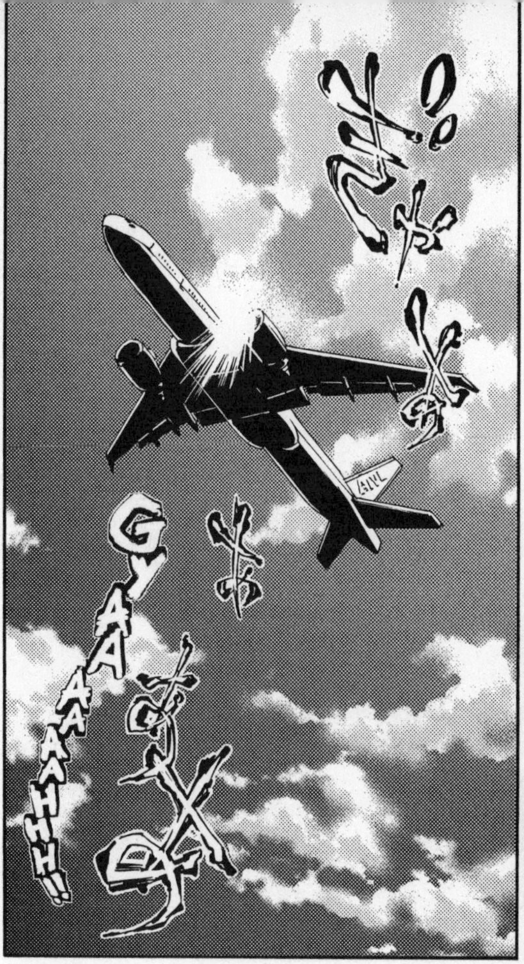
GYAAAAAAHHH!!
[redacted]
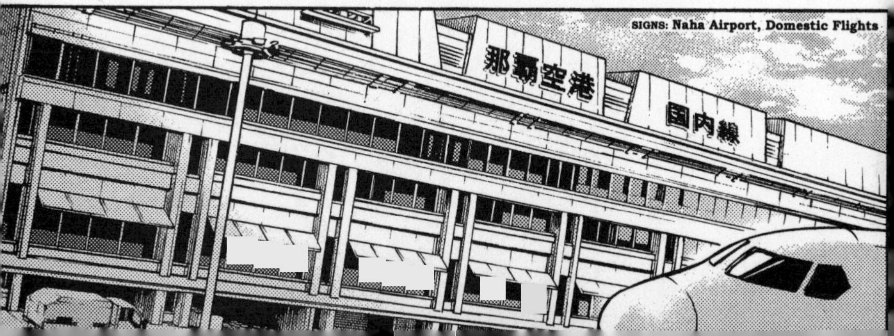
SIGNS: Naha Airport, Domestic Flights
那覇空港
国内線

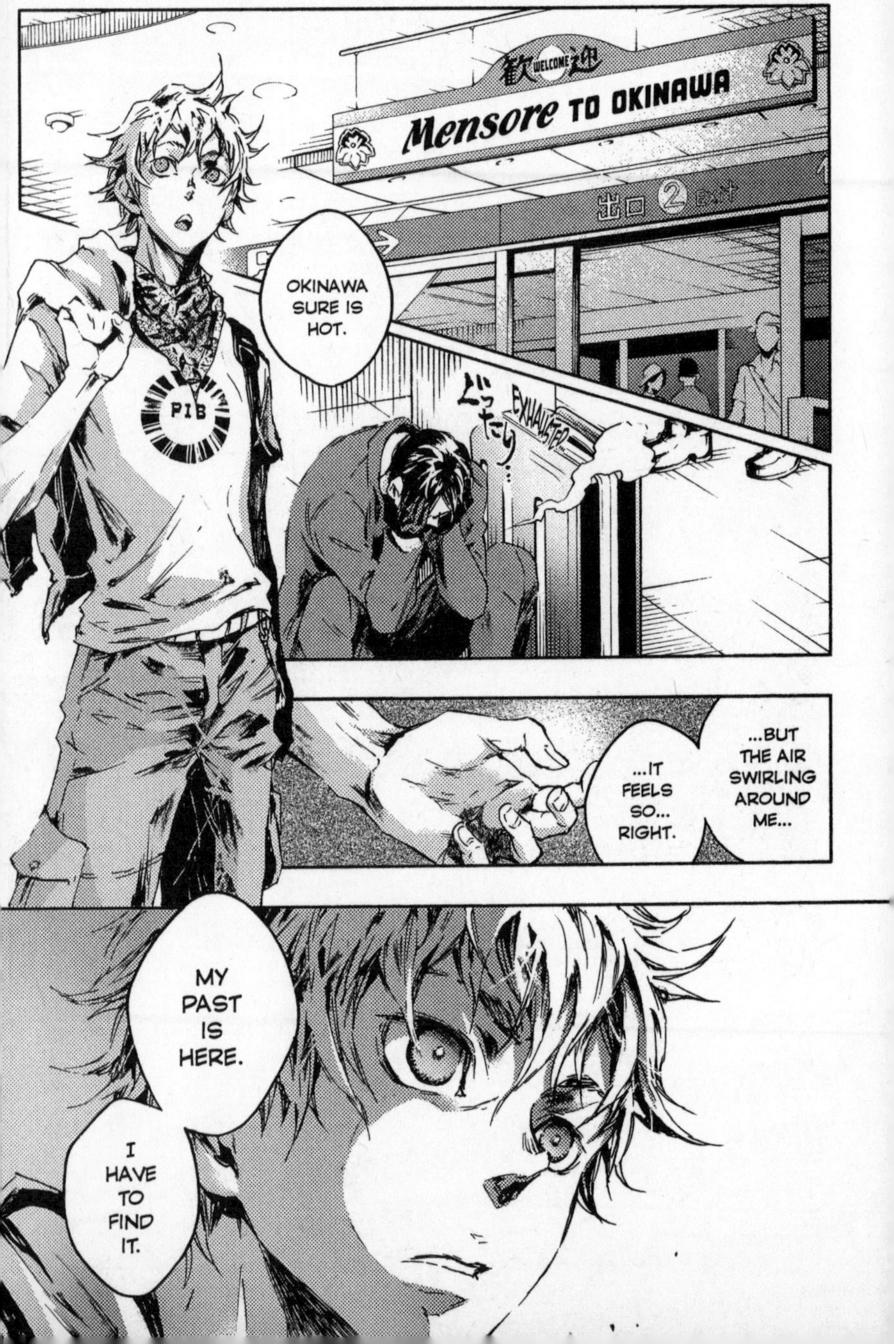
歓 WELCOME 迎
Mensore TO OKINAWA
出口 2 EXIT
OKINAWA SURE IS HOT.
ぐったり…
EXHAUSTED...
...BUT THE AIR SWIRLING AROUND ME...
...IT FEELS SO... RIGHT.
MY PAST IS HERE.
I HAVE TO FIND IT.

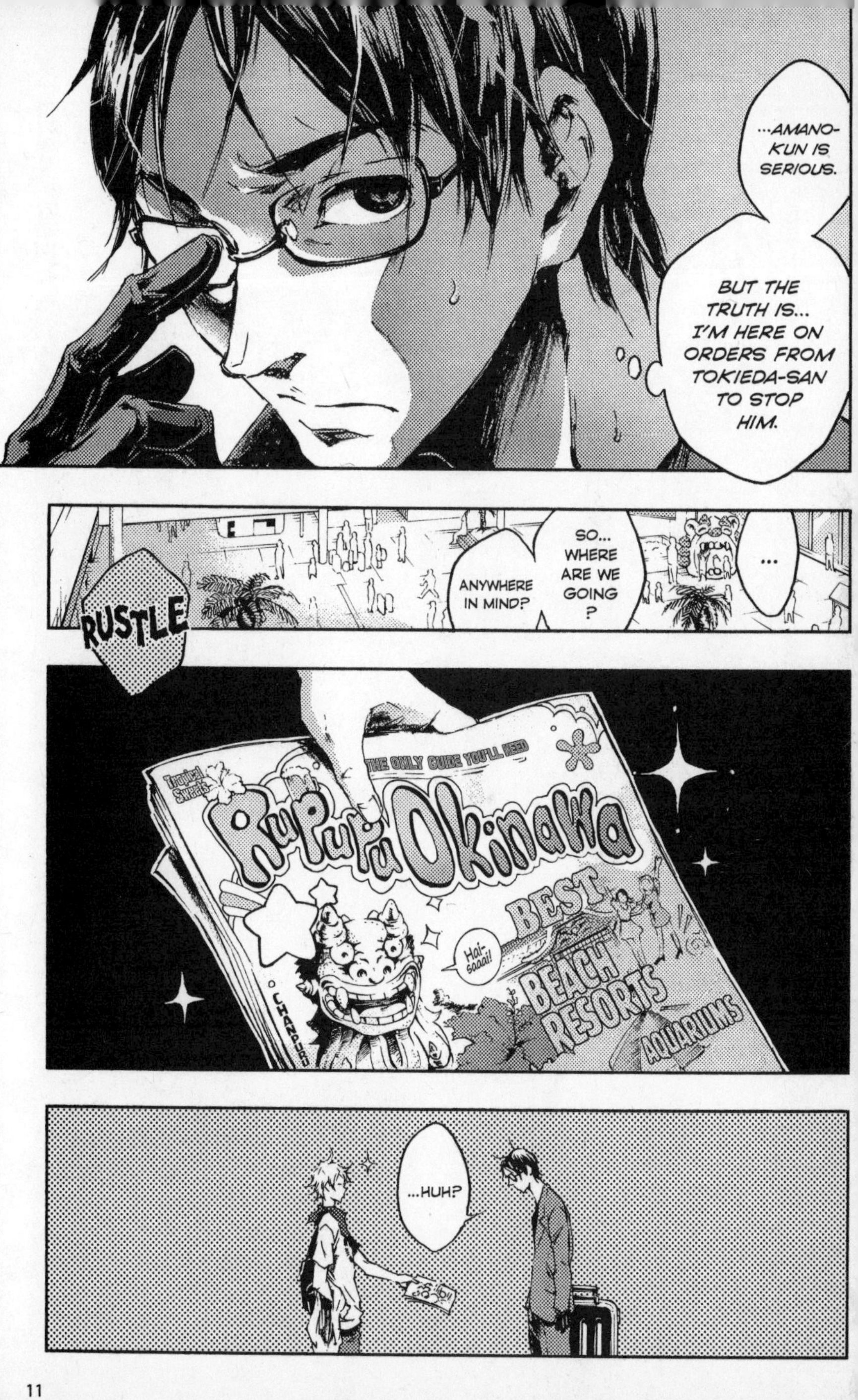
...AMANO-KUN IS SERIOUS.
BUT THE TRUTH IS... I'M HERE ON ORDERS FROM TOKIEDA-SAN TO STOP HIM.
...
SO... WHERE ARE WE GOING?
ANYWHERE IN MIND?
RUSTLE
THE ONLY GUIDE YOU'LL NEED
RuPuPu Okinawa
BEST BEACH RESORTS
Hai-saaai!
AQUARIUMS
...HUH?

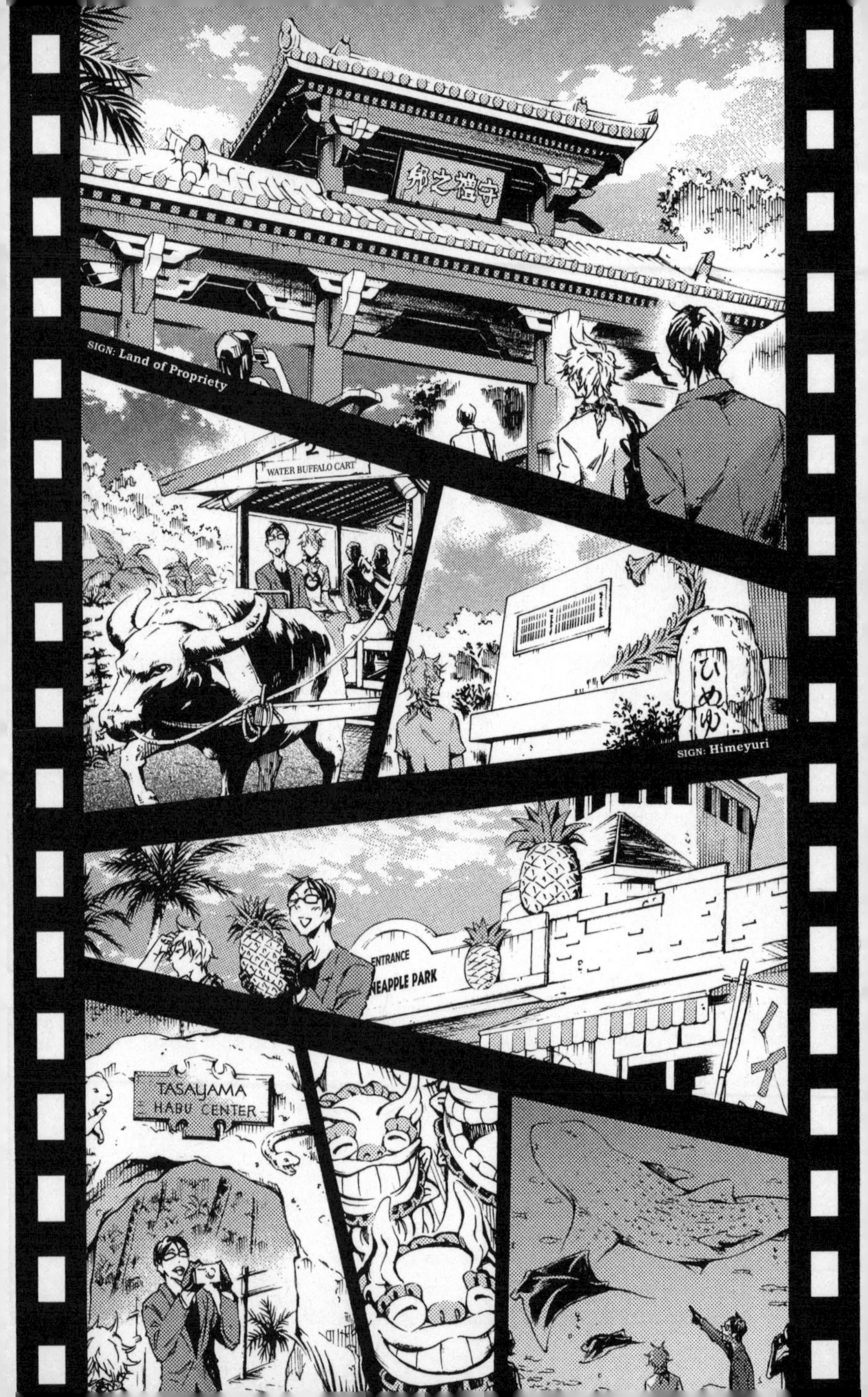
守禮之邦
SIGN: Land of Propriety
ひめゆ
SIGN: Himeyuri
2
WATER BUFFALO CART
ENTRANCE
NEAPPLE PARK
TASAYAMA
HABU CENTER

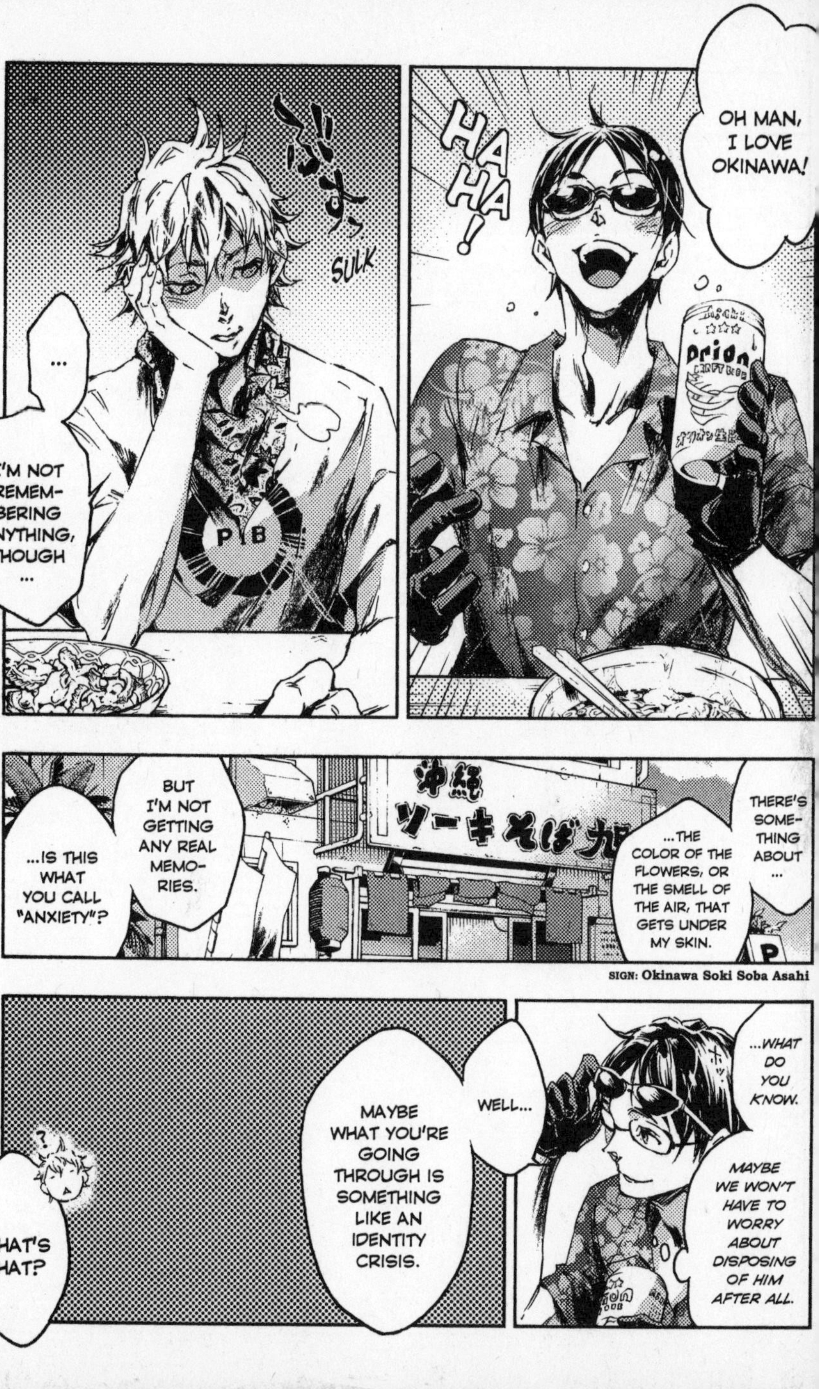
HAHA!
OH MAN, I LOVE OKINAWA!
Orion
ぶすっ
SULK
...
I'M NOT REMEMBERING ANYTHING, THOUGH ...
THERE'S SOMETHING ABOUT ...
...THE COLOR OF THE FLOWERS, OR THE SMELL OF THE AIR, THAT GETS UNDER MY SKIN.
沖縄
ソーキそば
BUT I'M NOT GETTING ANY REAL MEMORIES.
...IS THIS WHAT YOU CALL "ANXIETY"?
ホッ
...WHAT DO YOU KNOW.
MAYBE WE WON'T HAVE TO WORRY ABOUT DISPOSING OF HIM AFTER ALL.
WELL...
MAYBE WHAT YOU'RE GOING THROUGH IS SOMETHING LIKE AN IDENTITY CRISIS.
WHAT'S THAT?

SIGN: Okinawa Soki Soba Asahi

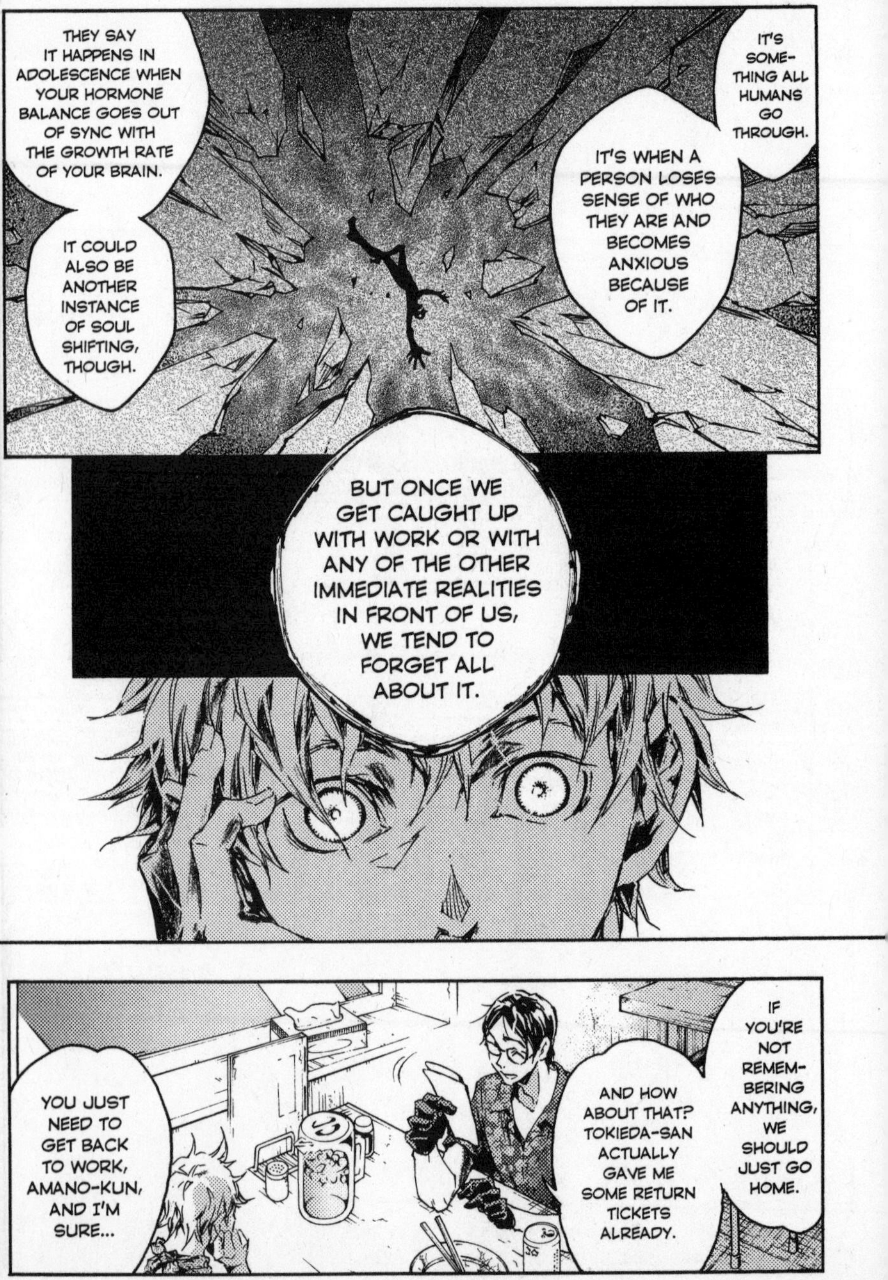
IT'S SOME-THING ALL HUMANS GO THROUGH.
IT'S WHEN A PERSON LOSES SENSE OF WHO THEY ARE AND BECOMES ANXIOUS BECAUSE OF IT.
THEY SAY IT HAPPENS IN ADOLESCENCE WHEN YOUR HORMONE BALANCE GOES OUT OF SYNC WITH THE GROWTH RATE OF YOUR BRAIN.
IT COULD ALSO BE ANOTHER INSTANCE OF SOUL SHIFTING, THOUGH.
BUT ONCE WE GET CAUGHT UP WITH WORK OR WITH ANY OF THE OTHER IMMEDIATE REALITIES IN FRONT OF US, WE TEND TO FORGET ALL ABOUT IT.
IF YOU'RE NOT REMEM-BERING ANYTHING, WE SHOULD JUST GO HOME.
AND HOW ABOUT THAT? TOKIEDA-SAN ACTUALLY GAVE ME SOME RETURN TICKETS ALREADY.
YOU JUST NEED TO GET BACK TO WORK, AMANO-KUN, AND I'M SURE...

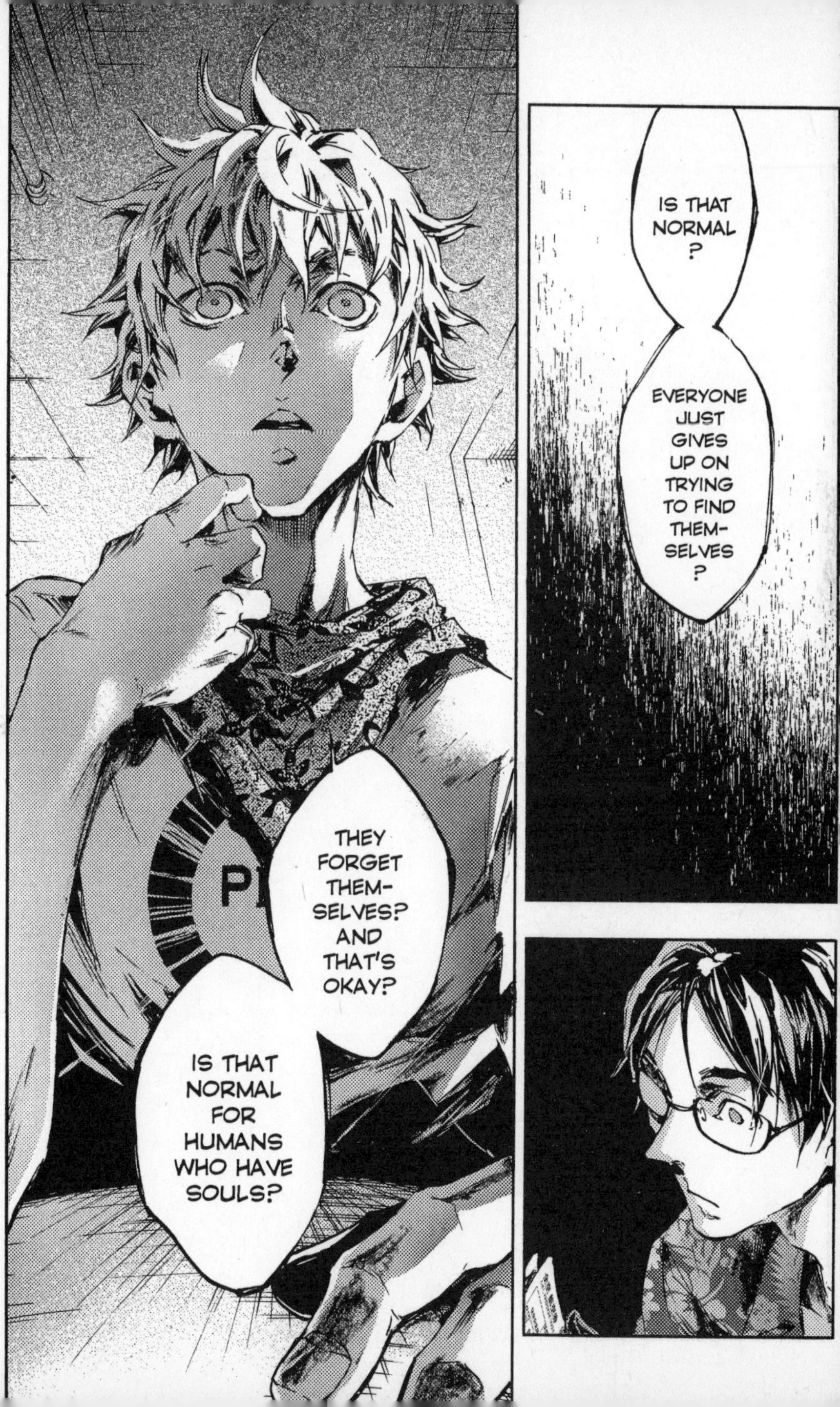
IS THAT NORMAL?
EVERYONE JUST GIVES UP ON TRYING TO FIND THEMSELVES?
THEY FORGET THEMSELVES? AND THAT'S OKAY?
IS THAT NORMAL FOR HUMANS WHO HAVE SOULS?

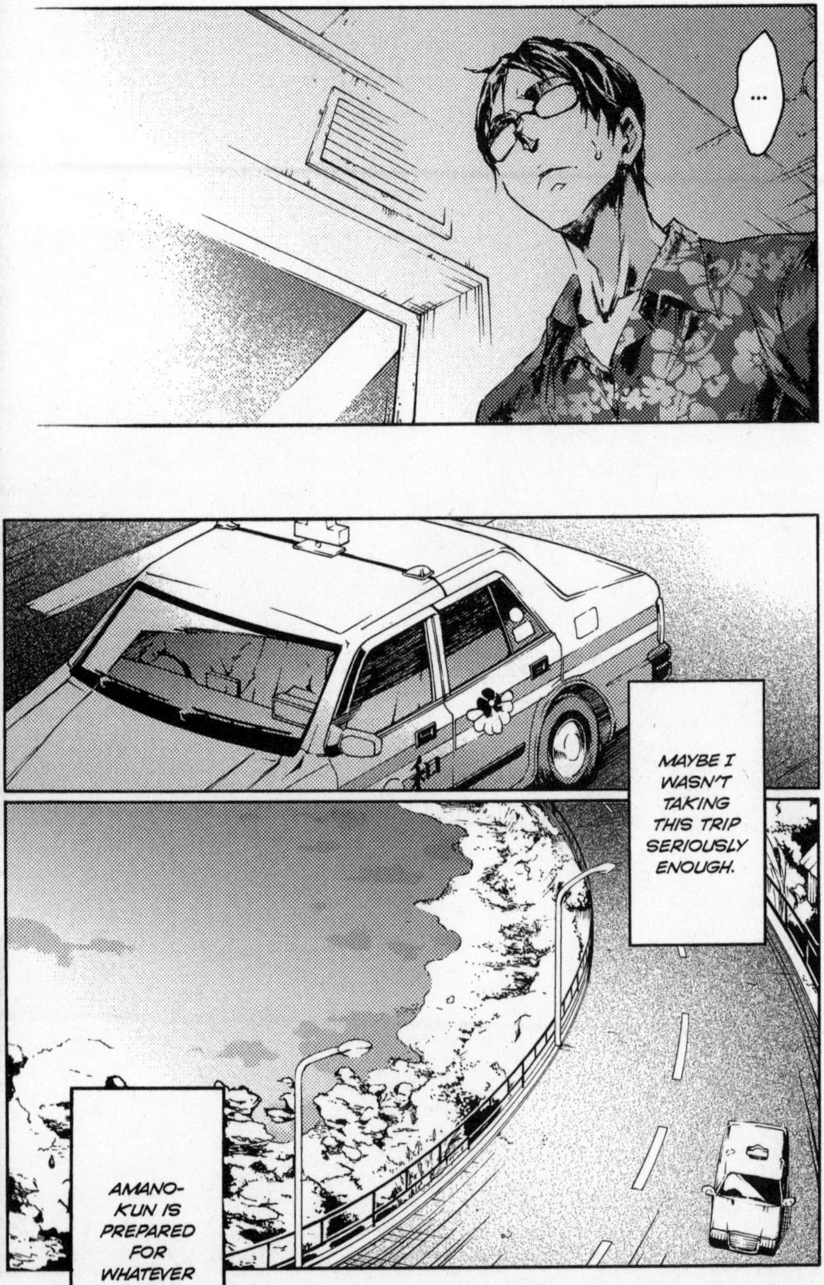
...
MAYBE I WASN'T TAKING THIS TRIP SERIOUSLY ENOUGH.
AMANO-KUN IS PREPARED FOR WHATEVER COMES.

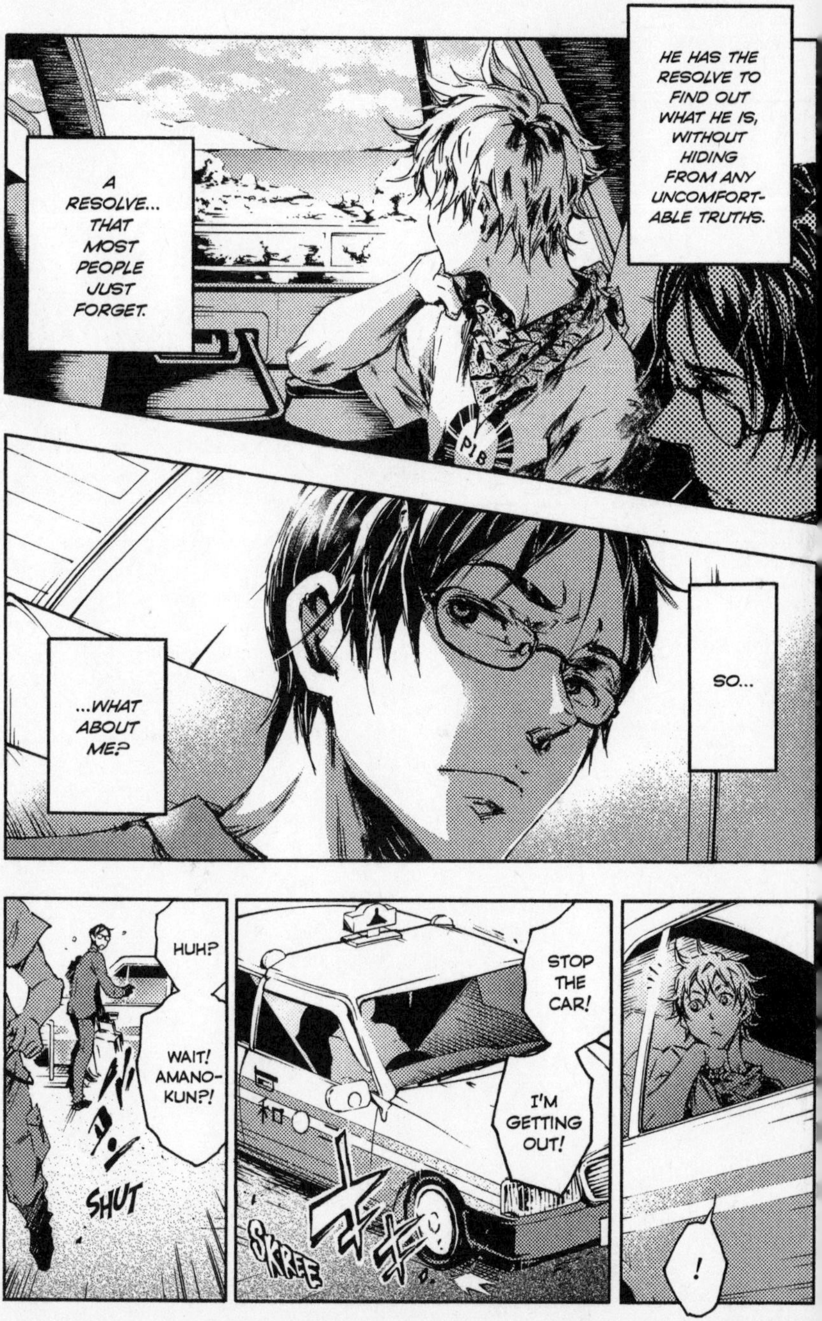
HE HAS THE RESOLVE TO FIND OUT WHAT HE IS, WITHOUT HIDING FROM ANY UNCOMFORTABLE TRUTHS.
A RESOLVE... THAT MOST PEOPLE JUST FORGET.
SO...
...WHAT ABOUT ME?
!
STOP THE CAR!
I'M GETTING OUT!
SKREE
HUH?
WAIT! AMANO-KUN?!
SHUT

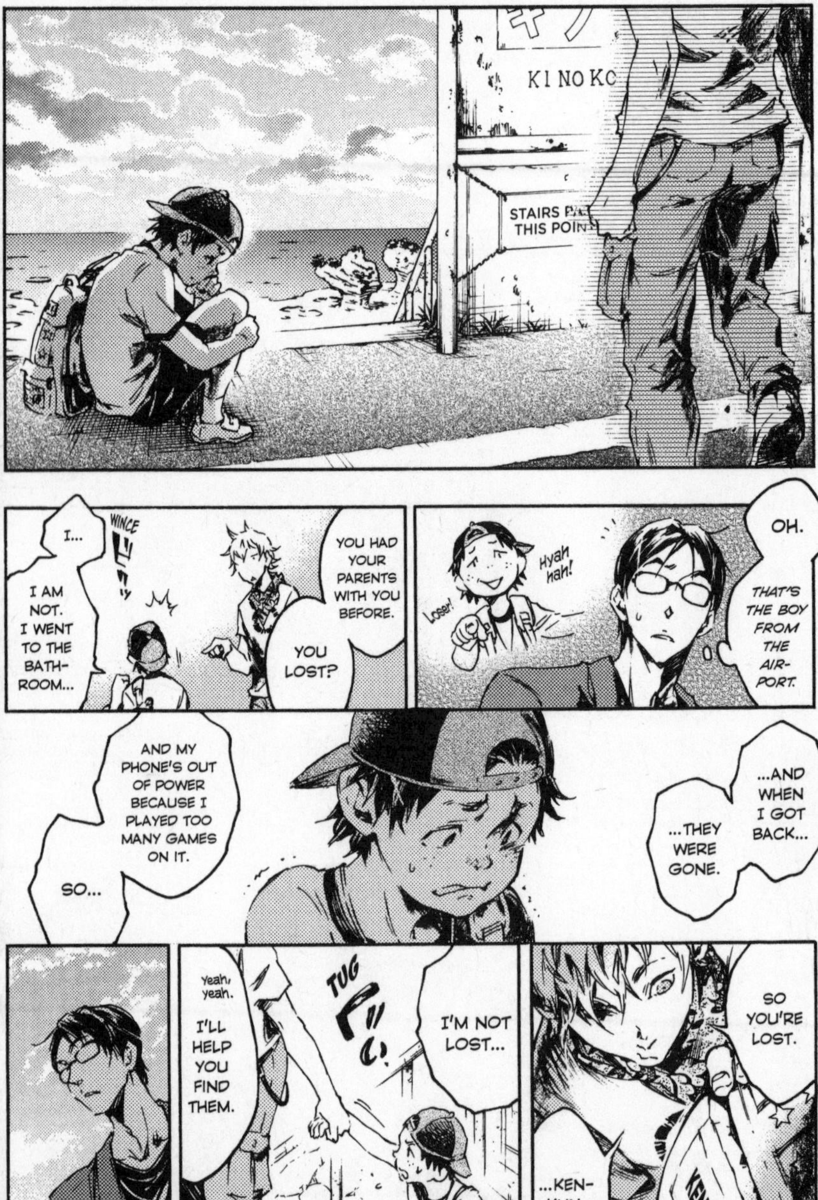

OH.
THAT'S THE BOY FROM THE AIRPORT.
Hyah hah!
Loser!
YOU HAD YOUR PARENTS WITH YOU BEFORE.
YOU LOST?
WINCE
I...
I AM NOT. I WENT TO THE BATHROOM...
...AND WHEN I GOT BACK...
...THEY WERE GONE.
AND MY PHONE'S OUT OF POWER BECAUSE I PLAYED TOO MANY GAMES ON IT.
SO...
SO YOU'RE LOST.
...KEN-KUN.
KEN SAITŌ
I'M NOT LOST...
TUG
Yeah, yeah.
I'LL HELP YOU FIND THEM.

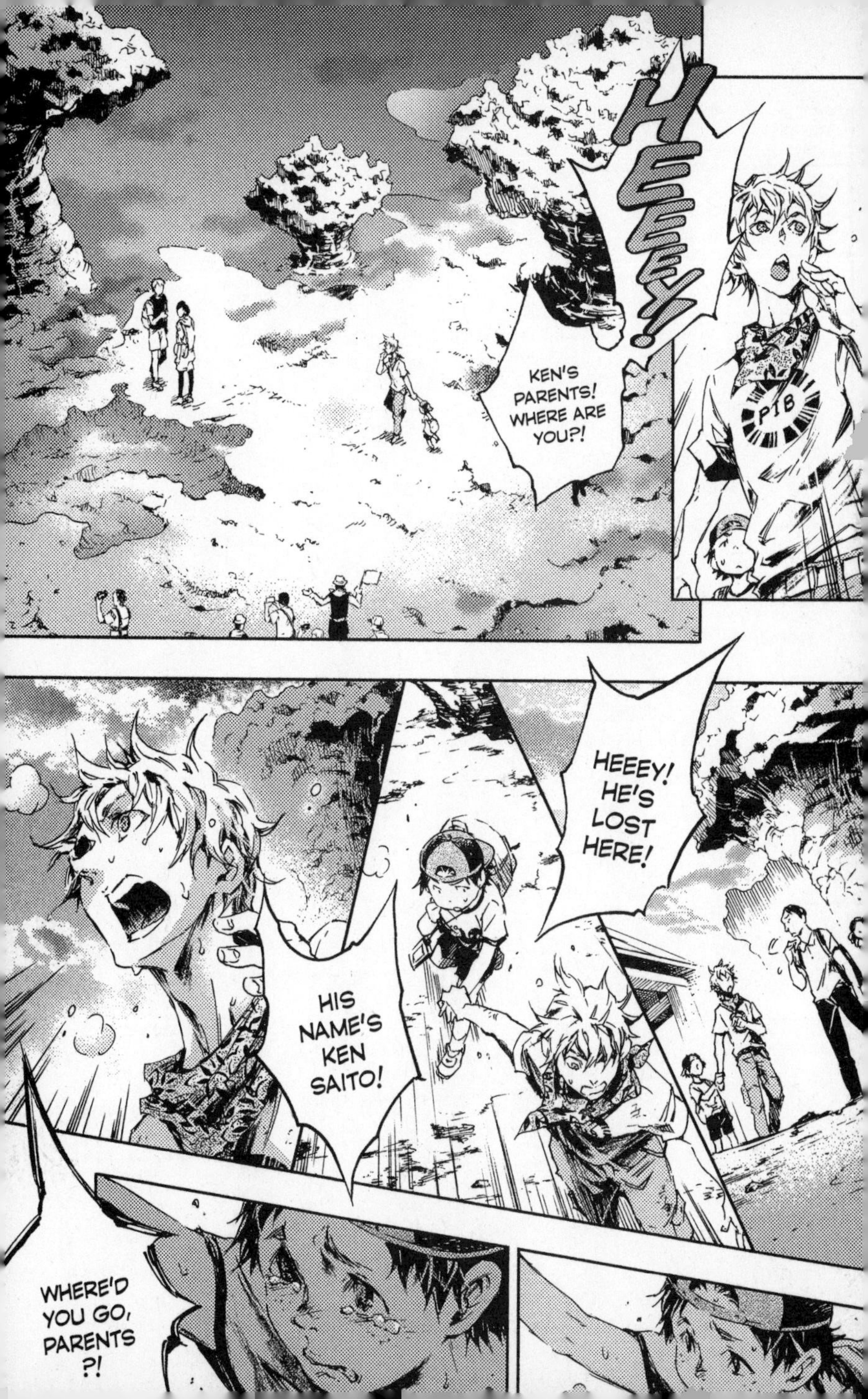
HEEEY!
KEN'S PARENTS! WHERE ARE YOU?!
HEEEY! HE'S LOST HERE!
HIS NAME'S KEN SAITO!
WHERE'D YOU GO, PARENTS?!

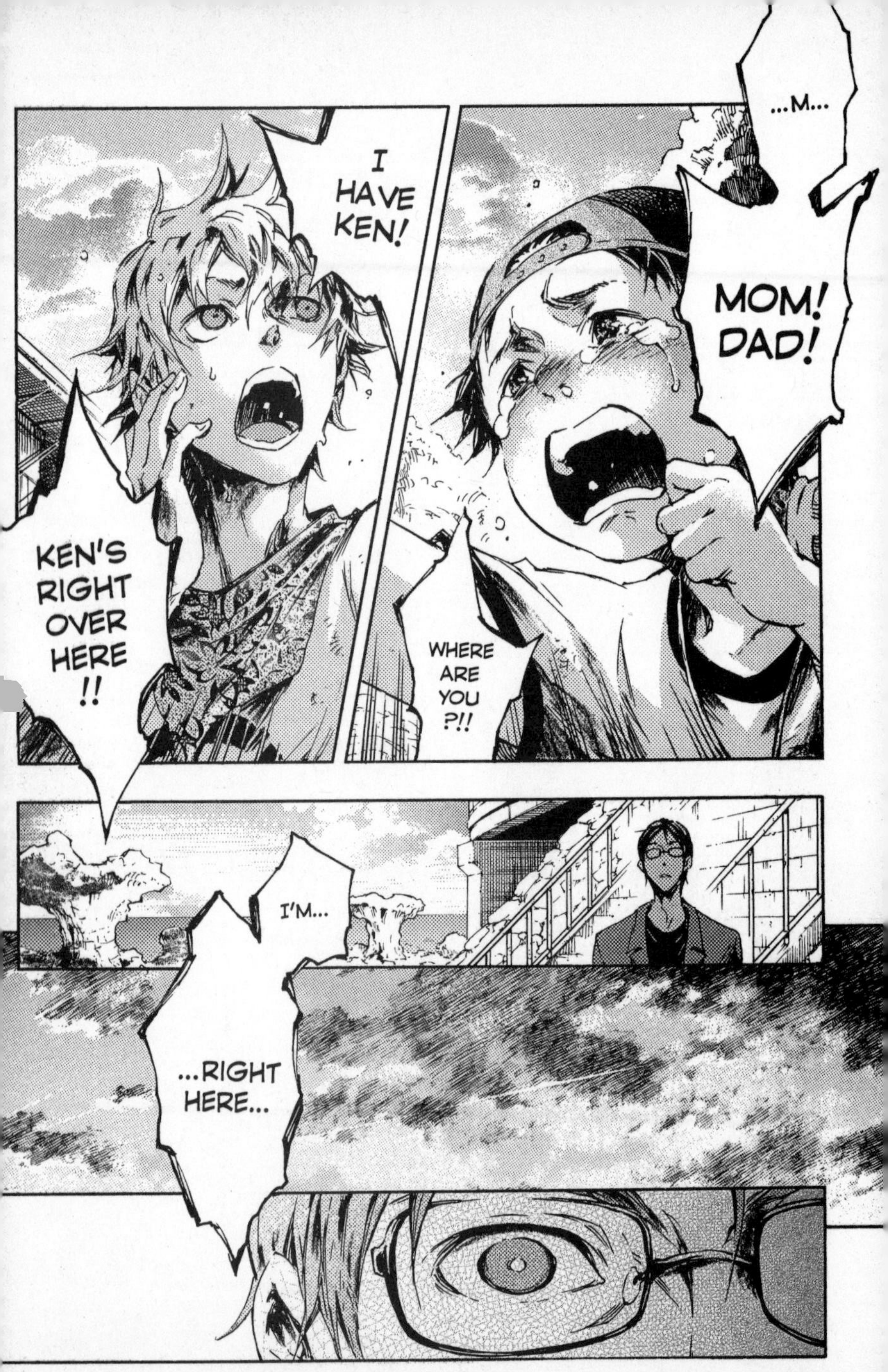
...M...
MOM! DAD!
WHERE ARE YOU ?!!
I HAVE KEN!
KEN'S RIGHT OVER HERE !!
I'M...
...RIGHT HERE...

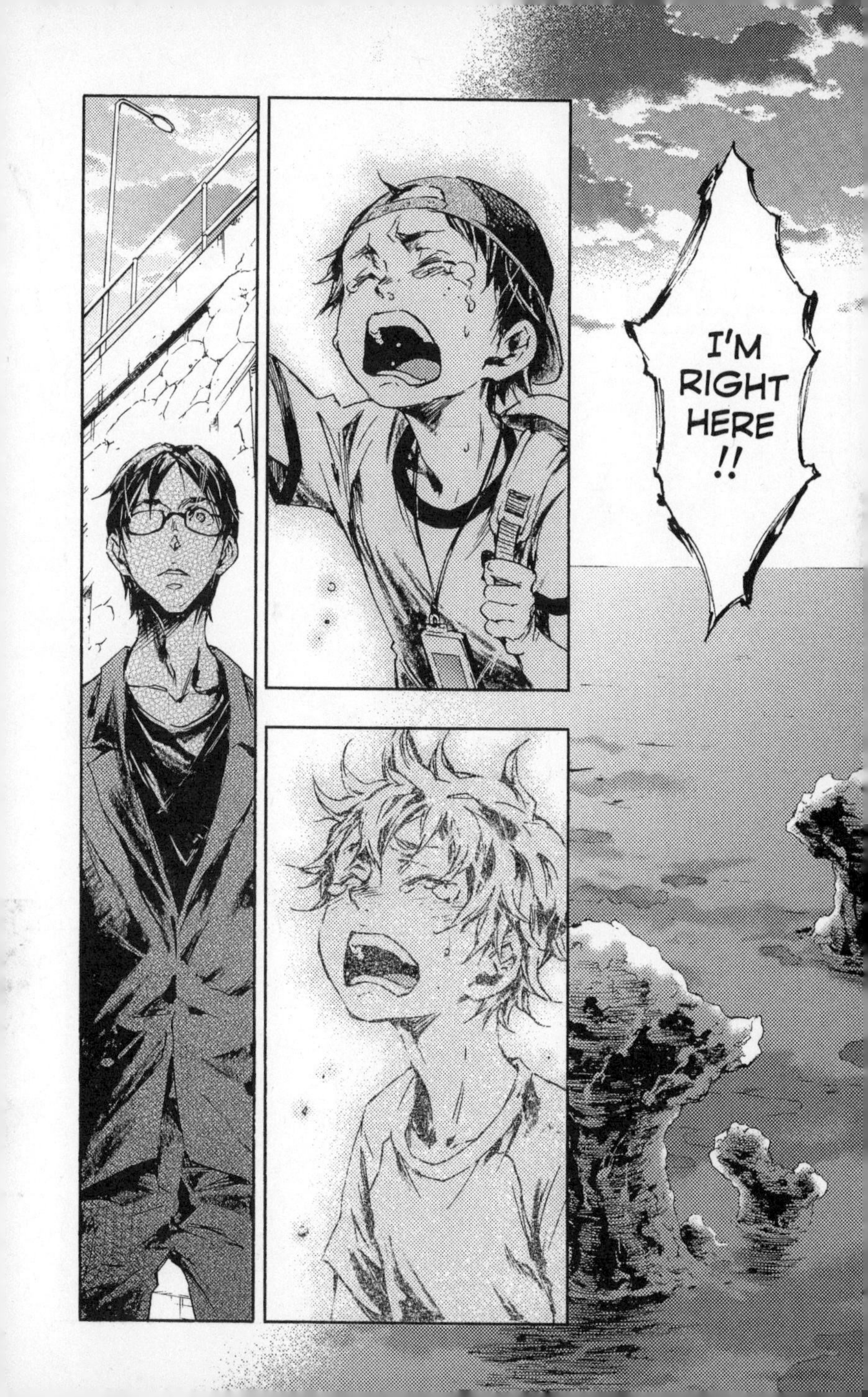
I'M RIGHT HERE !!

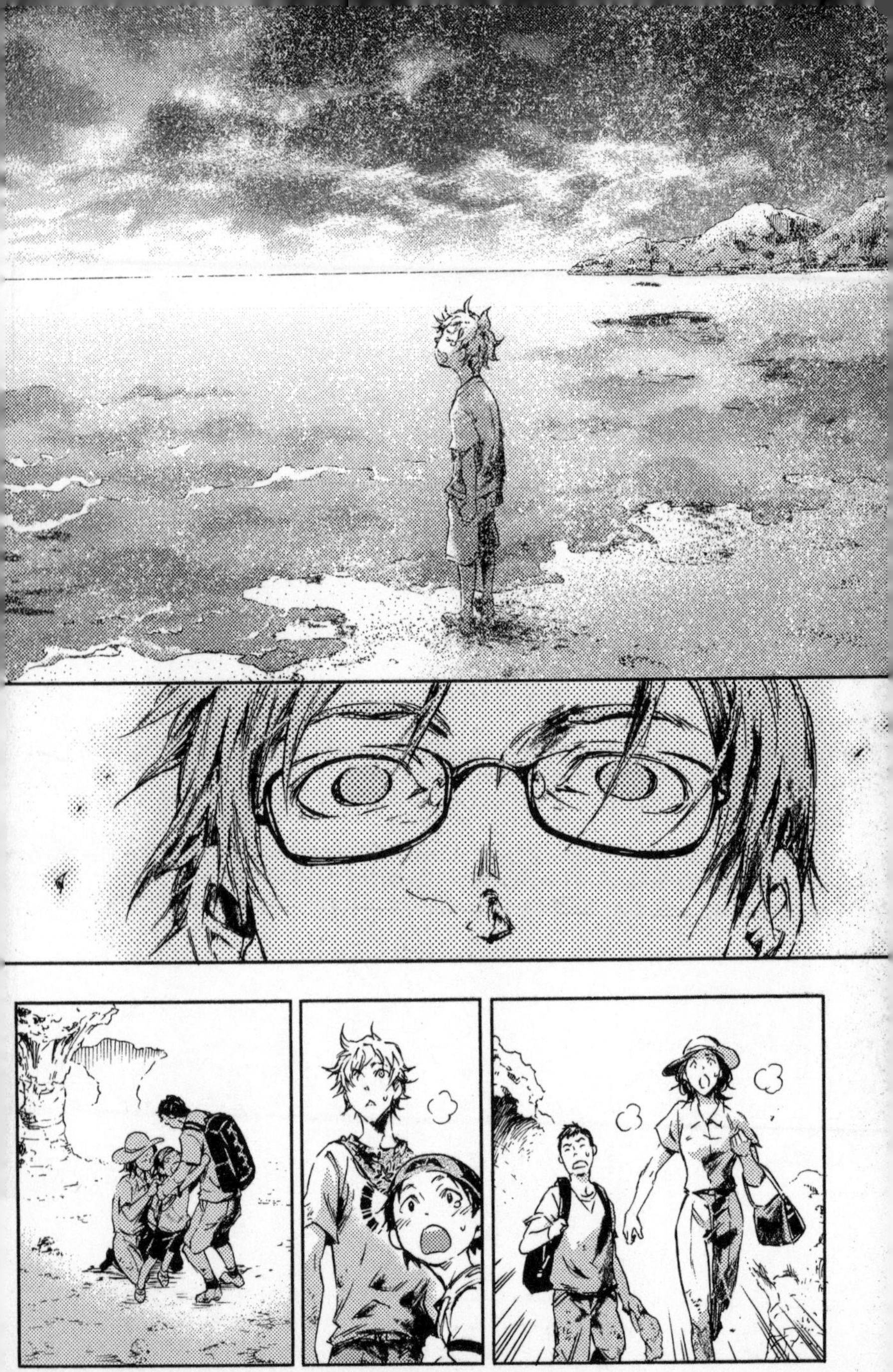

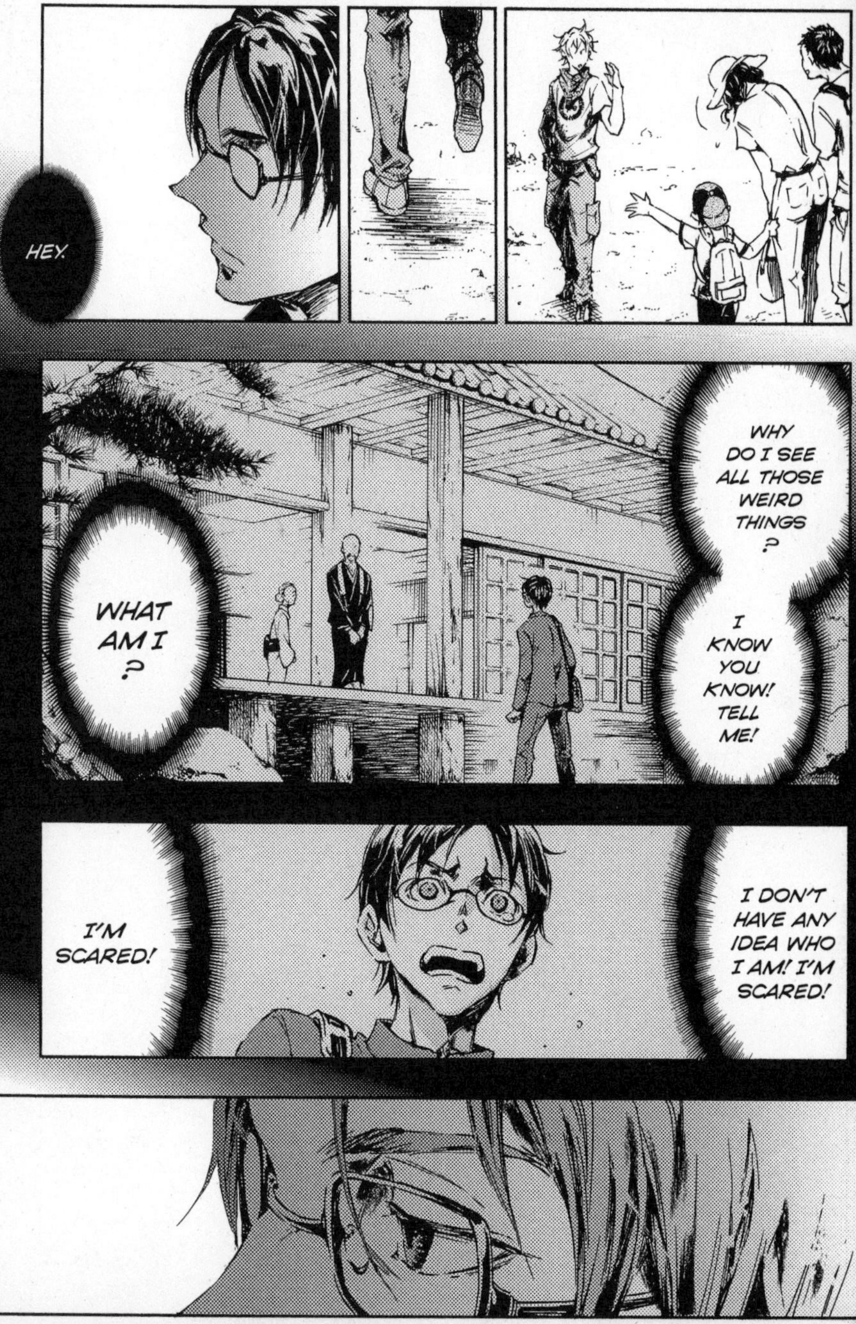
HEY.
WHY DO I SEE ALL THOSE WEIRD THINGS?
I KNOW YOU KNOW! TELL ME!
WHAT AM I?
I DON'T HAVE ANY IDEA WHO I AM! I'M SCARED!
I'M SCARED!

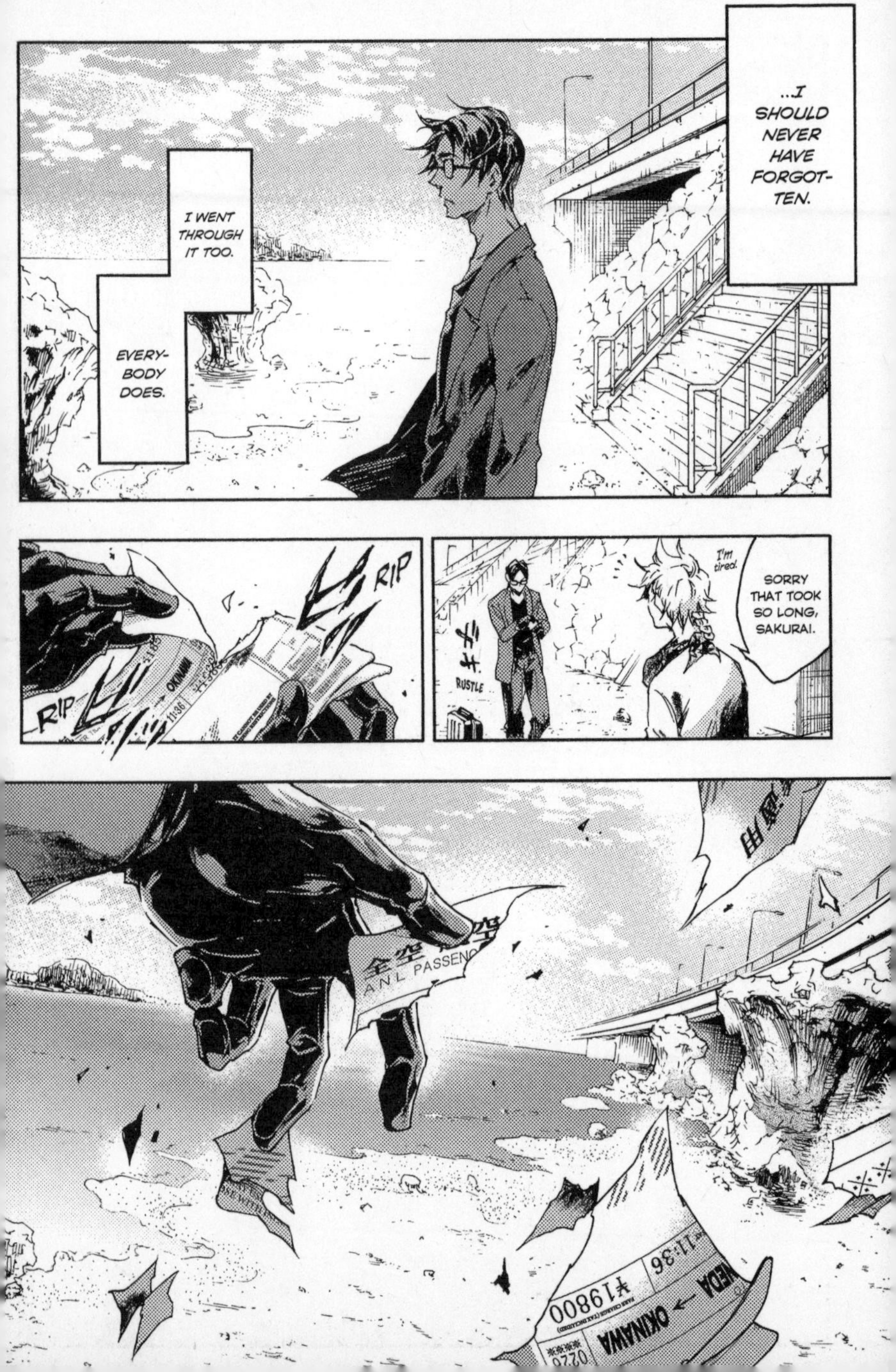
...I SHOULD NEVER HAVE FORGOT-TEN.
I WENT THROUGH IT TOO.
EVERY-BODY DOES.
I'm tired.
SORRY THAT TOOK SO LONG, SAKURAI.
RUSTLE
RIP
RIP
OKINAWA
11:36
¥19800

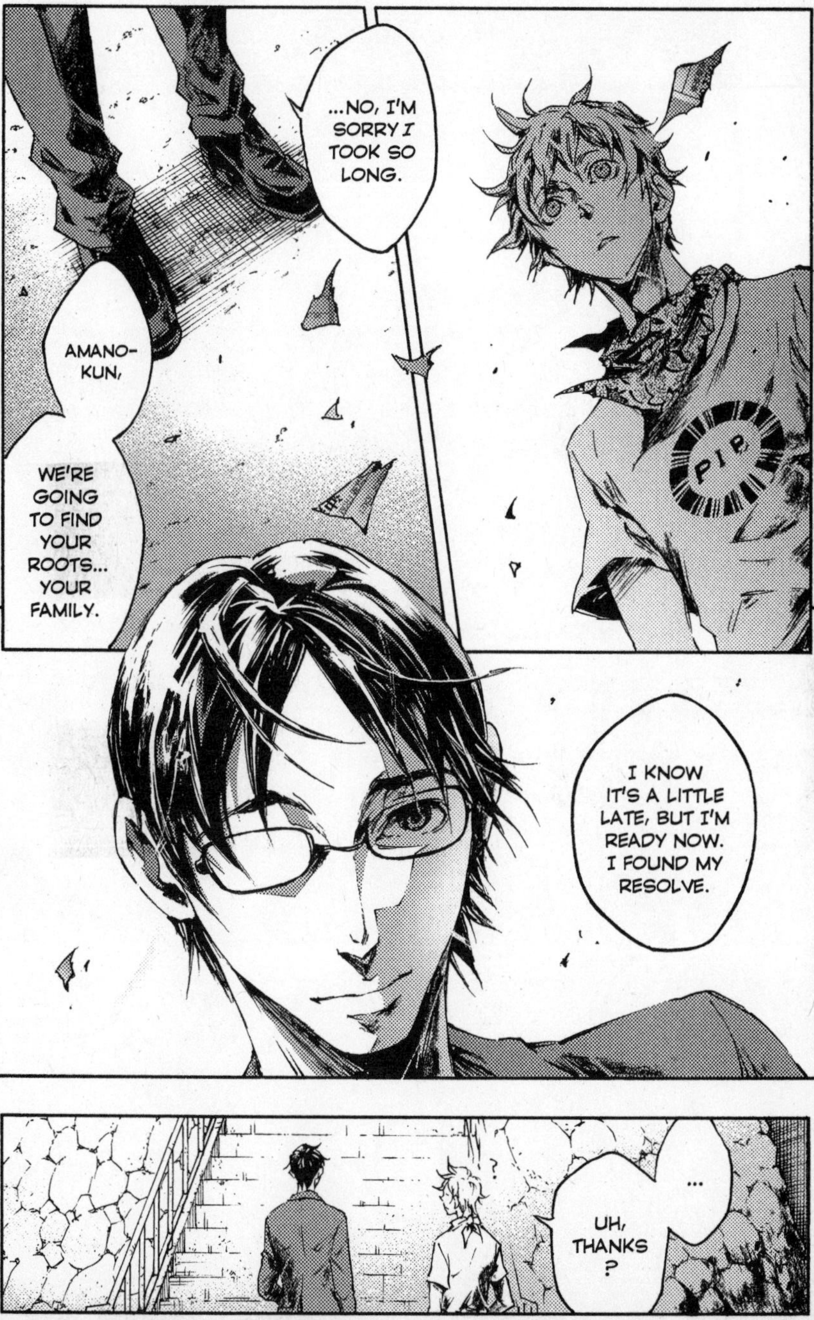
...NO, I'M SORRY I TOOK SO LONG.
AMANO-KUN,
WE'RE GOING TO FIND YOUR ROOTS... YOUR FAMILY.
I KNOW IT'S A LITTLE LATE, BUT I'M READY NOW. I FOUND MY RESOLVE.
...
UH, THANKS?
P.I.P.

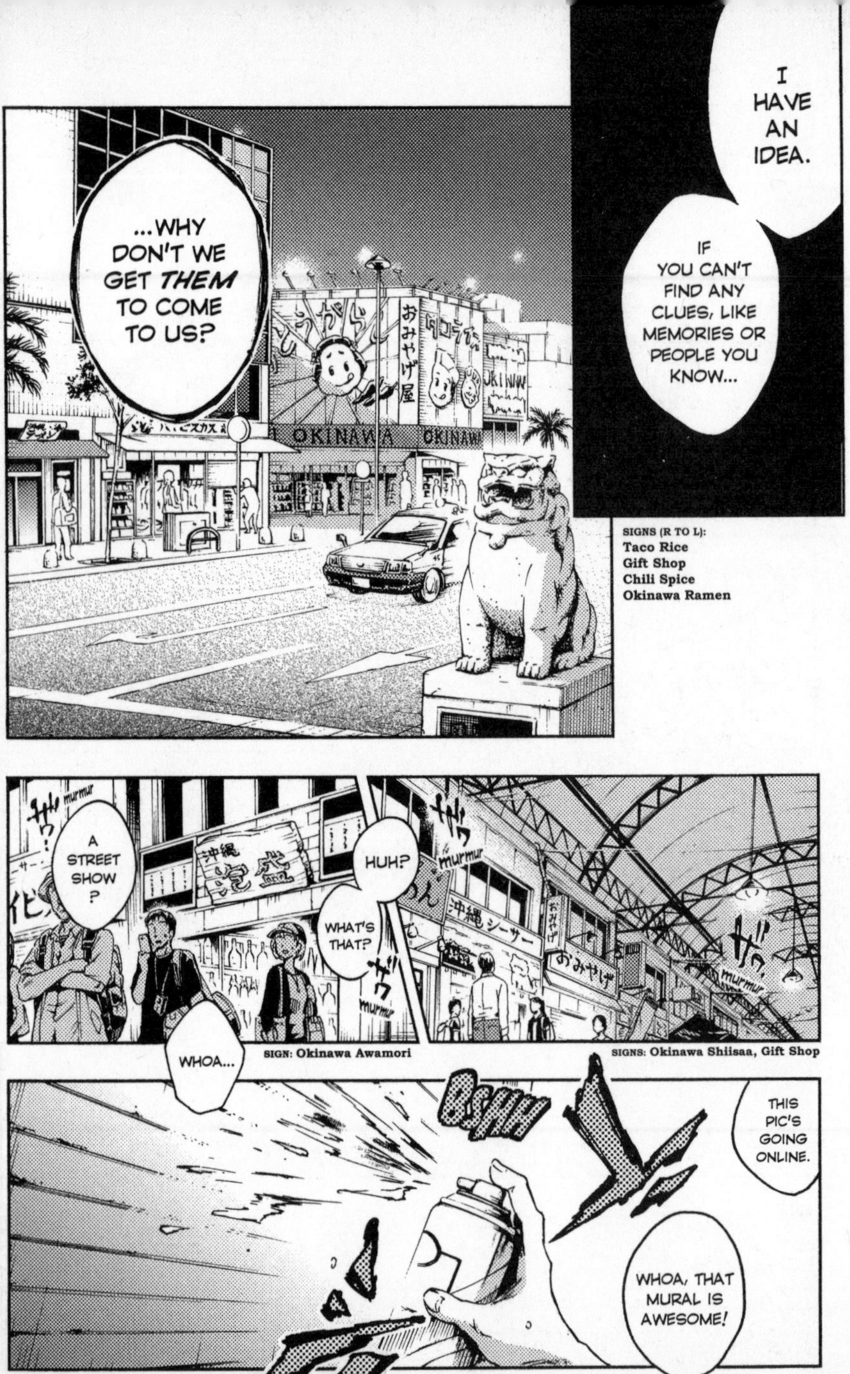
I HAVE AN IDEA.
IF YOU CAN'T FIND ANY CLUES, LIKE MEMORIES OR PEOPLE YOU KNOW...
...WHY DON'T WE GET *THEM* TO COME TO US?
murmur
murmur
murmur
HUH?
WHAT'S THAT?
murmur
A STREET SHOW?
WHOA...
BSHH
THIS PIC'S GOING ONLINE.
WHOA, THAT MURAL IS AWESOME!

SIGNS (R TO L):
Taco Rice
Gift Shop
Chili Spice
Okinawa Ramen

SIGN: Okinawa Awamori

SIGNS: Okinawa Shiisaa, Gift Shop

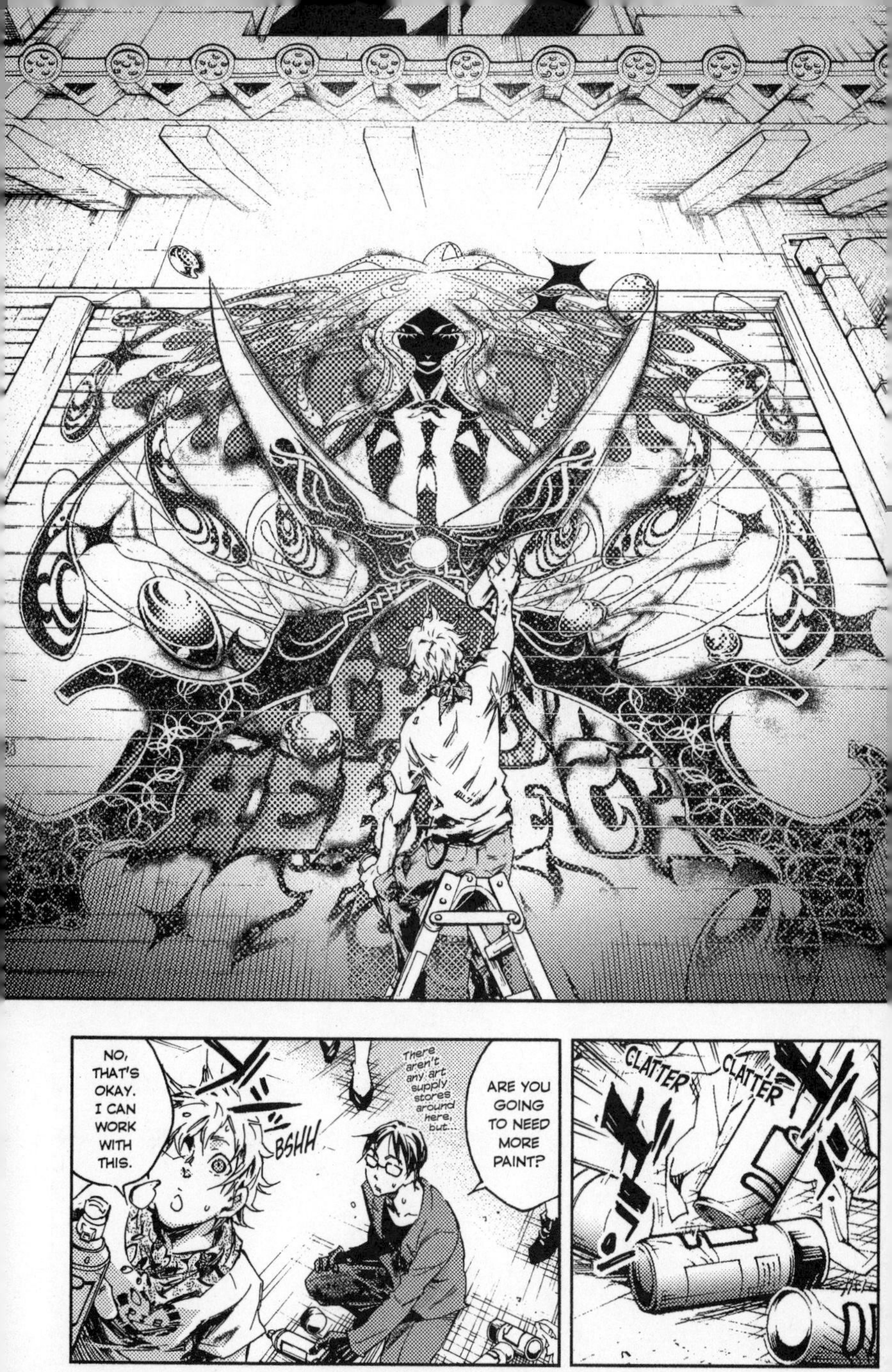
CLATTER
CLATTER
ARE YOU GOING TO NEED MORE PAINT?
There aren't any art supply stores around here, but...
BSHH
NO, THAT'S OKAY. I CAN WORK WITH THIS.

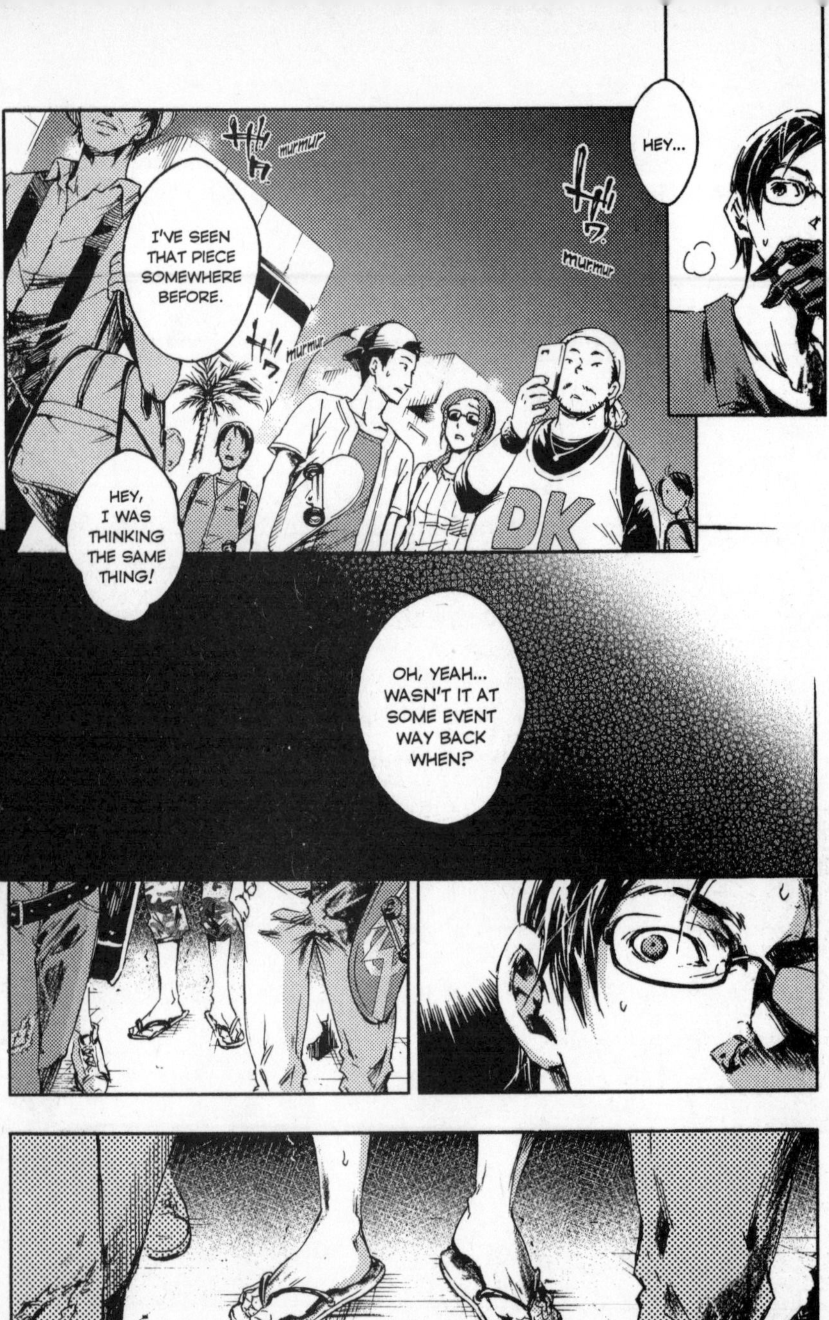
HEY...
murmur
murmur
I'VE SEEN THAT PIECE SOMEWHERE BEFORE.
murmur
HEY, I WAS THINKING THE SAME THING!
OH, YEAH... WASN'T IT AT SOME EVENT WAY BACK WHEN?

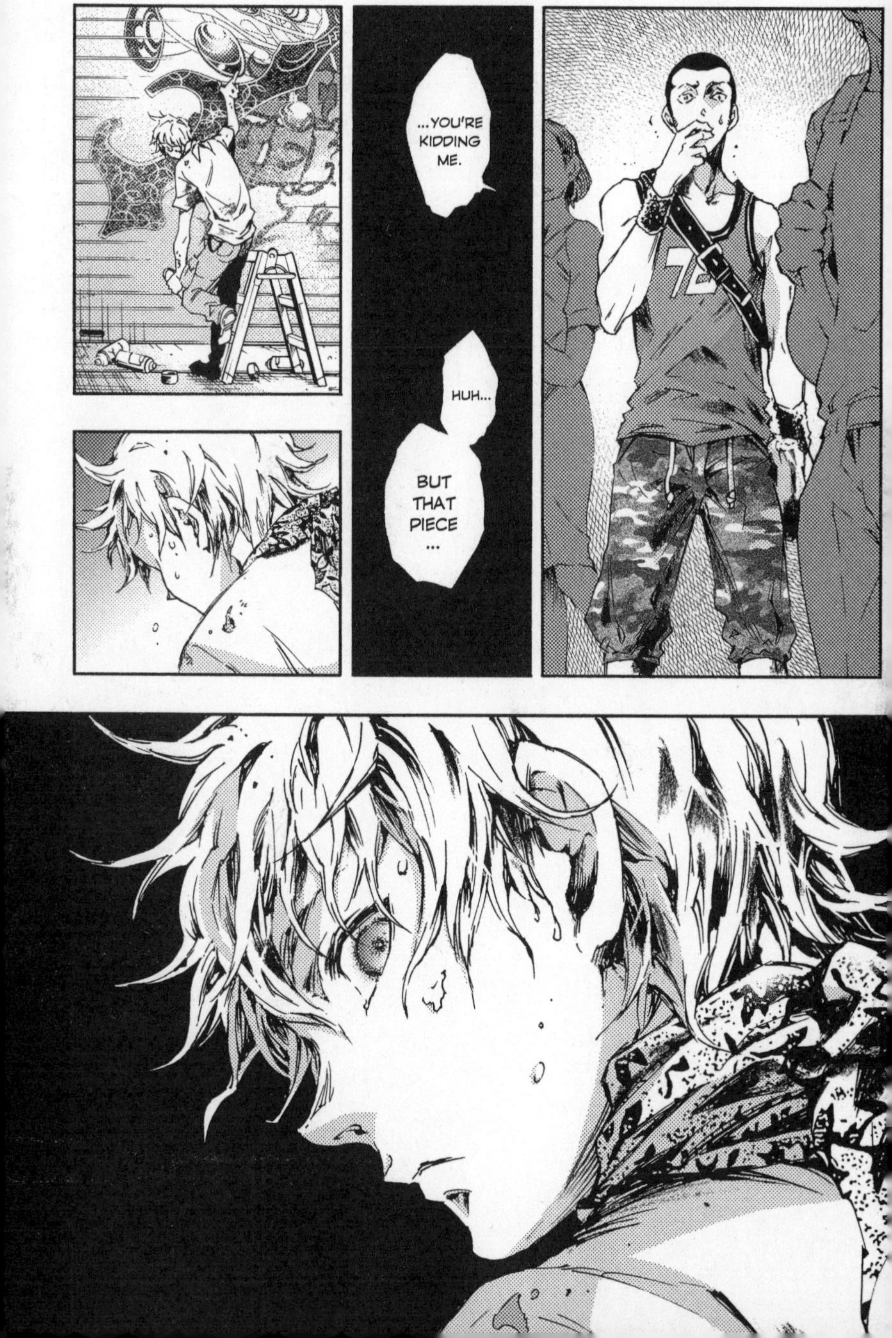
...YOU'RE KIDDING ME.
HUH...
BUT THAT PIECE ...

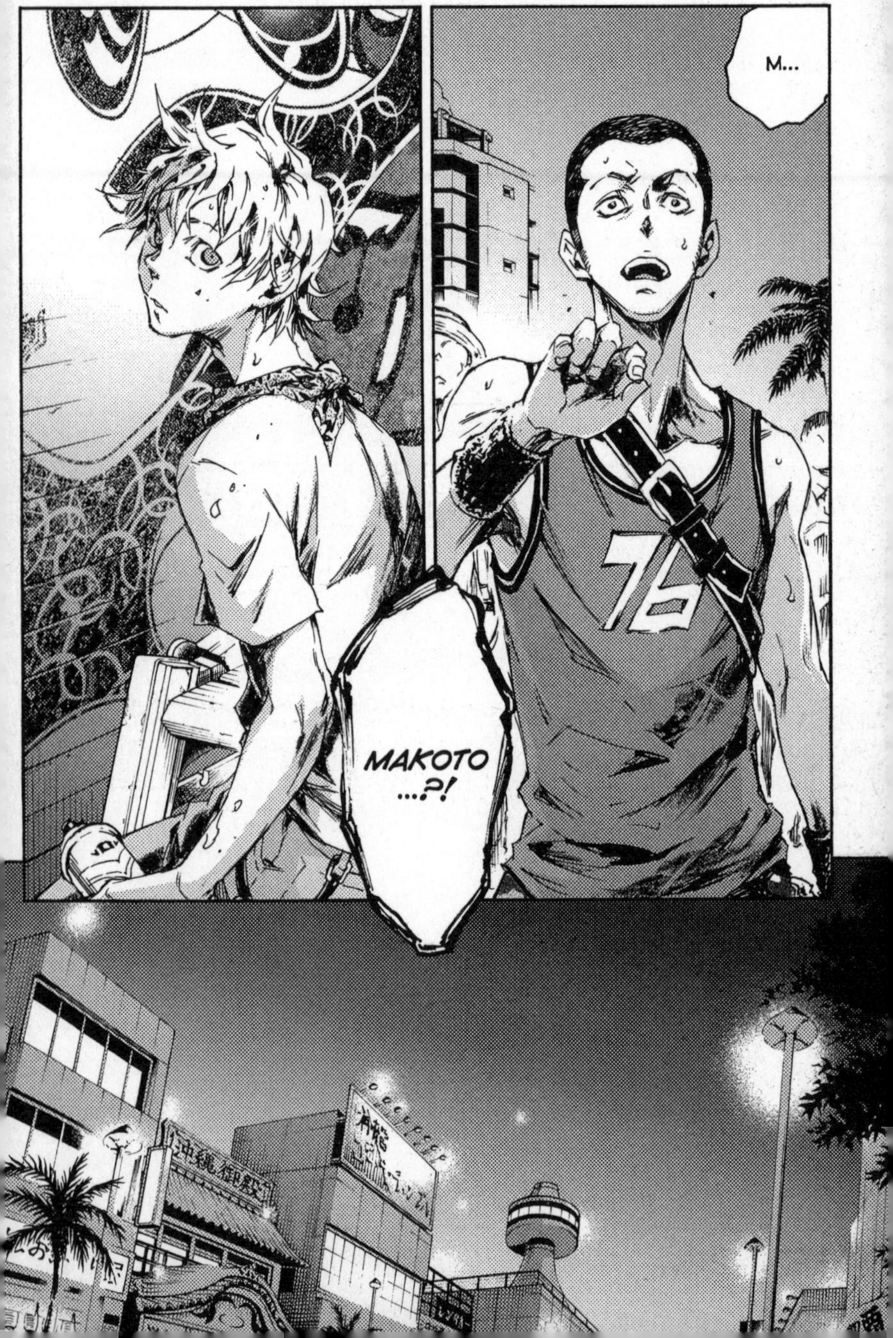
M...
MAKOTO ...?!
沖縄御殿

Chapter 19 ✚ Memory's Fuse

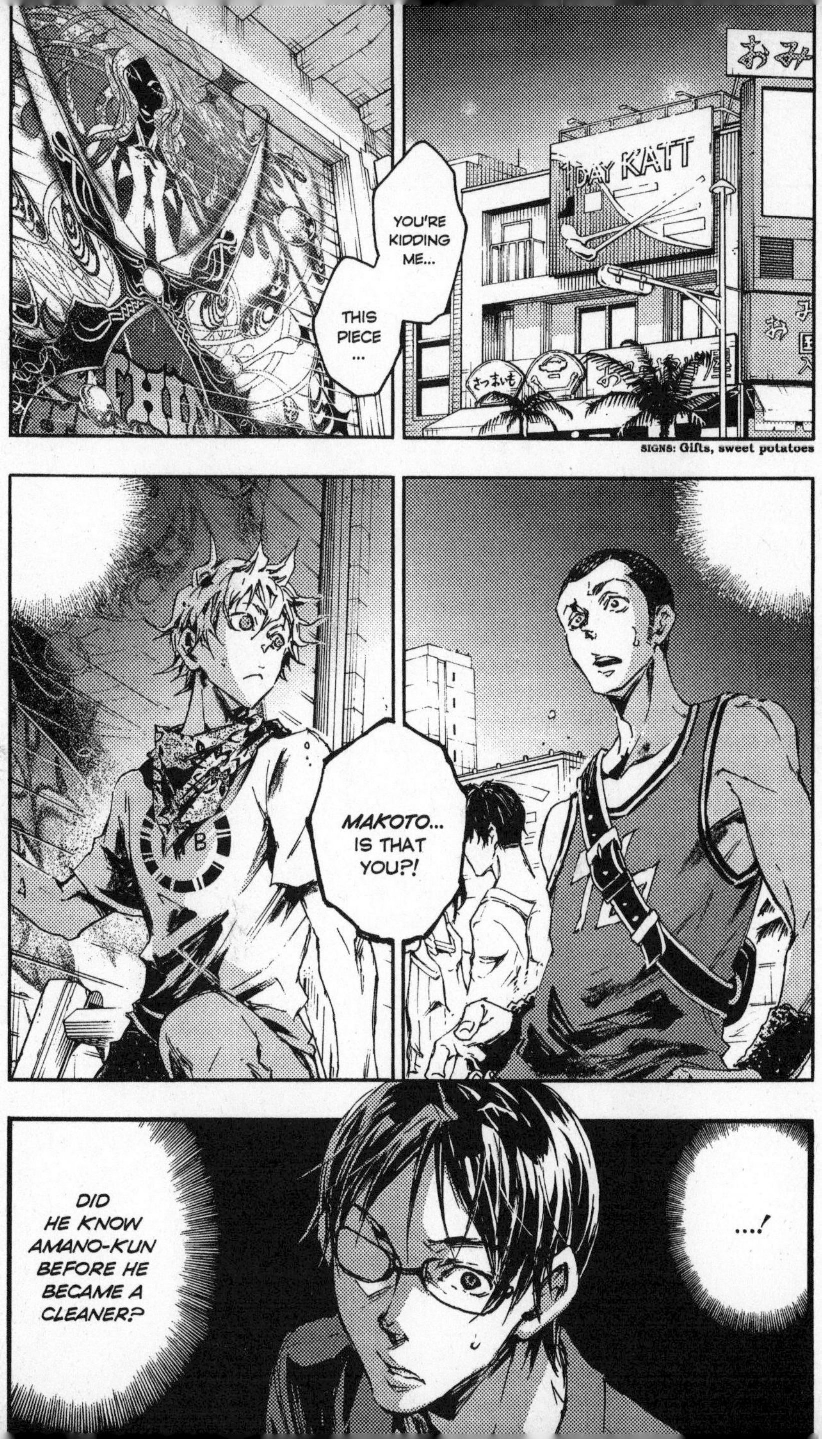
1DAY KATT
YOU'RE KIDDING ME...
THIS PIECE ...
SIGNS: Gifts, sweet potatoes
MAKOTO... IS THAT YOU?!
...!
DID HE KNOW AMANO-KUN BEFORE HE BECAME A CLEANER?

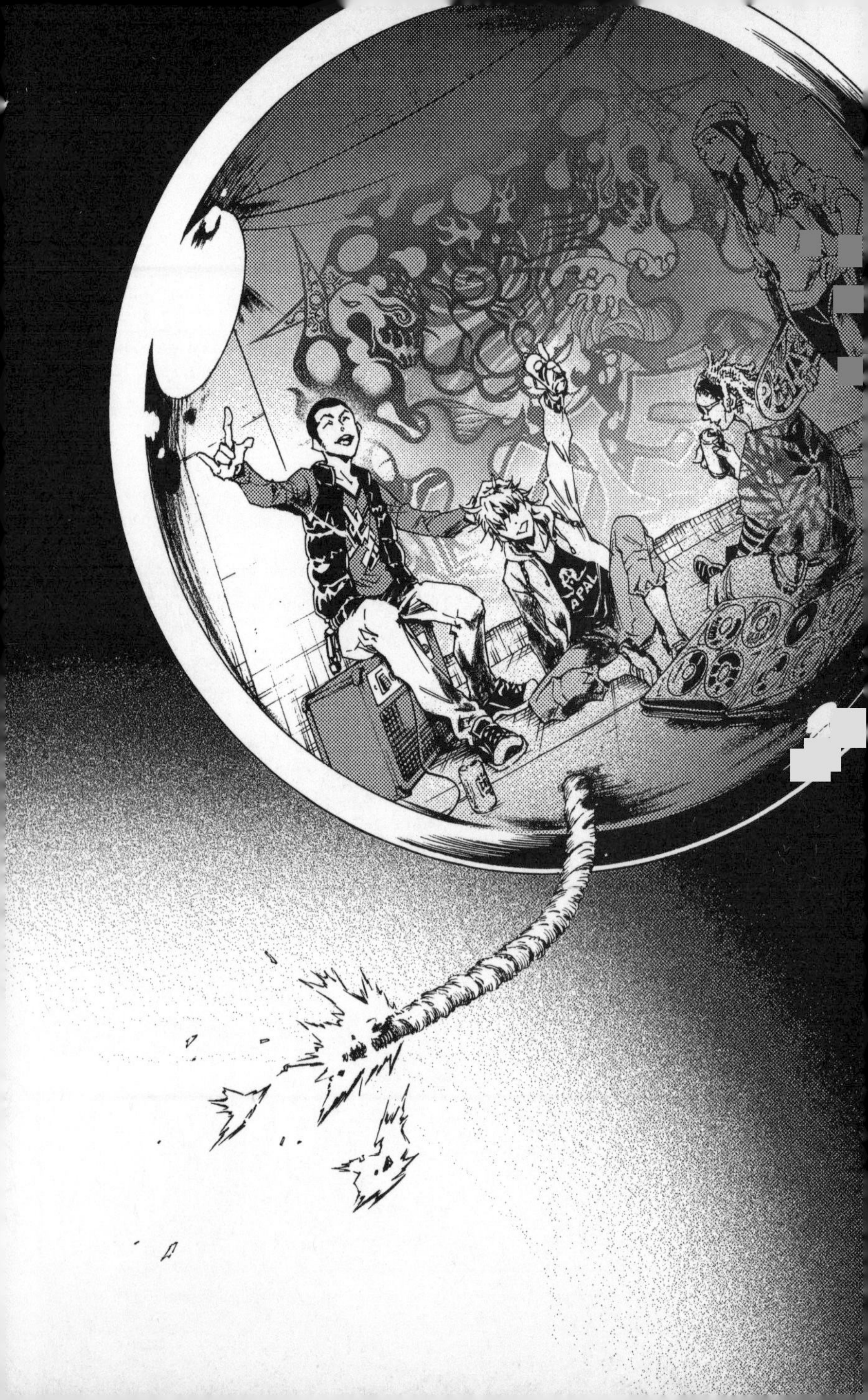
APAL

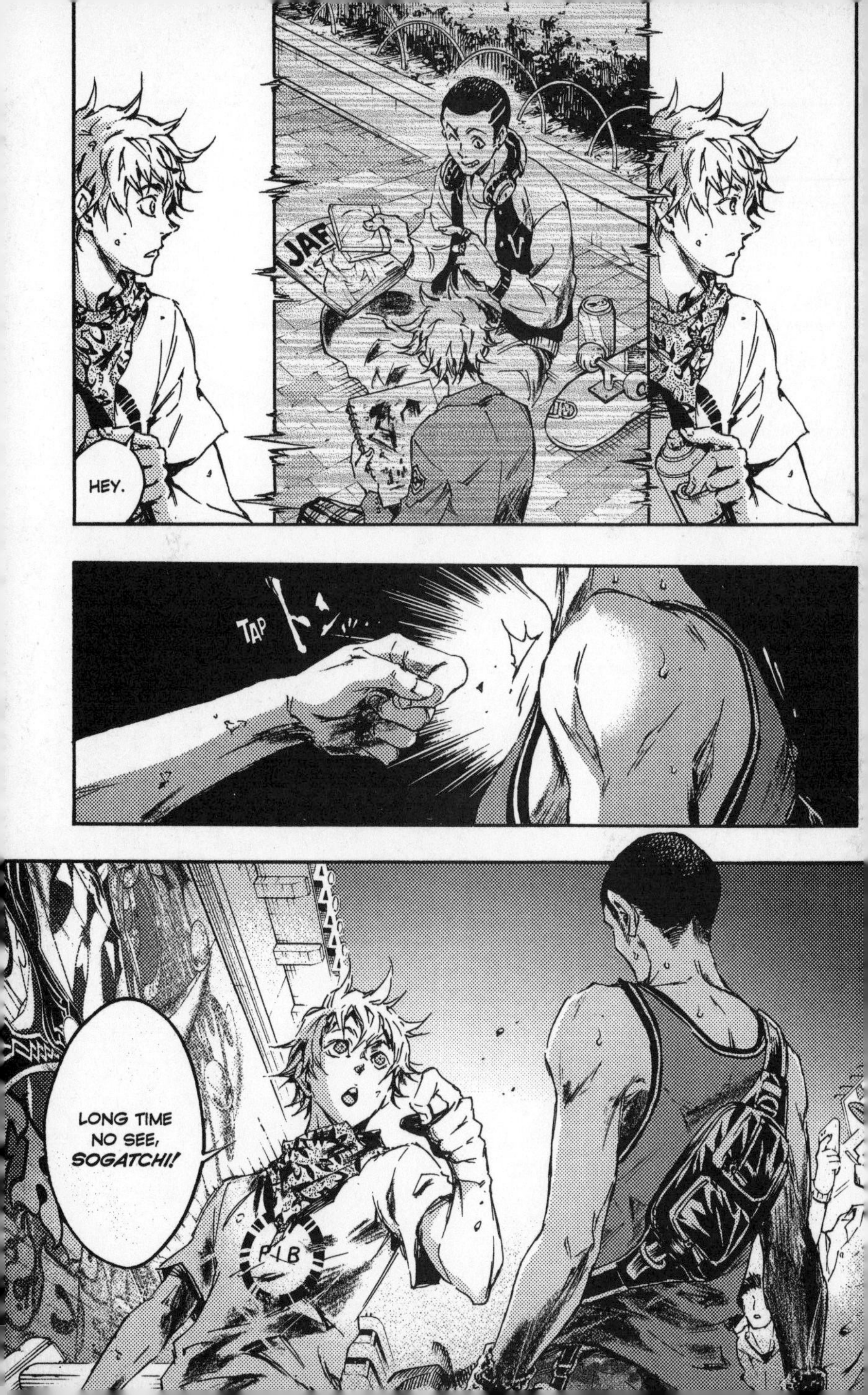
JAF
HEY.
TAP
LONG TIME NO SEE, SOGATCHI!

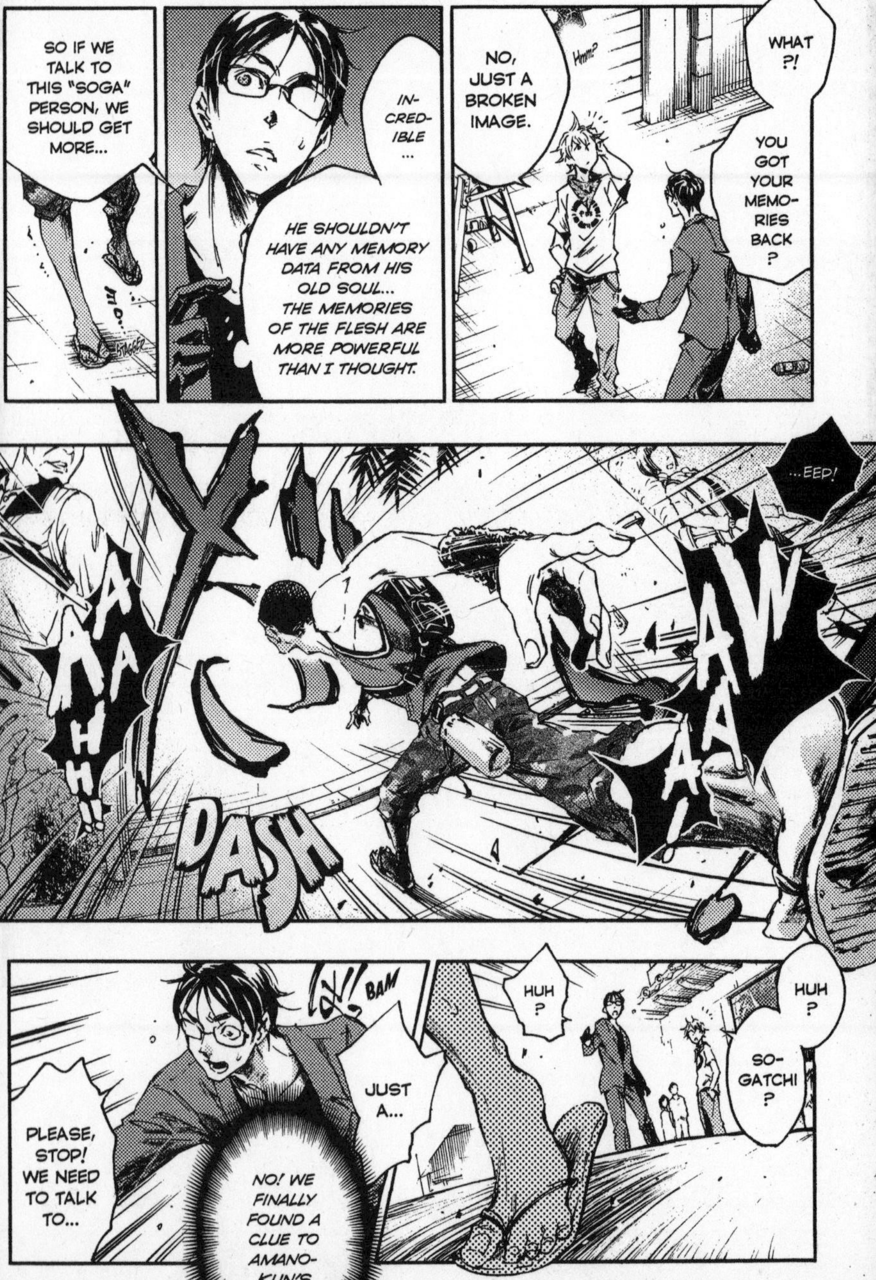
WHAT ?!
YOU GOT YOUR MEMORIES BACK ?
Hmm?
NO, JUST A BROKEN IMAGE.
INCREDIBLE ...
HE SHOULDN'T HAVE ANY MEMORY DATA FROM HIS OLD SOUL... THE MEMORIES OF THE FLESH ARE MORE POWERFUL THAN I THOUGHT.
SO IF WE TALK TO THIS "SOGA" PERSON, WE SHOULD GET MORE...
STAGGER
...EEP!
AWAAA!
AAAHHH!!
DASH
HUH ?
SO-GATCHI ?
HUH ?
BAM
JUST A...
NO! WE FINALLY FOUND A CLUE TO AMANO-KUN'S PAST!
PLEASE, STOP! WE NEED TO TALK TO...

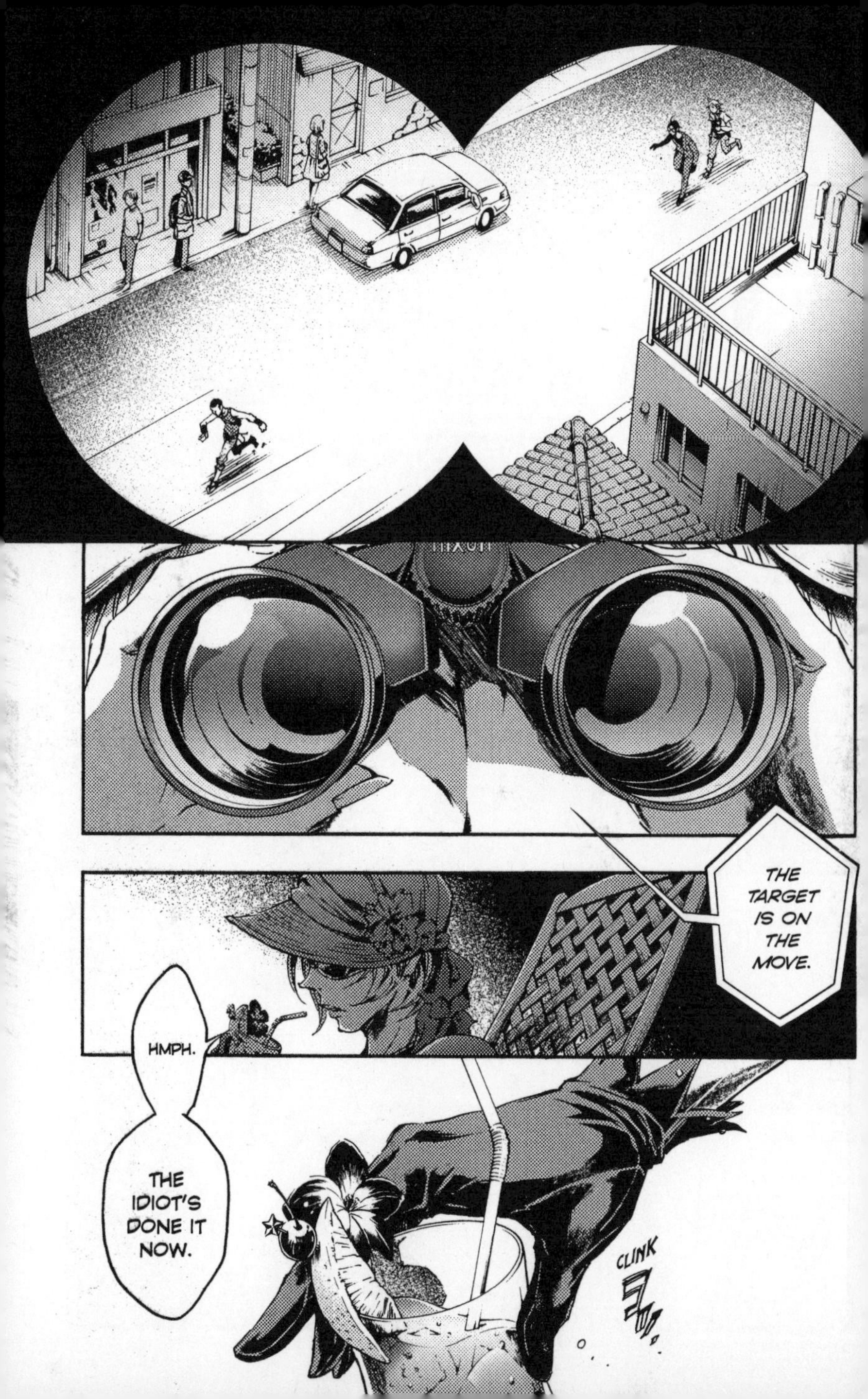
THE TARGET IS ON THE MOVE.
HMPH.
THE IDIOT'S DONE IT NOW.
CLINK

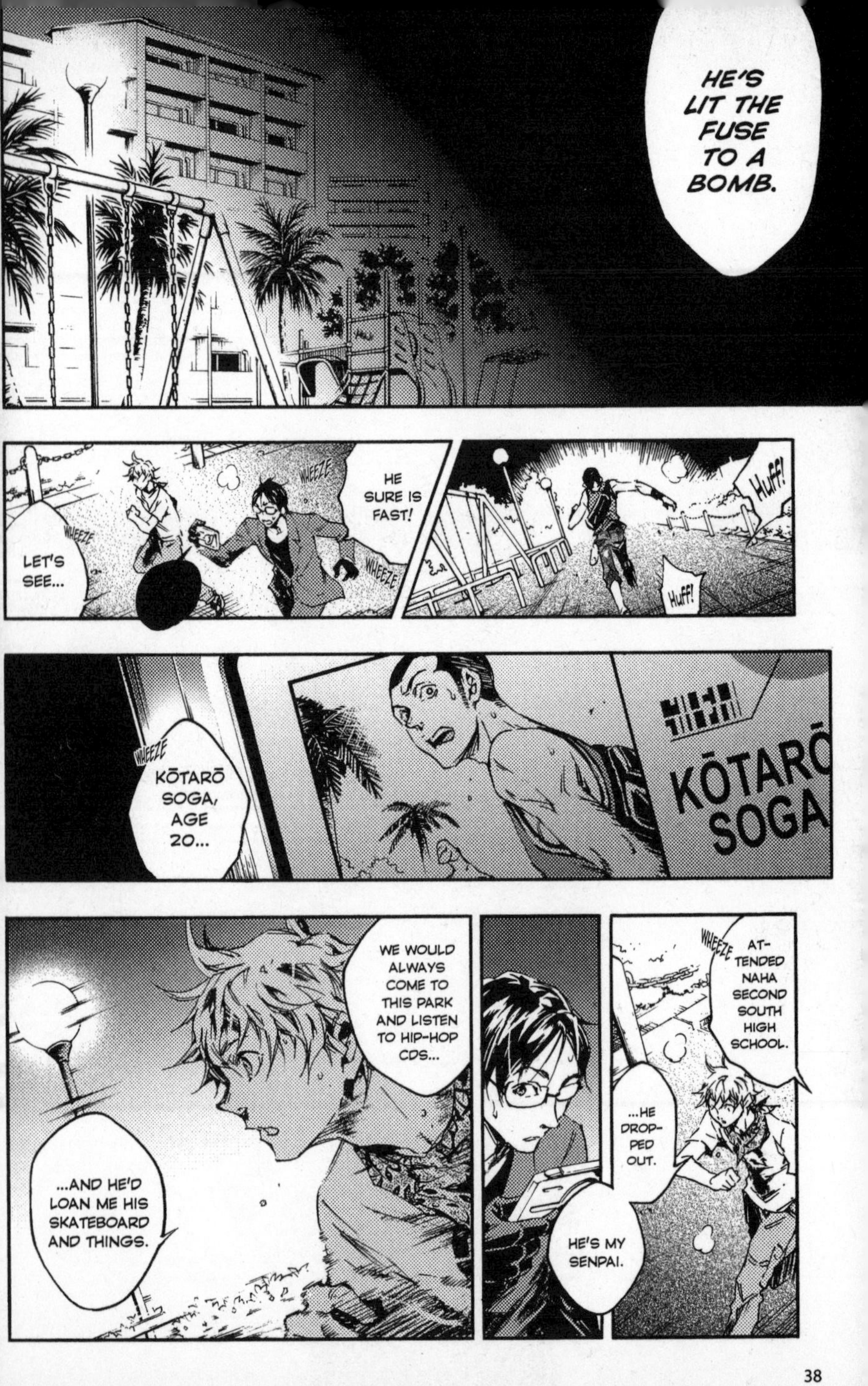
HE'S LIT THE FUSE TO A BOMB.
Huff!
Huff!
HE SURE IS FAST!
WHEEZE
WHEEZE
WHEEZE
LET'S SEE...
KŌTARŌ SOGA
WHEEZE
KŌTARŌ SOGA, AGE 20...
WHEEZE
AT-TENDED NAHA SECOND SOUTH HIGH SCHOOL.
...HE DROP-PED OUT.
HE'S MY SENPAI.
WE WOULD ALWAYS COME TO THIS PARK AND LISTEN TO HIP-HOP CDS...
...AND HE'D LOAN ME HIS SKATEBOARD AND THINGS.

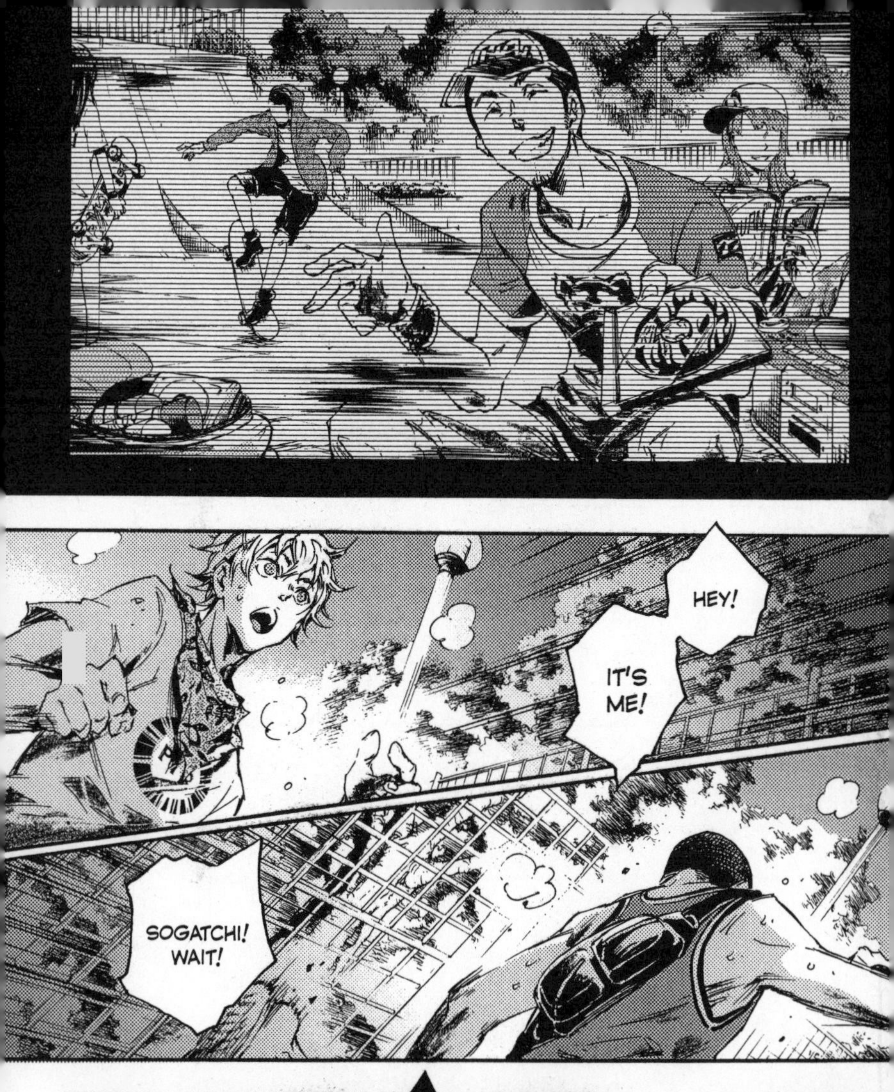
HEY!
IT'S ME!
SOGATCHI! WAIT!
BEEP
BEEP
BEEP
?!

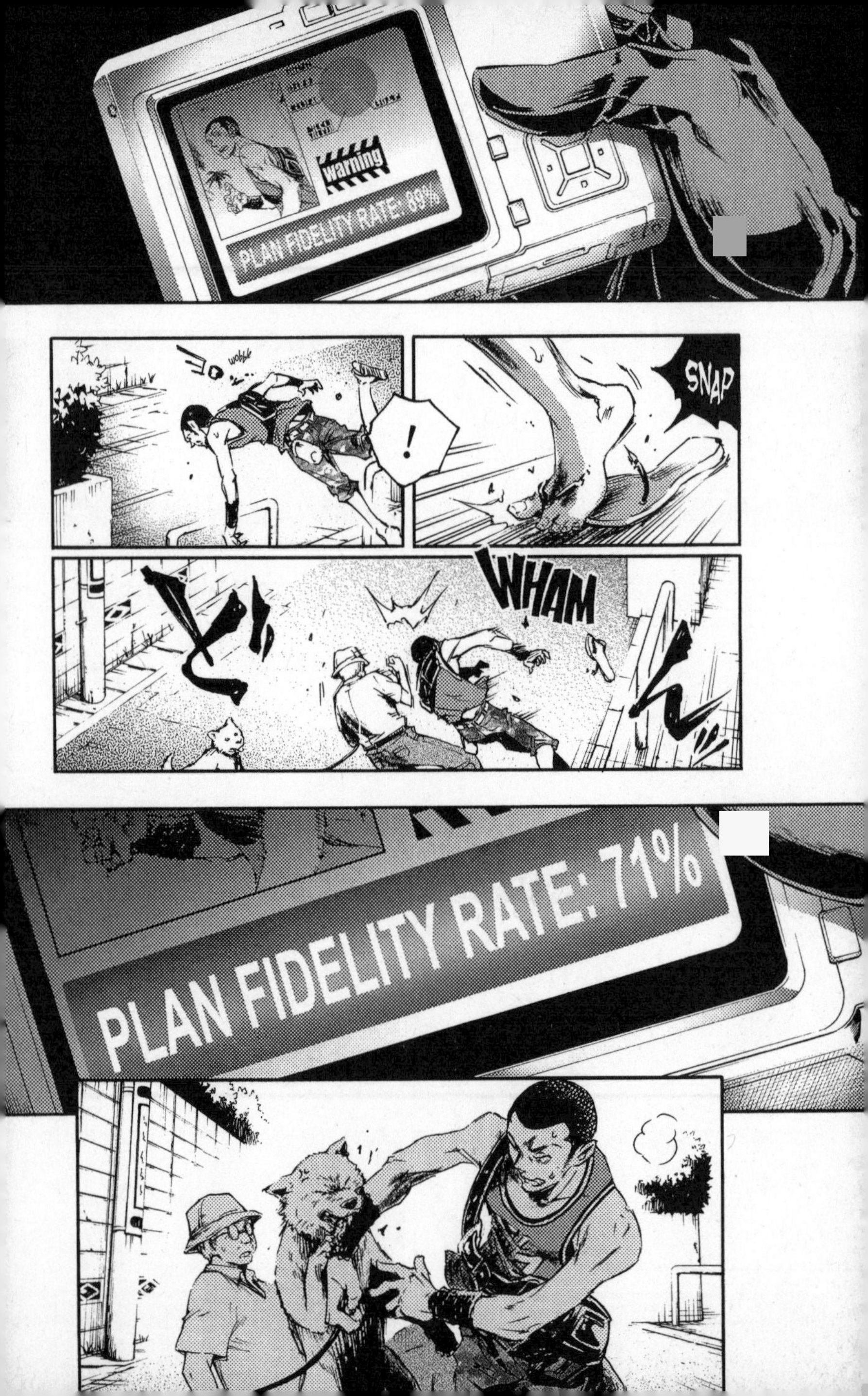
warning
PLAN FIDELITY RATE: 89%
SNAP
wobble
!
WHAM
PLAN FIDELITY RATE: 71%

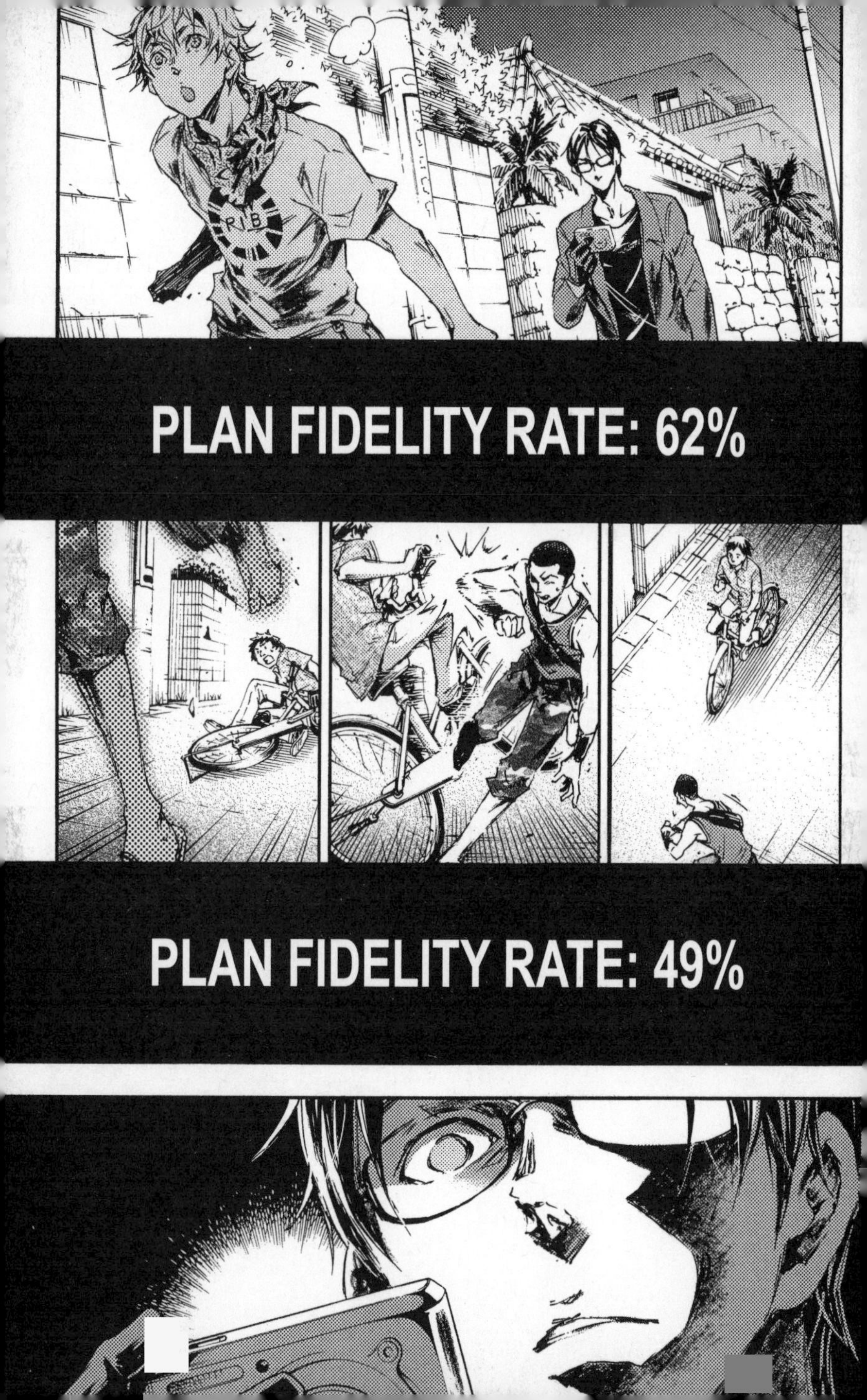
PLAN FIDELITY RATE: 62%
PLAN FIDELITY RATE: 49%

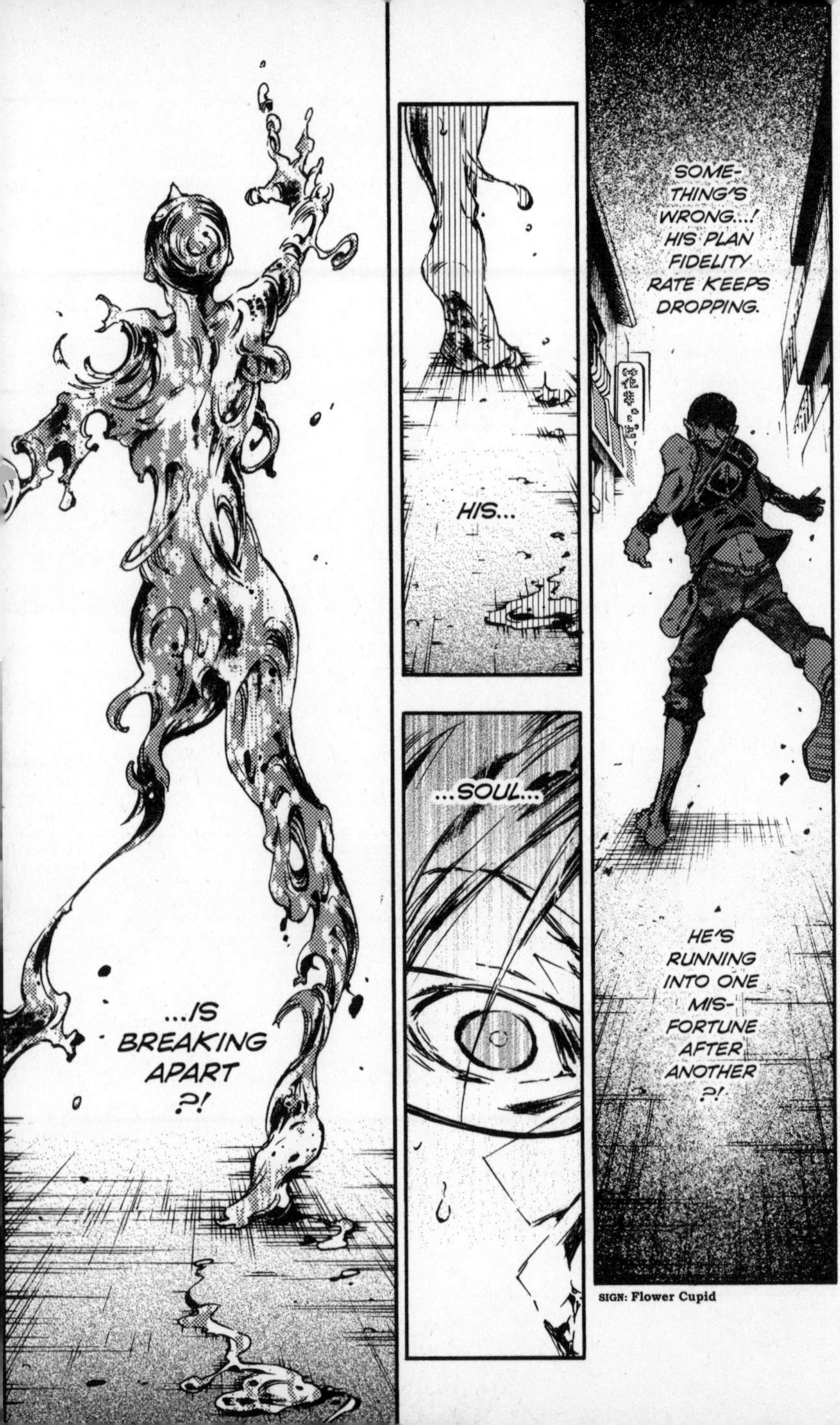
SOME-THING'S WRONG...! HIS PLAN FIDELITY RATE KEEPS DROPPING.
HE'S RUNNING INTO ONE MIS-FORTUNE AFTER ANOTHER ?!
HIS...
...SOUL...
...IS BREAKING APART ?!

SIGN: Flower Cupid

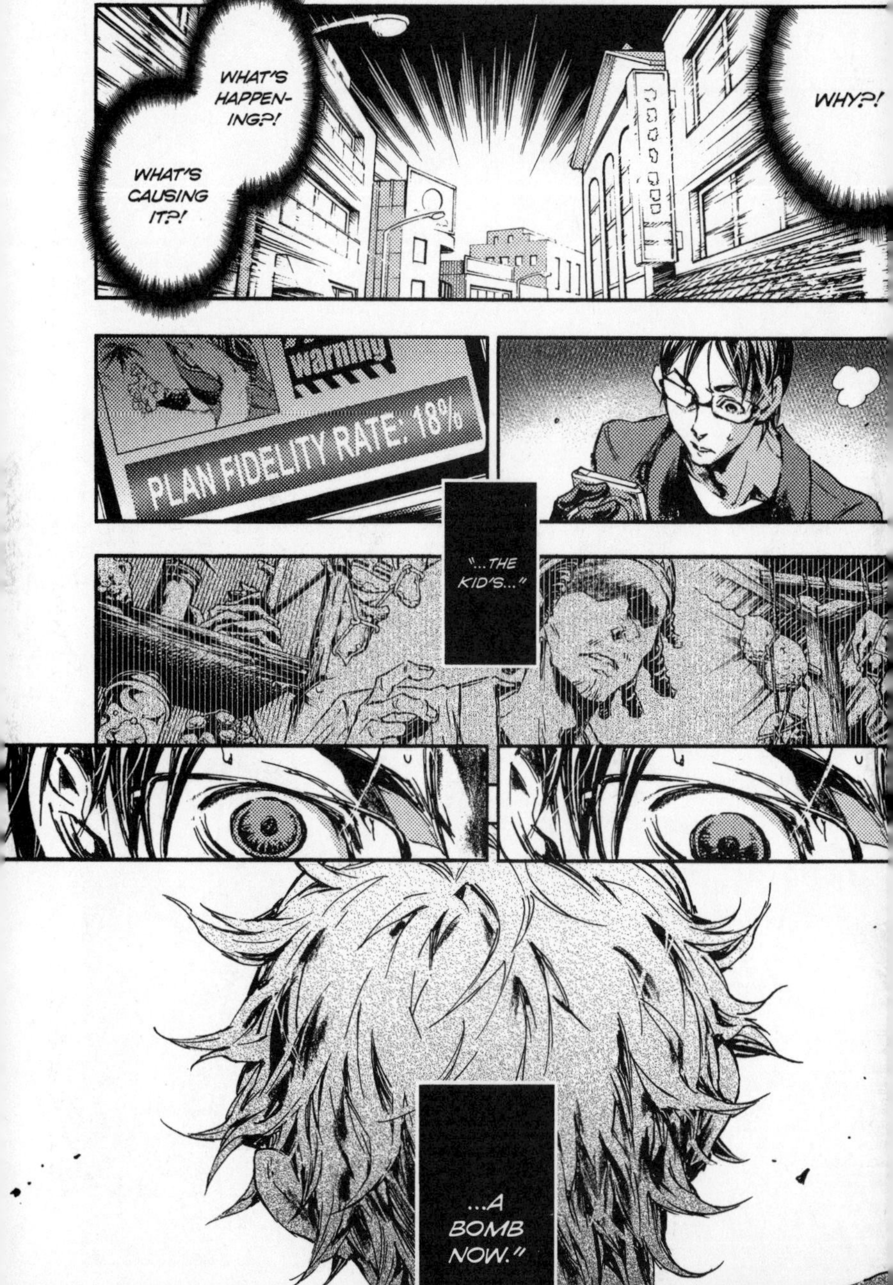
WHY?!
WHAT'S HAPPEN-ING?!
WHAT'S CAUSING IT?!
warning
PLAN FIDELITY RATE: 18%
"...THE KID'S..."
...A BOMB NOW."

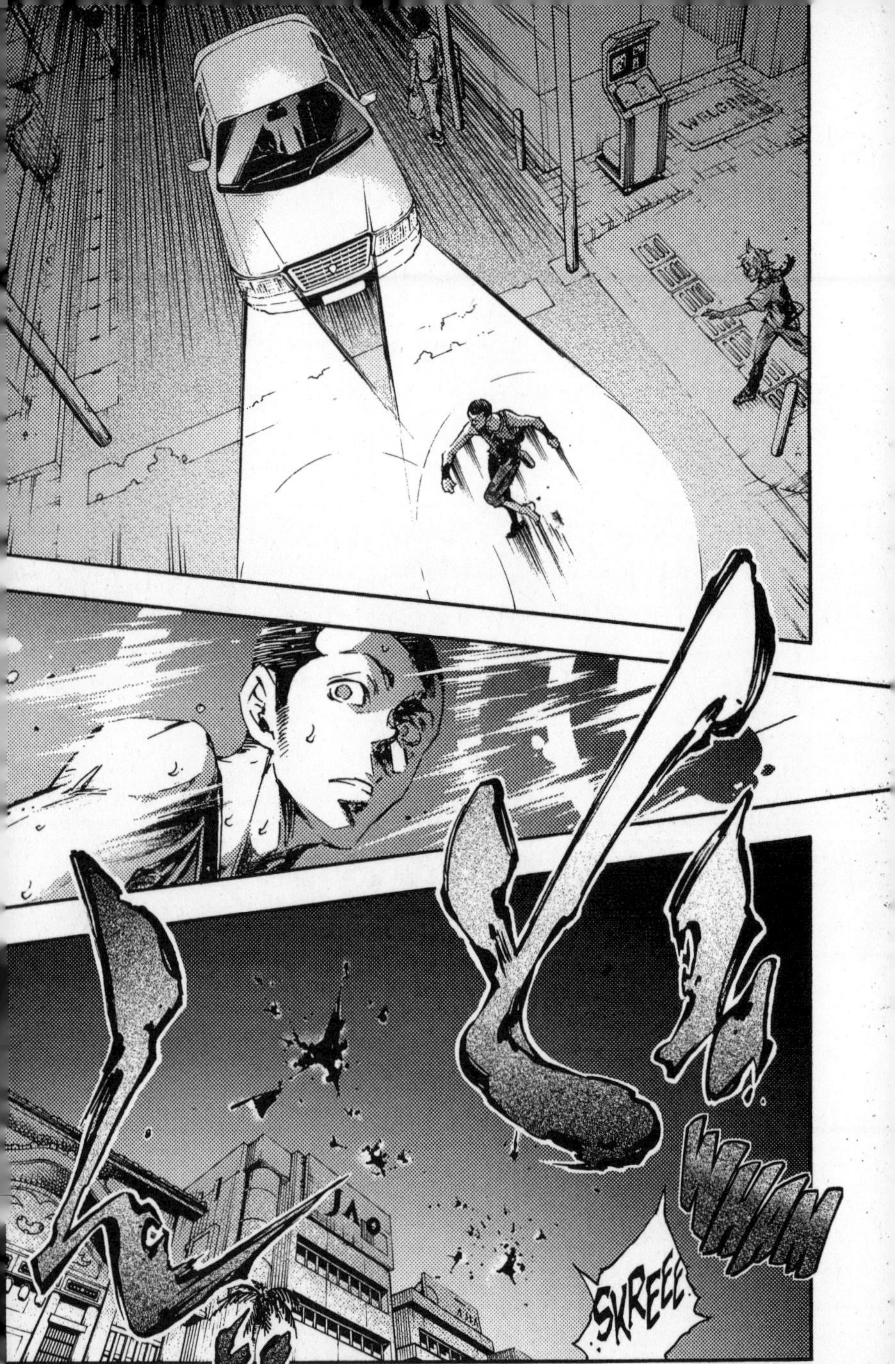
SKREEE

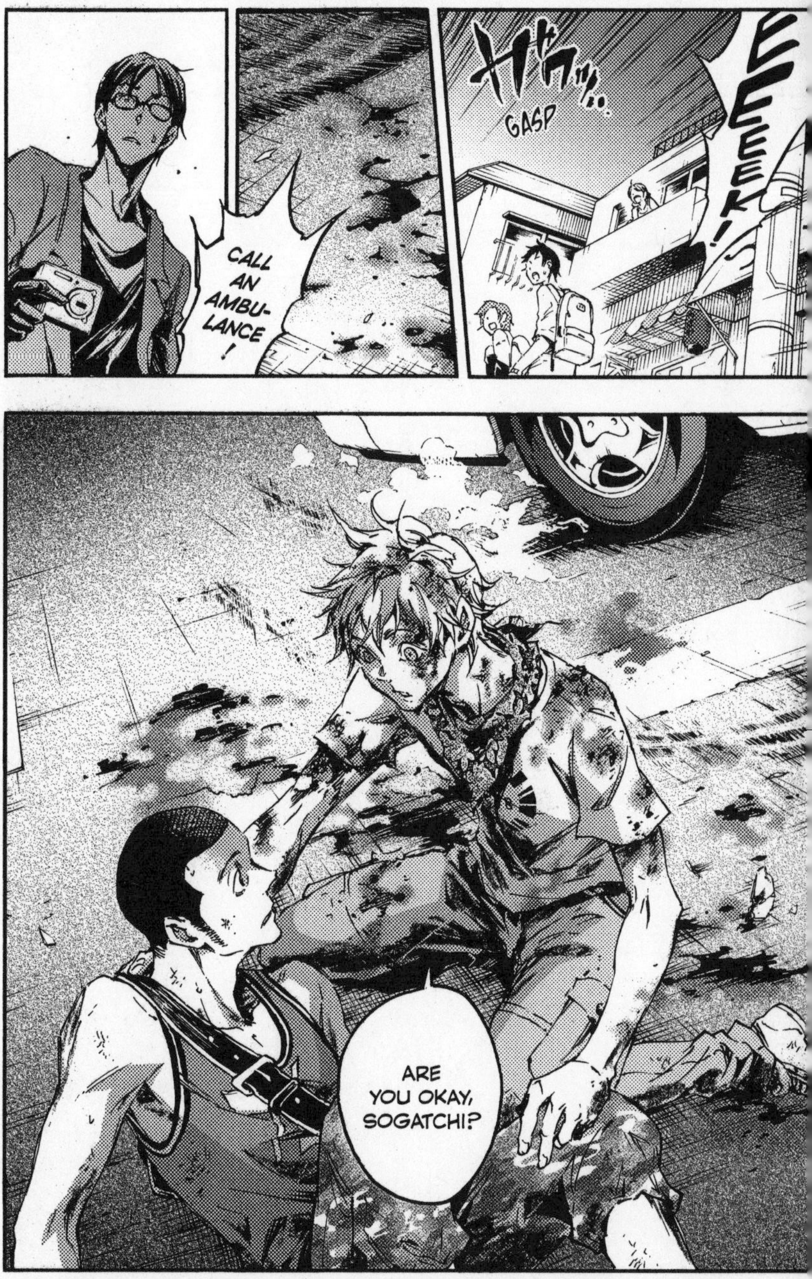
EEEEK!
GASP
CALL AN AMBULANCE!
ARE YOU OKAY, SOGATCHI?

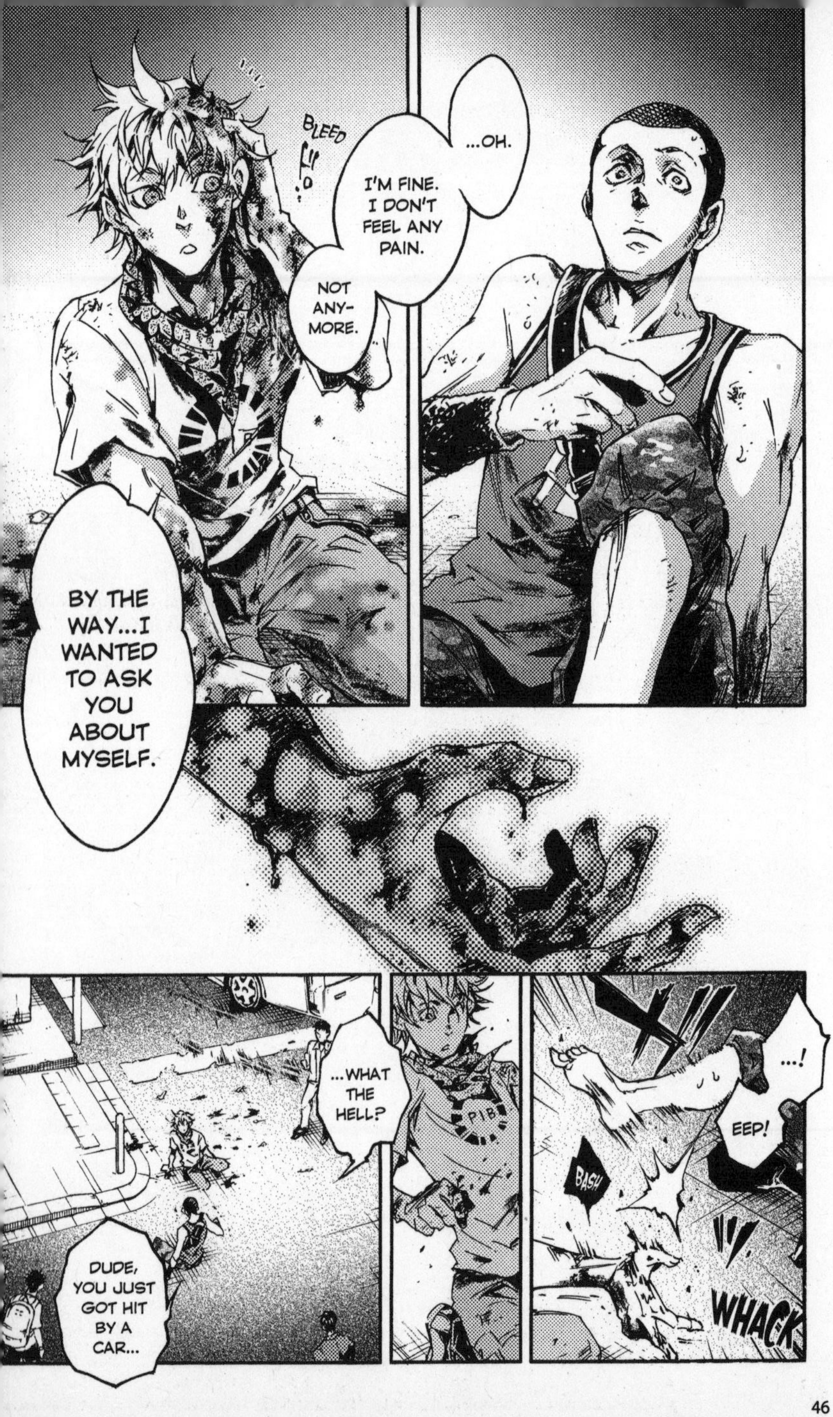

...OH.
BLEED
I'M FINE. I DON'T FEEL ANY PAIN.
NOT ANYMORE.
BY THE WAY...I WANTED TO ASK YOU ABOUT MYSELF.
...!
EEP!
BASH
WHACK
...WHAT THE HELL?
DUDE, YOU JUST GOT HIT BY A CAR...

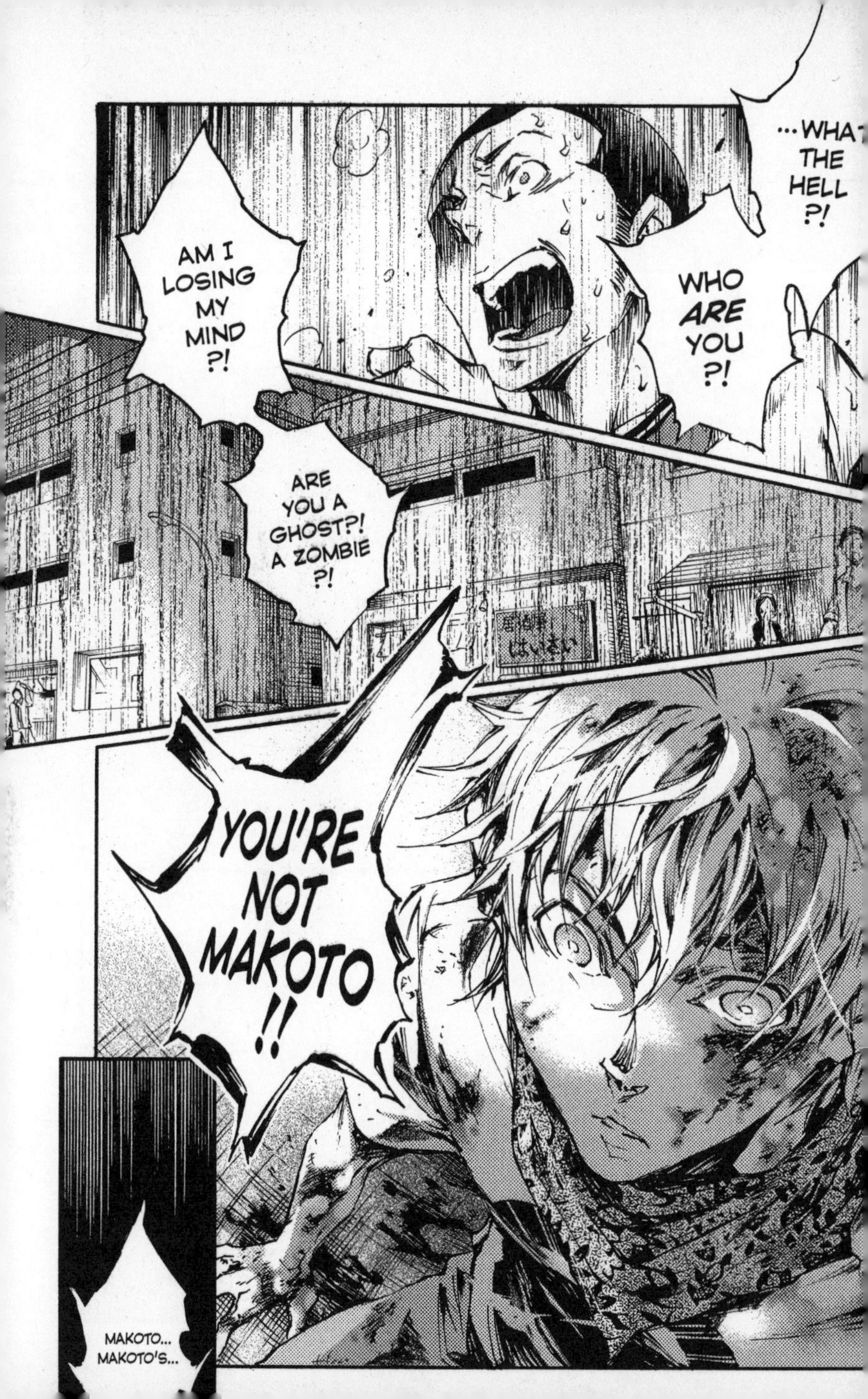
...WHAT THE HELL?!
WHO ARE YOU?!
AM I LOSING MY MIND?!
ARE YOU A GHOST?! A ZOMBIE?!
YOU'RE NOT MAKOTO!!
MAKOTO... MAKOTO'S...

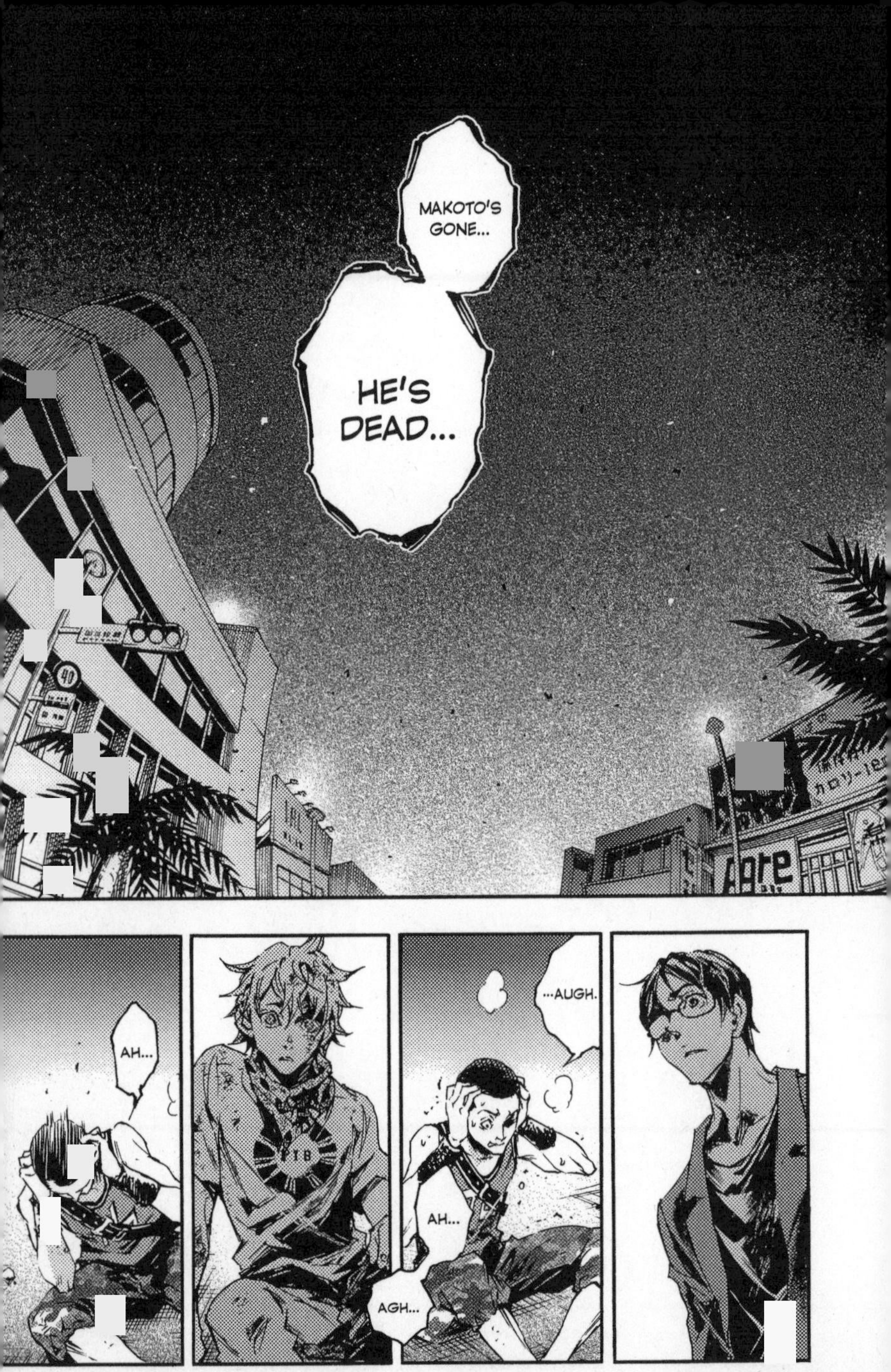
MAKOTO'S GONE...
HE'S DEAD...
...AUGH.
AH...
AGH...
AH...

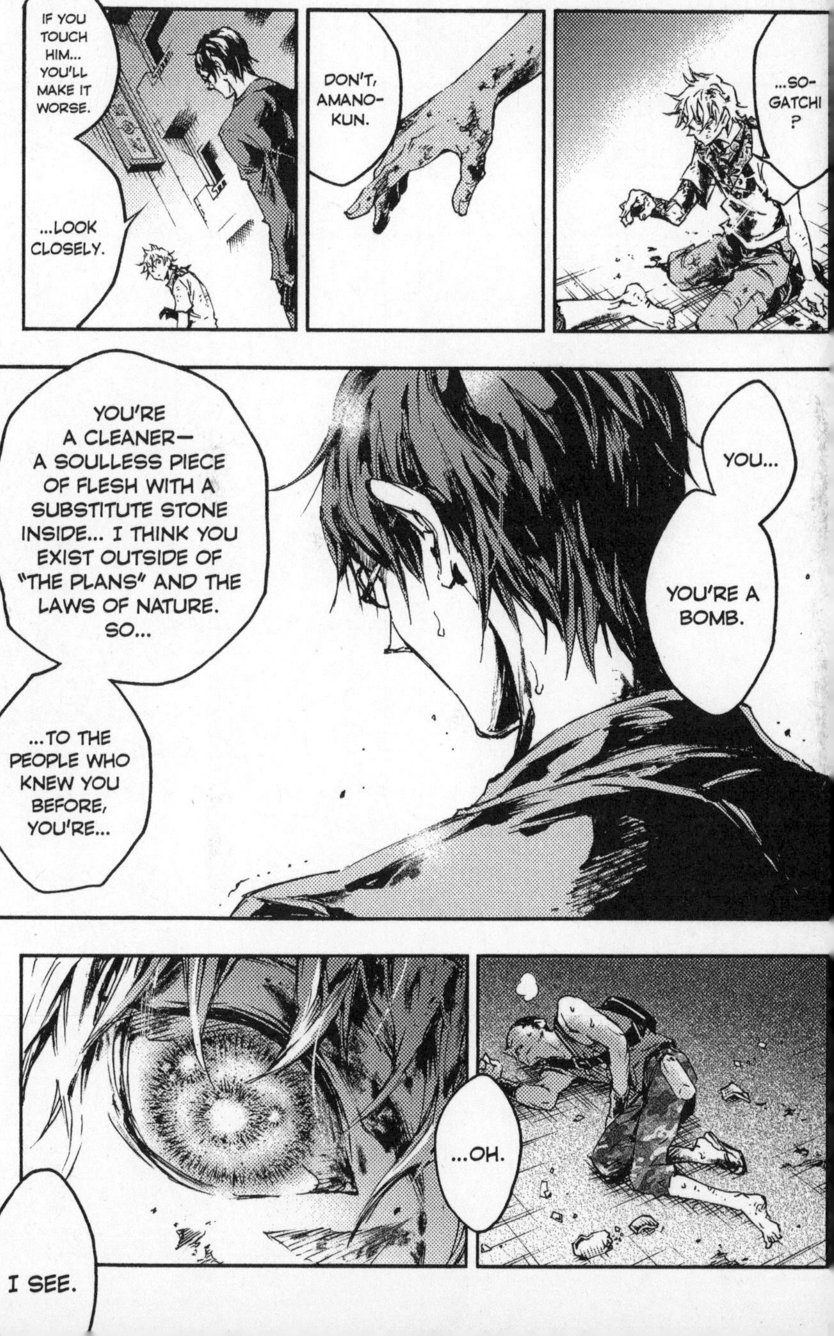
...SO-GATCHI?
DON'T, AMANO-KUN.
IF YOU TOUCH HIM... YOU'LL MAKE IT WORSE.
...LOOK CLOSELY.
YOU'RE A CLEANER— A SOULLESS PIECE OF FLESH WITH A SUBSTITUTE STONE INSIDE... I THINK YOU EXIST OUTSIDE OF "THE PLANS" AND THE LAWS OF NATURE. SO...
...TO THE PEOPLE WHO KNEW YOU BEFORE, YOU'RE...
YOU...
YOU'RE A BOMB.
...OH.
I SEE.

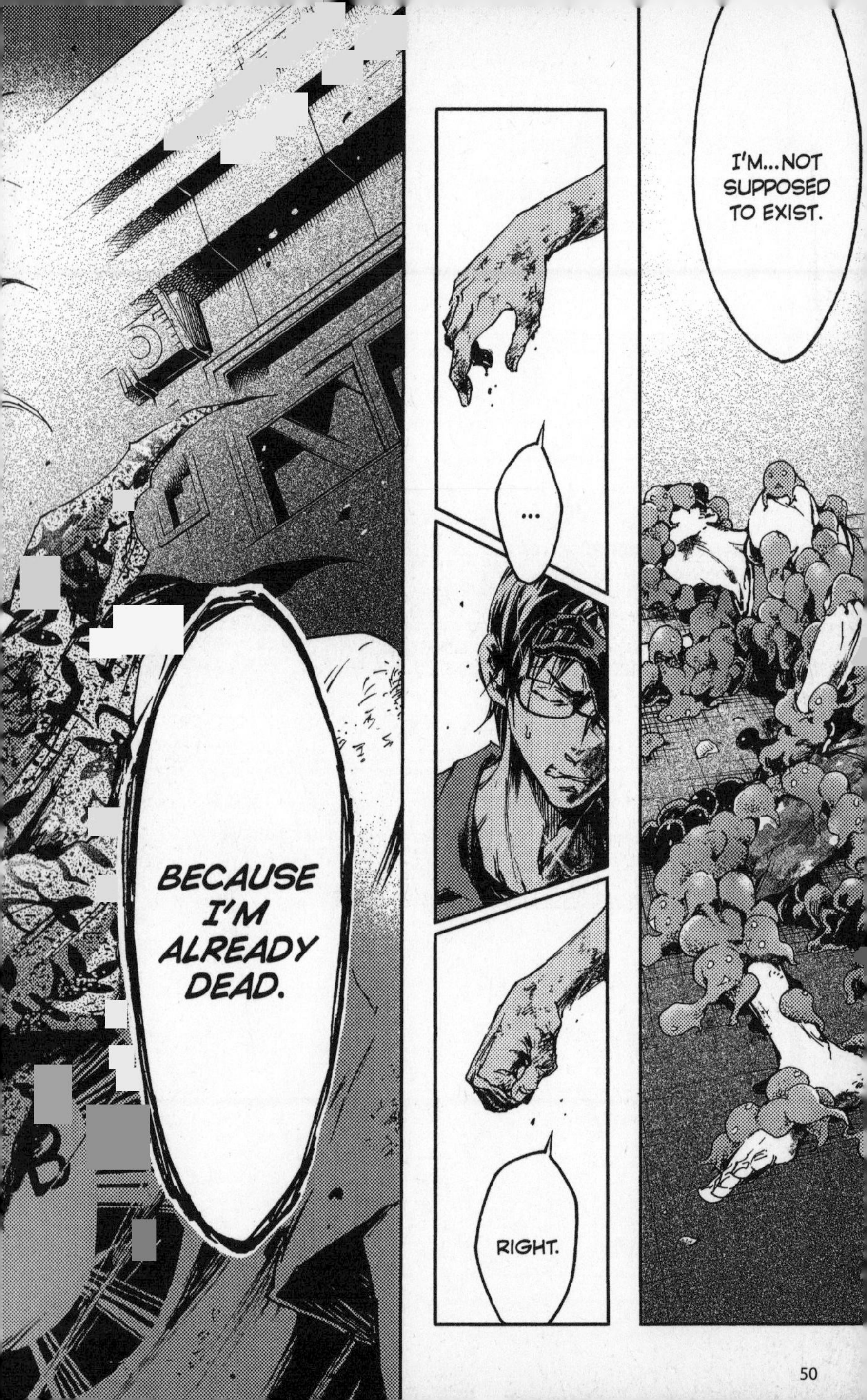
I'M...NOT SUPPOSED TO EXIST.
...
RIGHT.
BECAUSE I'M ALREADY DEAD.

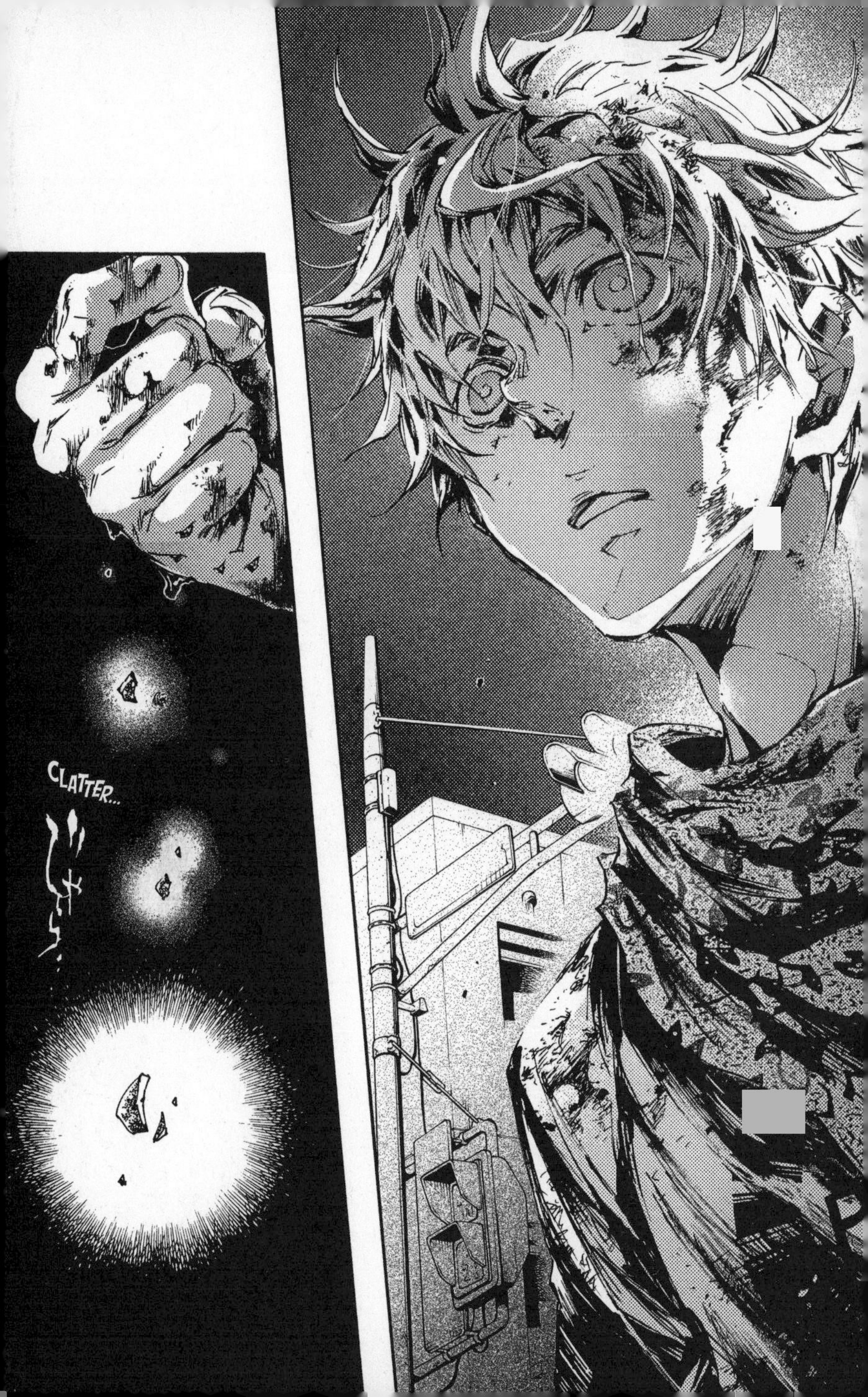
CLATTER...

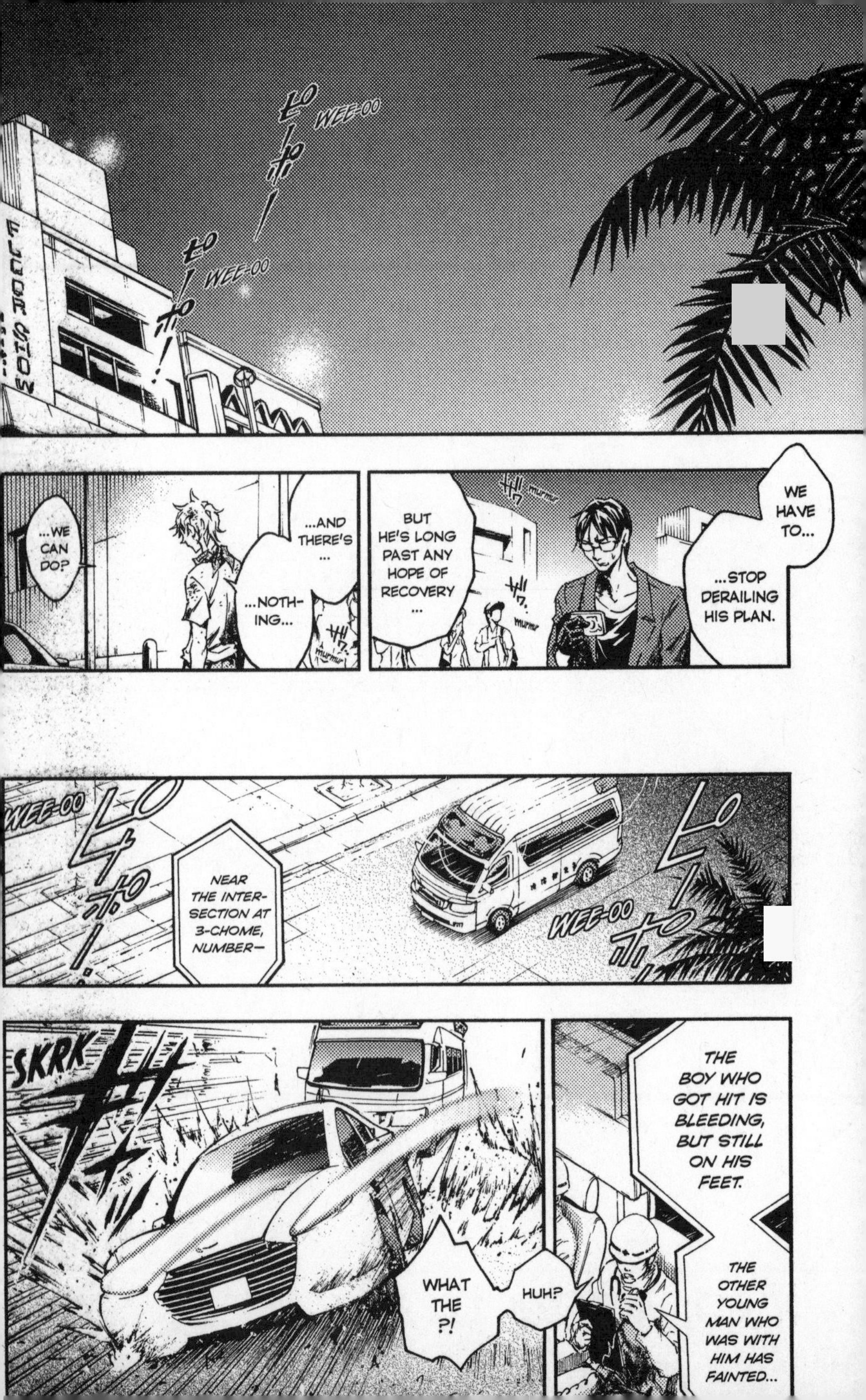

WEE-OO
WEE-OO
FLOOR SHOW
WE HAVE TO...
...STOP DERAILING HIS PLAN.
murmur
murmur
BUT HE'S LONG PAST ANY HOPE OF RECOVERY...
...AND THERE'S...
...NOTH-ING...
murmur
...WE CAN DO?
WEE-OO
NEAR THE INTER-SECTION AT 3-CHOME, NUMBER—
WEE-OO
THE BOY WHO GOT HIT IS BLEEDING, BUT STILL ON HIS FEET.
THE OTHER YOUNG MAN WHO WAS WITH HIM HAS FAINTED...
HUH?
WHAT THE ?!
SKRK

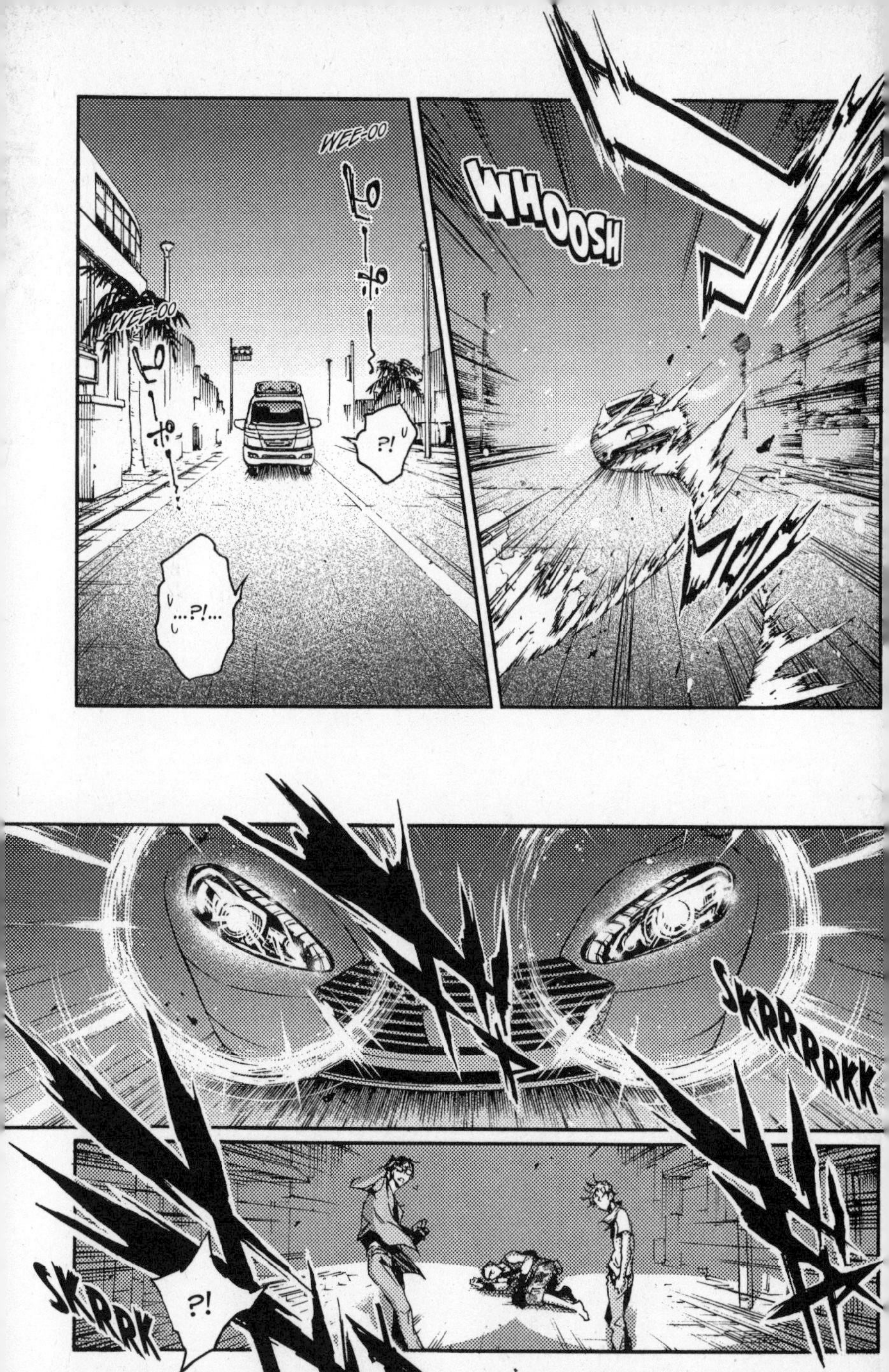
WHOOSH
WEE-OO
ピーポー
?!
WEE-OO
ピーポー
...?!...
SKRRRRKK
SKRRK
?!

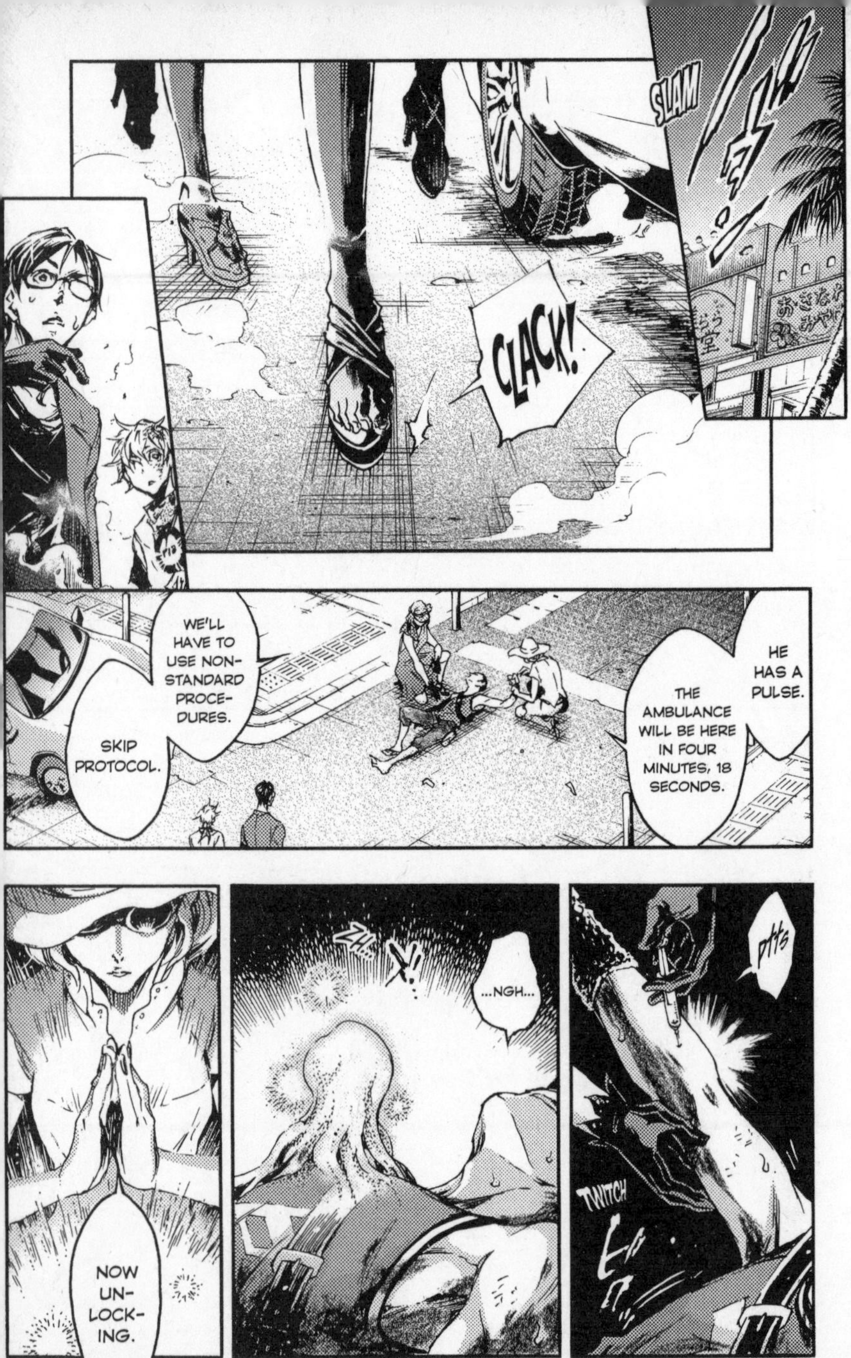
SLAM
CLACK!
HE HAS A PULSE.
THE AMBULANCE WILL BE HERE IN FOUR MINUTES, 18 SECONDS.
WE'LL HAVE TO USE NON-STANDARD PROCEDURES.
SKIP PROTOCOL.
ptts
TWITCH
ZH... X!..
...NGH...
NOW UNLOCKING.

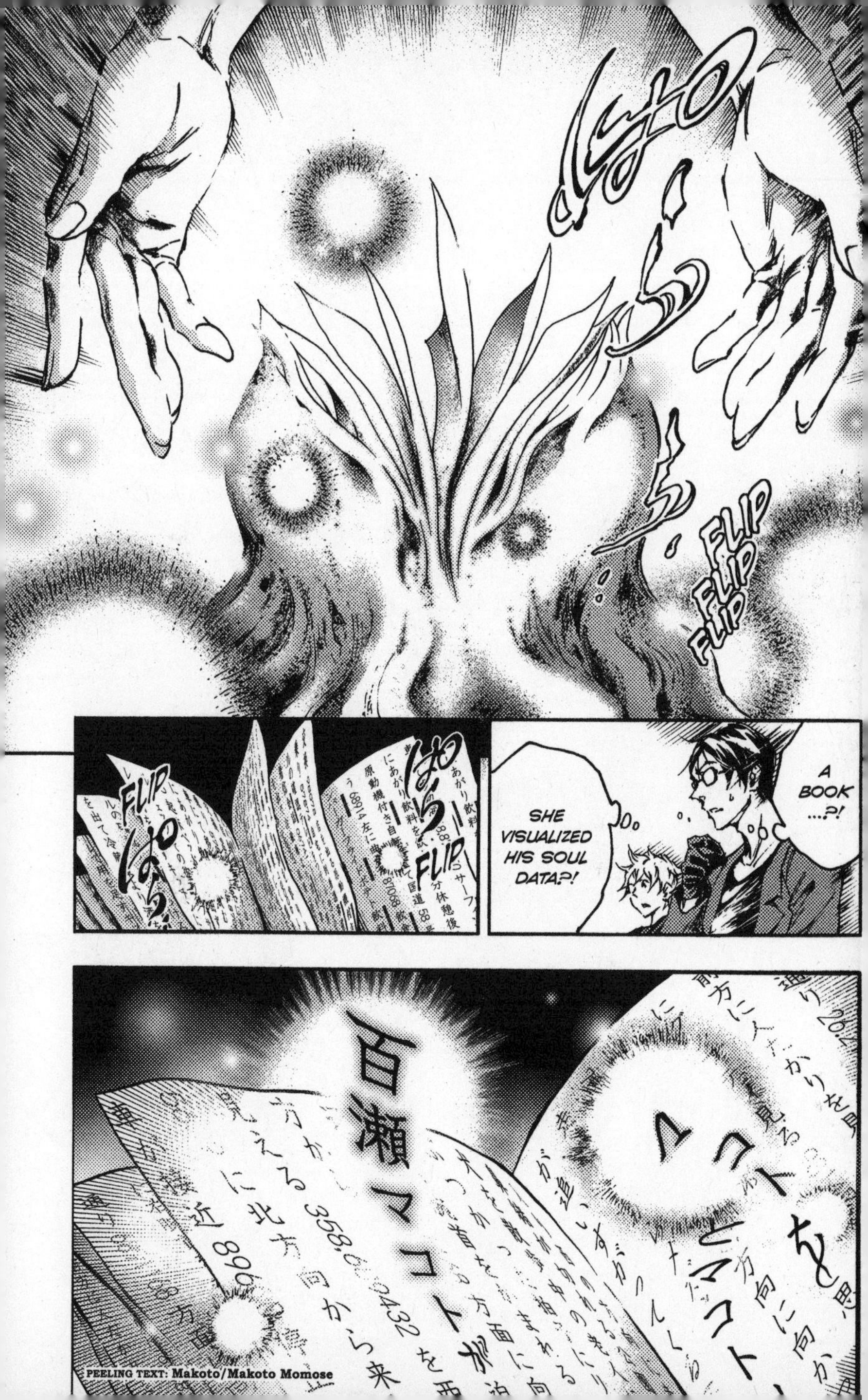
FLIP FLIP FLIP
A BOOK ...?!
SHE VISUALIZED HIS SOUL DATA?!
FLIP
FLIP
百瀬マコト
マコト
PEELING TEXT: Makoto/Makoto Momose

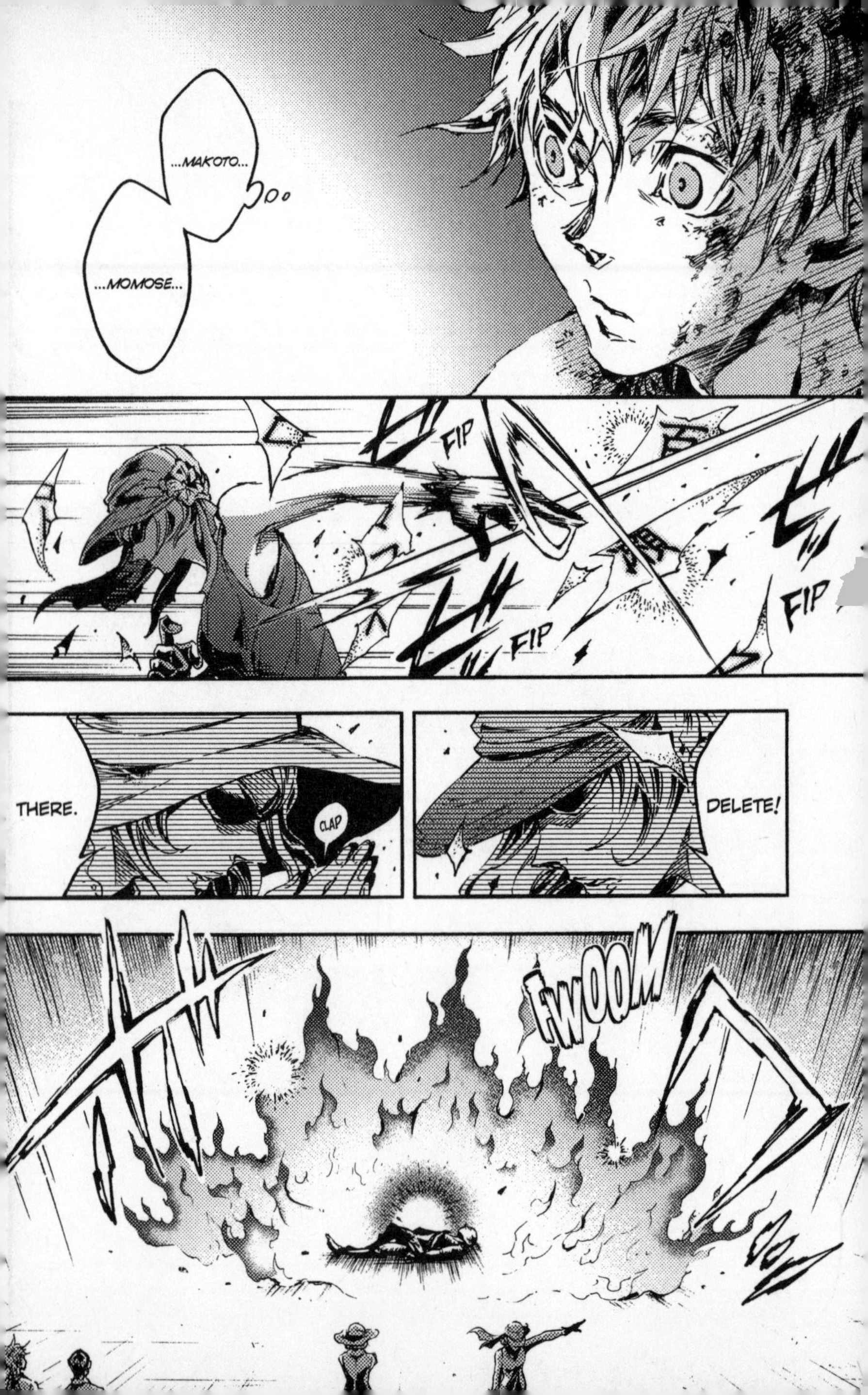
...MAKOTO...
...MOMOSE...
FIP
FIP
FIP
DELETE!
THERE.
CLAP
FWOOM

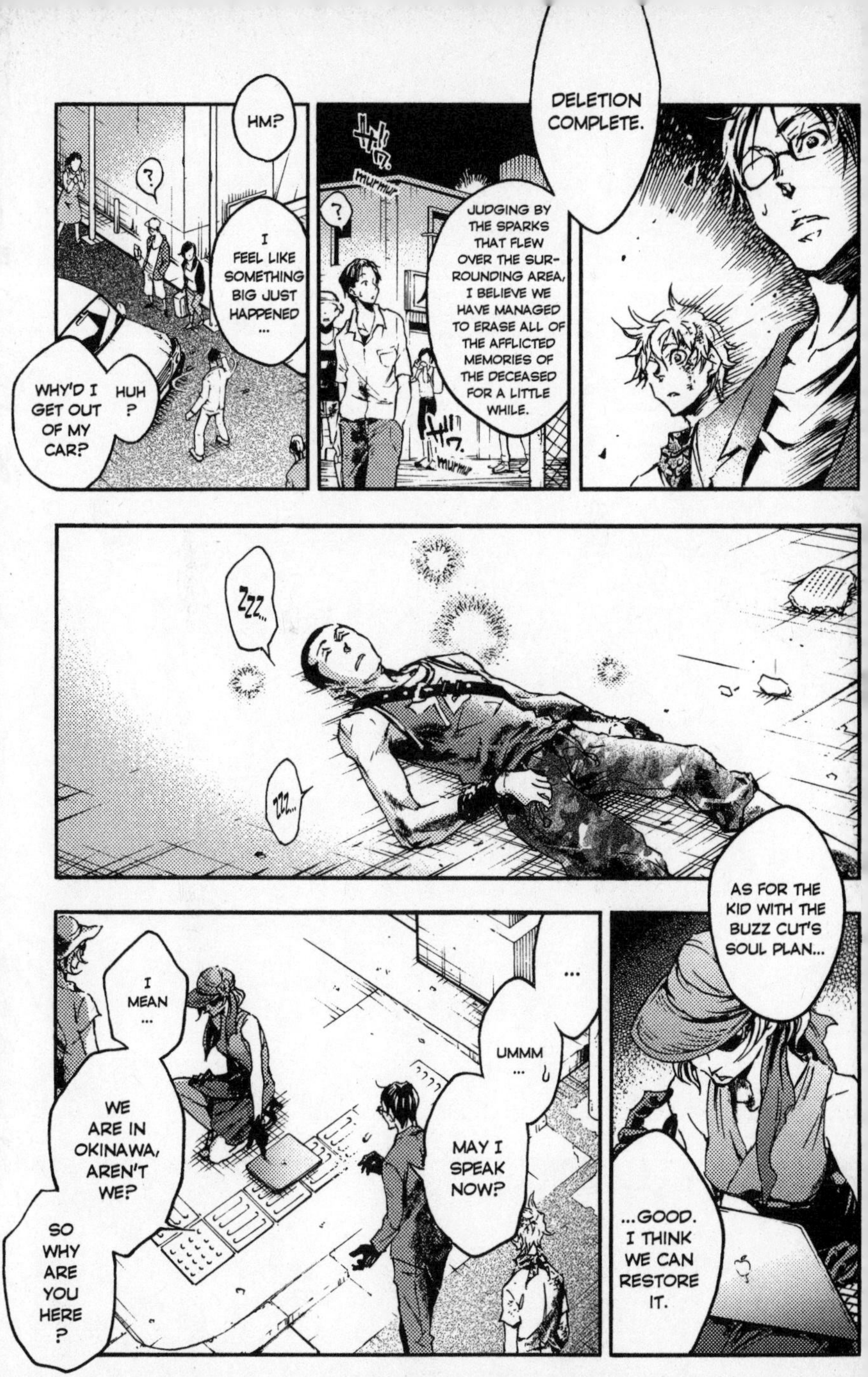
DELETION COMPLETE.
murmur
?
JUDGING BY THE SPARKS THAT FLEW OVER THE SURROUNDING AREA, I BELIEVE WE HAVE MANAGED TO ERASE ALL OF THE AFFLICTED MEMORIES OF THE DECEASED FOR A LITTLE WHILE.
murmur
HM?
?
I FEEL LIKE SOMETHING BIG JUST HAPPENED...
HUH?
WHY'D I GET OUT OF MY CAR?
Zzz...
Zzz...
AS FOR THE KID WITH THE BUZZ CUT'S SOUL PLAN...
...GOOD. I THINK WE CAN RESTORE IT.
...
UMMM...
MAY I SPEAK NOW?
I MEAN...
WE ARE IN OKINAWA, AREN'T WE?
SO WHY ARE YOU HERE?

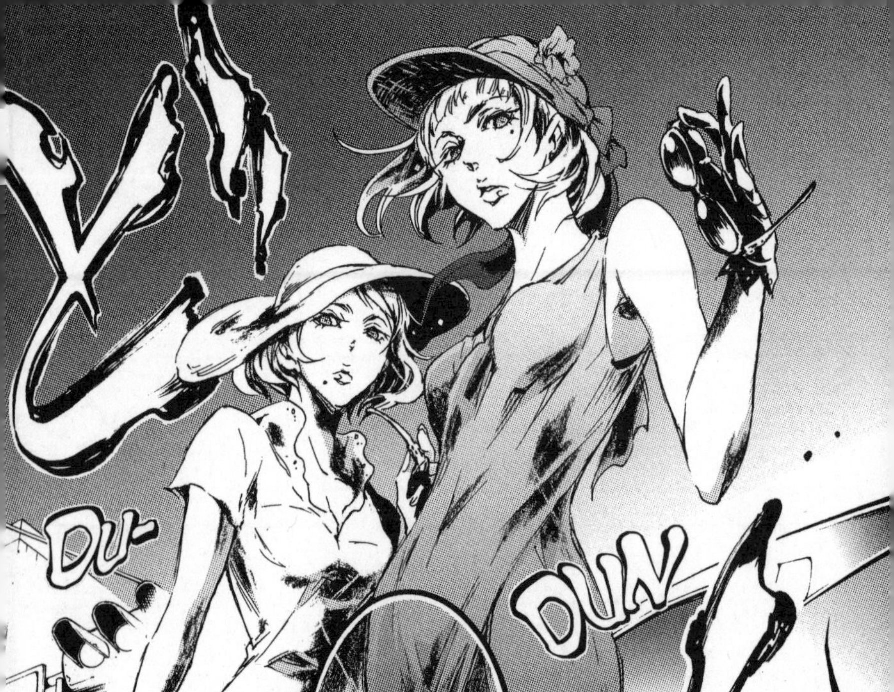
DU-
DUN
...EBINA-SAN?

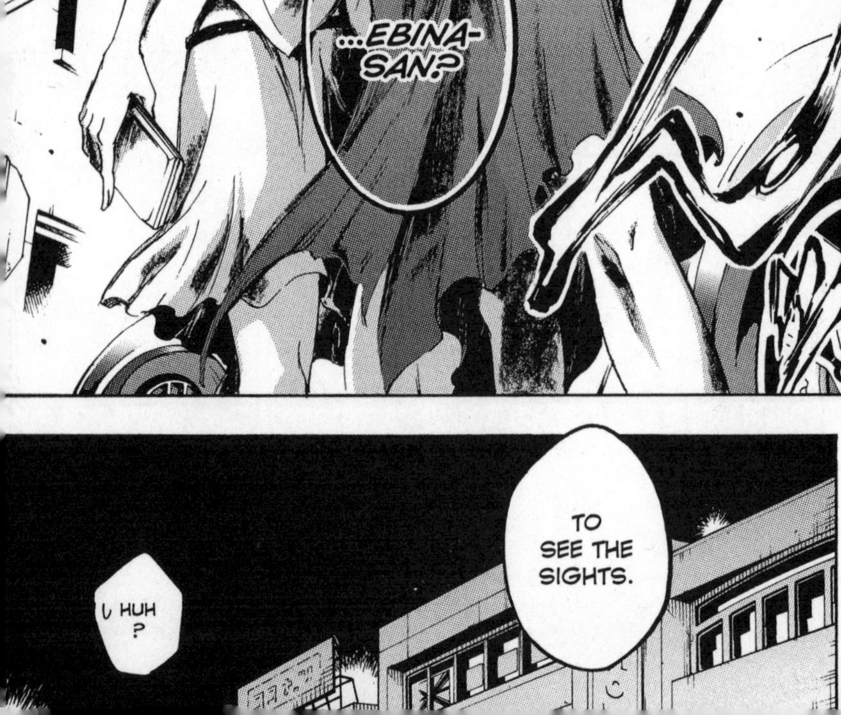
TO SEE THE SIGHTS.
HUH ?

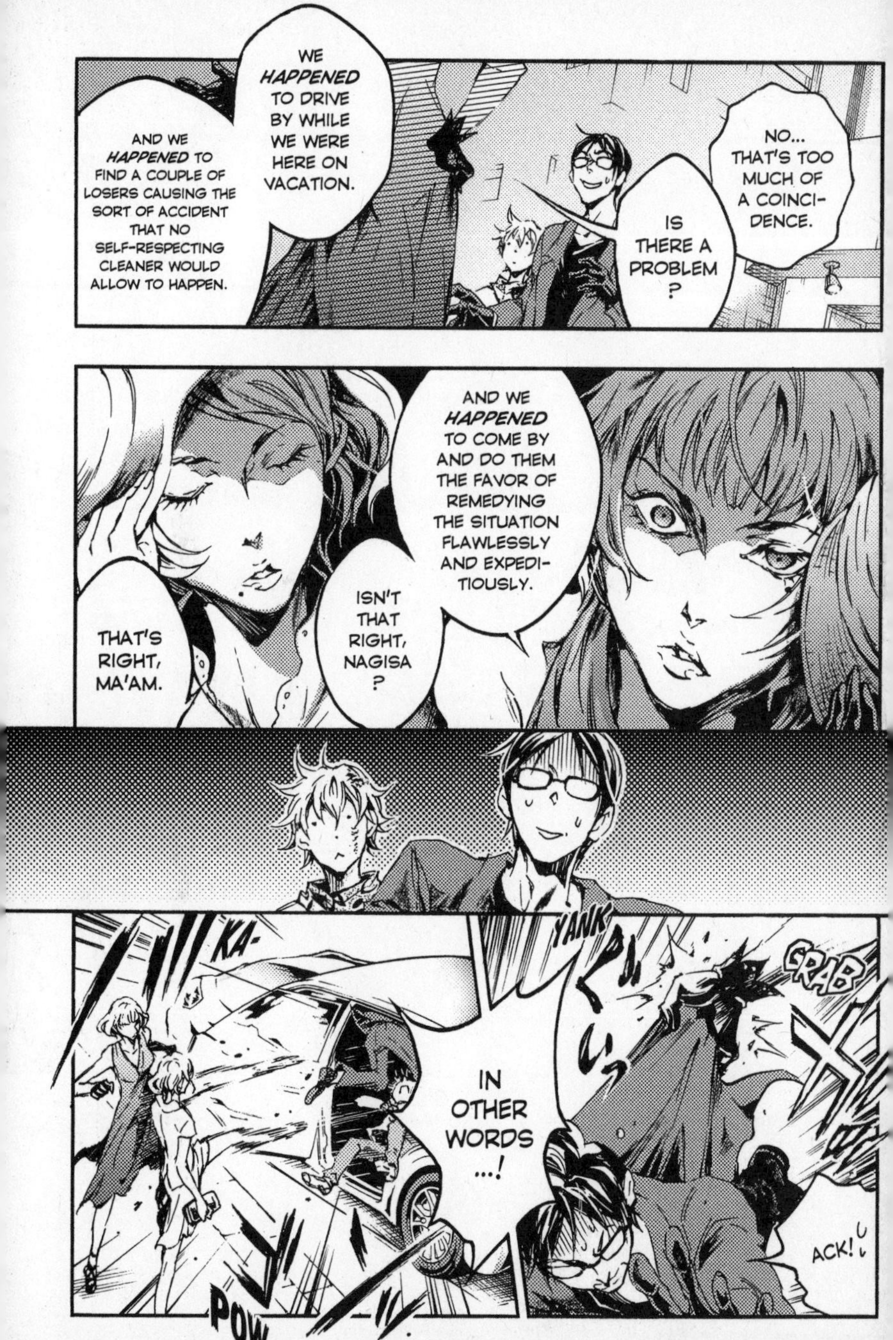
NO... THAT'S TOO MUCH OF A COINCI-DENCE.
IS THERE A PROBLEM?
WE *HAPPENED* TO DRIVE BY WHILE WE WERE HERE ON VACATION.
AND WE *HAPPENED* TO FIND A COUPLE OF LOSERS CAUSING THE SORT OF ACCIDENT THAT NO SELF-RESPECTING CLEANER WOULD ALLOW TO HAPPEN.
AND WE *HAPPENED* TO COME BY AND DO THEM THE FAVOR OF REMEDYING THE SITUATION FLAWLESSLY AND EXPEDI-TIOUSLY.
ISN'T THAT RIGHT, NAGISA?
THAT'S RIGHT, MA'AM.
GRAB
ACK!
YANK
IN OTHER WORDS ...!
KA-
POW

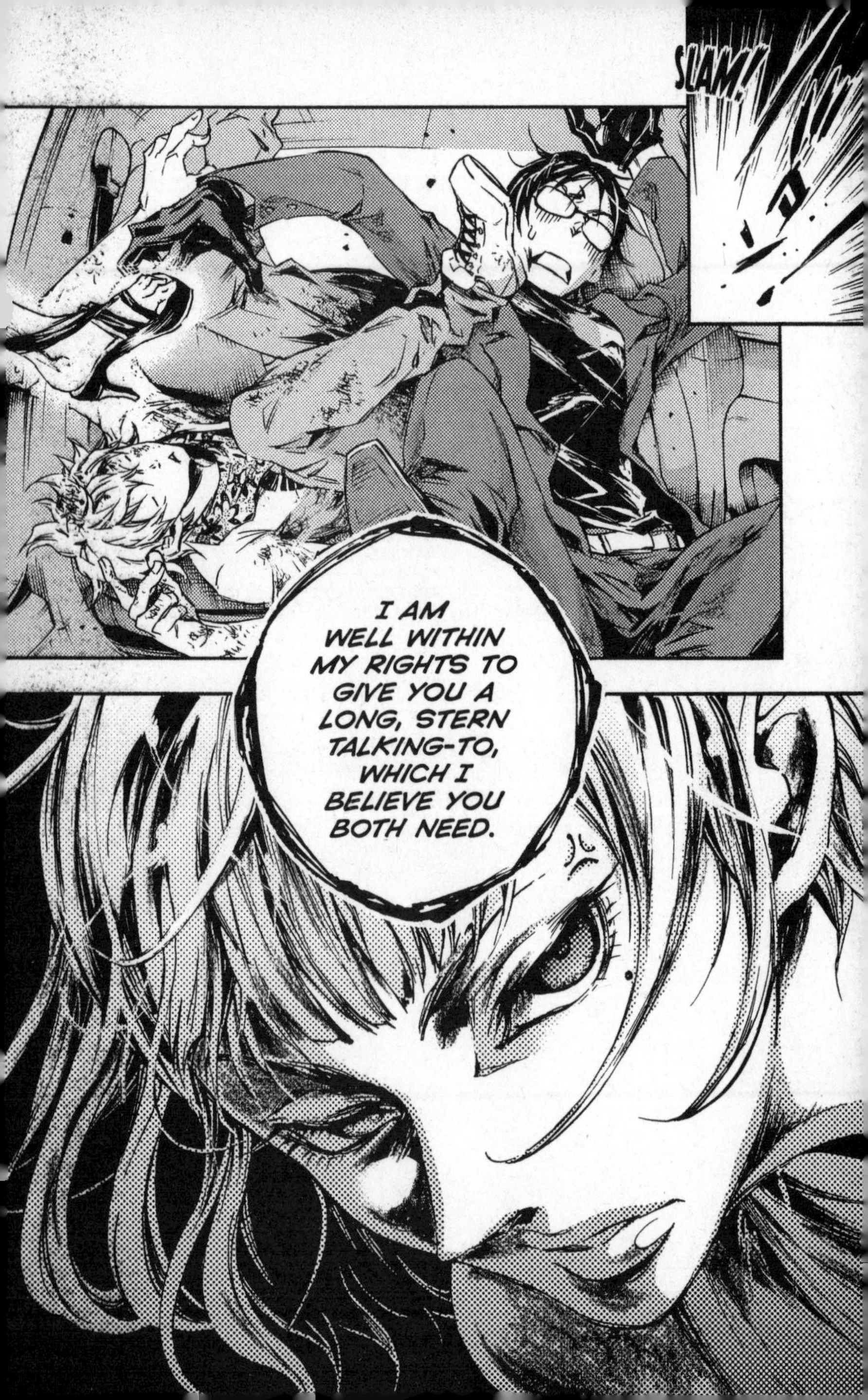
SLAM!!
I AM WELL WITHIN MY RIGHTS TO GIVE YOU A LONG, STERN TALKING-TO, WHICH I BELIEVE YOU BOTH NEED.

Chapter 20   Second Death

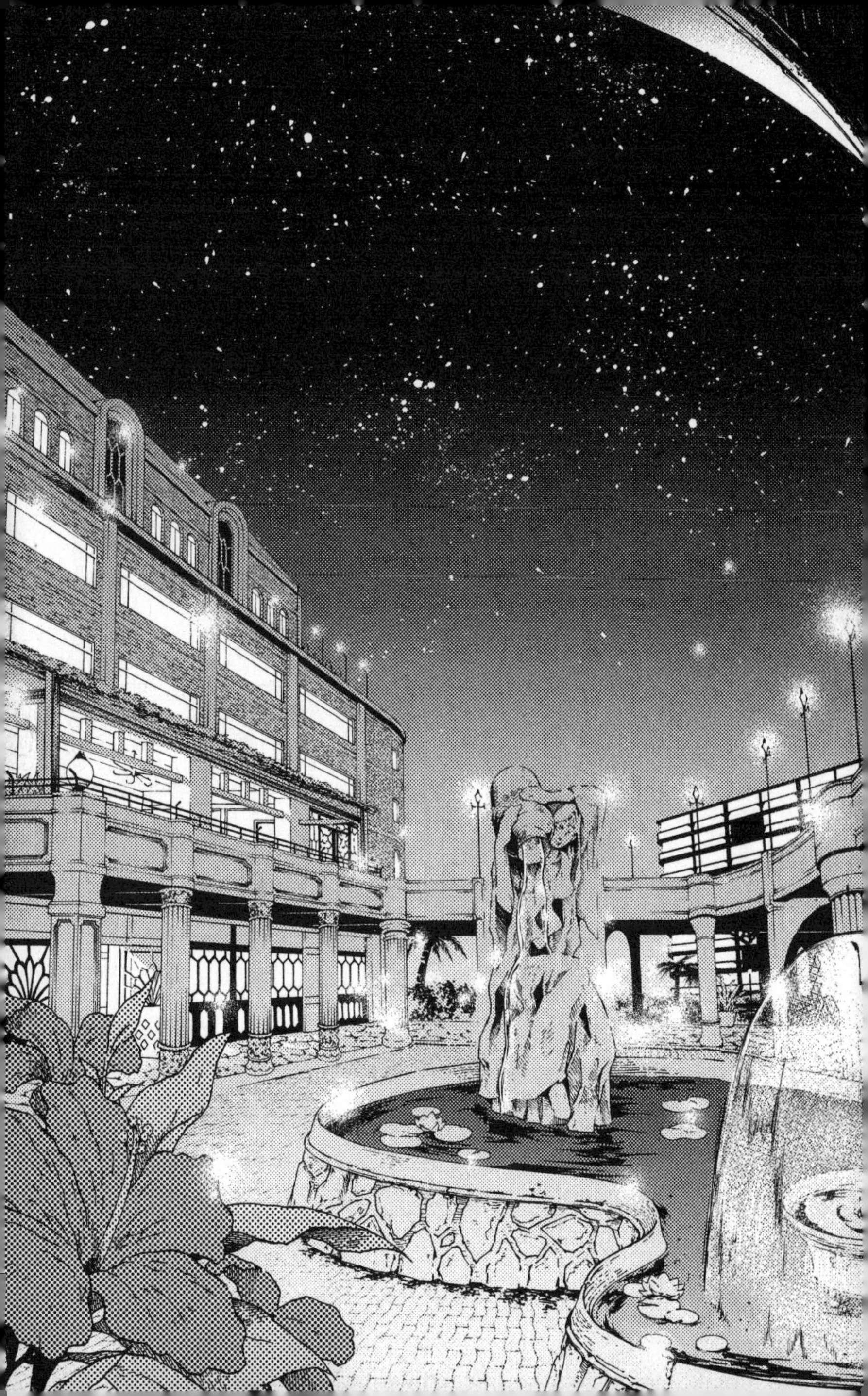

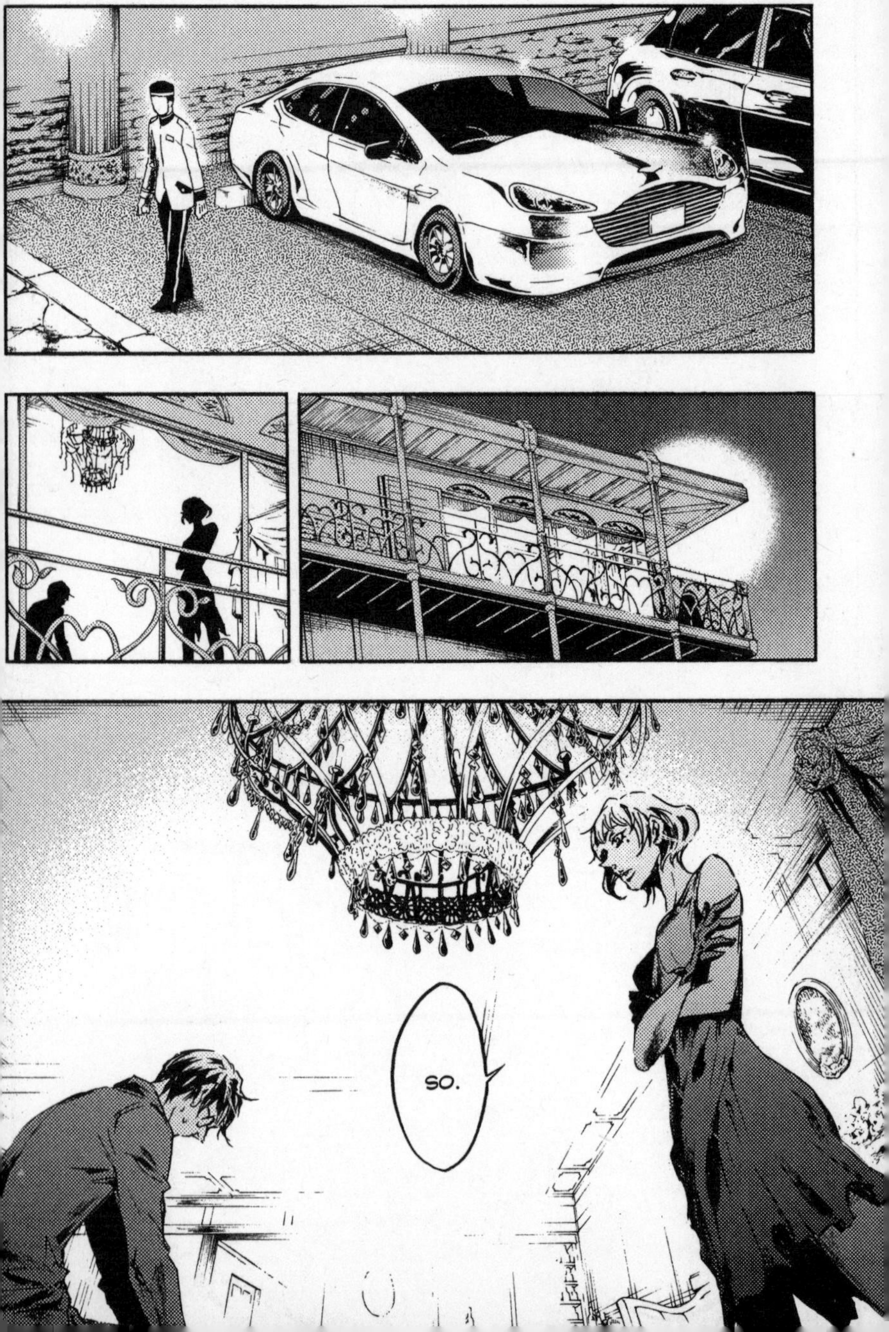
SO.

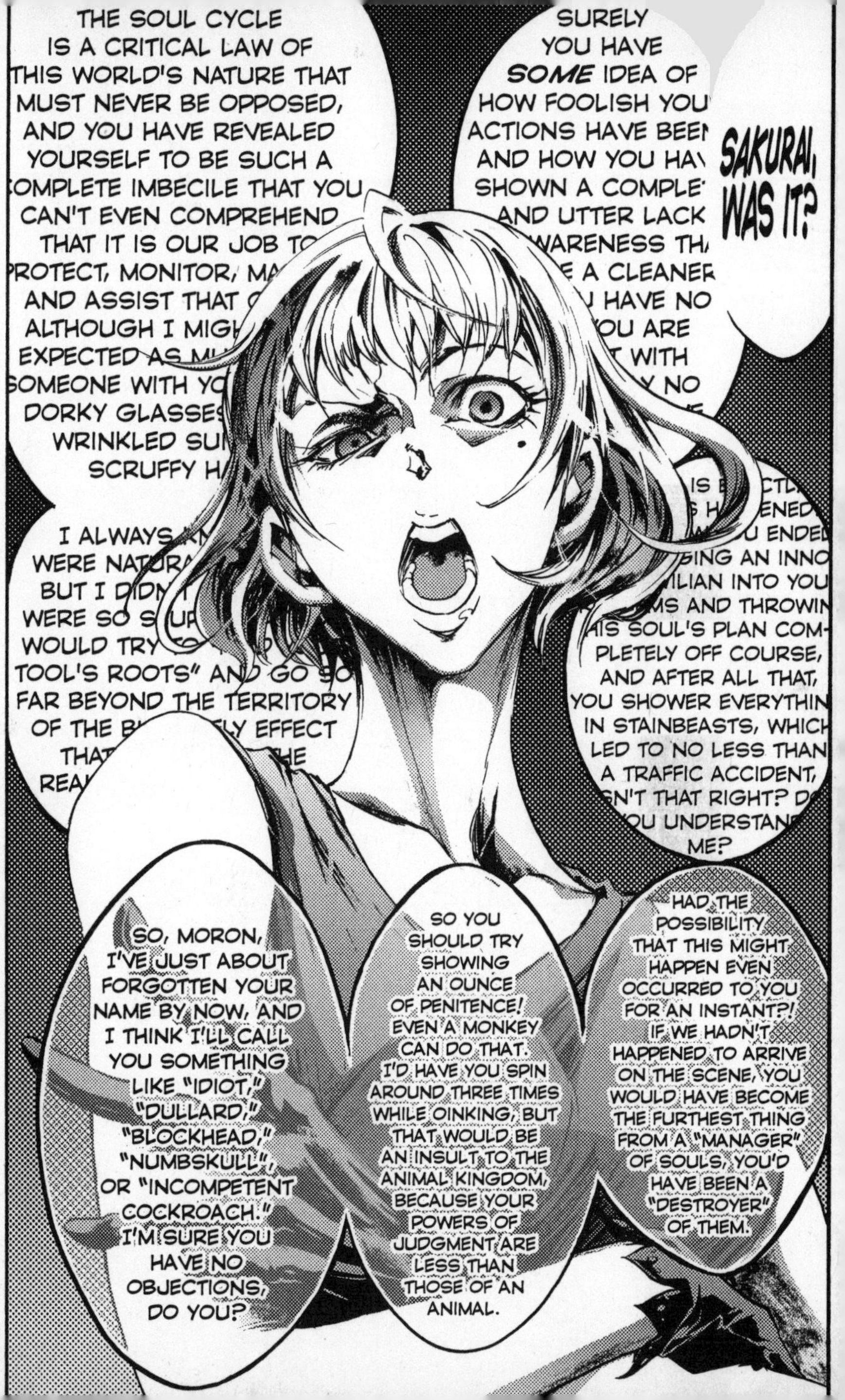
SAKURAI, WAS IT?
SURELY YOU HAVE *SOME* IDEA OF HOW FOOLISH YOU ACTIONS HAVE BEEN AND HOW YOU HA SHOWN A COMPLE AND UTTER LACK WARENESS TH E A CLEANER U HAVE NO OU ARE WITH NO
IS ENED U ENDED ING AN INNO ILIAN INTO YOU MS AND THROWIN IS SOUL'S PLAN COMPLETELY OFF COURSE, AND AFTER ALL THAT, YOU SHOWER EVERYTHIN IN STAINBEASTS, WHICH LED TO NO LESS THAN A TRAFFIC ACCIDENT, N'T THAT RIGHT? D YOU UNDERSTAN ME?
THE SOUL CYCLE IS A CRITICAL LAW OF THIS WORLD'S NATURE THAT MUST NEVER BE OPPOSED, AND YOU HAVE REVEALED YOURSELF TO BE SUCH A OMPLETE IMBECILE THAT YOU CAN'T EVEN COMPREHEND THAT IT IS OUR JOB TO ROTECT, MONITOR, MA AND ASSIST THAT ALTHOUGH I MIGH EXPECTED AS OMEONE WITH YO DORKY GLASSES WRINKLED SU SCRUFFY H
I ALWAYS WERE NAT BUT I WERE SO WOULD TRY TOOL'S ROOTS" AN GO FAR BEYOND THE TERRITORY OF THE EFFECT THA REA
HAD THE POSSIBILITY THAT THIS MIGHT HAPPEN EVEN OCCURRED TO YOU FOR AN INSTANT?! IF WE HADN'T HAPPENED TO ARRIVE ON THE SCENE, YOU WOULD HAVE BECOME THE FURTHEST THING FROM A "MANAGER" OF SOULS, YOU'D HAVE BEEN A "DESTROYER" OF THEM.
SO YOU SHOULD TRY SHOWING AN OUNCE OF PENITENCE! EVEN A MONKEY CAN DO THAT. I'D HAVE YOU SPIN AROUND THREE TIMES WHILE OINKING, BUT THAT WOULD BE AN INSULT TO THE ANIMAL KINGDOM, BECAUSE YOUR POWERS OF JUDGMENT ARE LESS THAN THOSE OF AN ANIMAL.
SO, MORON, I'VE JUST ABOUT FORGOTTEN YOUR NAME BY NOW, AND I THINK I'LL CALL YOU SOMETHING LIKE "IDIOT," "DULLARD," "BLOCKHEAD," "NUMBSKULL", OR "INCOMPETENT COCKROACH." I'M SURE YOU HAVE NO OBJECTIONS, DO YOU?

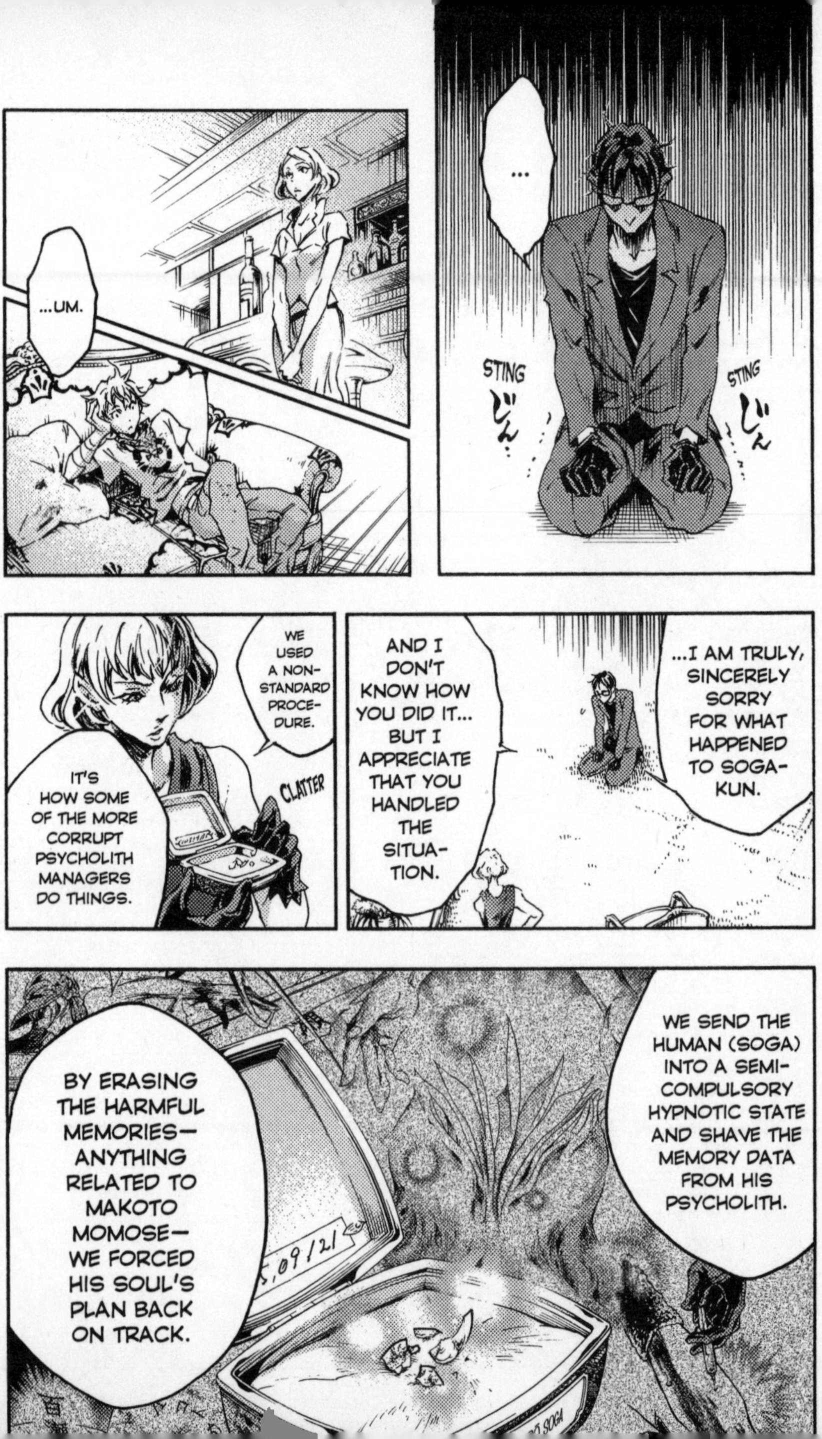
...
STING じん
STING じん
...UM.
...I AM TRULY, SINCERELY SORRY FOR WHAT HAPPENED TO SOGA-KUN.
AND I DON'T KNOW HOW YOU DID IT... BUT I APPRECIATE THAT YOU HANDLED THE SITUATION.
WE USED A NON-STANDARD PROCEDURE.
CLATTER
IT'S HOW SOME OF THE MORE CORRUPT PSYCHOLITH MANAGERS DO THINGS.
WE SEND THE HUMAN (SOGA) INTO A SEMI-COMPULSORY HYPNOTIC STATE AND SHAVE THE MEMORY DATA FROM HIS PSYCHOLITH.
BY ERASING THE HARMFUL MEMORIES—ANYTHING RELATED TO MAKOTO MOMOSE—WE FORCED HIS SOUL'S PLAN BACK ON TRACK.

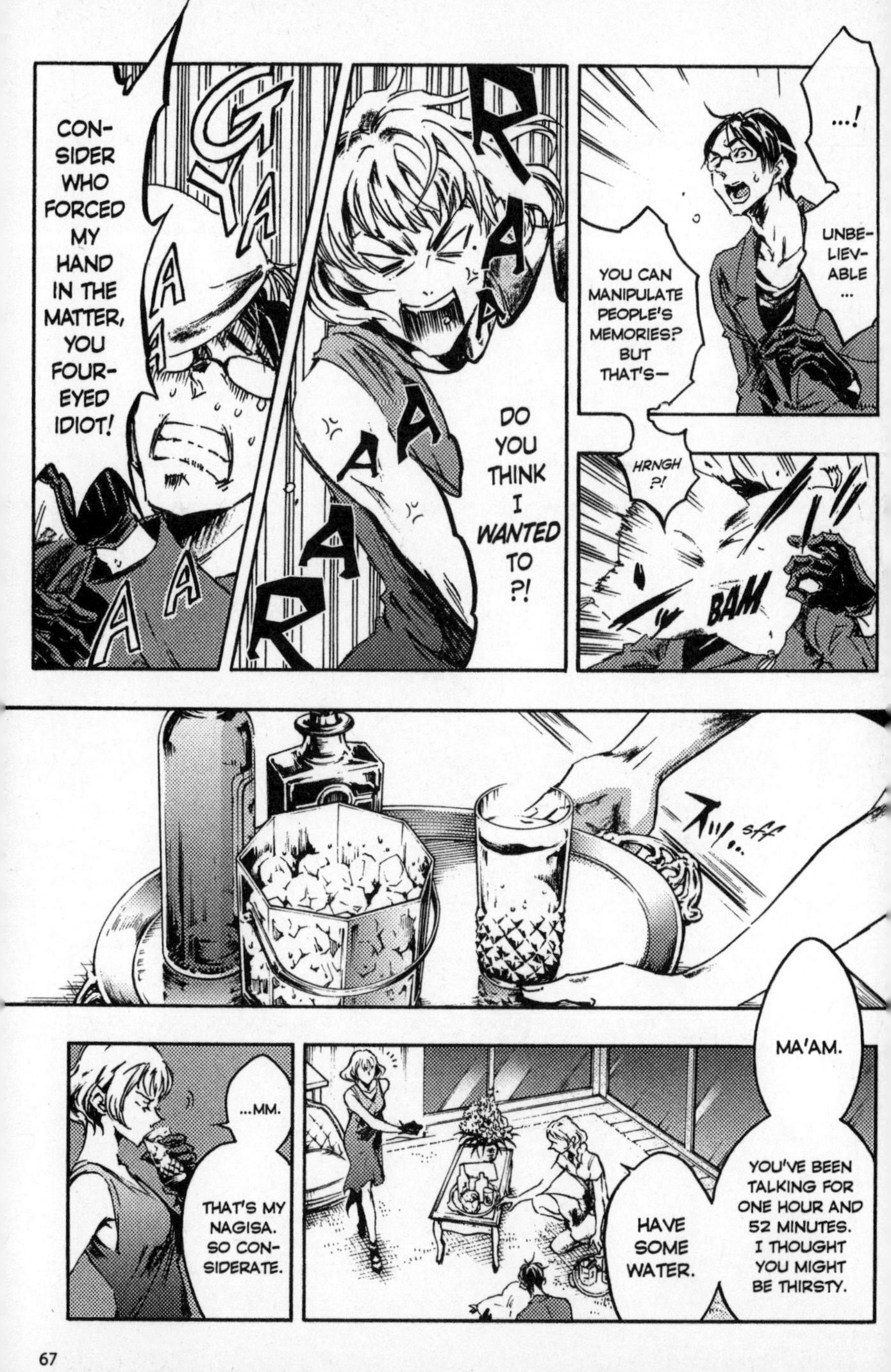
...!
UNBELIEVABLE...
YOU CAN MANIPULATE PEOPLE'S MEMORIES? BUT THAT'S—
HRNGH?!
BAM
DO YOU THINK I WANTED TO?!
CONSIDER WHO FORCED MY HAND IN THE MATTER, YOU FOUR-EYED IDIOT!
sff
MA'AM.
YOU'VE BEEN TALKING FOR ONE HOUR AND 52 MINUTES. I THOUGHT YOU MIGHT BE THIRSTY.
HAVE SOME WATER.
...MM.
THAT'S MY NAGISA. SO CONSIDERATE.

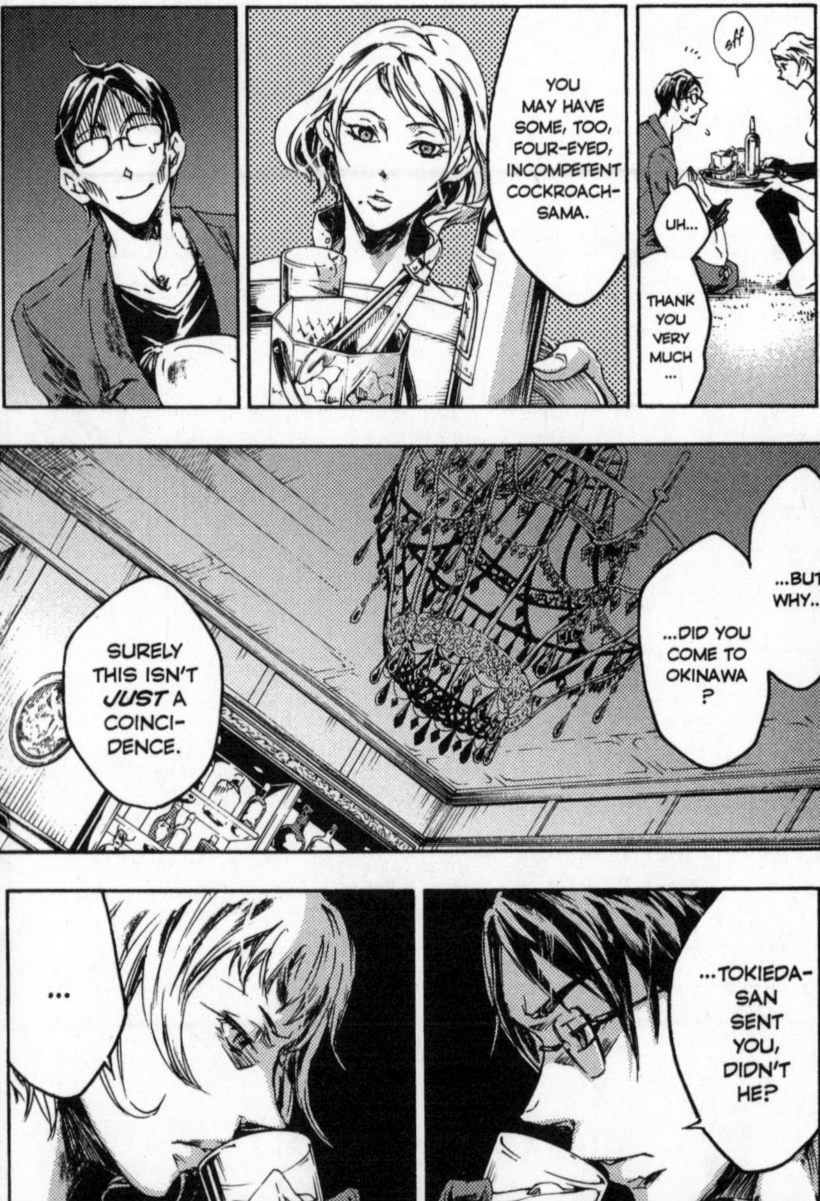
sff
UH...
THANK YOU VERY MUCH ...
YOU MAY HAVE SOME, TOO, FOUR-EYED, INCOMPETENT COCKROACH-SAMA.
...BUT WHY...
...DID YOU COME TO OKINAWA ?
SURELY THIS ISN'T *JUST* A COINCI-DENCE.
...TOKIEDA-SAN SENT YOU, DIDN'T HE?
...

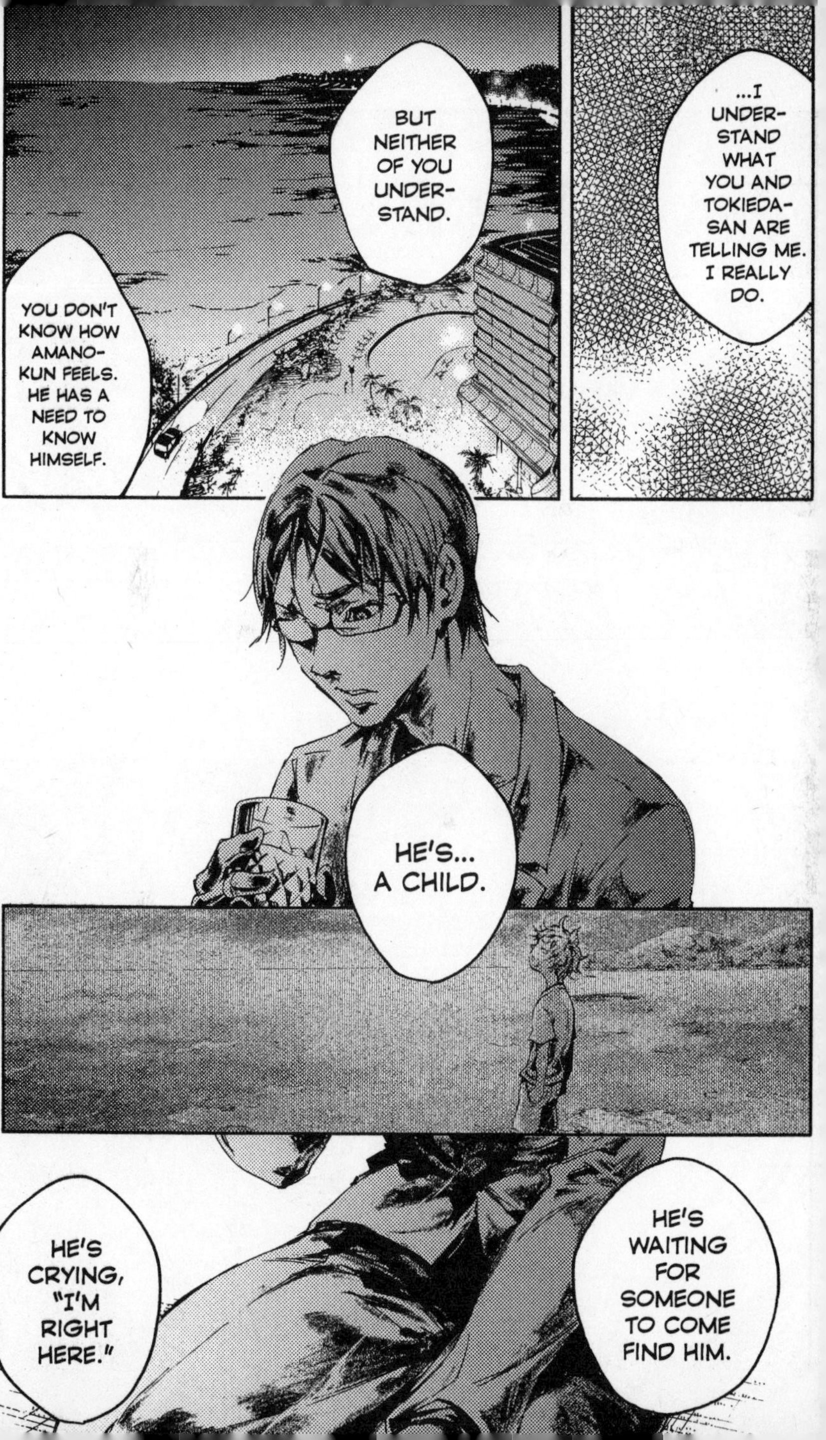
...I UNDERSTAND WHAT YOU AND TOKIEDA-SAN ARE TELLING ME. I REALLY DO.
BUT NEITHER OF YOU UNDERSTAND.
YOU DON'T KNOW HOW AMANO-KUN FEELS. HE HAS A NEED TO KNOW HIMSELF.
HE'S... A CHILD.
HE'S WAITING FOR SOMEONE TO COME FIND HIM.
HE'S CRYING, "I'M RIGHT HERE."

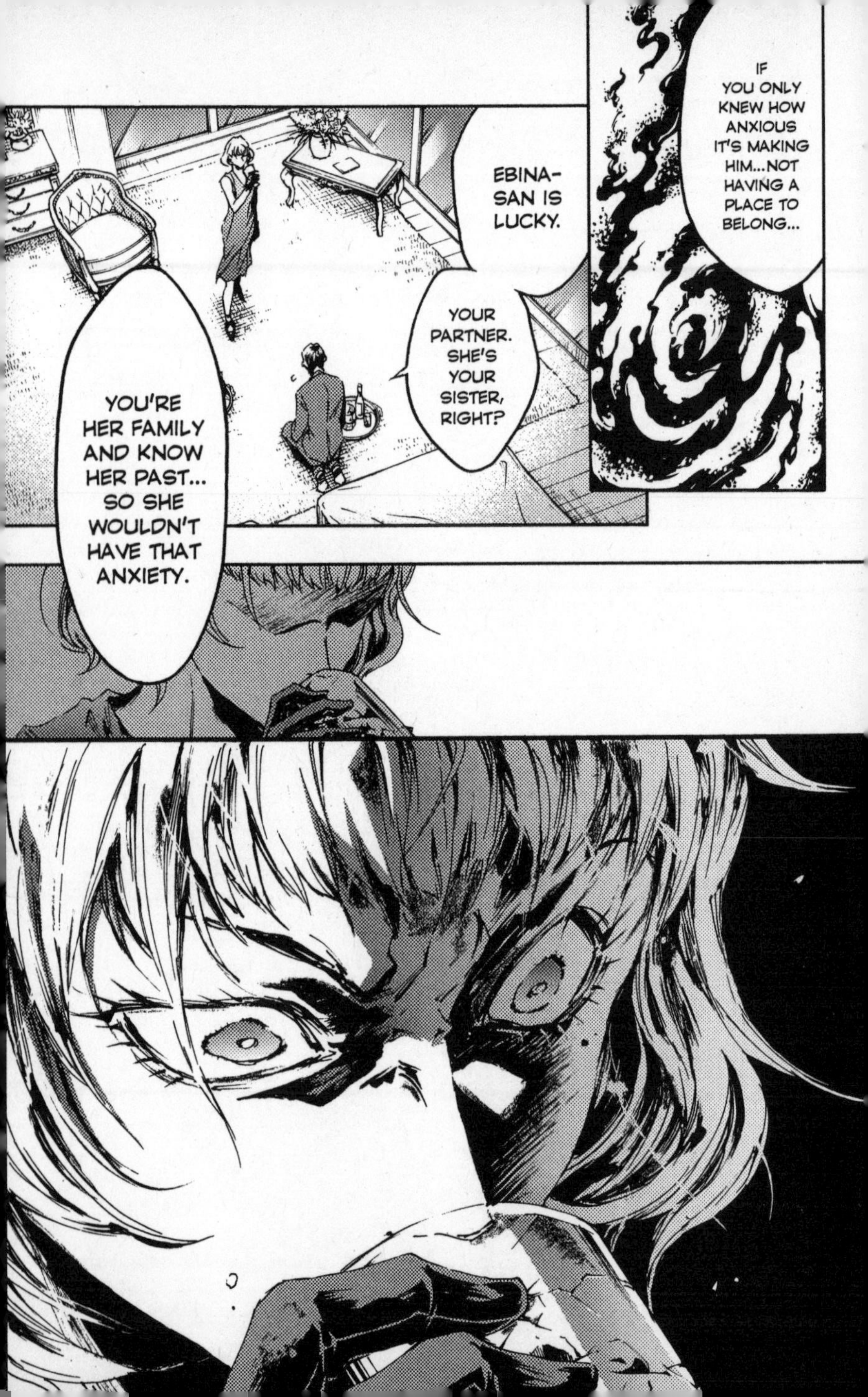
IF YOU ONLY KNEW HOW ANXIOUS IT'S MAKING HIM...NOT HAVING A PLACE TO BELONG...
EBINA-SAN IS LUCKY.
YOUR PARTNER. SHE'S YOUR SISTER, RIGHT?
YOU'RE HER FAMILY AND KNOW HER PAST... SO SHE WOULDN'T HAVE THAT ANXIETY.

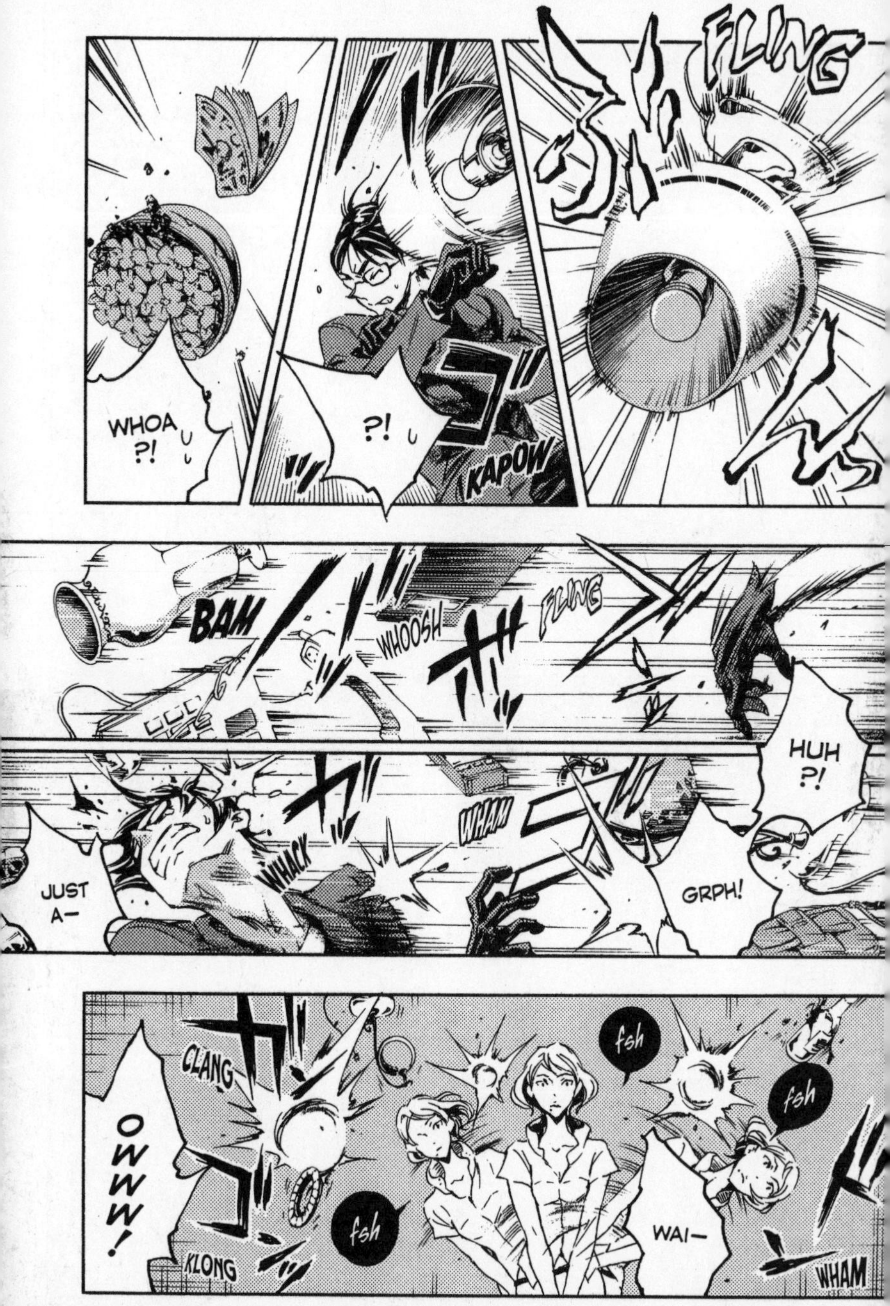
FLING
?!
KAPOW
WHOA ?!
HUH ?!
FLING
WHOOSH
BAM
GRPH!
WHAM
WHACK
JUST A—
fsh
fsh
WAI—
WHAM
fsh
CLANG
OWWW!
KLONG

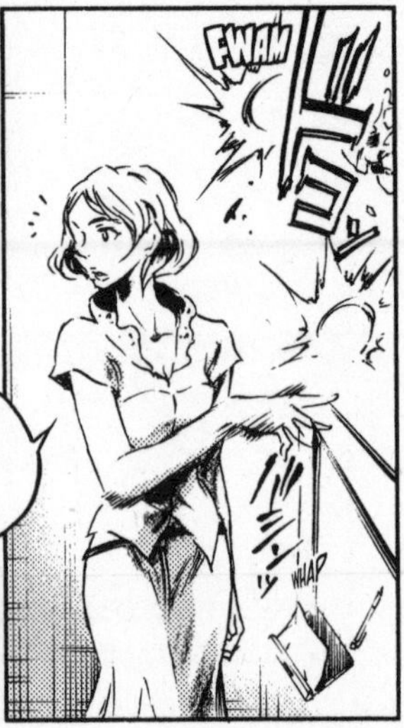
FWAM
WHAP
?
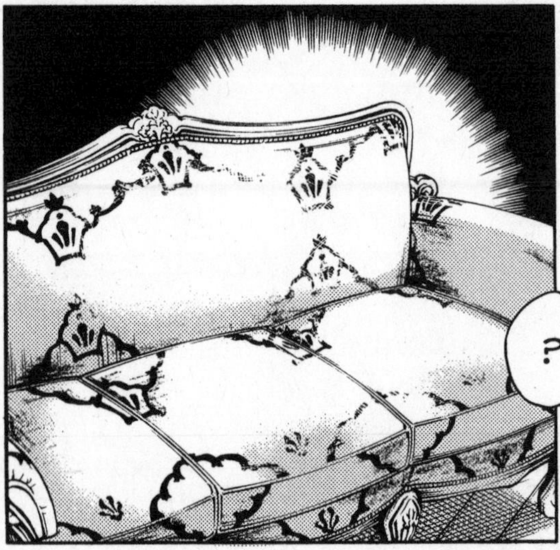
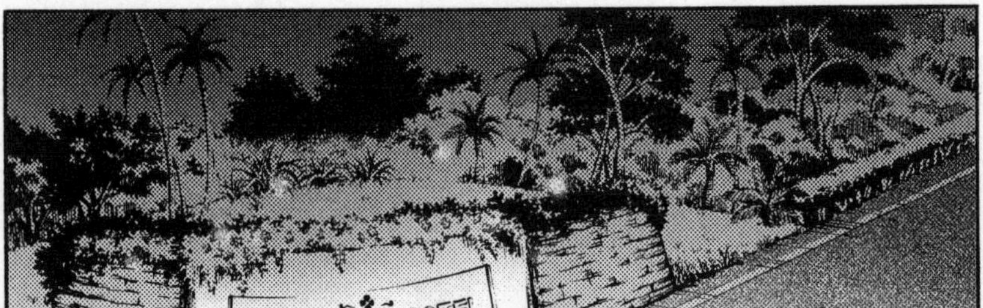
RESORT HOTEL
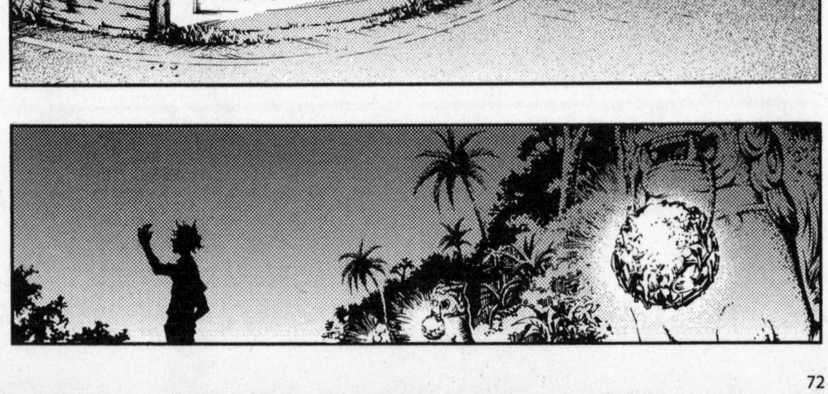

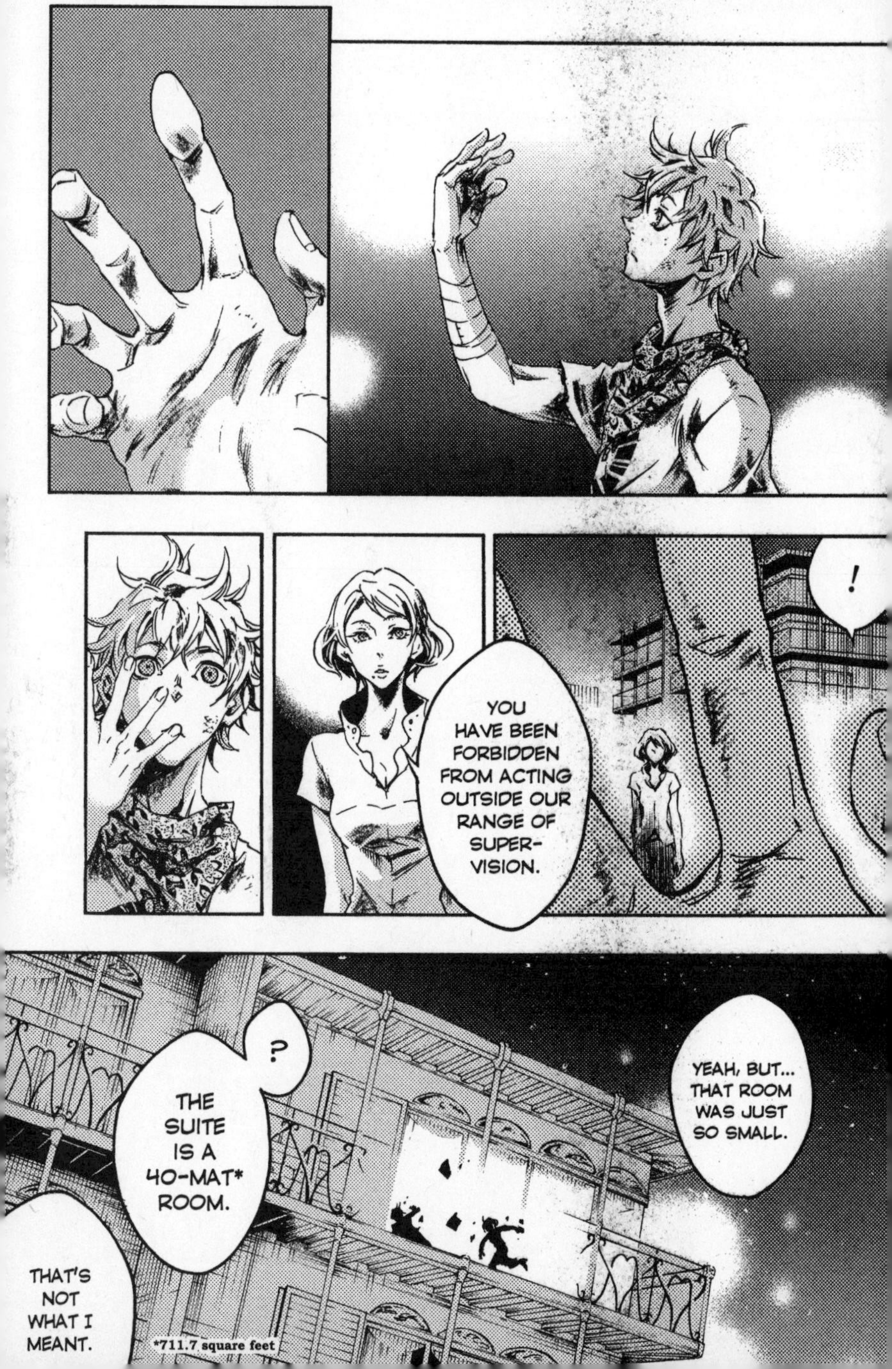
!
YOU HAVE BEEN FORBIDDEN FROM ACTING OUTSIDE OUR RANGE OF SUPER-VISION.
YEAH, BUT... THAT ROOM WAS JUST SO SMALL.
?
THE SUITE IS A 40-MAT* ROOM.
THAT'S NOT WHAT I MEANT.
*711.7 square feet

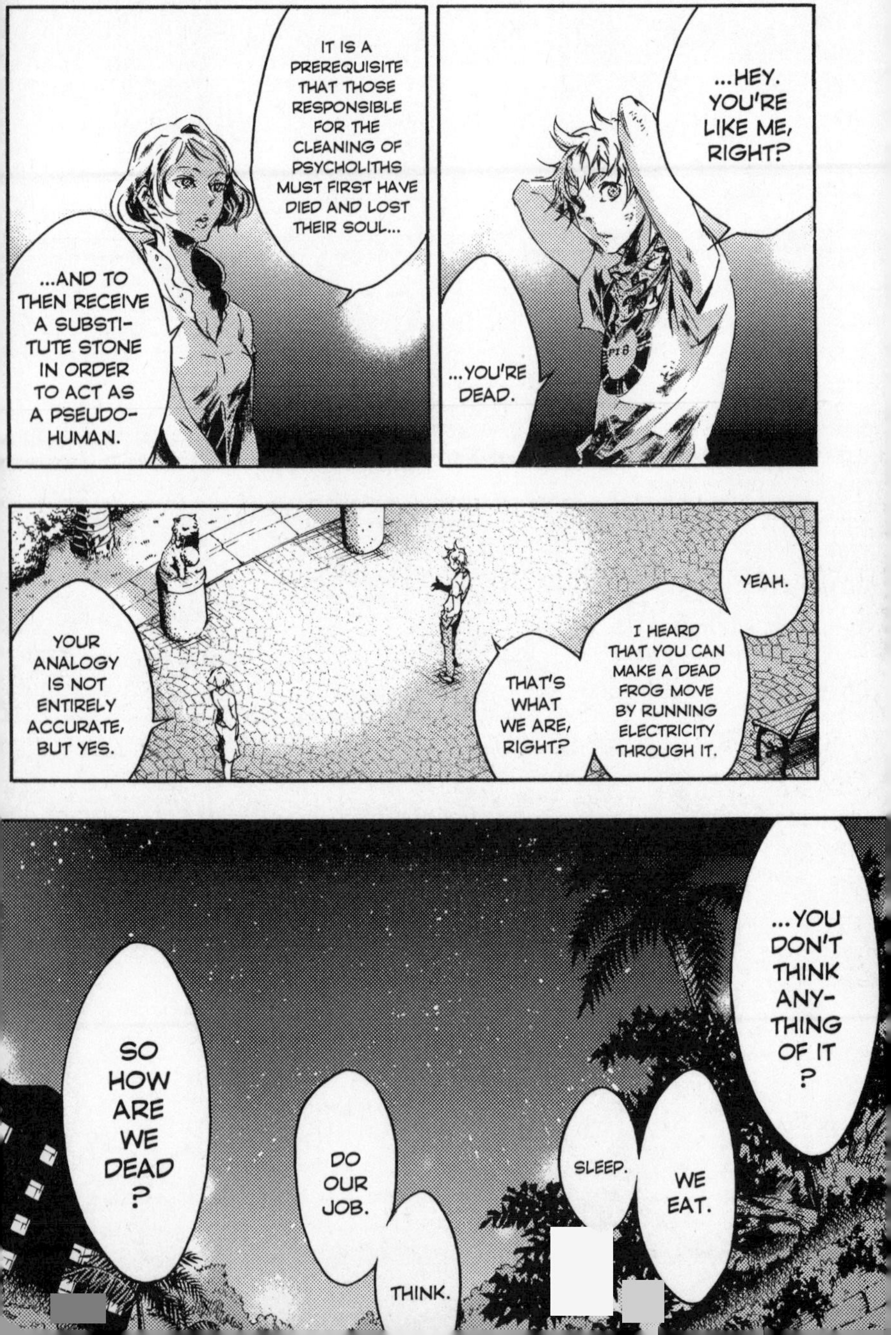
...HEY. YOU'RE LIKE ME, RIGHT?
...YOU'RE DEAD.
IT IS A PREREQUISITE THAT THOSE RESPONSIBLE FOR THE CLEANING OF PSYCHOLITHS MUST FIRST HAVE DIED AND LOST THEIR SOUL...
...AND TO THEN RECEIVE A SUBSTITUTE STONE IN ORDER TO ACT AS A PSEUDO-HUMAN.
YEAH.
I HEARD THAT YOU CAN MAKE A DEAD FROG MOVE BY RUNNING ELECTRICITY THROUGH IT.
THAT'S WHAT WE ARE, RIGHT?
YOUR ANALOGY IS NOT ENTIRELY ACCURATE, BUT YES.
...YOU DON'T THINK ANYTHING OF IT?
WE EAT.
SLEEP.
THINK.
DO OUR JOB.
SO HOW ARE WE DEAD?

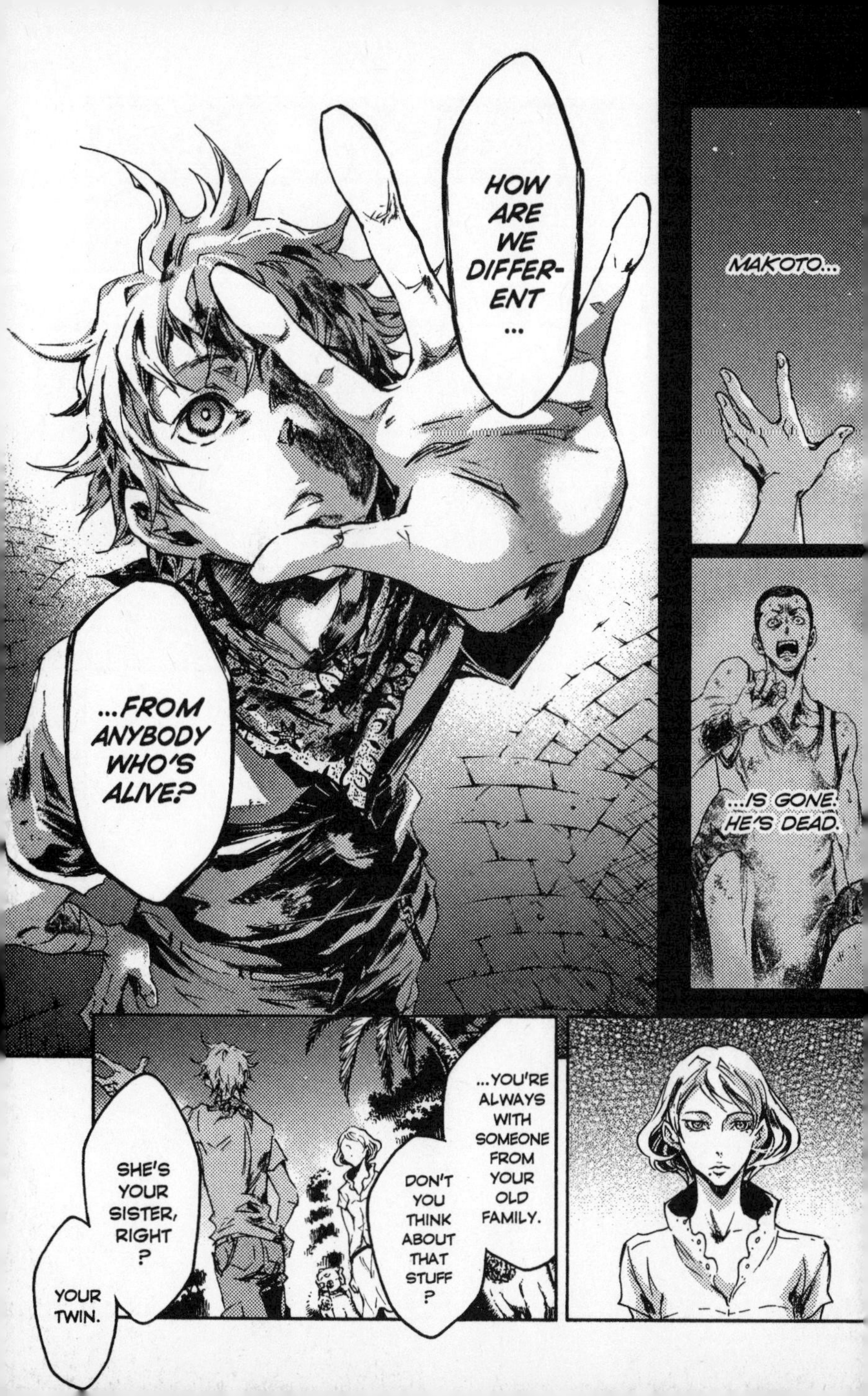
MAKOTO...
...IS GONE. HE'S DEAD.
HOW ARE WE DIFFERENT...
...FROM ANYBODY WHO'S ALIVE?
...YOU'RE ALWAYS WITH SOMEONE FROM YOUR OLD FAMILY.
DON'T YOU THINK ABOUT THAT STUFF?
SHE'S YOUR SISTER, RIGHT?
YOUR TWIN.

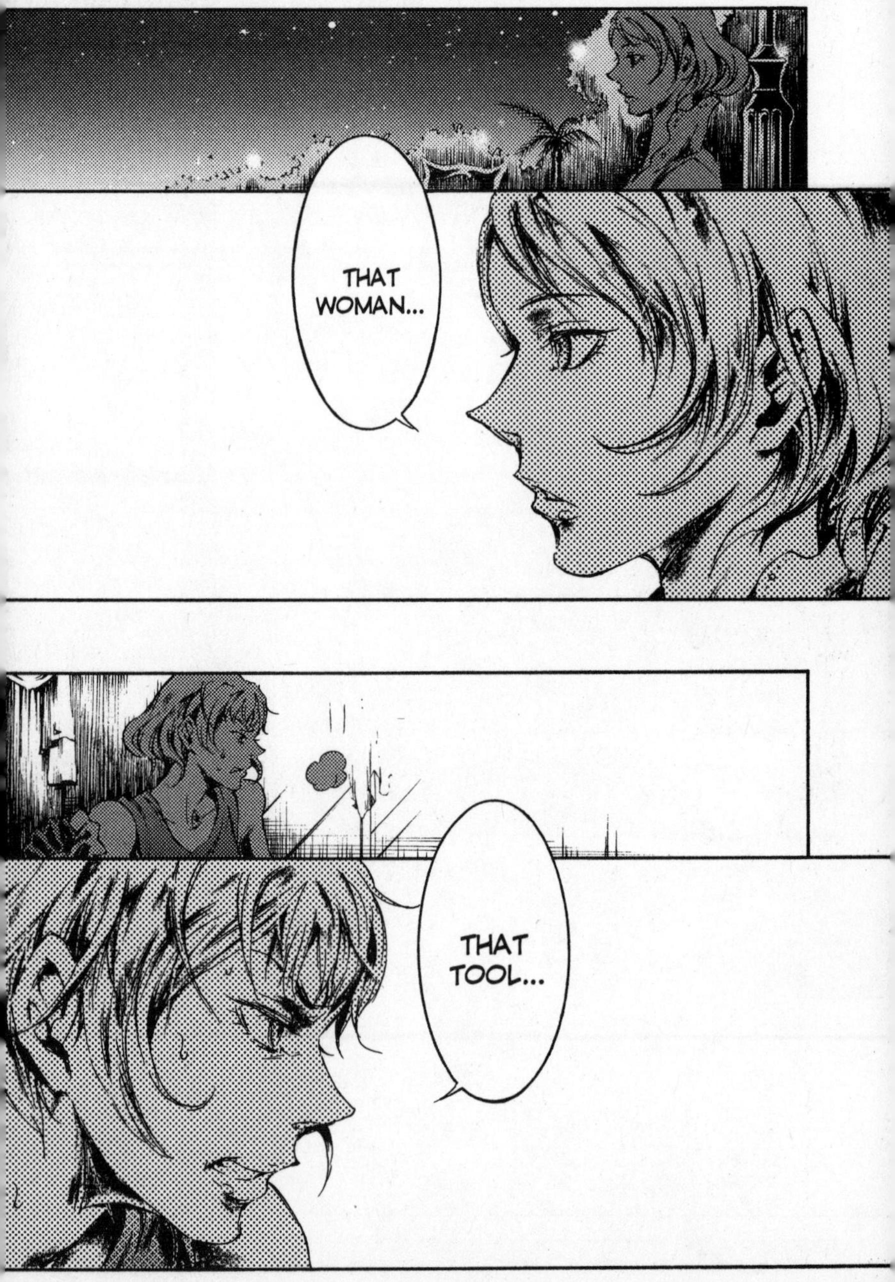
THAT WOMAN...
THAT TOOL...

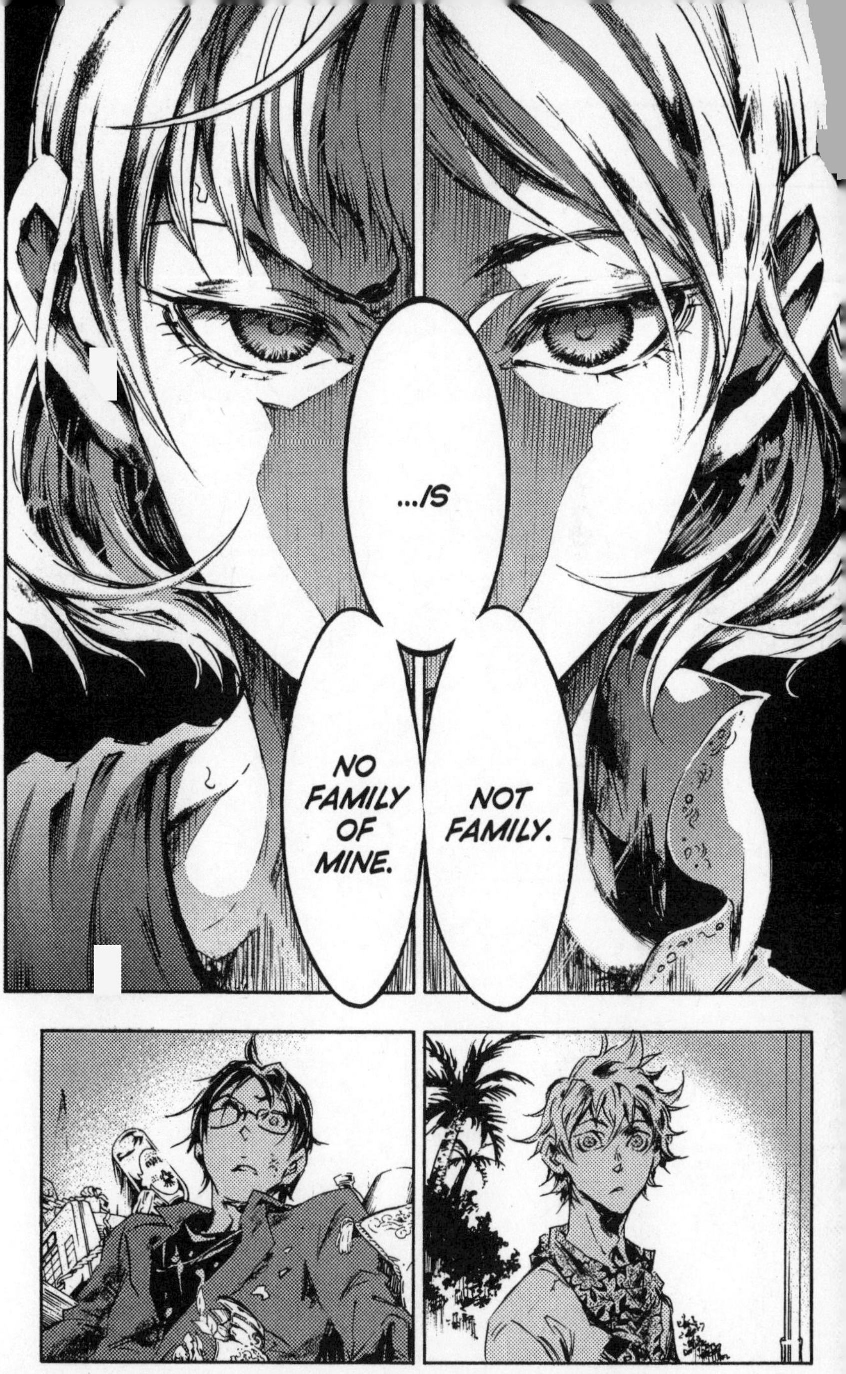
...IS
NOT FAMILY.
NO FAMILY OF MINE.

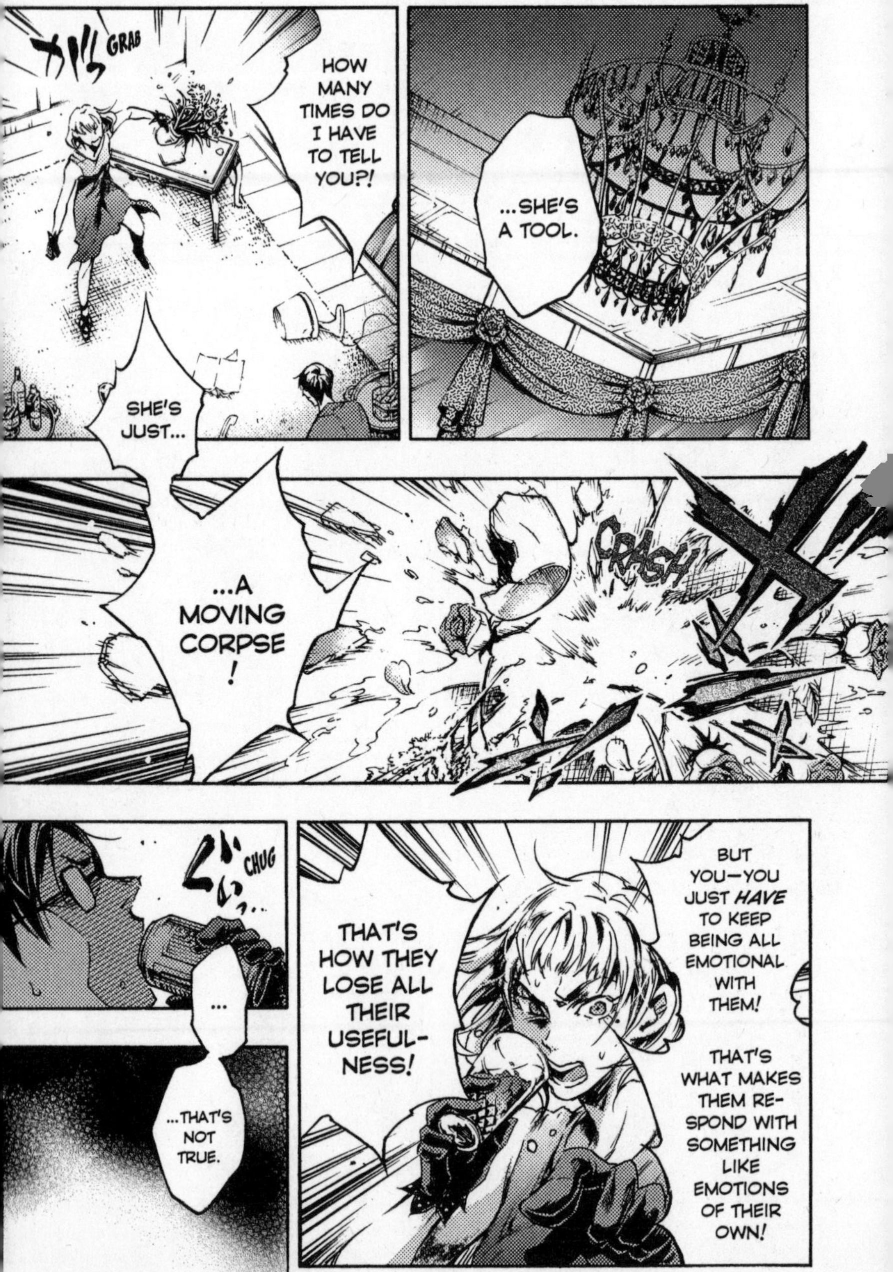
...SHE'S A TOOL.
GRAB
HOW MANY TIMES DO I HAVE TO TELL YOU?!
SHE'S JUST...
CRASH
...A MOVING CORPSE!
BUT YOU—YOU JUST *HAVE* TO KEEP BEING ALL EMOTIONAL WITH THEM!
THAT'S WHAT MAKES THEM RE-SPOND WITH SOMETHING LIKE EMOTIONS OF THEIR OWN!
THAT'S HOW THEY LOSE ALL THEIR USEFUL-NESS!
CHUG
...
...THAT'S NOT TRUE.

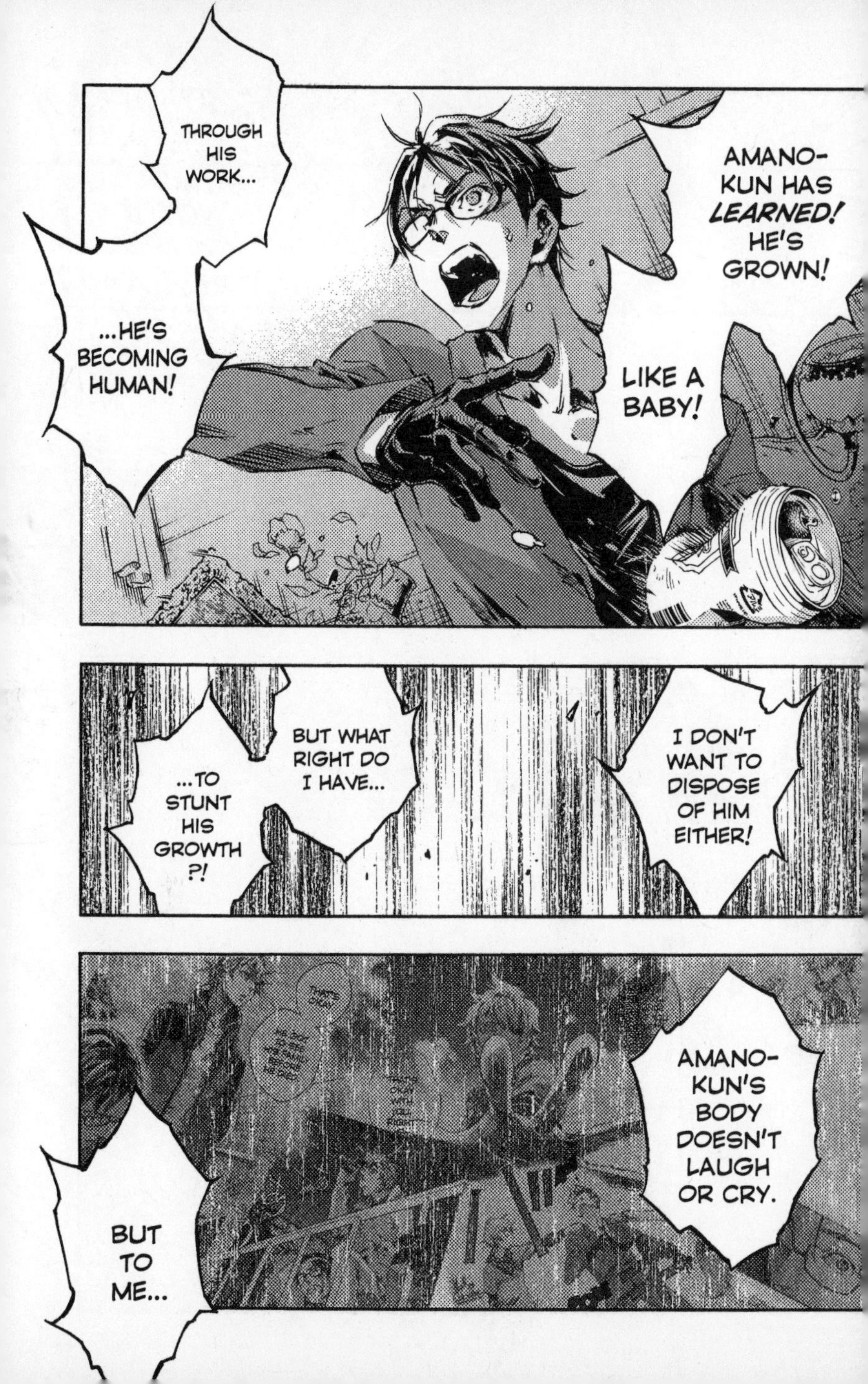
AMANO-KUN HAS *LEARNED!* HE'S GROWN!
LIKE A BABY!
THROUGH HIS WORK...
...HE'S BECOMING HUMAN!
I DON'T WANT TO DISPOSE OF HIM EITHER!
BUT WHAT RIGHT DO I HAVE...
...TO STUNT HIS GROWTH?!
AMANO-KUN'S BODY DOESN'T LAUGH OR CRY.
THAT'S OKAY WITH YOU, RIGHT
THAT'S OKAY
HE GOT TO SEE HIS FAMILY BEFORE HE DIED
BUT TO ME...

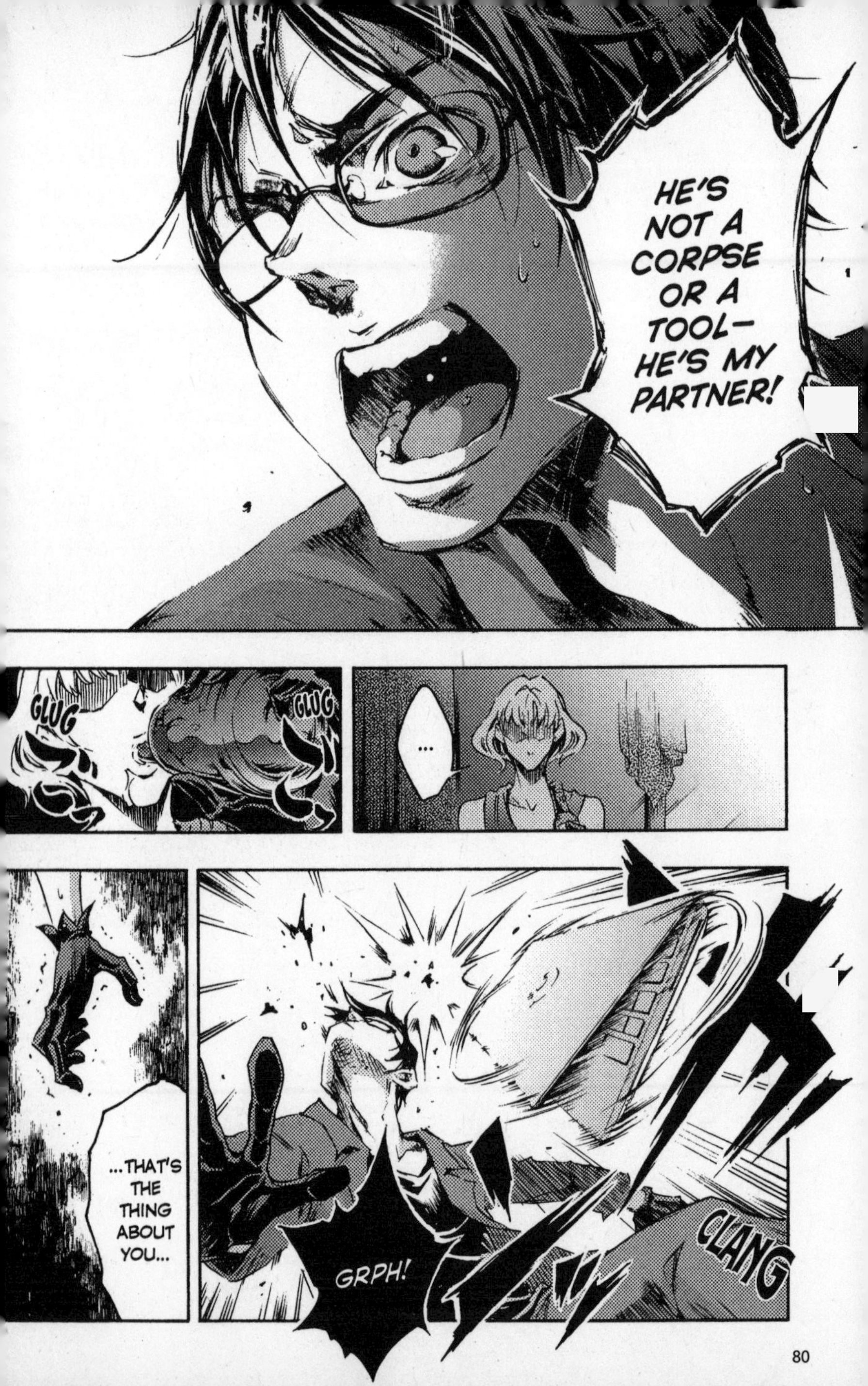

HE'S NOT A CORPSE OR A TOOL— HE'S MY PARTNER!
...
GLUG
GLUG
CLANG
GRPH!
...THAT'S THE THING ABOUT YOU...

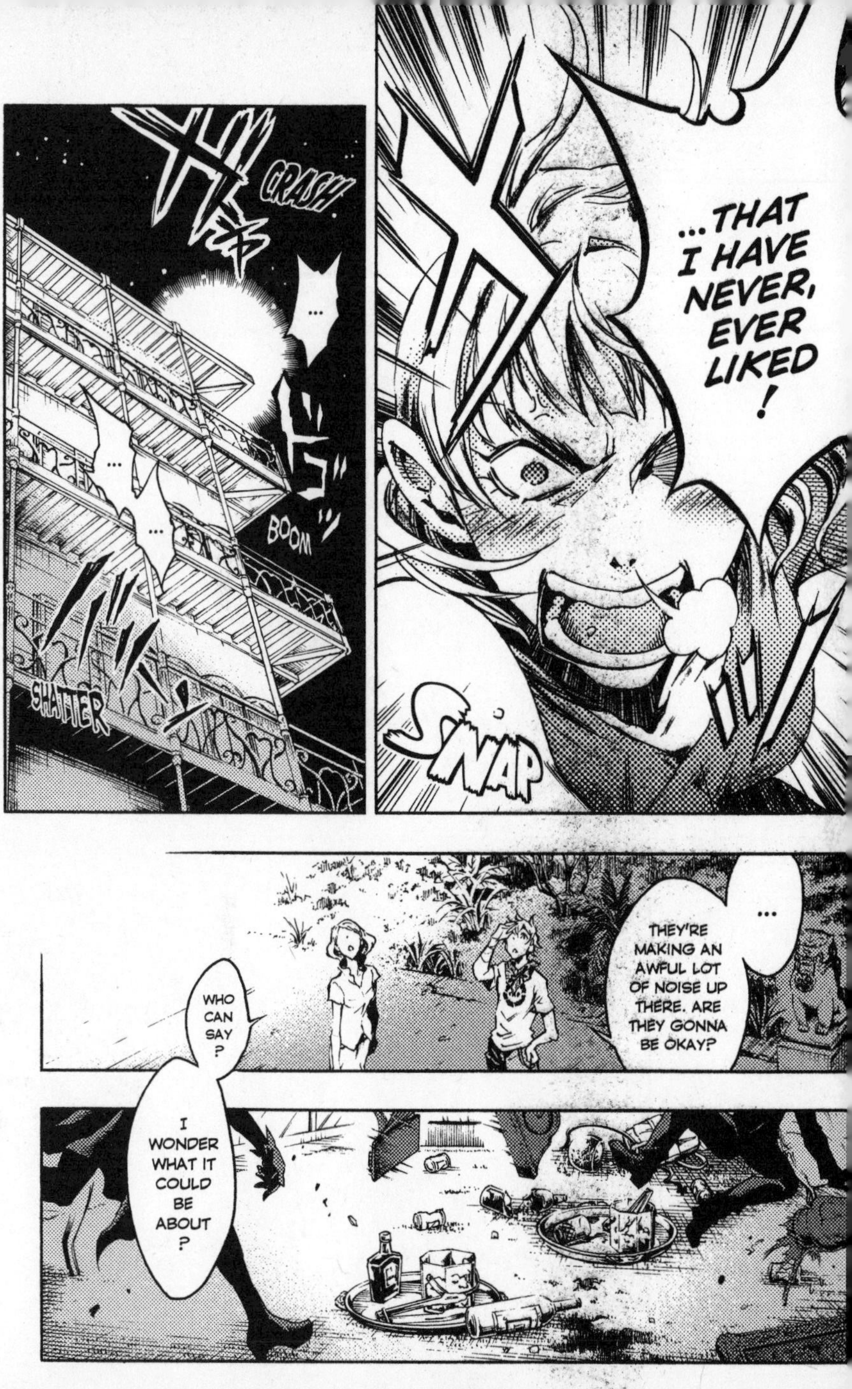
...THAT I HAVE NEVER, EVER LIKED!
SNAP
CRASH
...
BOOM
...
...
SHATTER
...
THEY'RE MAKING AN AWFUL LOT OF NOISE UP THERE. ARE THEY GONNA BE OKAY?
WHO CAN SAY?
I WONDER WHAT IT COULD BE ABOUT?

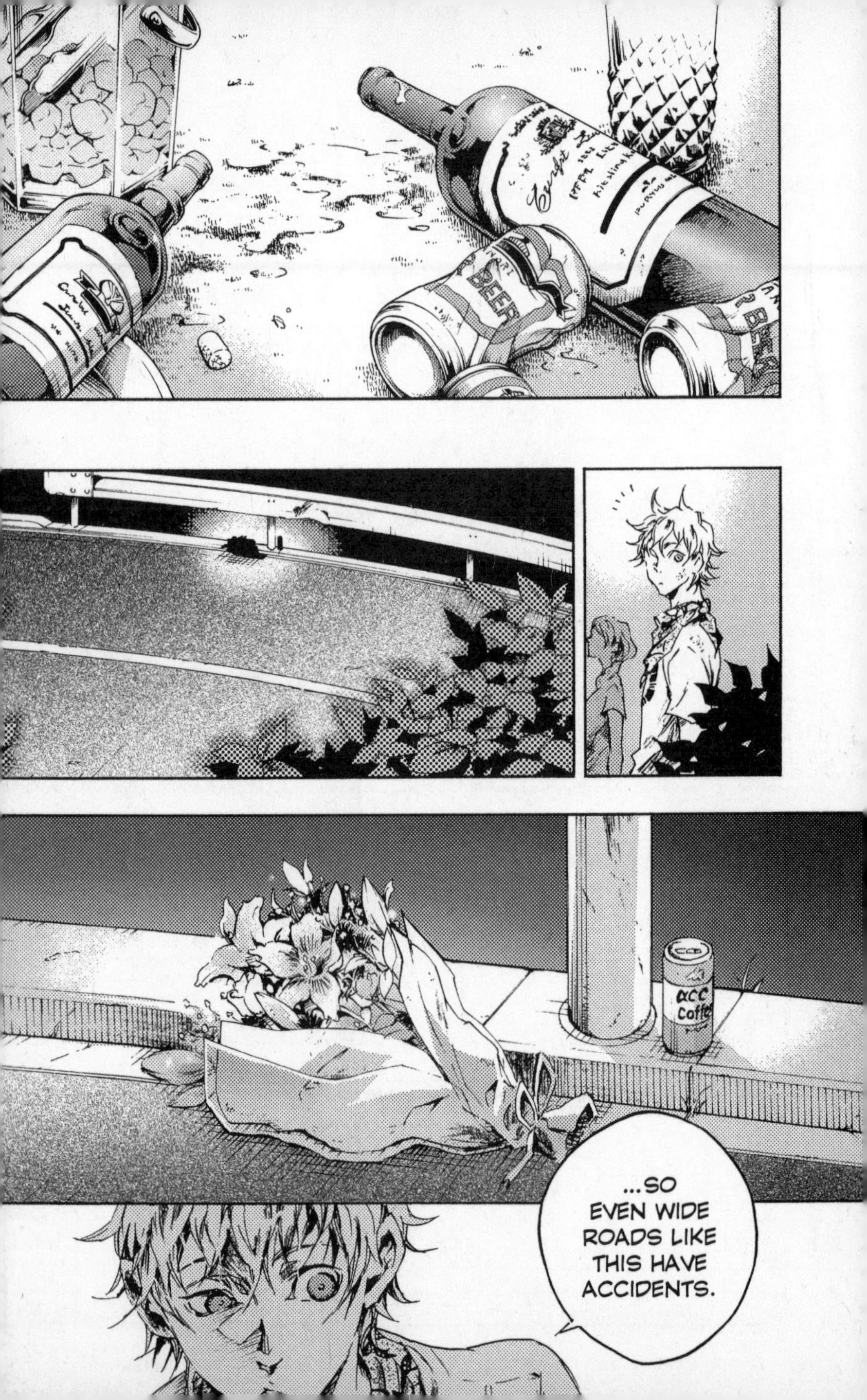
BEER
...SO EVEN WIDE ROADS LIKE THIS HAVE ACCIDENTS.

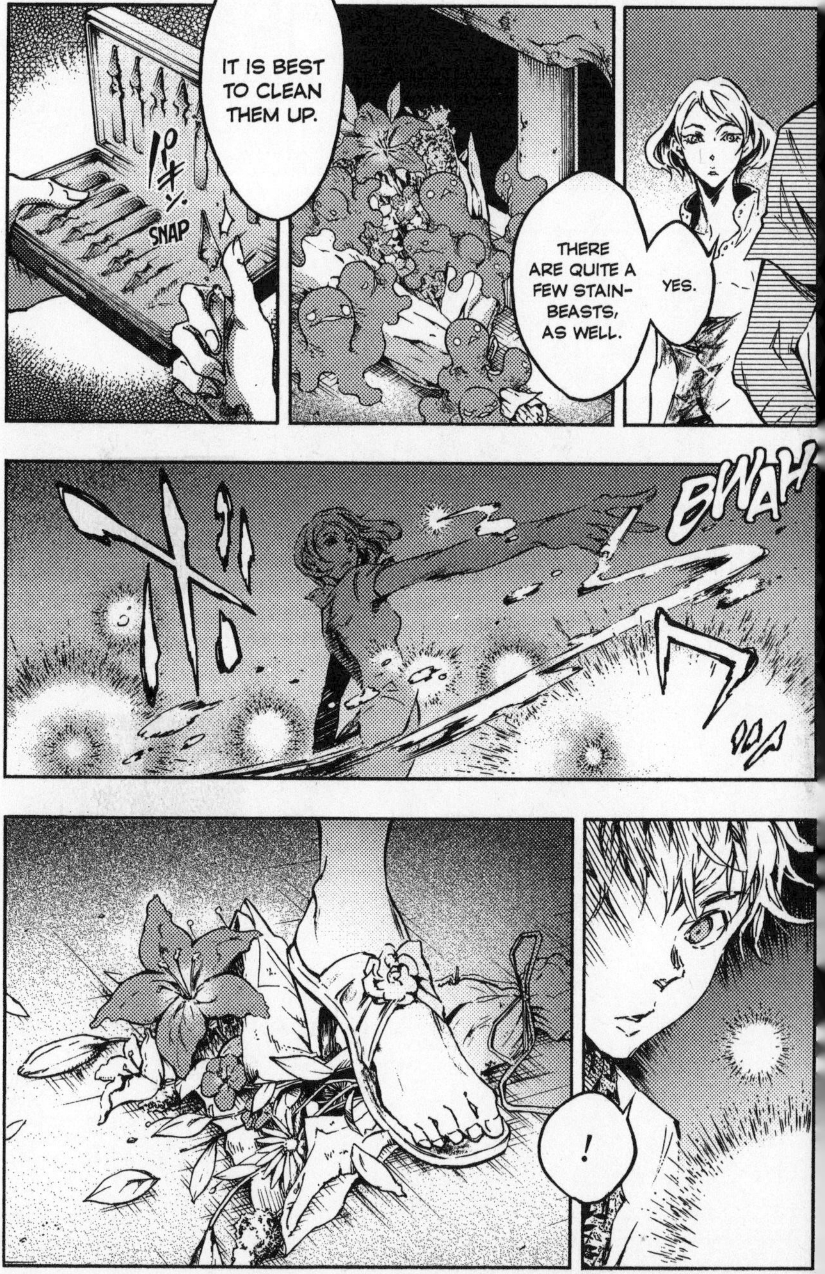
YES.
THERE ARE QUITE A FEW STAIN-BEASTS, AS WELL.
IT IS BEST TO CLEAN THEM UP.
SNAP
BWAH
!

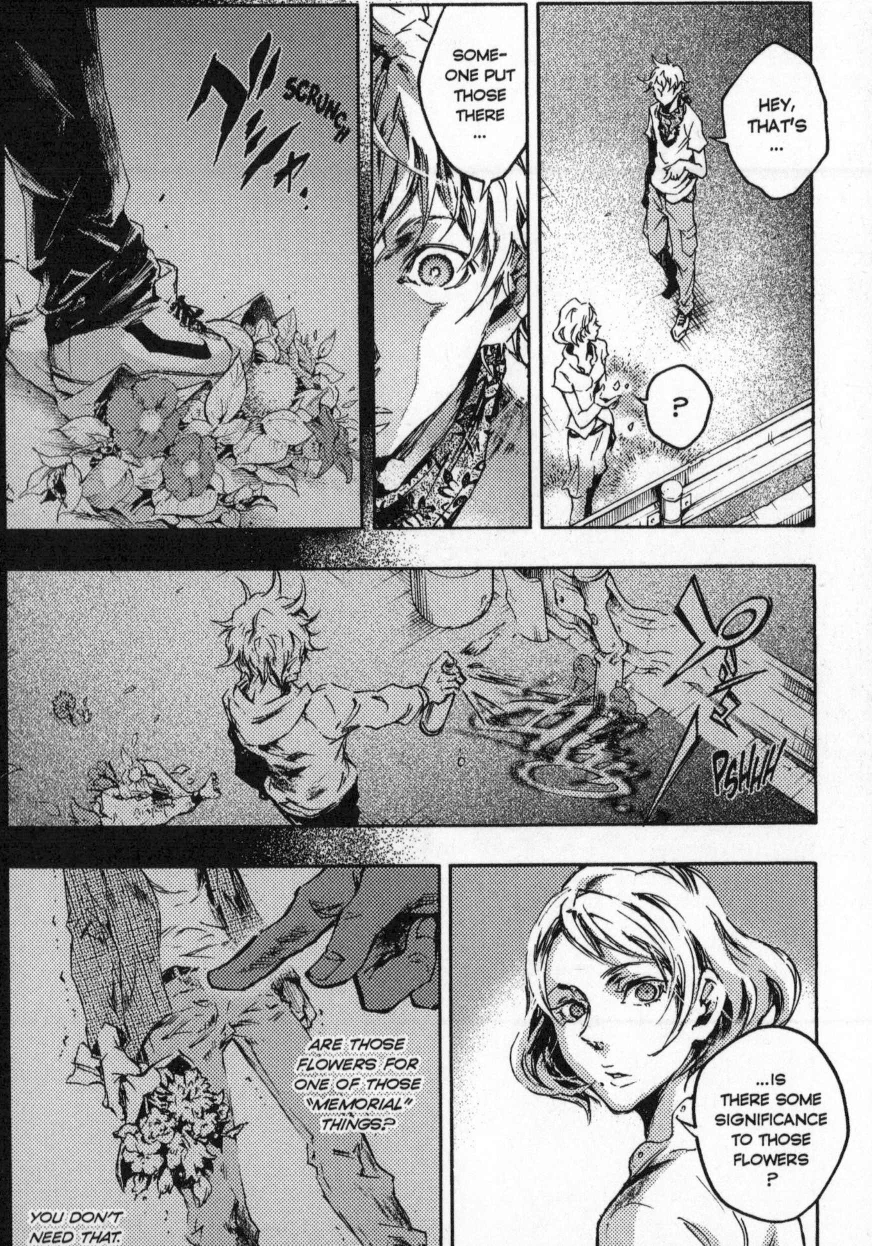
HEY, THAT'S ...
?
SOME-ONE PUT THOSE THERE ...
SCRUNCH
PSHHK
...IS THERE SOME SIGNIFICANCE TO THOSE FLOWERS ?
ARE THOSE FLOWERS FOR ONE OF THOSE "MEMORIAL" THINGS?
YOU DON'T NEED THAT.

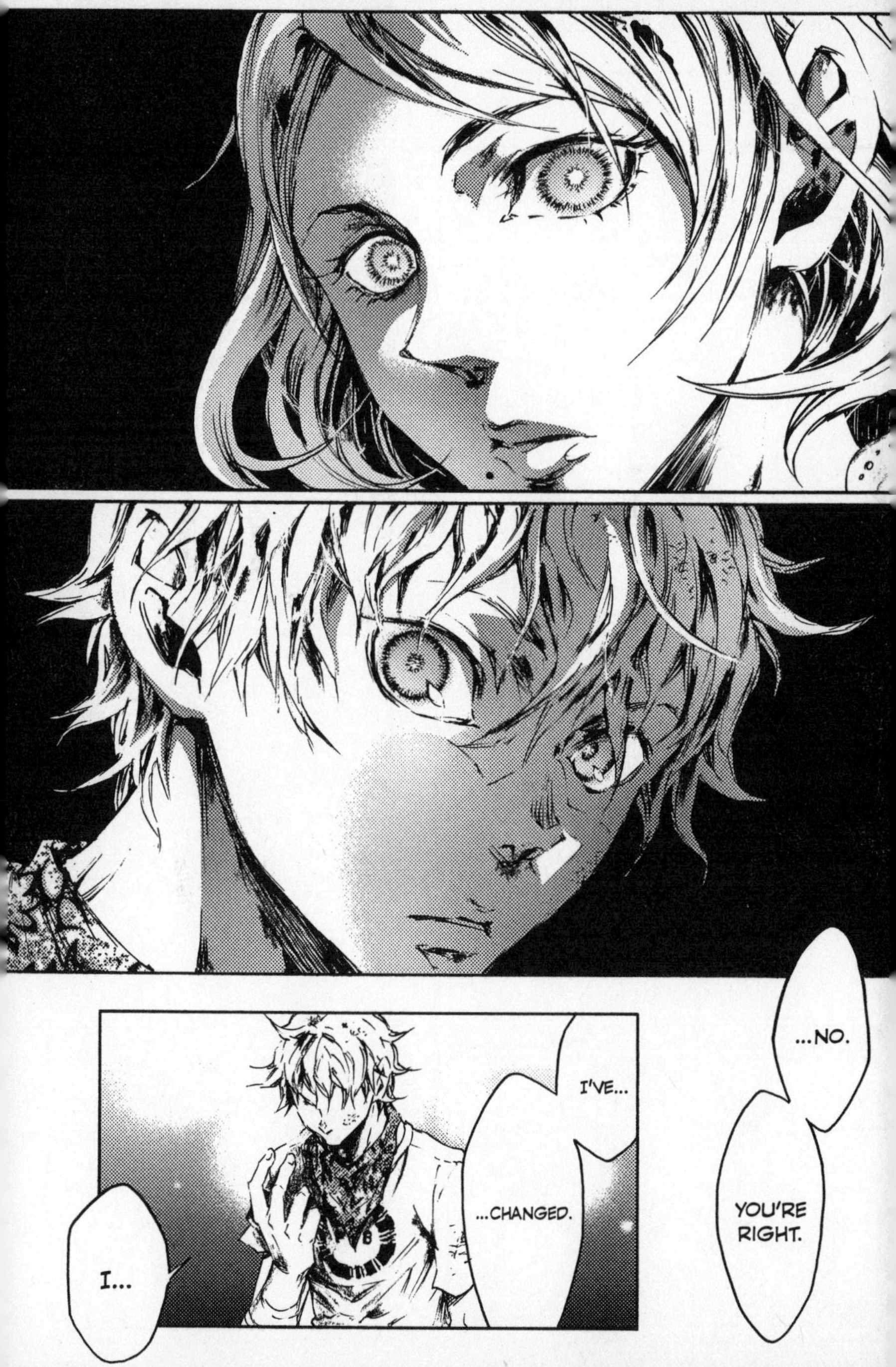
...NO.
YOU'RE RIGHT.
I'VE...
...CHANGED.
I...

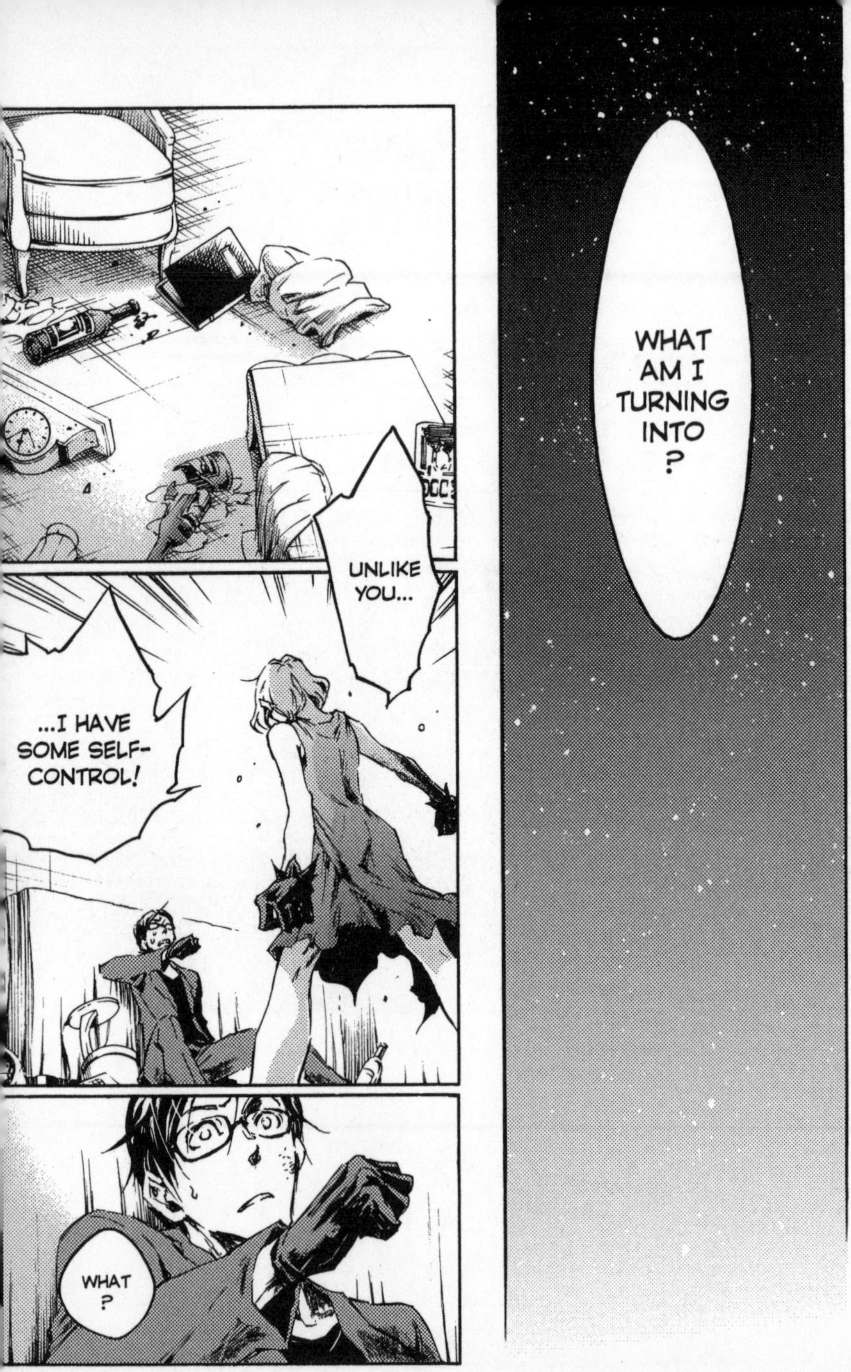
WHAT AM I TURNING INTO?
UNLIKE YOU...
...I HAVE SOME SELF-CONTROL!
WHAT?

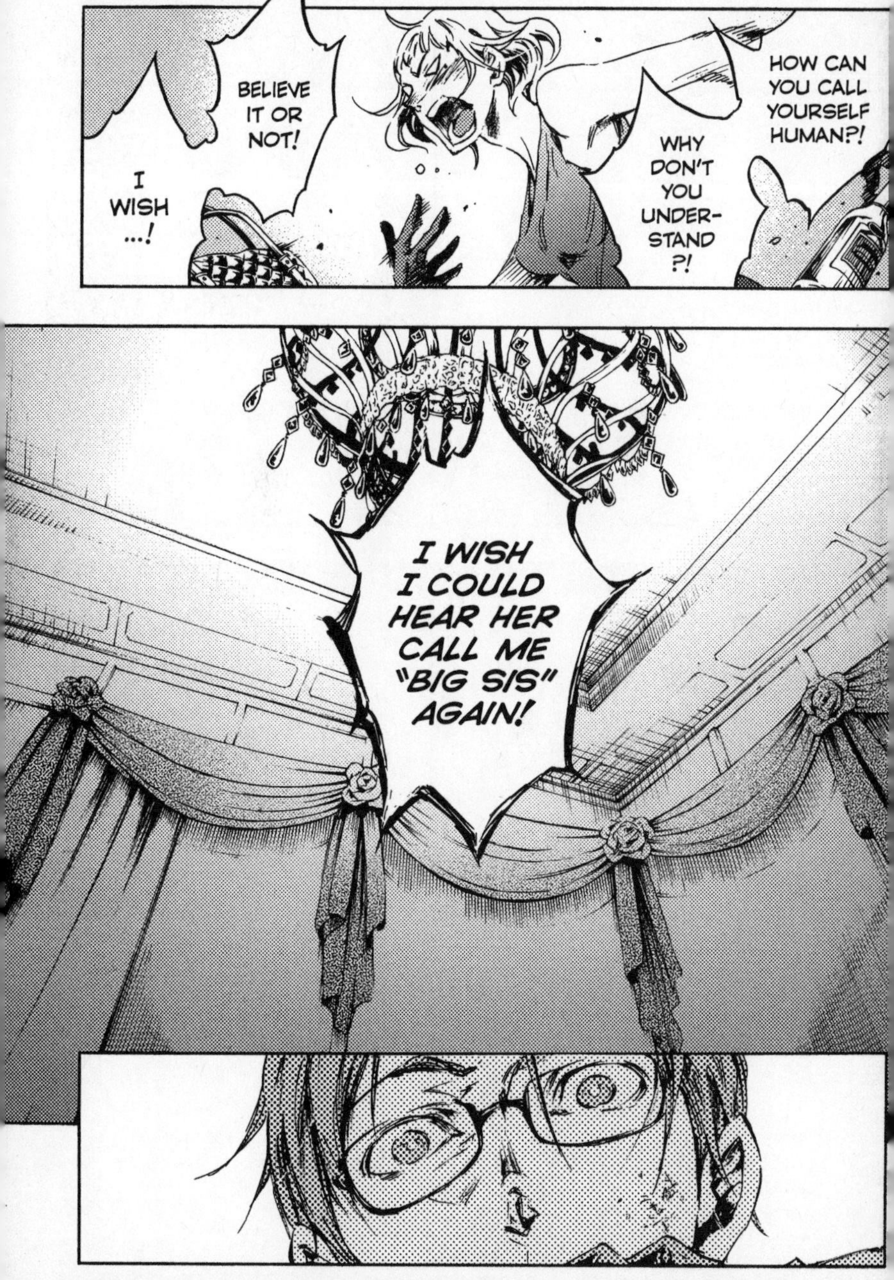
HOW CAN YOU CALL YOURSELF HUMAN?!
WHY DON'T YOU UNDERSTAND ?!
BELIEVE IT OR NOT!
I WISH ...!
I WISH I COULD HEAR HER CALL ME "BIG SIS" AGAIN!

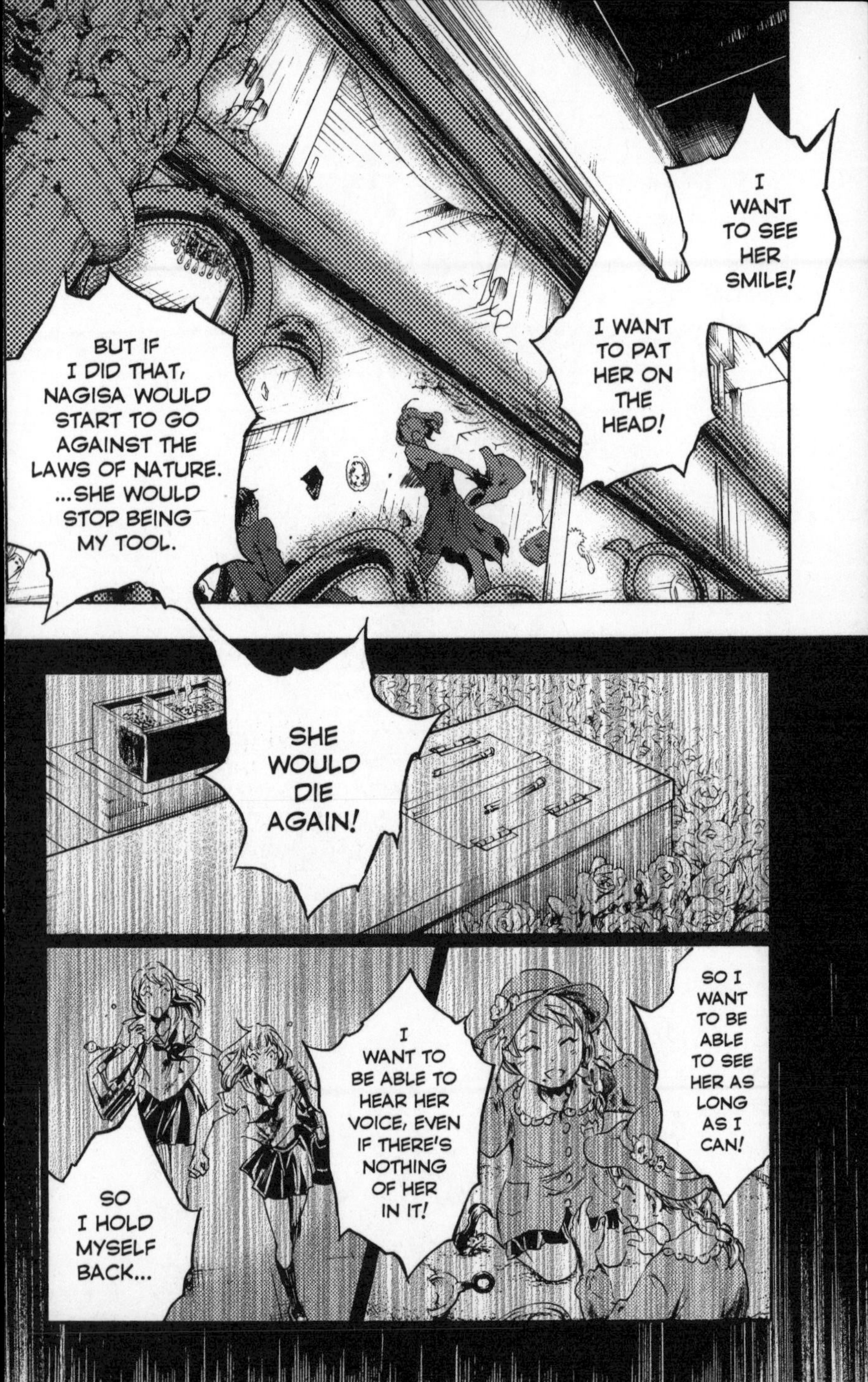
I WANT TO SEE HER SMILE!
I WANT TO PAT HER ON THE HEAD!
BUT IF I DID THAT, NAGISA WOULD START TO GO AGAINST THE LAWS OF NATURE. ...SHE WOULD STOP BEING MY TOOL.
SHE WOULD DIE AGAIN!
SO I WANT TO BE ABLE TO SEE HER AS LONG AS I CAN!
I WANT TO BE ABLE TO HEAR HER VOICE, EVEN IF THERE'S NOTHING OF HER IN IT!
SO I HOLD MYSELF BACK...

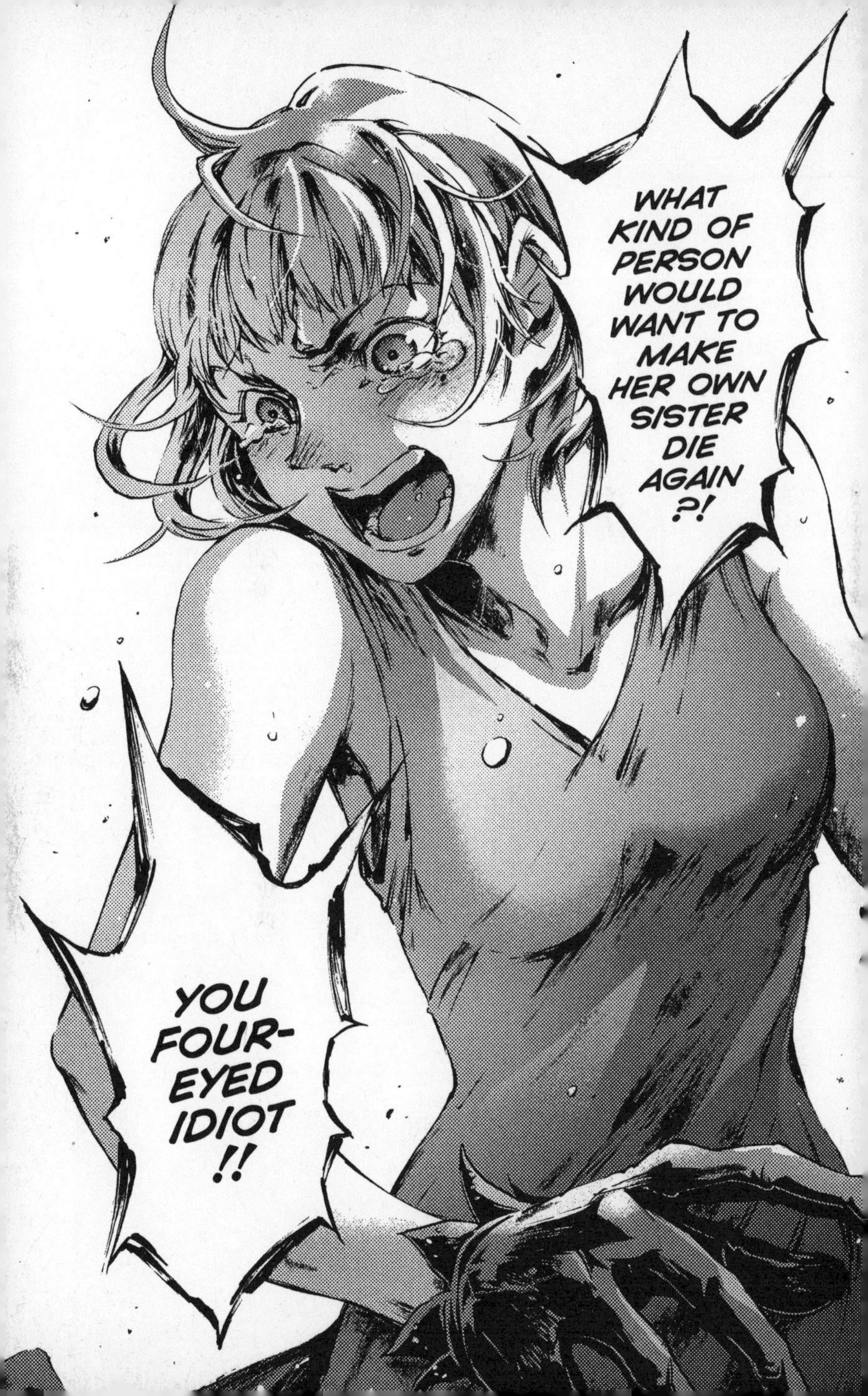
WHAT KIND OF PERSON WOULD WANT TO MAKE HER OWN SISTER DIE AGAIN ?!
YOU FOUR-EYED IDIOT !!

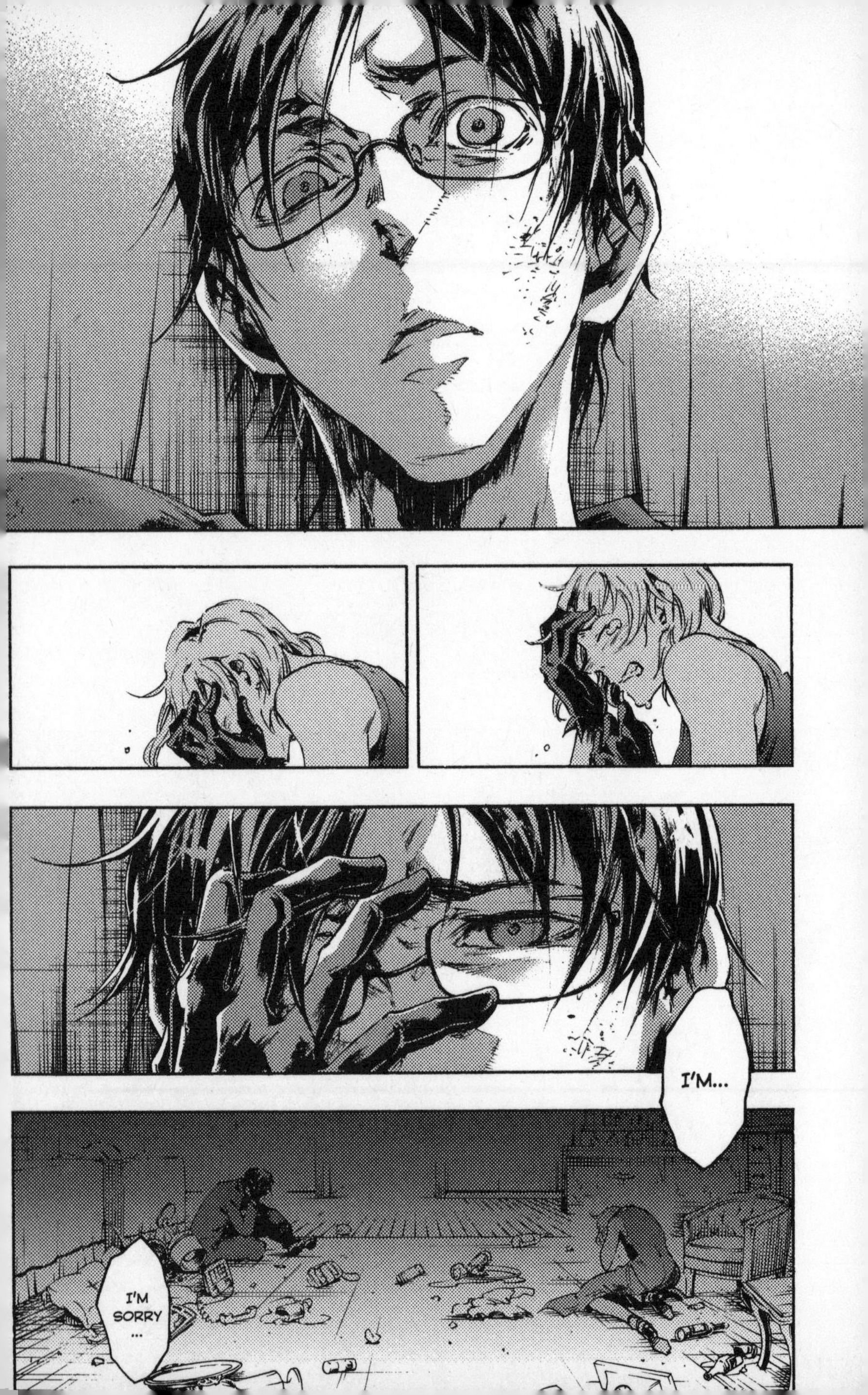
I'M...
I'M SORRY ...

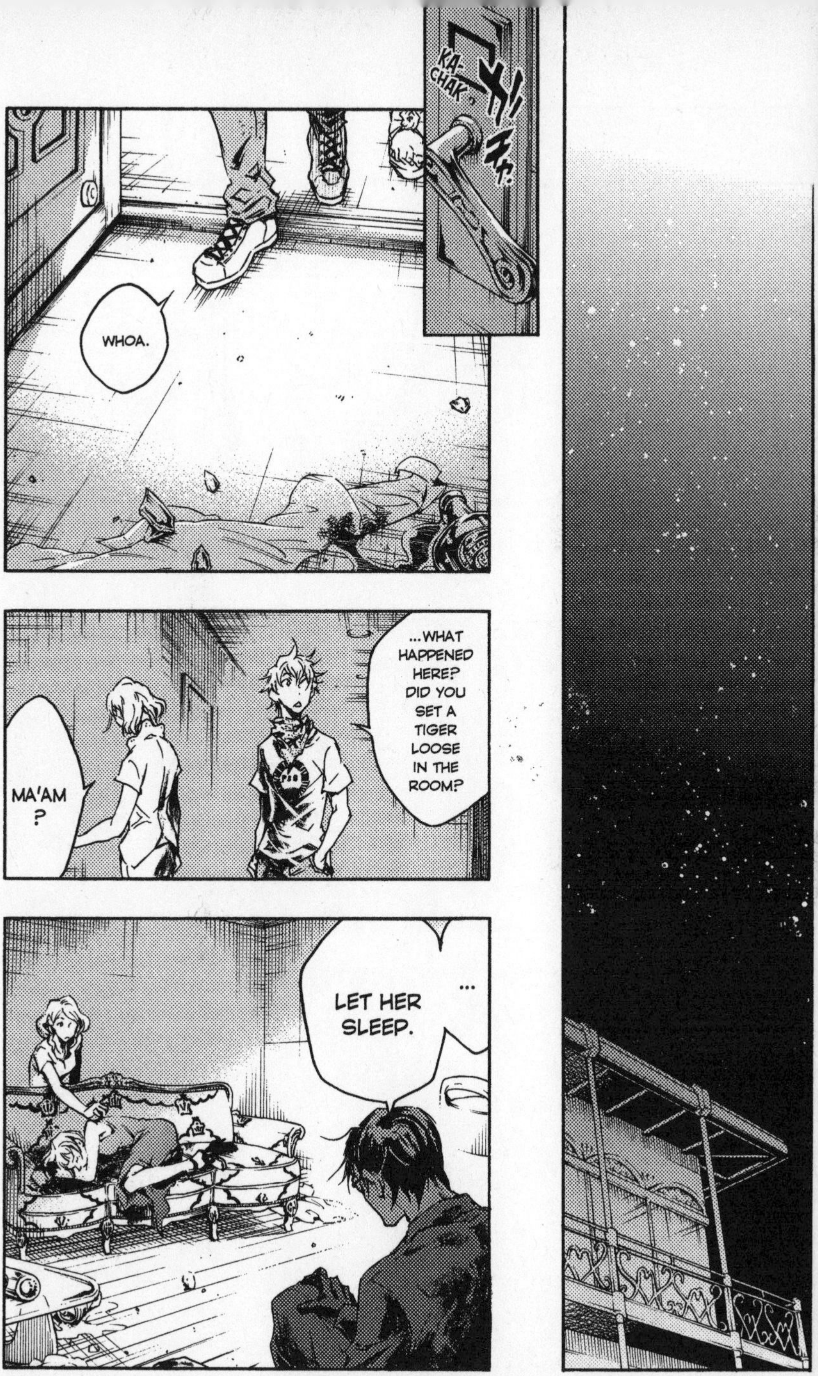
KA-CHAK,
WHOA.
...WHAT HAPPENED HERE? DID YOU SET A TIGER LOOSE IN THE ROOM?
MA'AM ?
...
LET HER SLEEP.

...YES, SIR.

SHE DOES APPEAR TO BE TIRED.

YOU BOTH MAY REST IN THAT VICINITY, AS WELL.

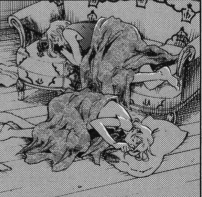

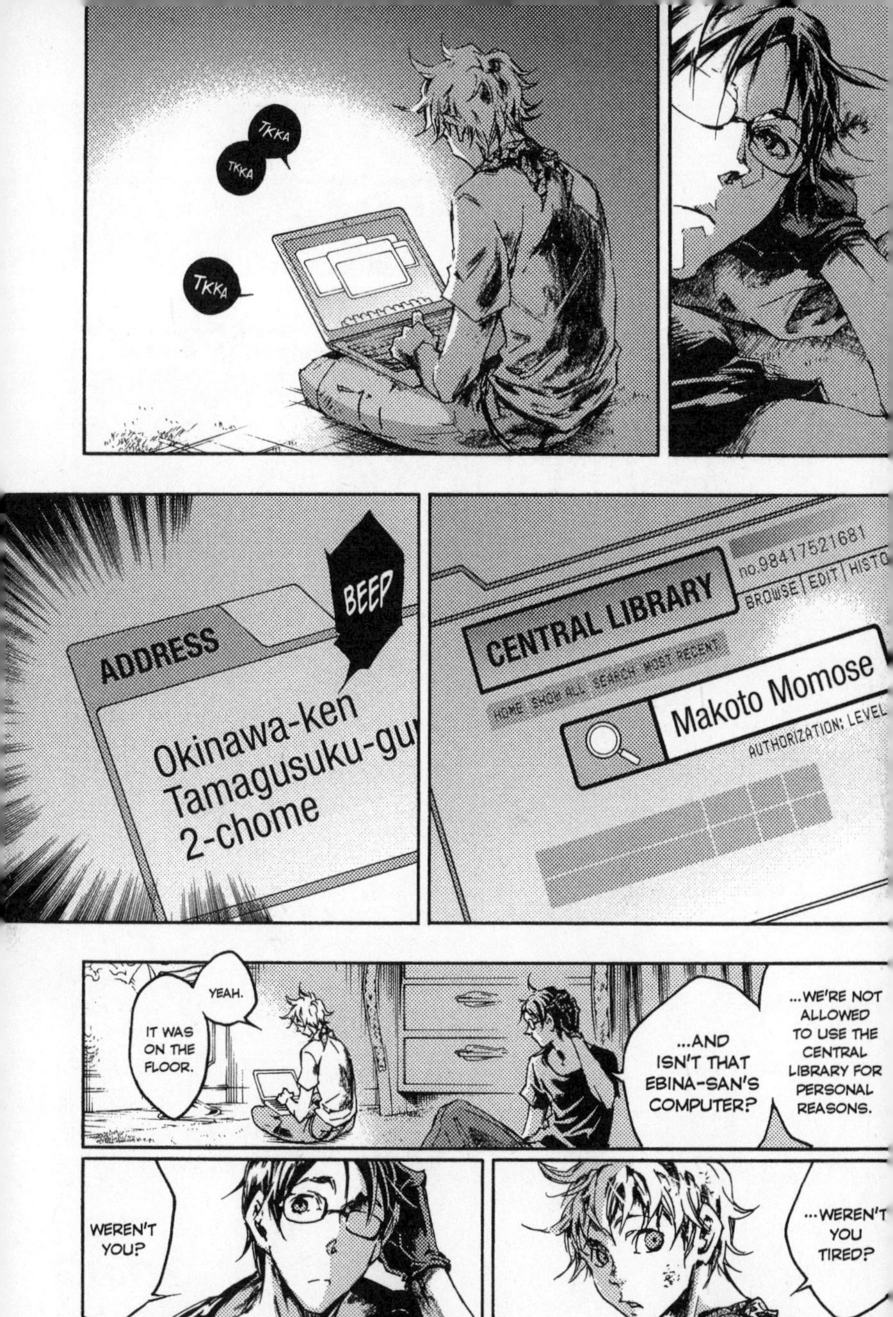
TKKA
TKKA
TKKA
no.98417521681
CENTRAL LIBRARY
BROWSE | EDIT | HISTO
HOME SHOW ALL SEARCH MOST RECENT
Makoto Momose
AUTHORIZATION; LEVEL
BEEP
ADDRESS
Okinawa-ken
Tamagusuku-gu
2-chome
...WE'RE NOT ALLOWED TO USE THE CENTRAL LIBRARY FOR PERSONAL REASONS.
...AND ISN'T THAT EBINA-SAN'S COMPUTER?
YEAH.
IT WAS ON THE FLOOR.
...WEREN'T YOU TIRED?
WEREN'T YOU?

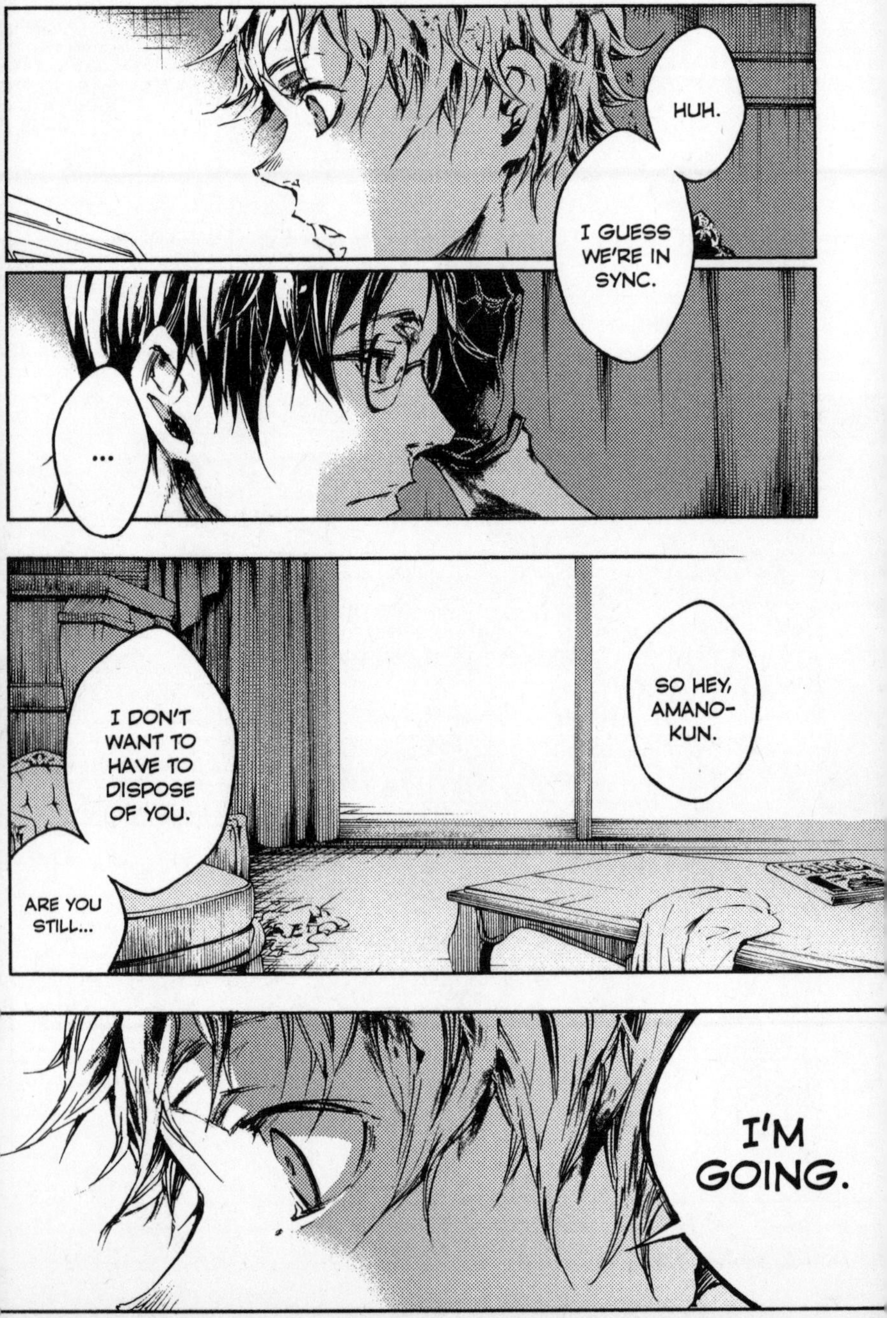
HUH.
I GUESS WE'RE IN SYNC.
...
SO HEY, AMANO-KUN.
I DON'T WANT TO HAVE TO DISPOSE OF YOU.
ARE YOU STILL...
I'M GOING.

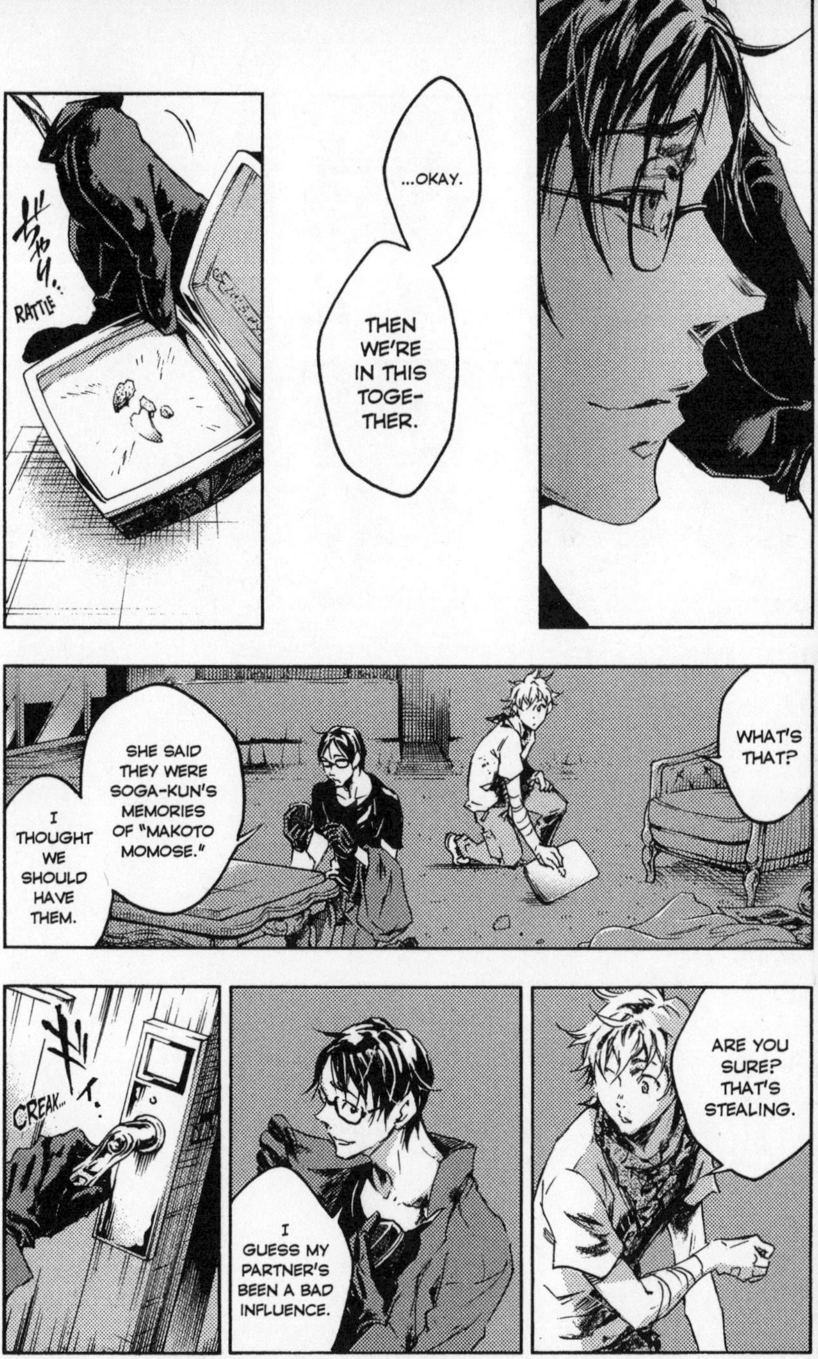
...OKAY.
THEN WE'RE IN THIS TOGE-THER.
RATTLE
WHAT'S THAT?
SHE SAID THEY WERE SOGA-KUN'S MEMORIES OF "MAKOTO MOMOSE."
I THOUGHT WE SHOULD HAVE THEM.
ARE YOU SURE? THAT'S STEALING.
I GUESS MY PARTNER'S BEEN A BAD INFLUENCE.
CREAK...

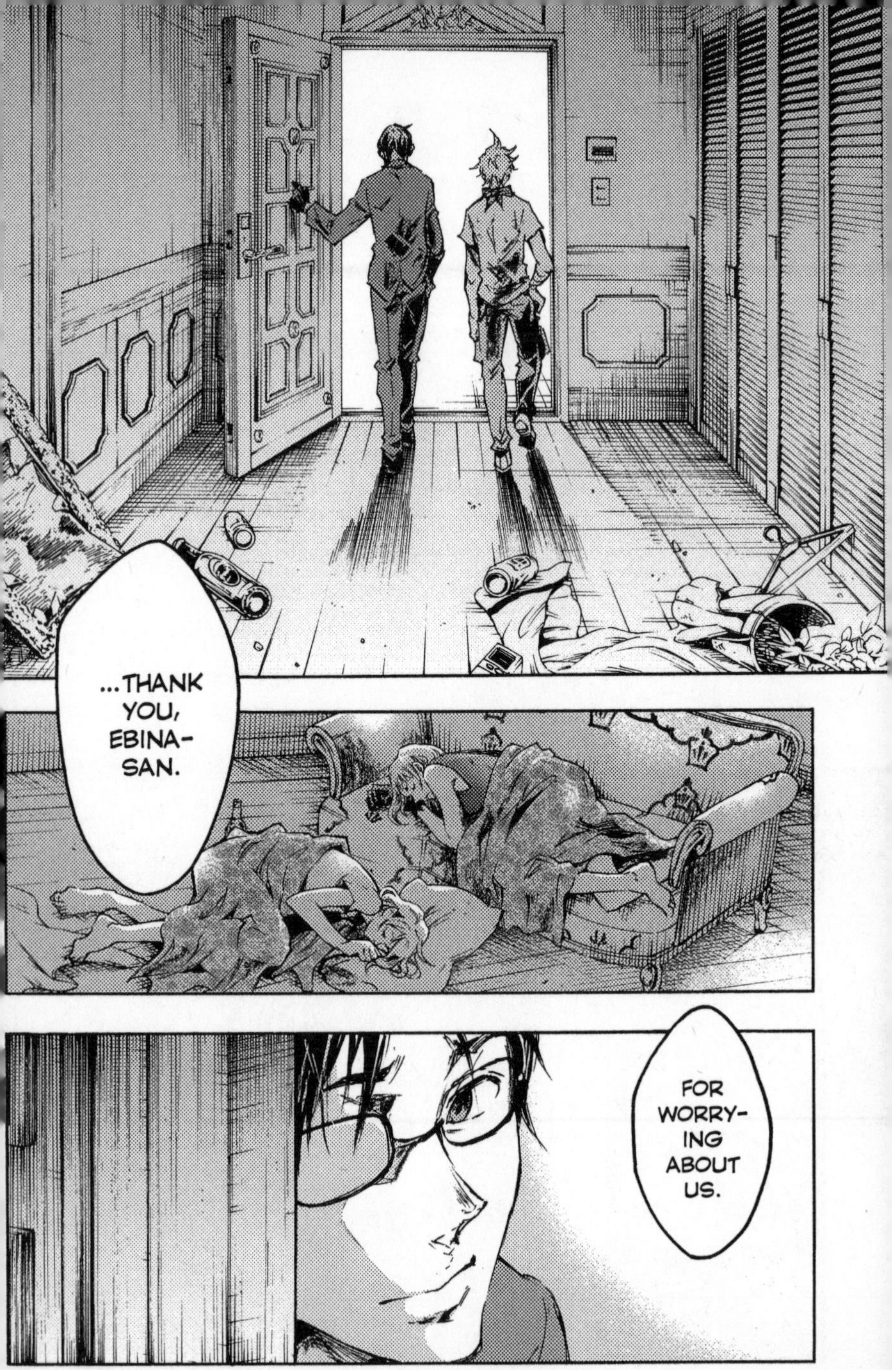
...THANK YOU, EBINA-SAN.
FOR WORRYING ABOUT US.

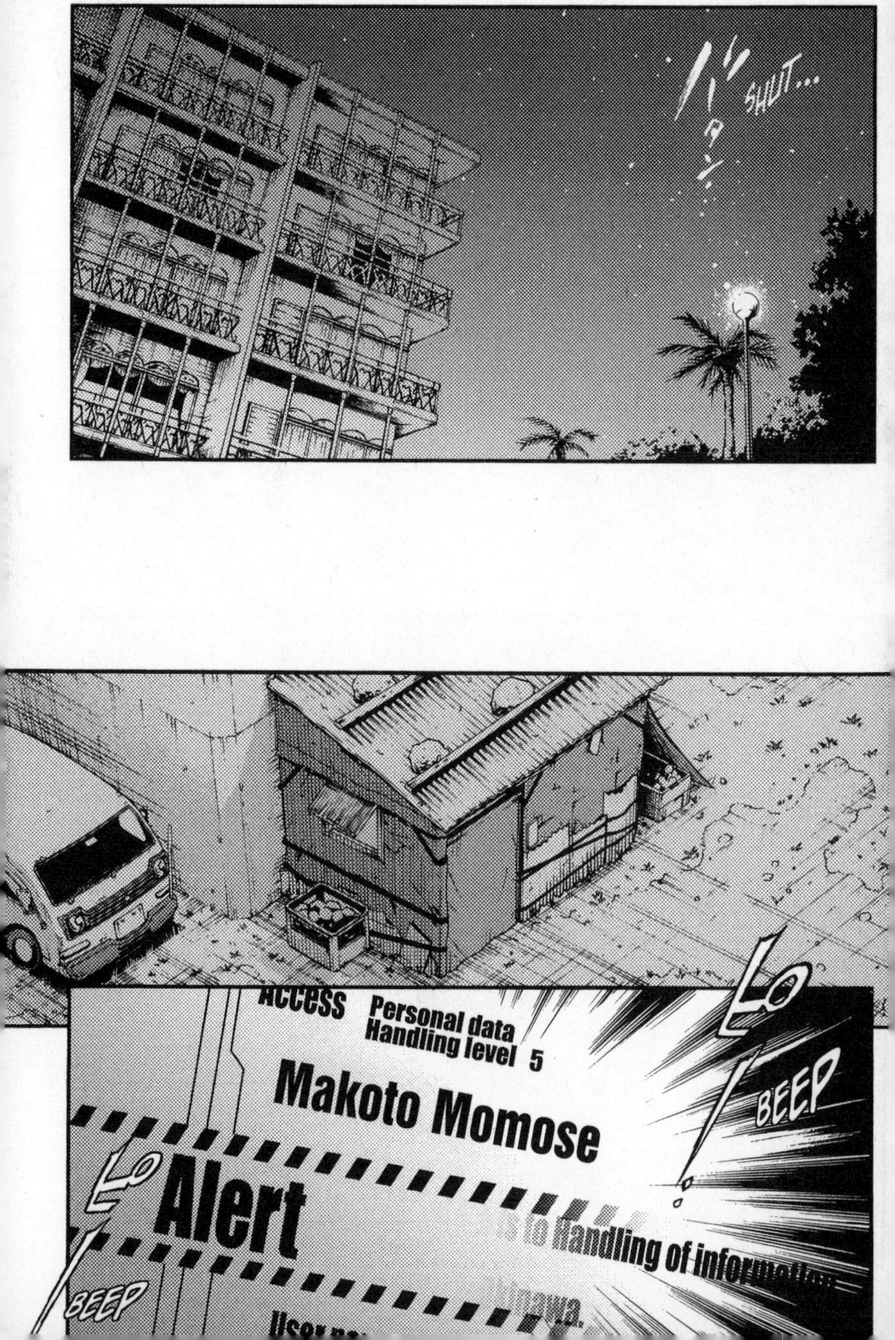

SHUT...
ACCESS
Personal data
Handling level 5
Makoto Momose
BEEP
Alert
BEEP

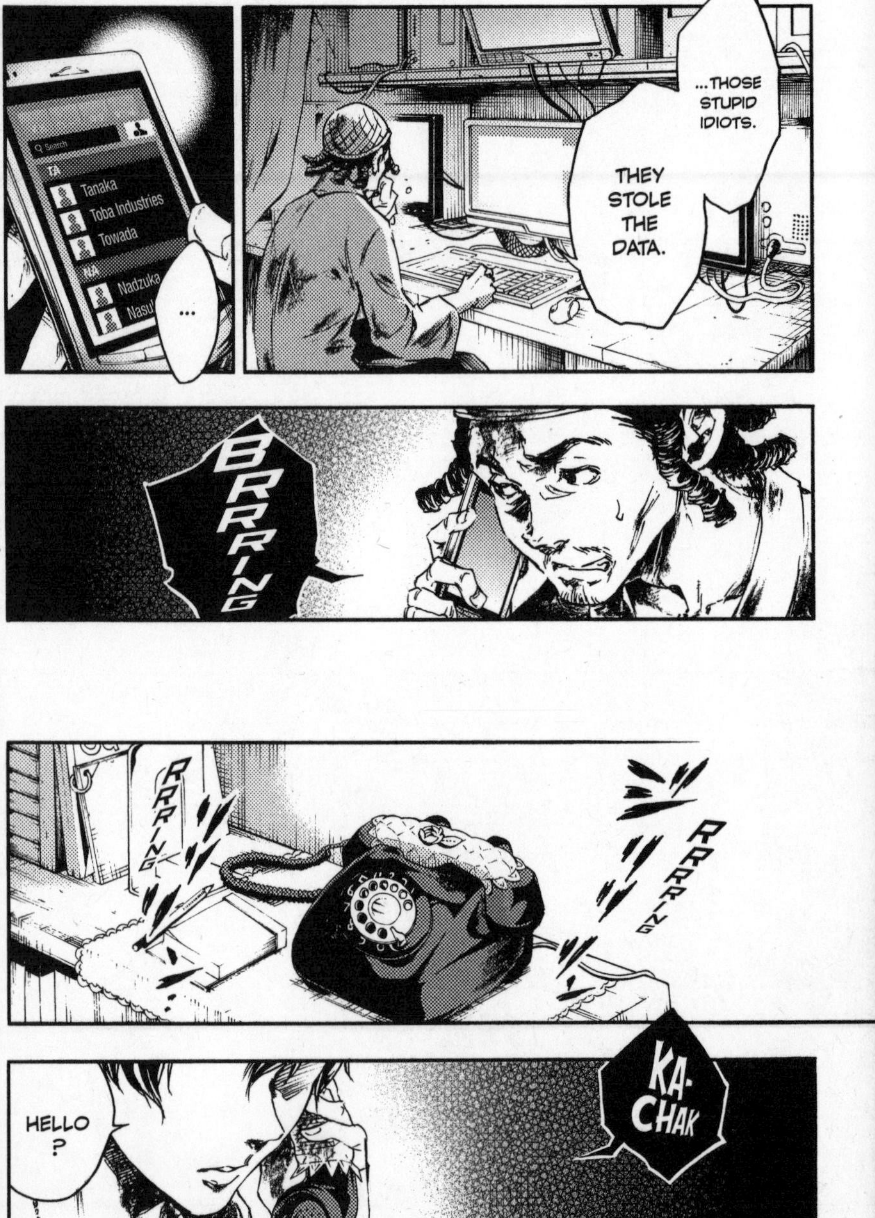
...THOSE STUPID IDIOTS.
THEY STOLE THE DATA.
Search
TA
Tanaka
Toba Industries
Towada
NA
Nadzuka
...
BRRRING
RRRING
RRRING
KA-CHAK
HELLO?

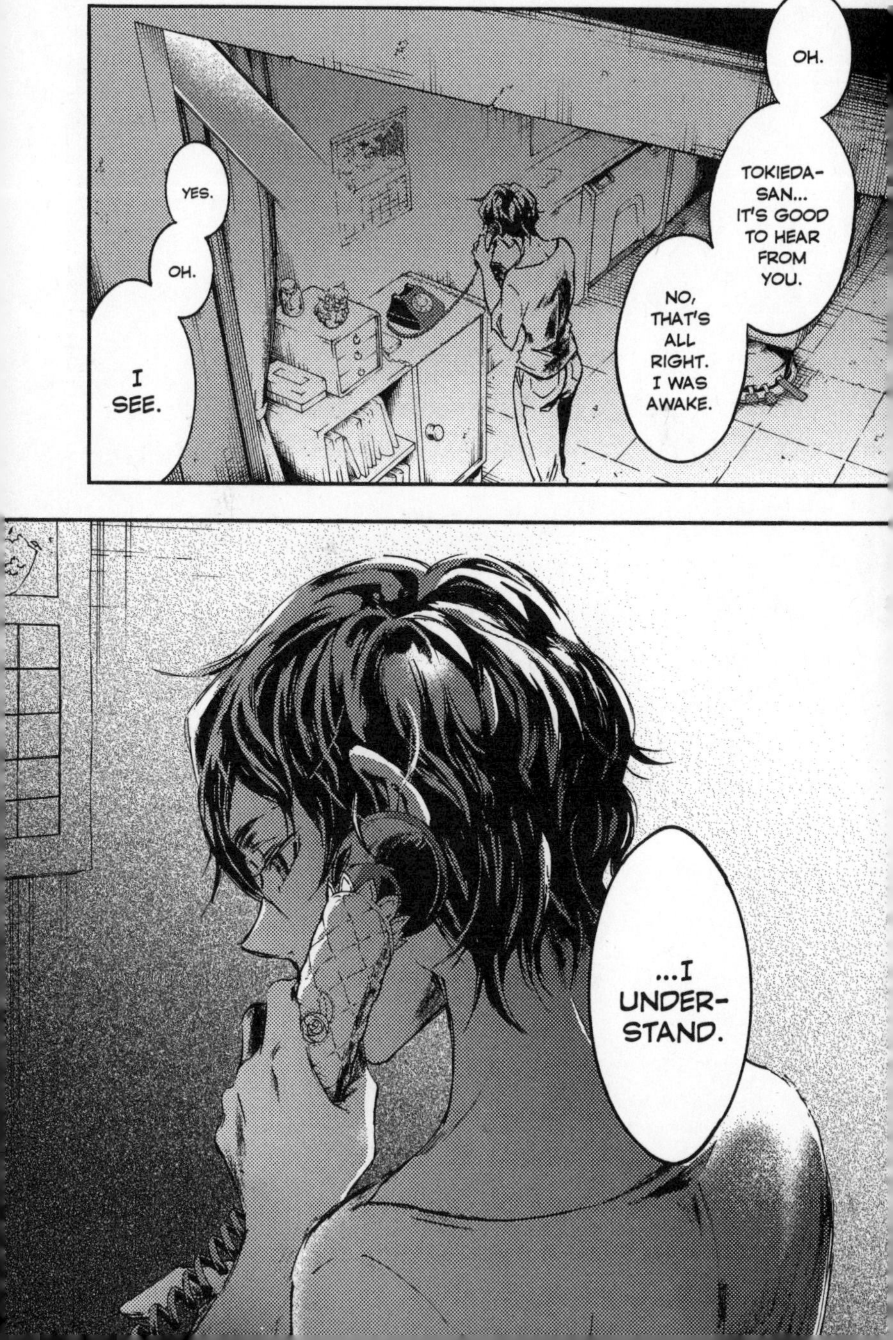
OH.
TOKIEDA-SAN... IT'S GOOD TO HEAR FROM YOU.
NO, THAT'S ALL RIGHT. I WAS AWAKE.
YES.
OH.
I SEE.
...I UNDERSTAND.

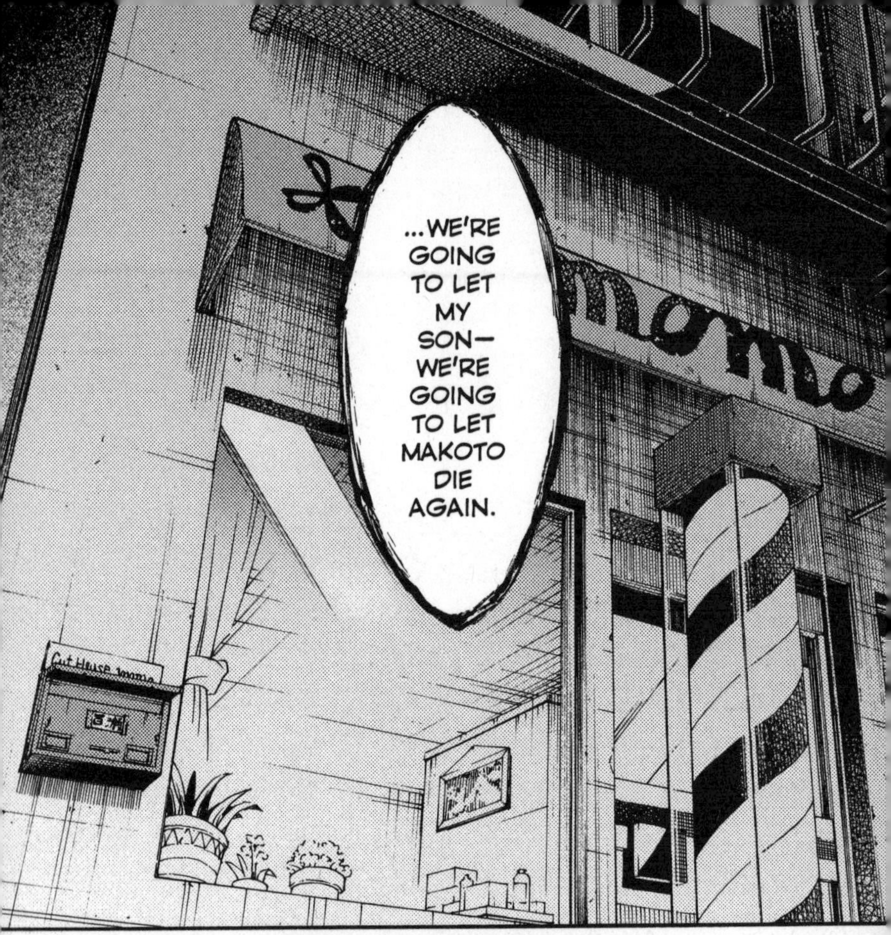
...WE'RE GOING TO LET MY SON— WE'RE GOING TO LET MAKOTO DIE AGAIN.
Cut House momo

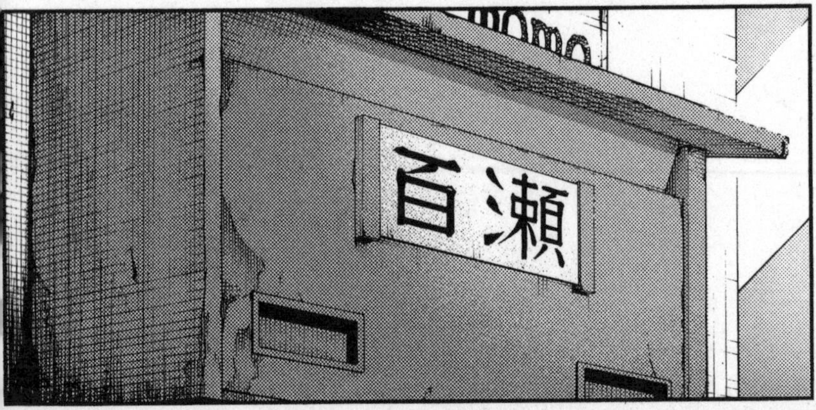
百瀬

SIGN: Momose

Chapter 21   Two Realities

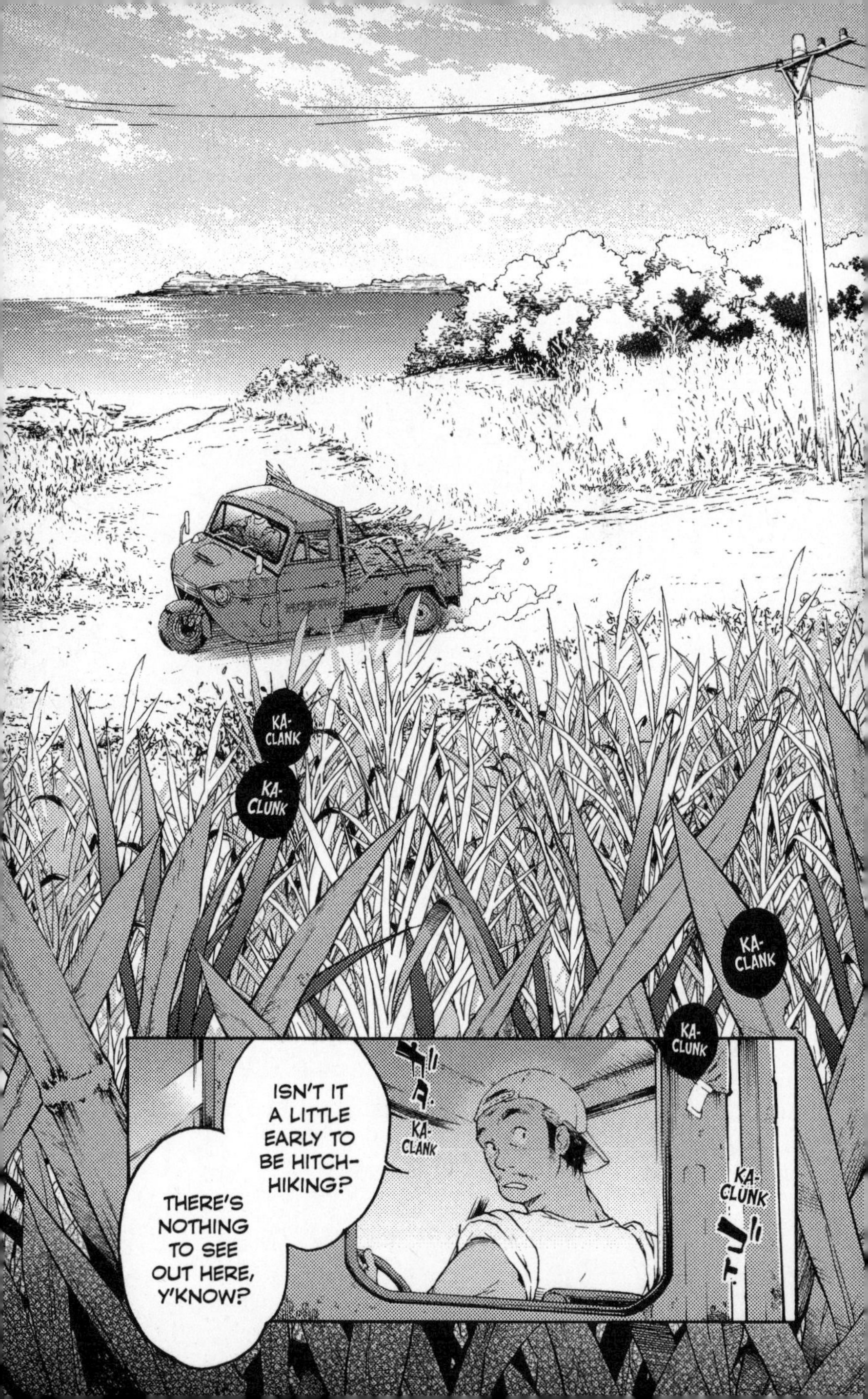
KA-CLANK
KA-CLUNK
KA-CLANK
KA-CLUNK
KA-CLANK
KA-CLUNK
ISN'T IT A LITTLE EARLY TO BE HITCH-HIKING?
THERE'S NOTHING TO SEE OUT HERE, Y'KNOW?

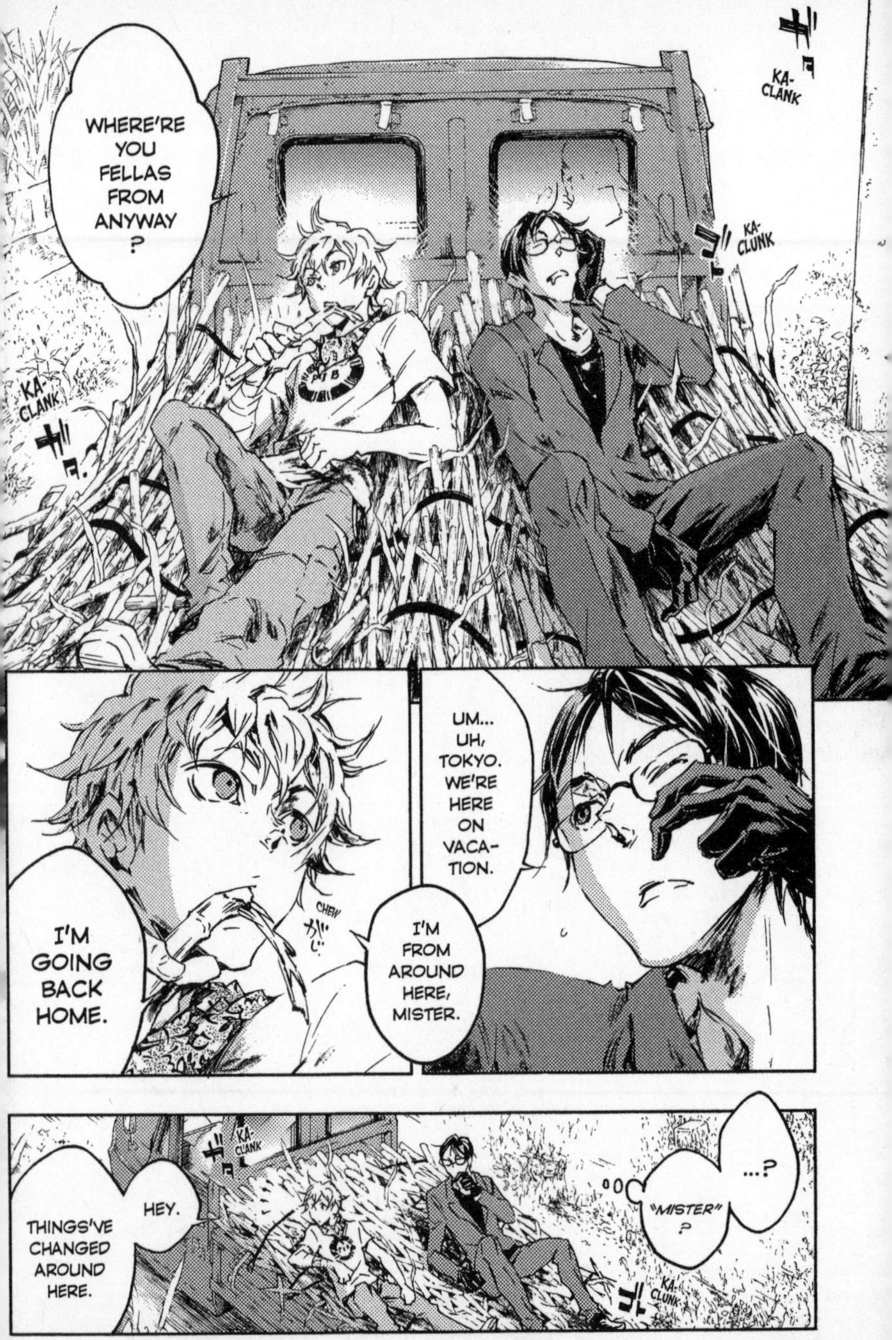
KA-CLANK
KA-CLUNK
WHERE'RE YOU FELLAS FROM ANYWAY?
KA-CLANK
UM... UH, TOKYO. WE'RE HERE ON VACA-TION.
I'M FROM AROUND HERE, MISTER.
CHEW
I'M GOING BACK HOME.
...?
"MISTER"?
KA-CLUNK
KA-CLANK
HEY.
THINGS'VE CHANGED AROUND HERE.

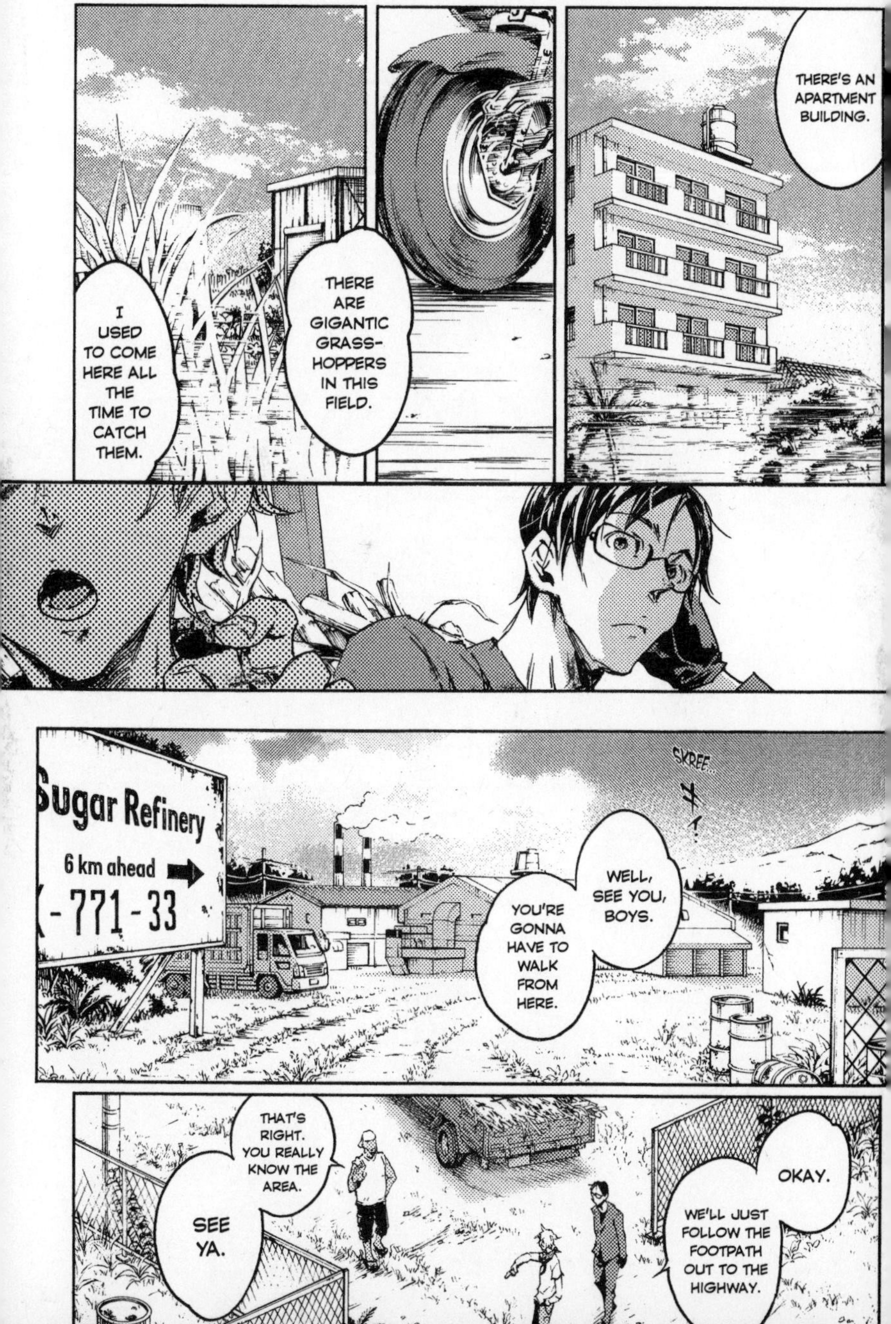
THERE'S AN APARTMENT BUILDING.
THERE ARE GIGANTIC GRASS-HOPPERS IN THIS FIELD.
I USED TO COME HERE ALL THE TIME TO CATCH THEM.
SKREE...
WELL, SEE YOU, BOYS.
YOU'RE GONNA HAVE TO WALK FROM HERE.
Sugar Refinery
6 km ahead
-771-33
OKAY.
WE'LL JUST FOLLOW THE FOOTPATH OUT TO THE HIGHWAY.
THAT'S RIGHT. YOU REALLY KNOW THE AREA.
SEE YA.

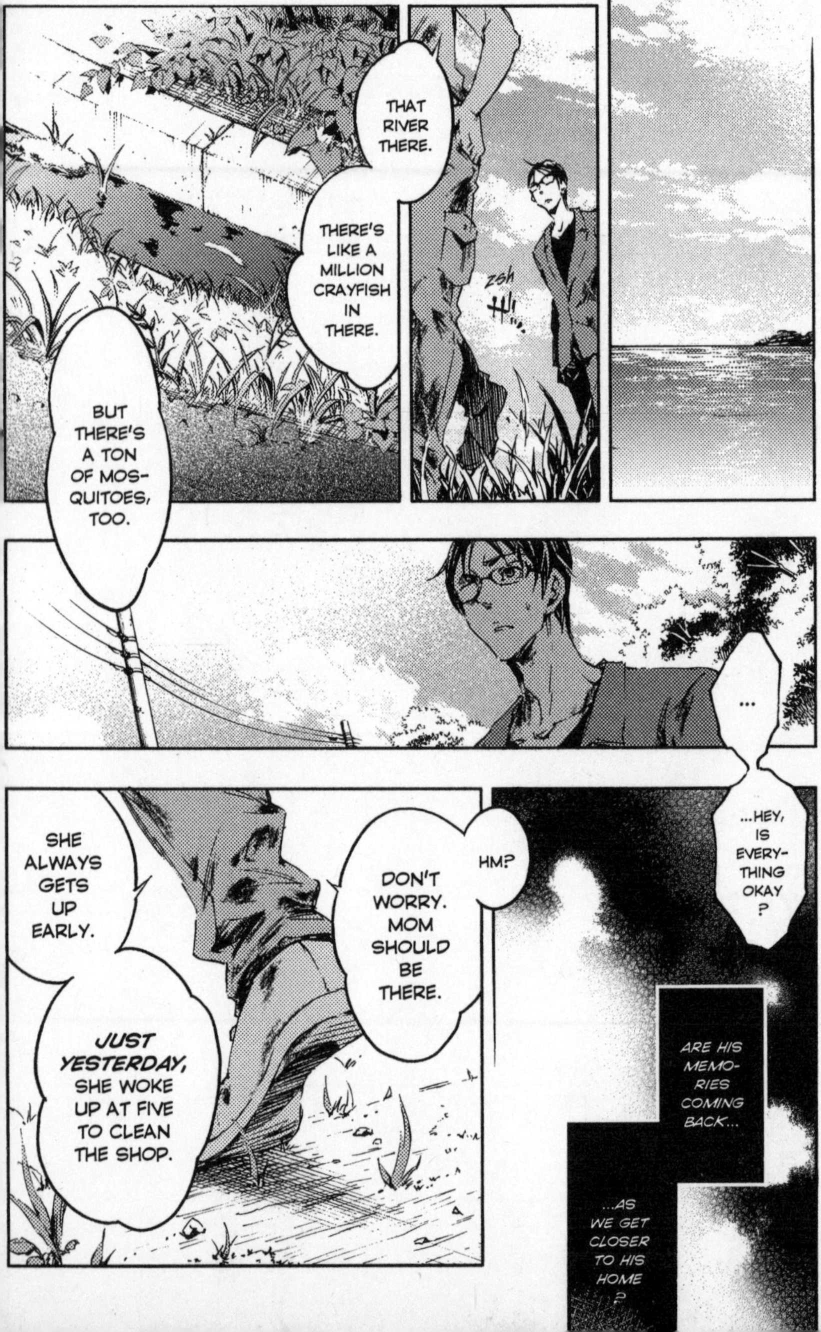
THAT RIVER THERE.
THERE'S LIKE A MILLION CRAYFISH IN THERE.
ZSH
BUT THERE'S A TON OF MOS-QUITOES, TOO.
...
...HEY, IS EVERY-THING OKAY?
ARE HIS MEMO-RIES COMING BACK...
...AS WE GET CLOSER TO HIS HOME?
HM?
DON'T WORRY. MOM SHOULD BE THERE.
SHE ALWAYS GETS UP EARLY.
JUST YESTERDAY, SHE WOKE UP AT FIVE TO CLEAN THE SHOP.

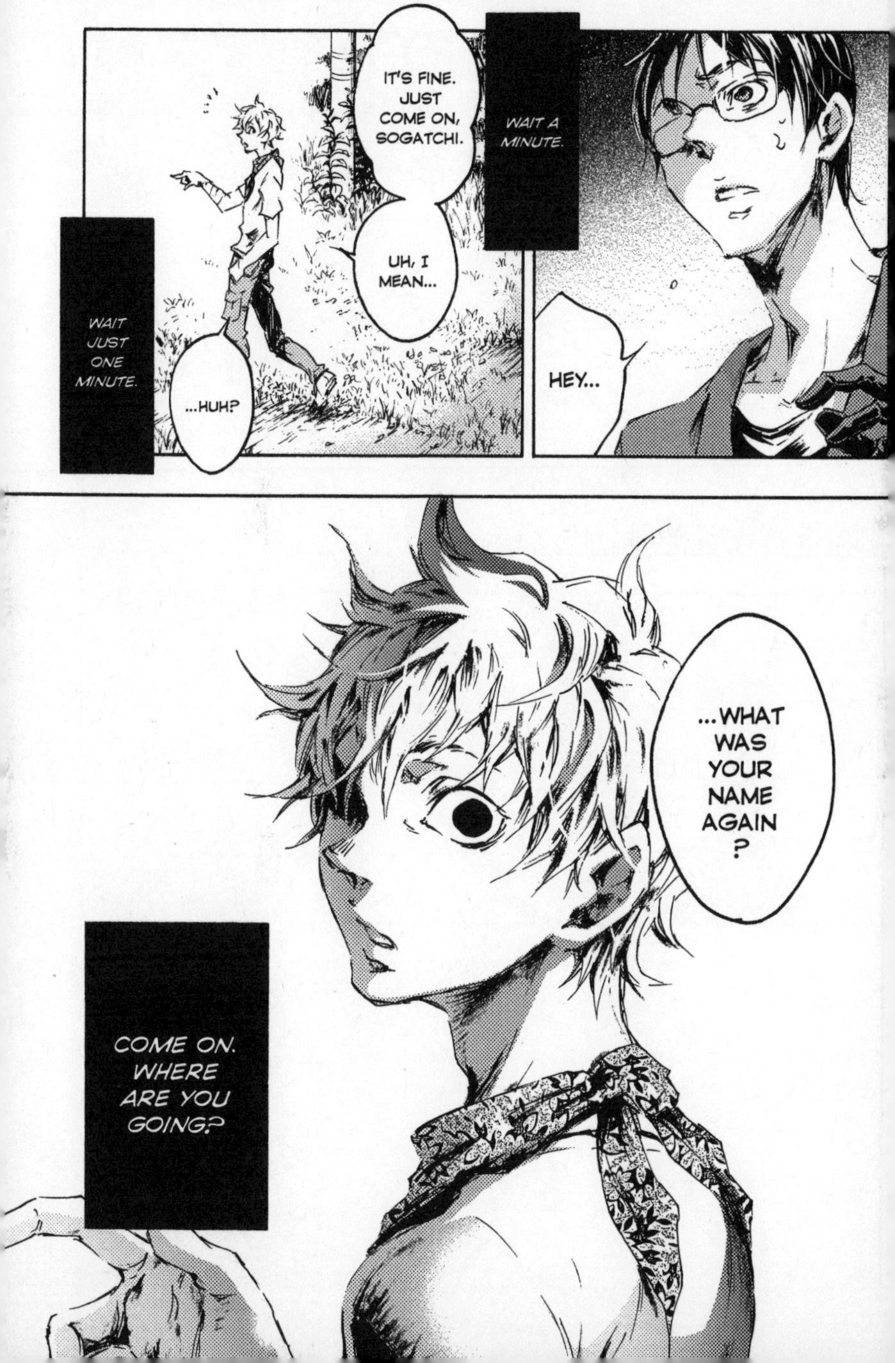
WAIT A MINUTE.
HEY...
IT'S FINE. JUST COME ON, SOGATCHI.
UH, I MEAN...
...HUH?
WAIT JUST ONE MINUTE.
...WHAT WAS YOUR NAME AGAIN?
COME ON. WHERE ARE YOU GOING?

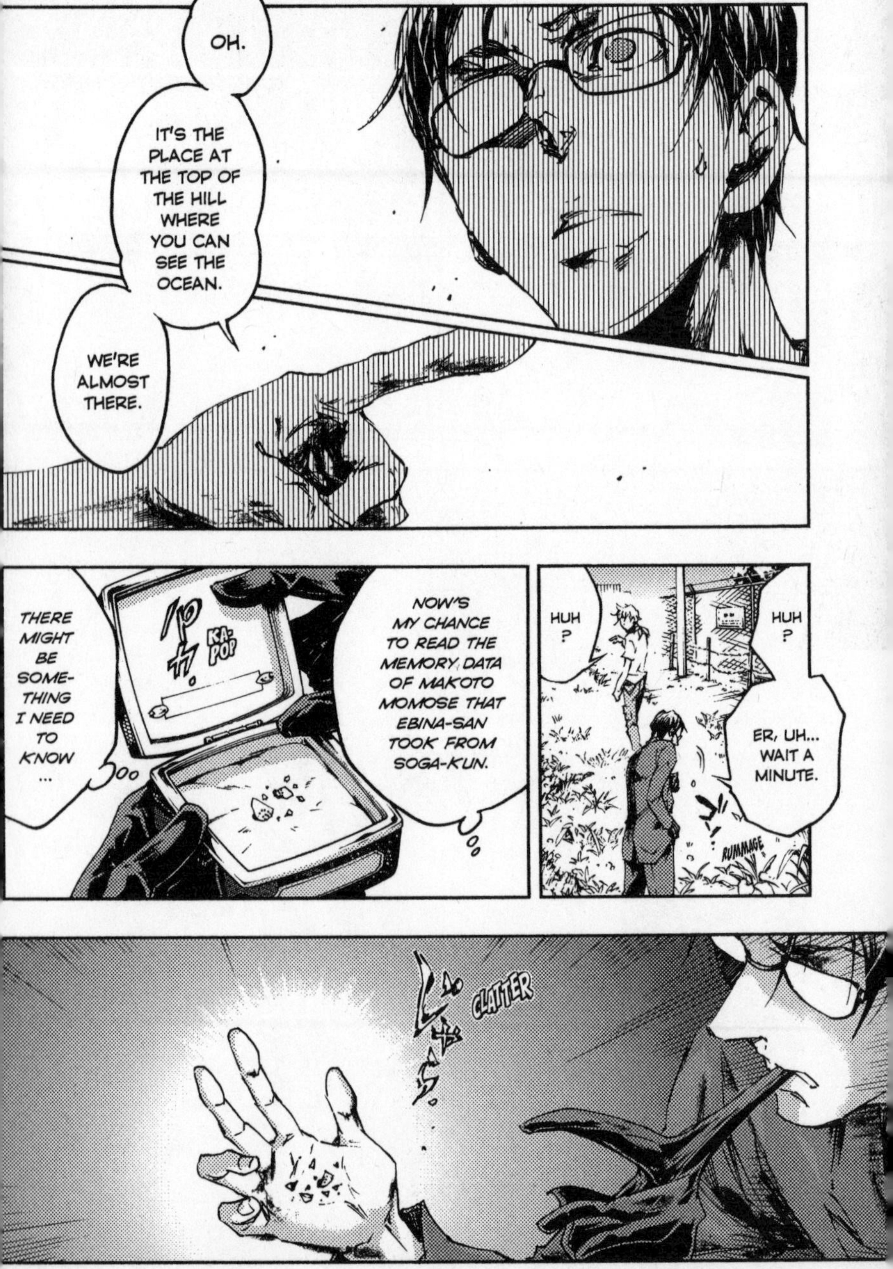
OH.
IT'S THE PLACE AT THE TOP OF THE HILL WHERE YOU CAN SEE THE OCEAN.
WE'RE ALMOST THERE.
HUH ?
HUH ?
ER, UH... WAIT A MINUTE.
RUMMAGE
NOW'S MY CHANCE TO READ THE MEMORY DATA OF MAKOTO MOMOSE THAT EBINA-SAN TOOK FROM SOGA-KUN.
KA-POP
THERE MIGHT BE SOME-THING I NEED TO KNOW ...
CLATTER

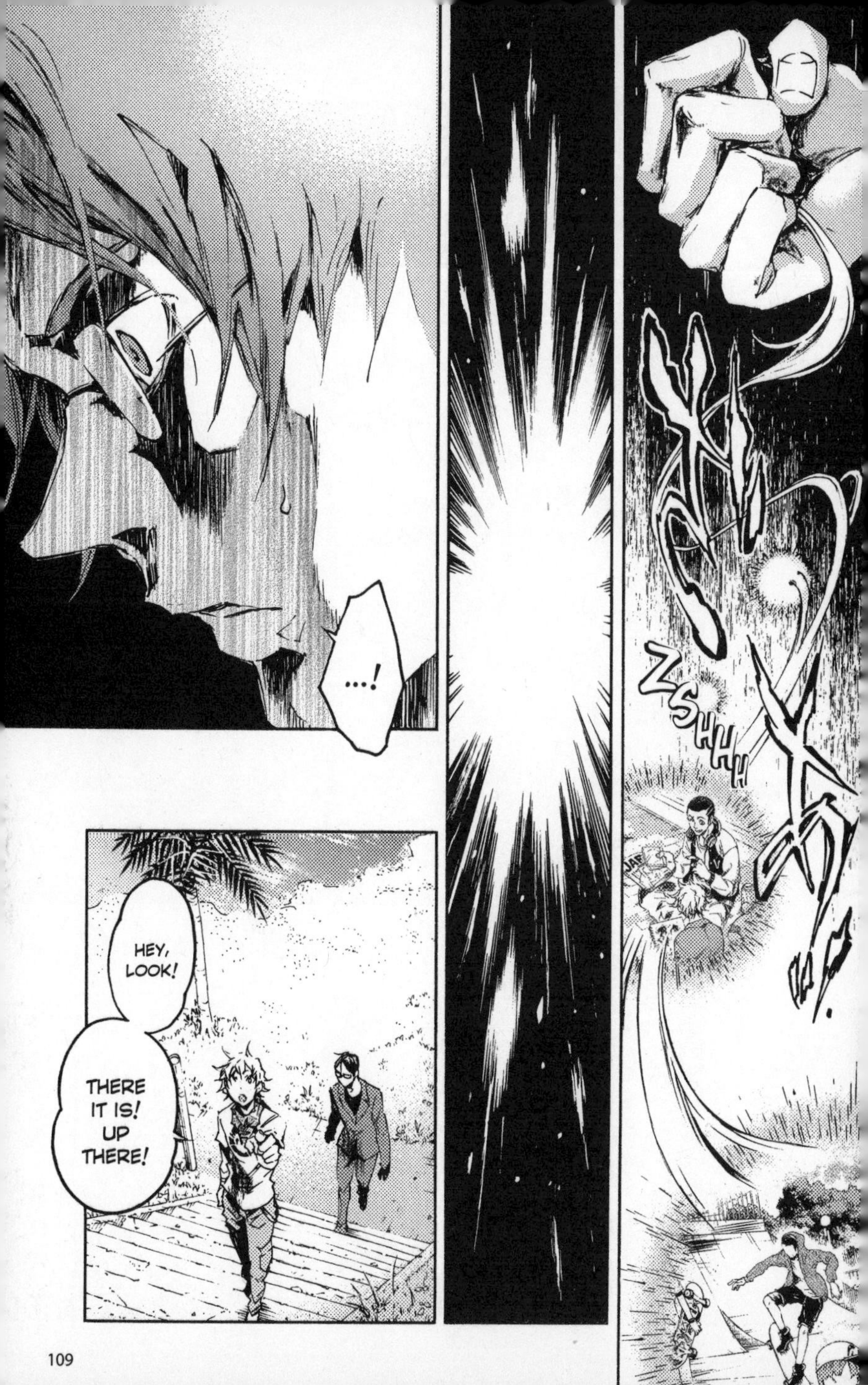
ZSHHHH
...!
HEY, LOOK!
THERE IT IS! UP THERE!

CUT HOUSE MoMo
THAT'S MY PLACE!
CUT HOUSE MoMo

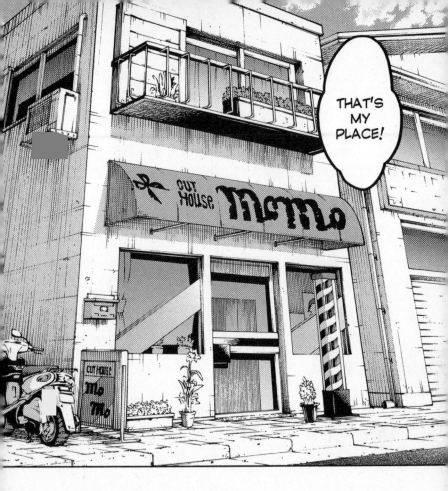

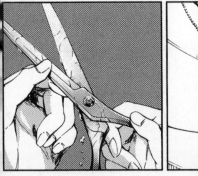

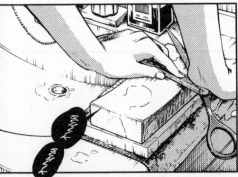

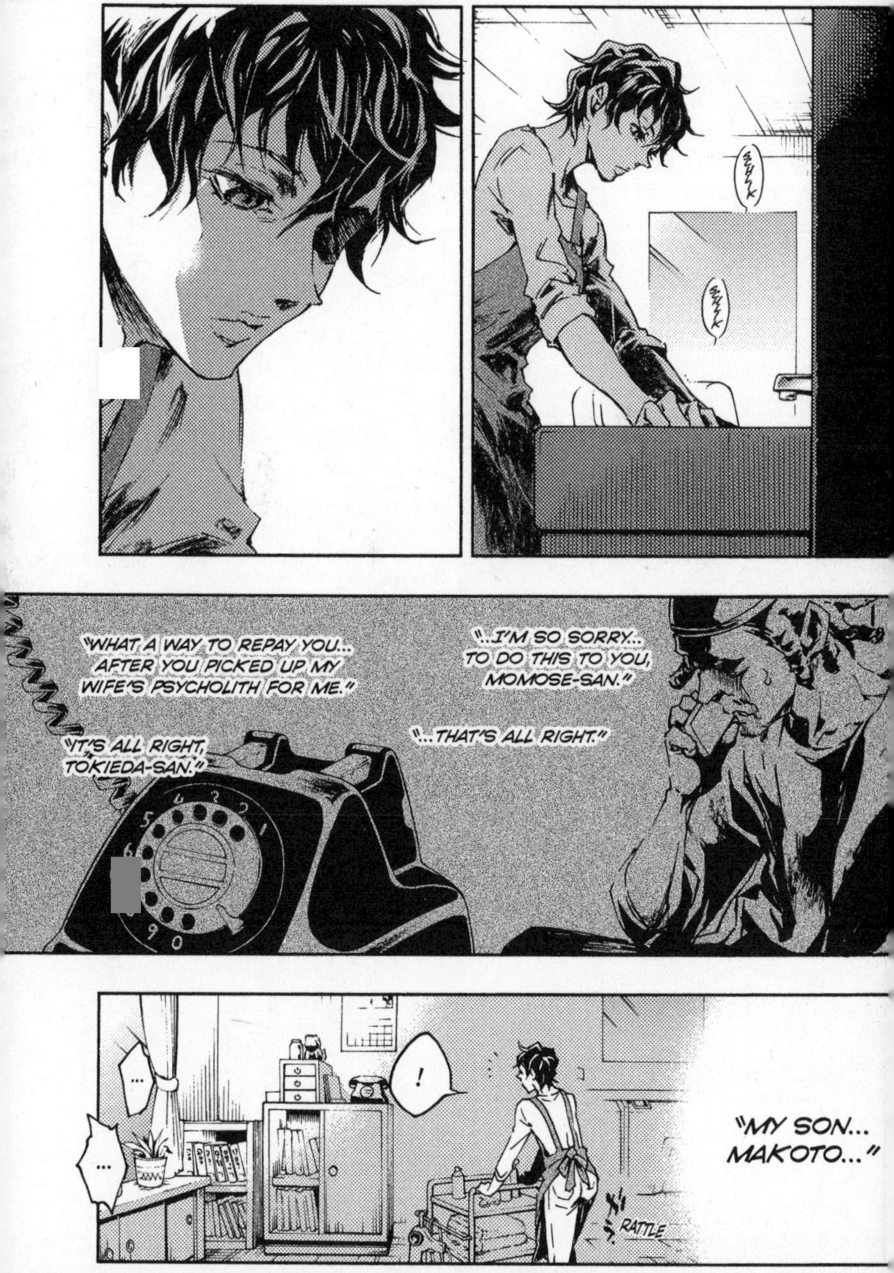
"...I'M SO SORRY... TO DO THIS TO YOU, MOMOSE-SAN."
"WHAT A WAY TO REPAY YOU... AFTER YOU PICKED UP MY WIFE'S PSYCHOLITH FOR ME."
"...THAT'S ALL RIGHT."
"IT'S ALL RIGHT, TOKIEDA-SAN."
"MY SON... MAKOTO..."
RATTLE
!
...
...

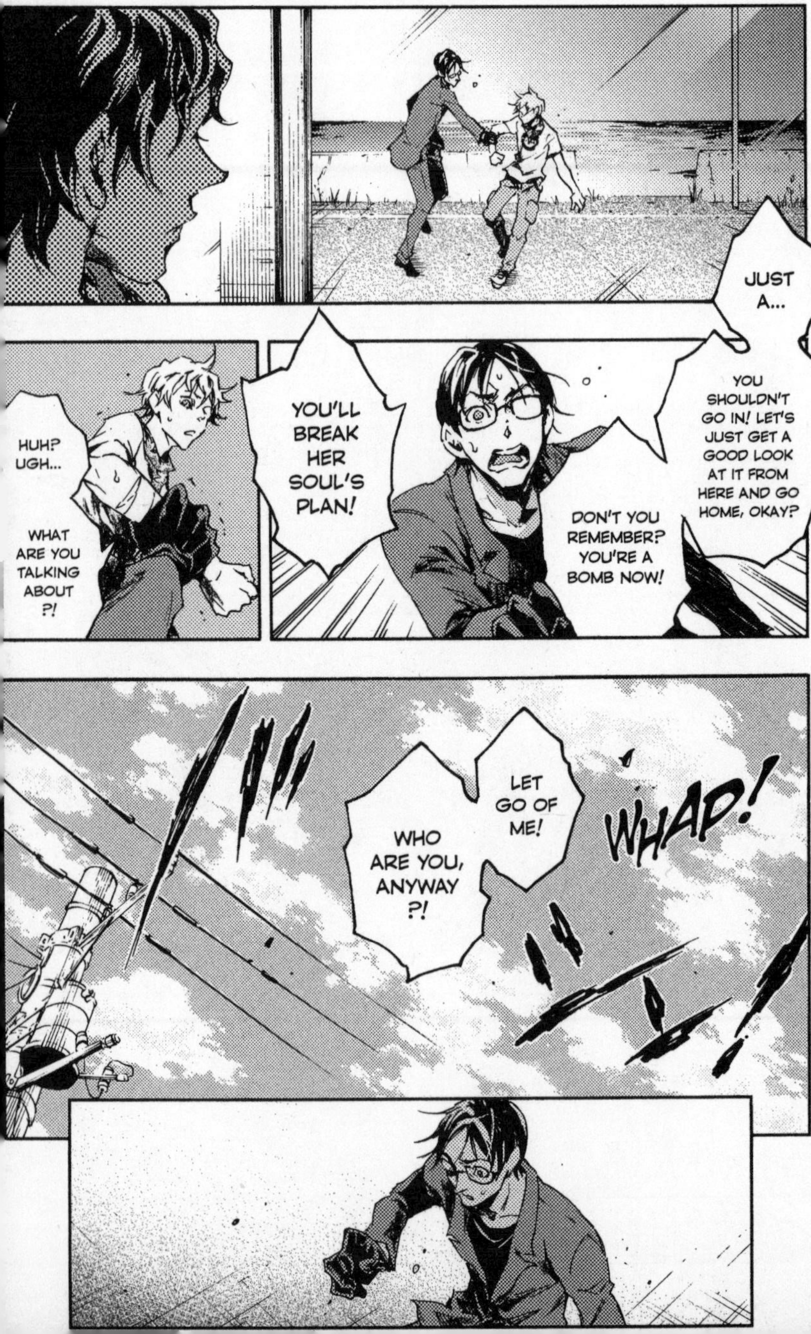
JUST A...
YOU SHOULDN'T GO IN! LET'S JUST GET A GOOD LOOK AT IT FROM HERE AND GO HOME, OKAY?
DON'T YOU REMEMBER? YOU'RE A BOMB NOW!
YOU'LL BREAK HER SOUL'S PLAN!
HUH? UGH...
WHAT ARE YOU TALKING ABOUT ?!
LET GO OF ME!
WHO ARE YOU, ANYWAY ?!
WHAP!

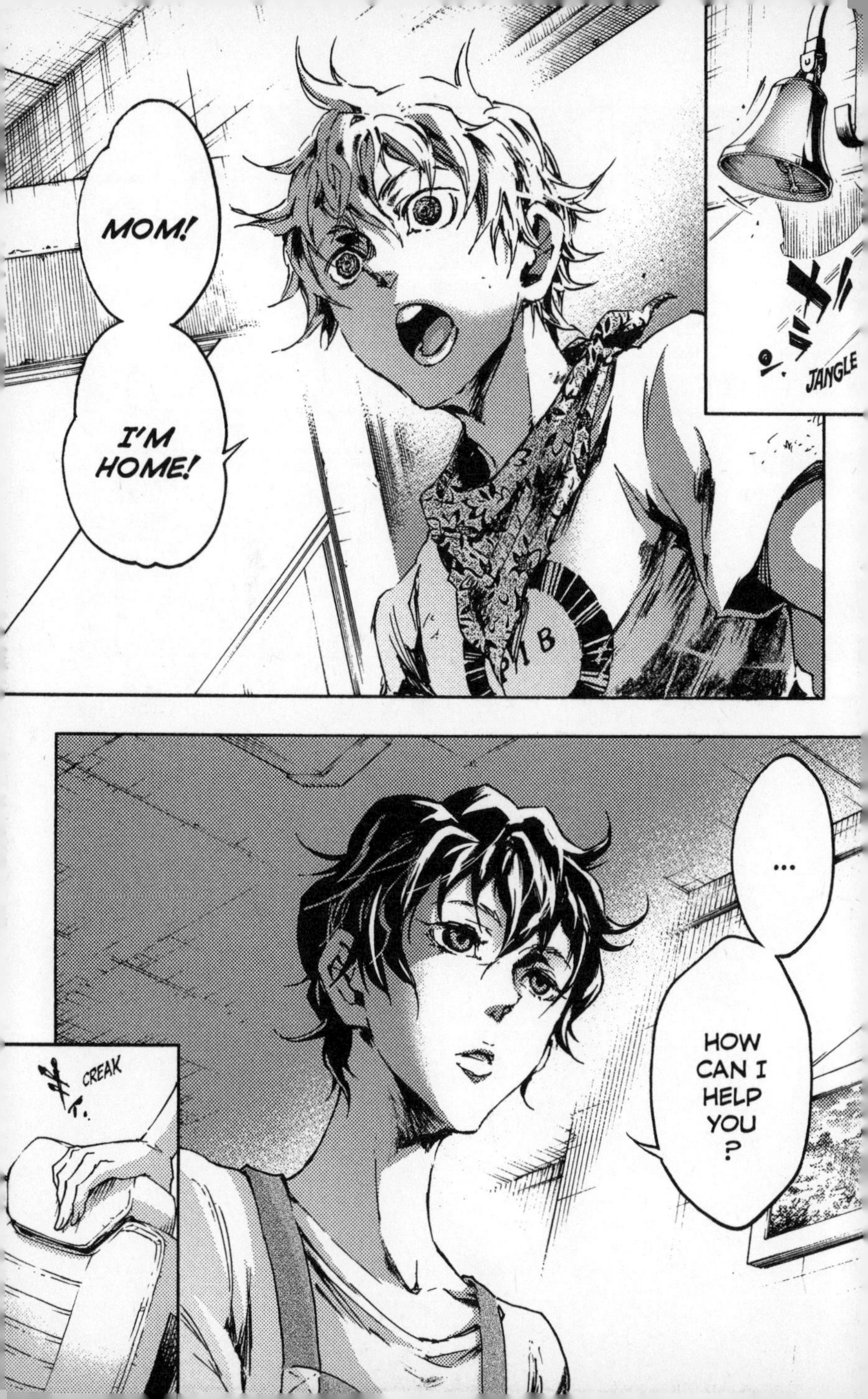
JANGLE
MOM!
I'M HOME!
...
HOW CAN I HELP YOU?
CREAK

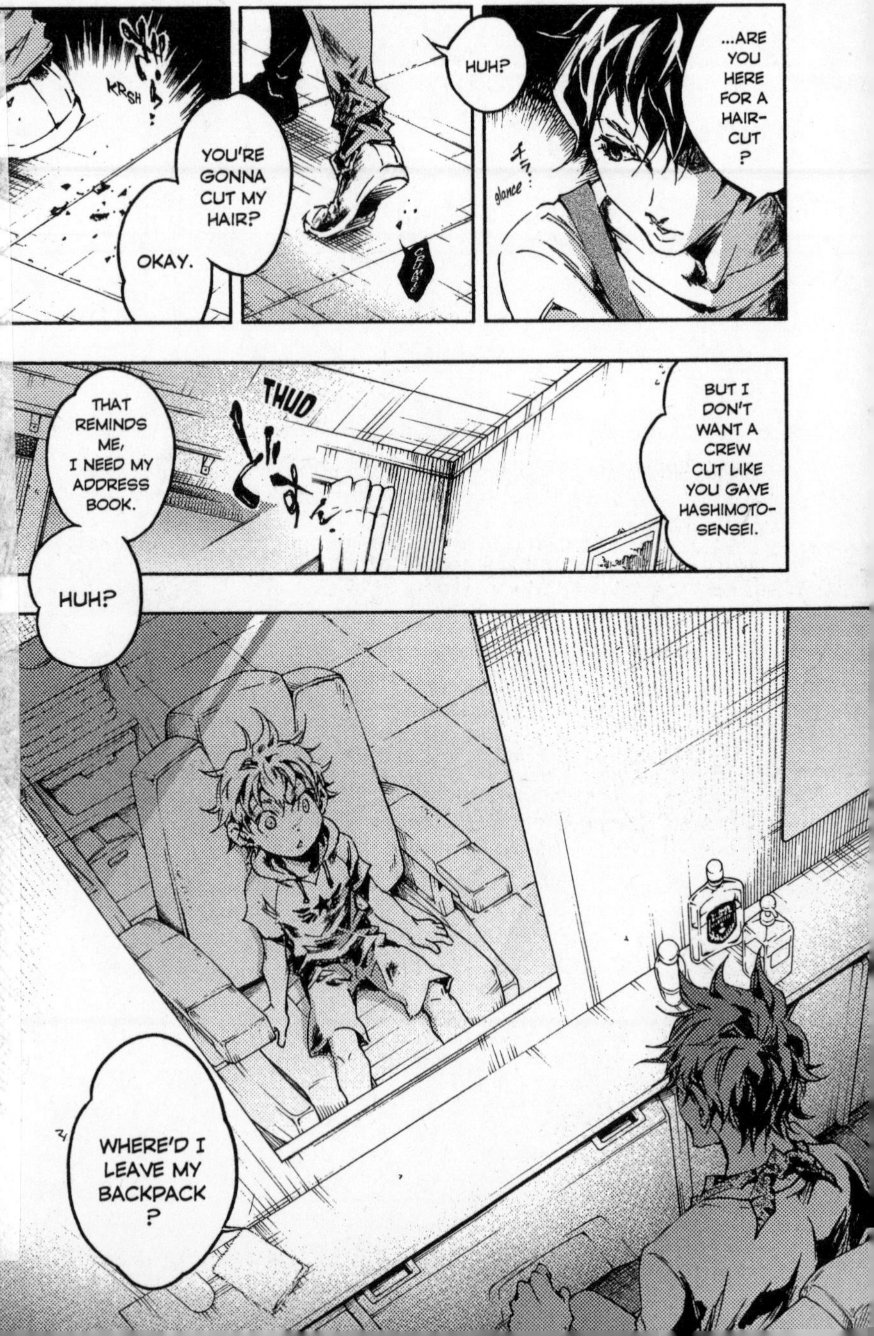
...ARE YOU HERE FOR A HAIR-CUT?
glance
HUH?
CRUMBLE
KRSH
YOU'RE GONNA CUT MY HAIR?
OKAY.
BUT I DON'T WANT A CREW CUT LIKE YOU GAVE HASHIMOTO-SENSEI.
THUD
THAT REMINDS ME, I NEED MY ADDRESS BOOK.
HUH?
WHERE'D I LEAVE MY BACKPACK?

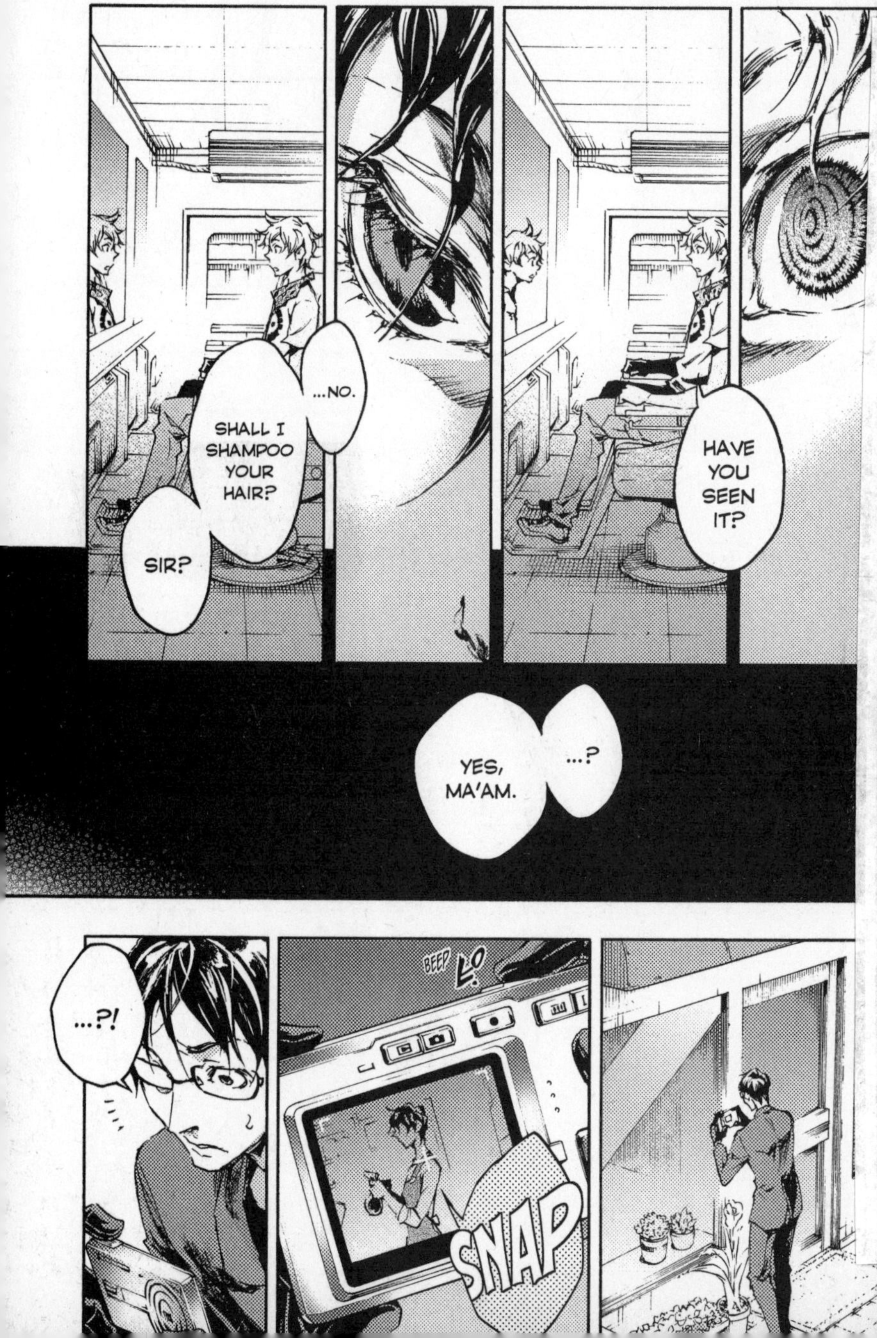
HAVE YOU SEEN IT?
...NO.
SHALL I SHAMPOO YOUR HAIR?
SIR?
...?
YES, MA'AM.
BEEP
SNAP
...?!

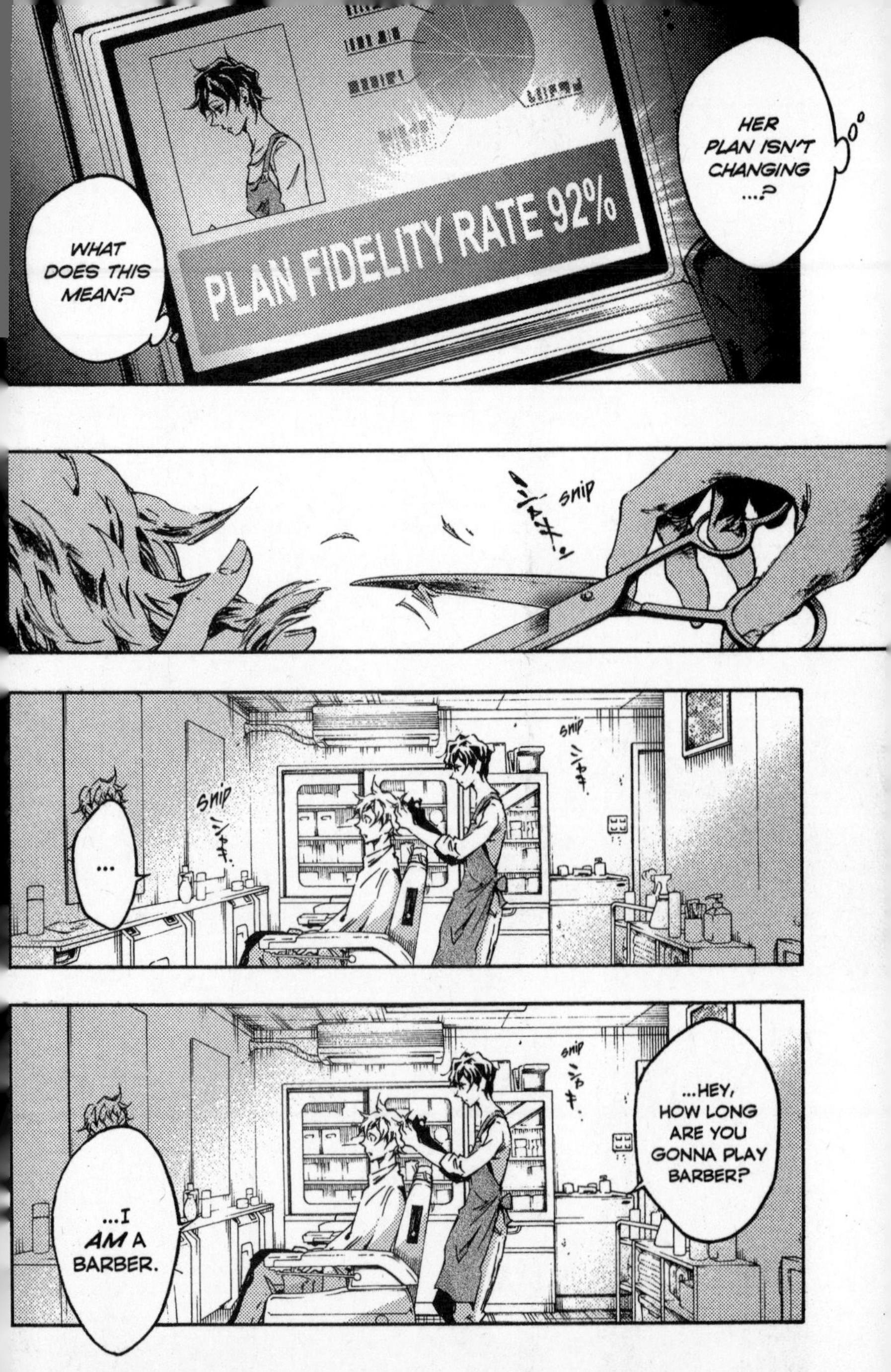
HER PLAN ISN'T CHANGING ...?
PLAN FIDELITY RATE 92%
WHAT DOES THIS MEAN?
snip
snip
snip
...
snip
...HEY, HOW LONG ARE YOU GONNA PLAY BARBER?
...I *AM* A BARBER.

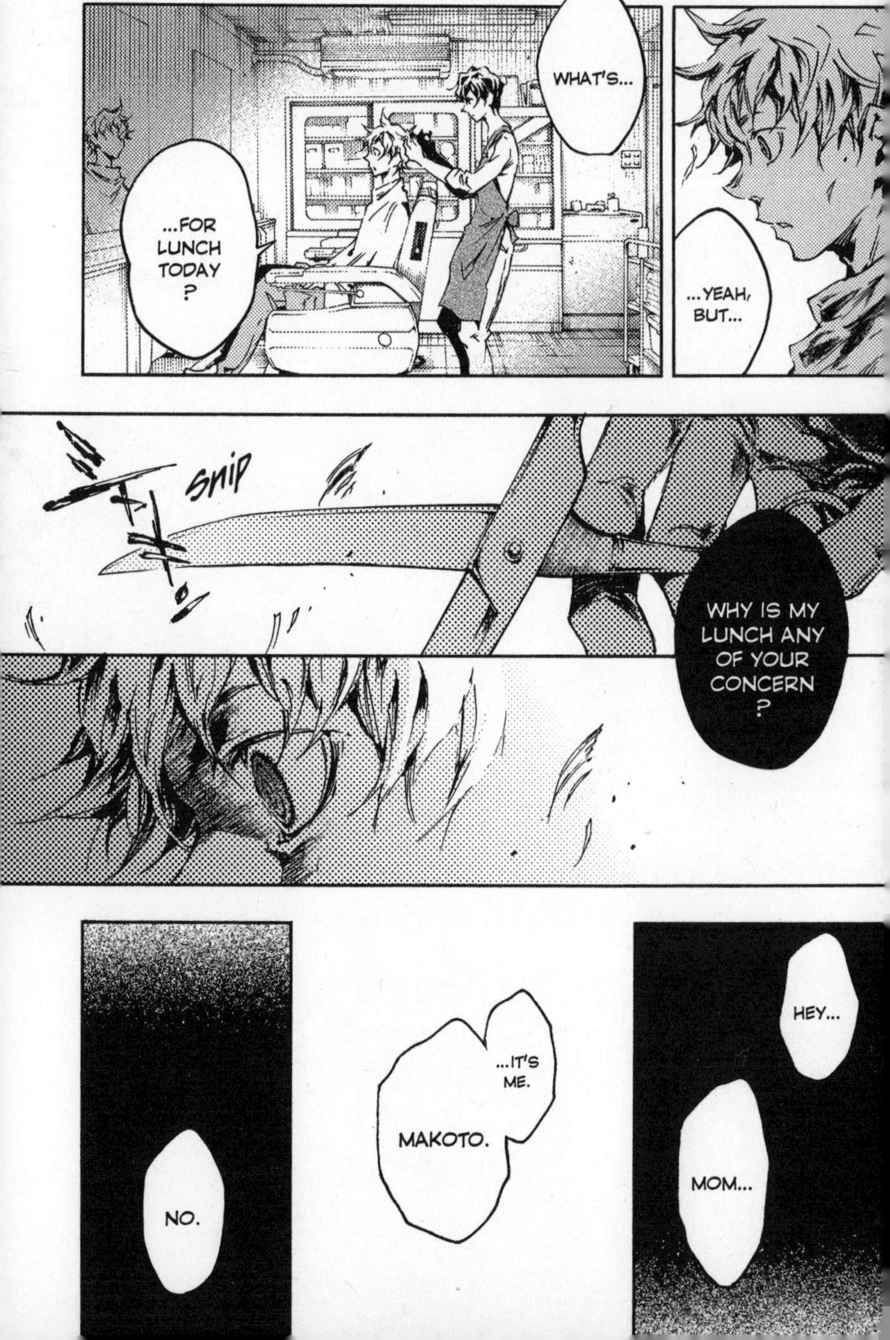
...YEAH, BUT...
WHAT'S...
...FOR LUNCH TODAY?
Snip
WHY IS MY LUNCH ANY OF YOUR CONCERN?
HEY...
MOM...
...IT'S ME.
MAKOTO.
NO.

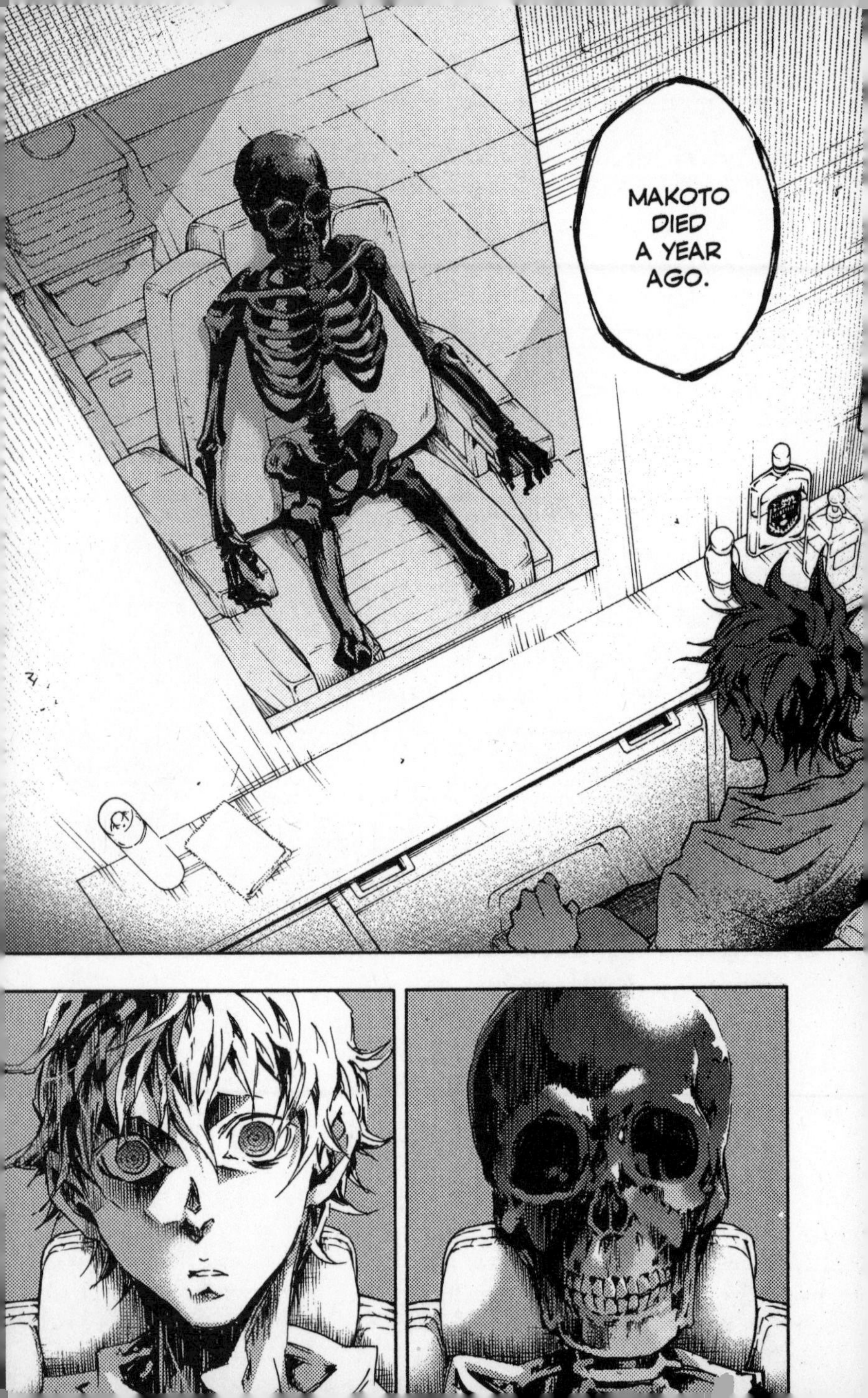
MAKOTO DIED A YEAR AGO.

KA-THUNK
...IS SOMETHING THE MATTER?
NO I DIDN'T.
WHAT ARE YOU TALKING ABOUT? ...I MEAN, LOOK.
THAT PICTURE THERE. I DREW THAT.
CRASH
YEAH. I GOT AN AWARD FOR IT.
BUT I DIDN'T HAVE ENOUGH TIME TO FINISH IT.
GRAB
I WANTED TO ADD JUST A LITTLE MORE.
HERE. SEE? ON THIS BIRD...

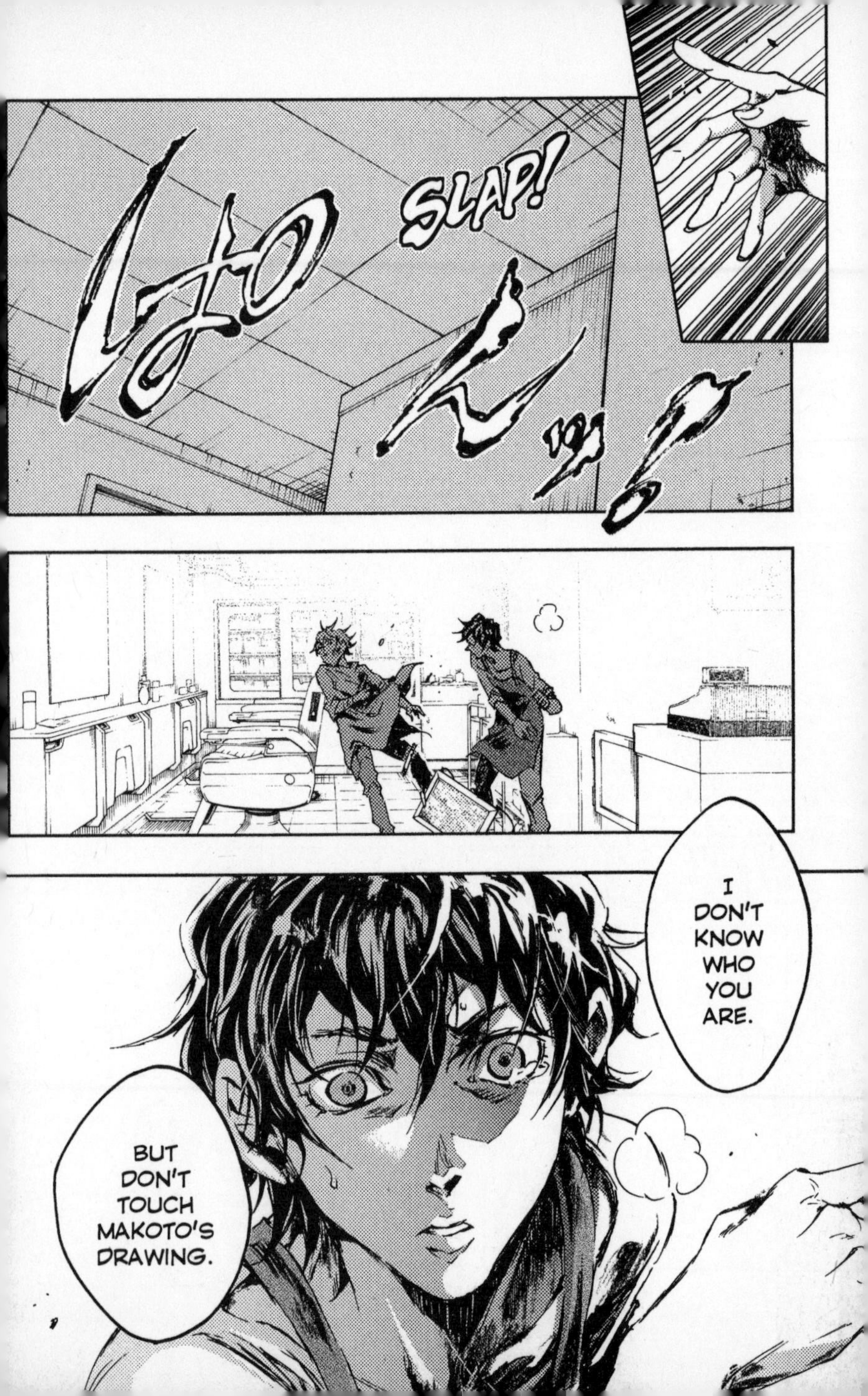
SLAP!
I DON'T KNOW WHO YOU ARE.
BUT DON'T TOUCH MAKOTO'S DRAWING.

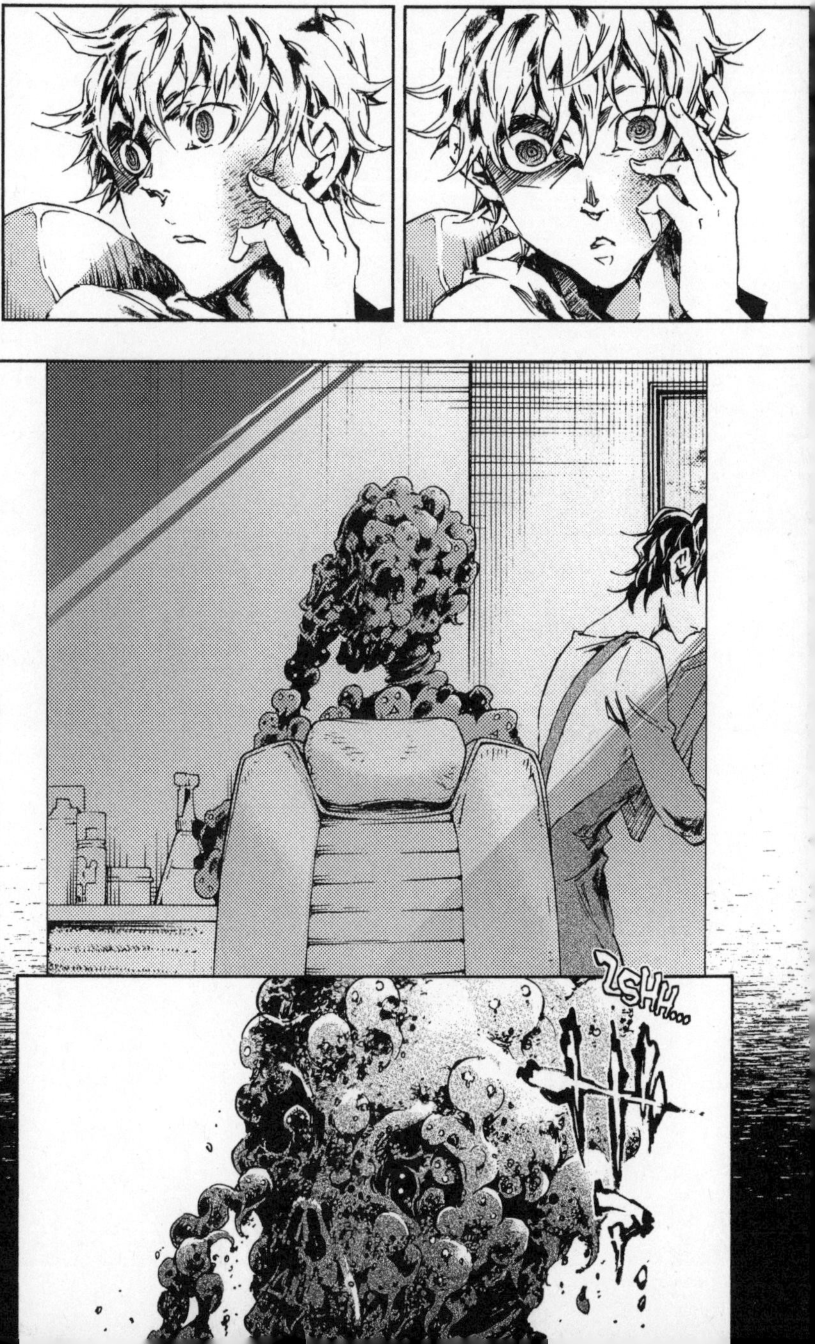
ZSHH...

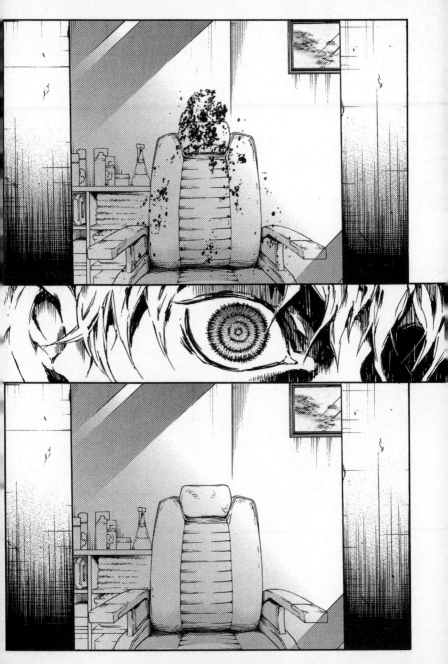

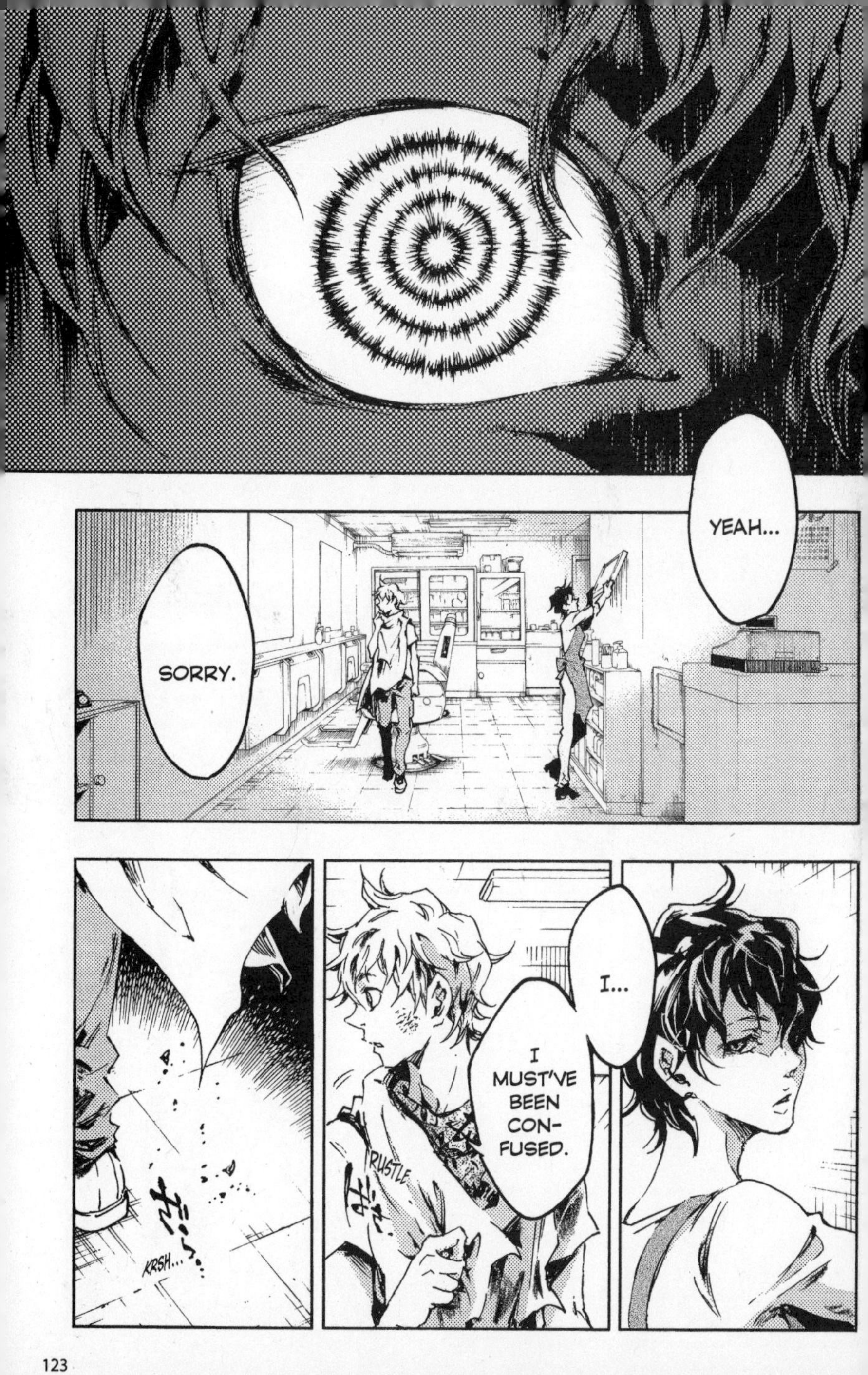
YEAH...
SORRY.
I...
I MUST'VE BEEN CON- FUSED.
RUSTLE
KRSH...

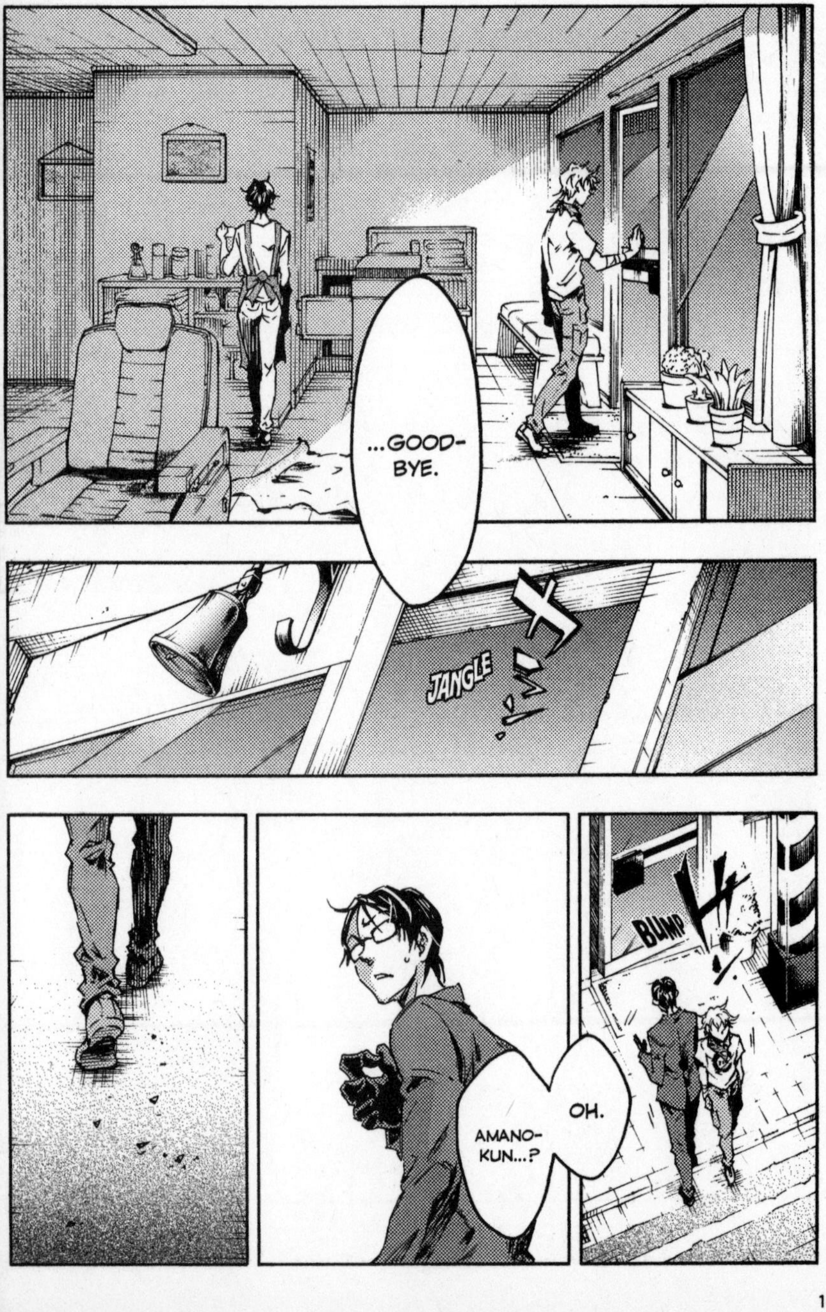
...GOOD-BYE.
JANGLE
BUMP
OH.
AMANO-KUN...?

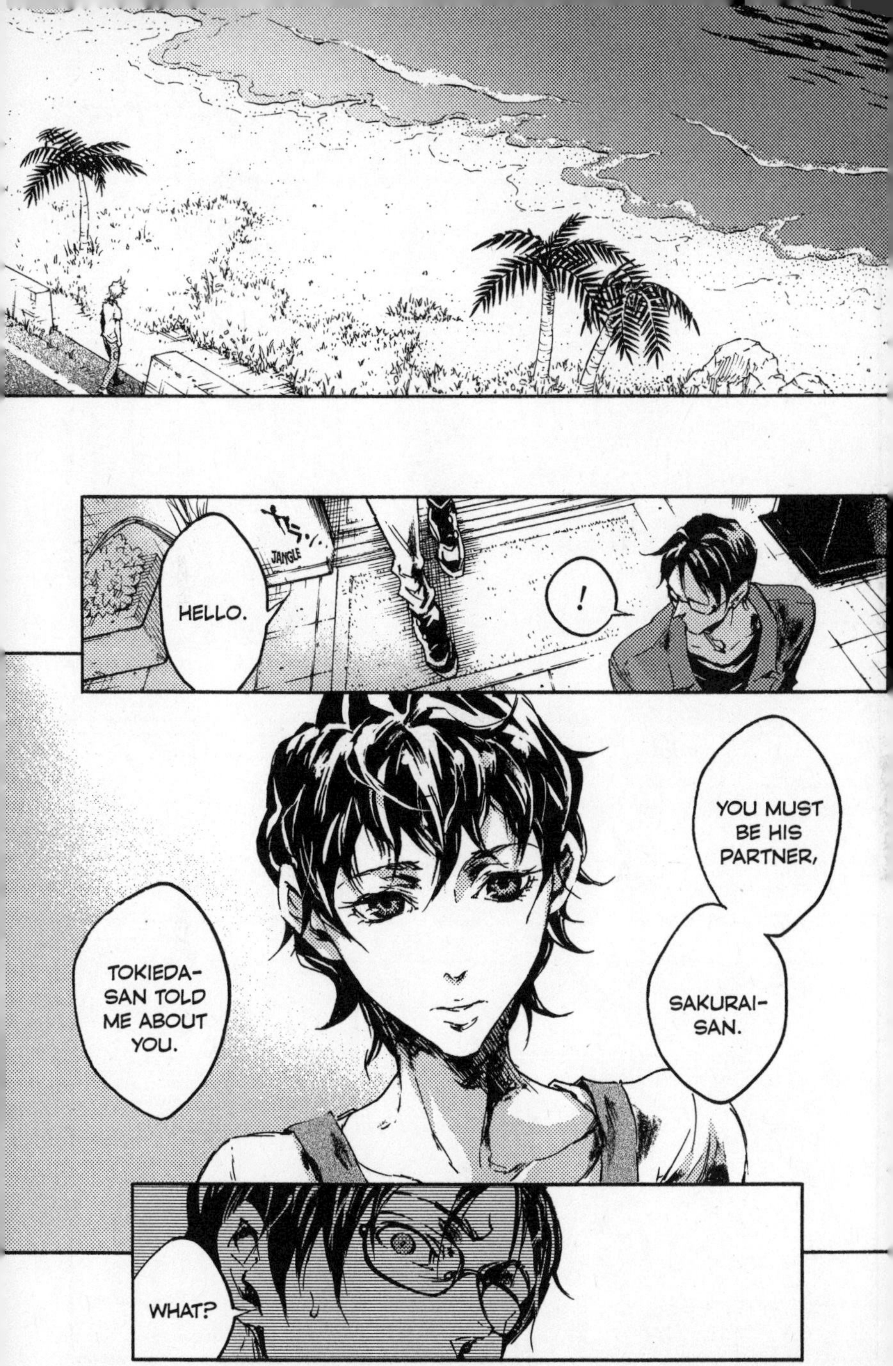
!
JANGLE
HELLO.
YOU MUST BE HIS PARTNER,
SAKURAI-SAN.
TOKIEDA-SAN TOLD ME ABOUT YOU.
WHAT?

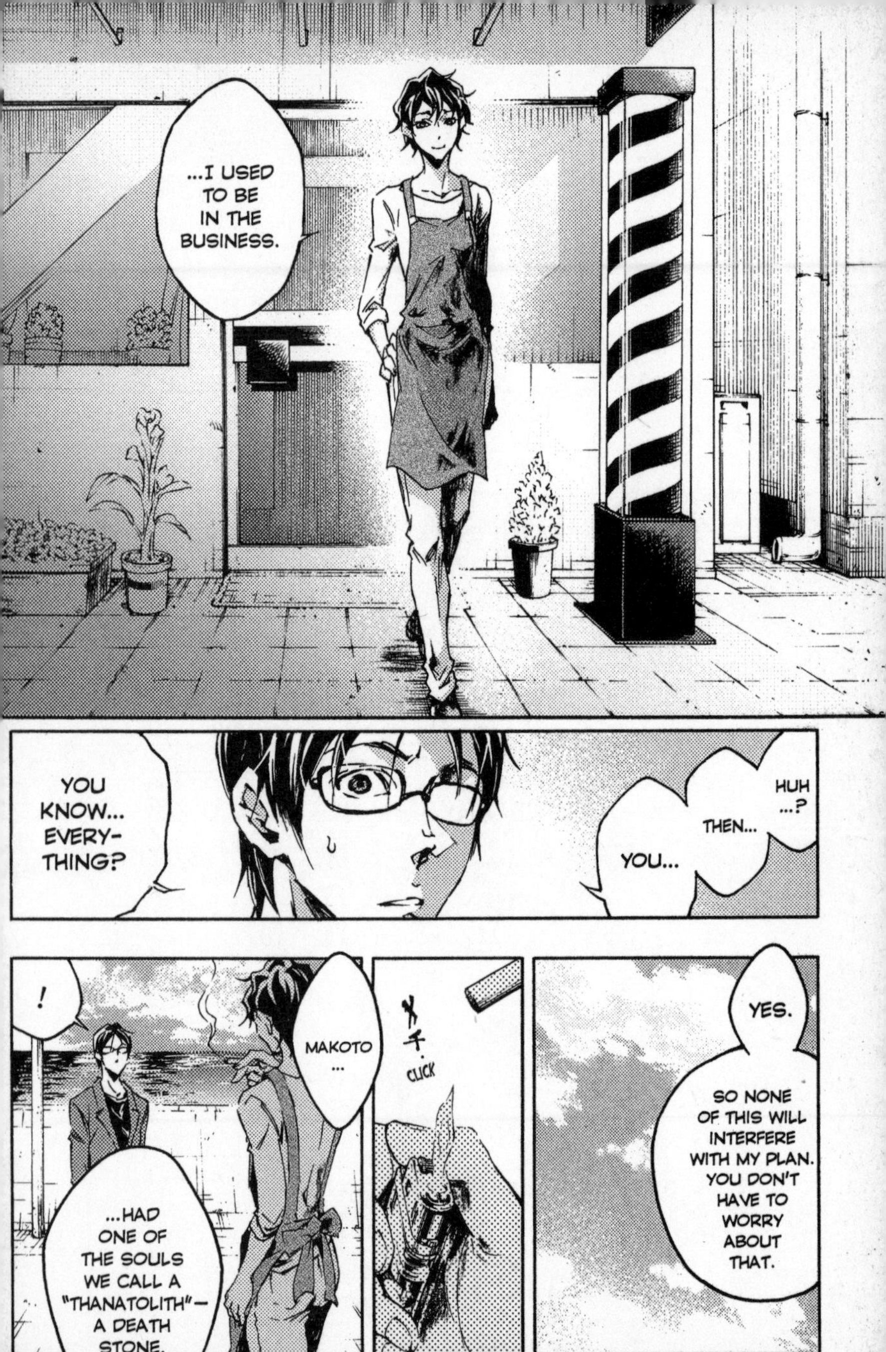

...I USED TO BE IN THE BUSINESS.
HUH ...?
THEN...
YOU...
YOU KNOW... EVERY-THING?
YES.
SO NONE OF THIS WILL INTERFERE WITH MY PLAN. YOU DON'T HAVE TO WORRY ABOUT THAT.
カチ
CLICK
MAKOTO ...
!
...HAD ONE OF THE SOULS WE CALL A "THANATOLITH"— A DEATH STONE.

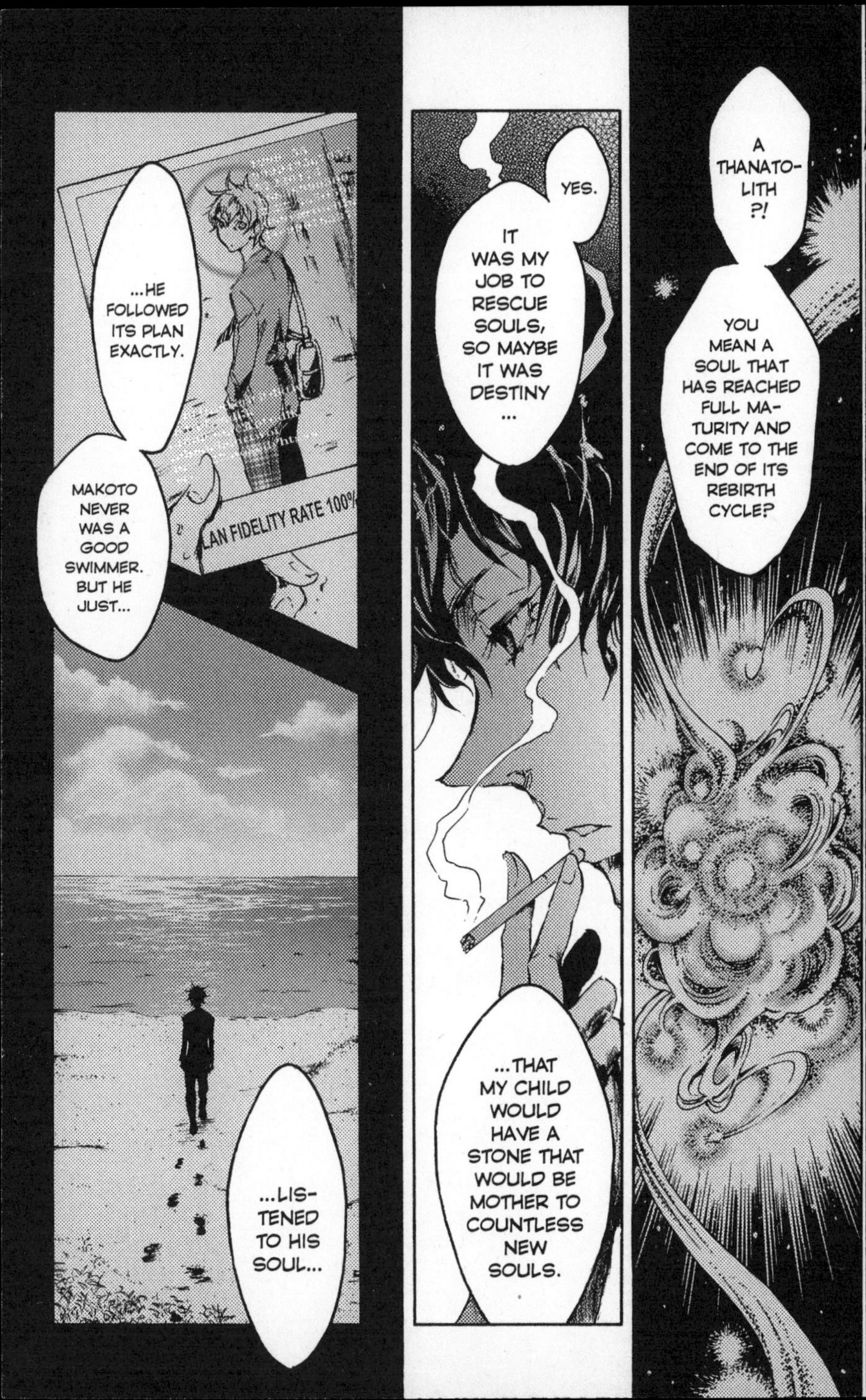
A THANATO-LITH ?!
YOU MEAN A SOUL THAT HAS REACHED FULL MATURITY AND COME TO THE END OF ITS REBIRTH CYCLE?
YES.
IT WAS MY JOB TO RESCUE SOULS, SO MAYBE IT WAS DESTINY ...
...THAT MY CHILD WOULD HAVE A STONE THAT WOULD BE MOTHER TO COUNTLESS NEW SOULS.
...HE FOLLOWED ITS PLAN EXACTLY.
LAN FIDELITY RATE 100%
MAKOTO NEVER WAS A GOOD SWIMMER. BUT HE JUST...
...LISTENED TO HIS SOUL...

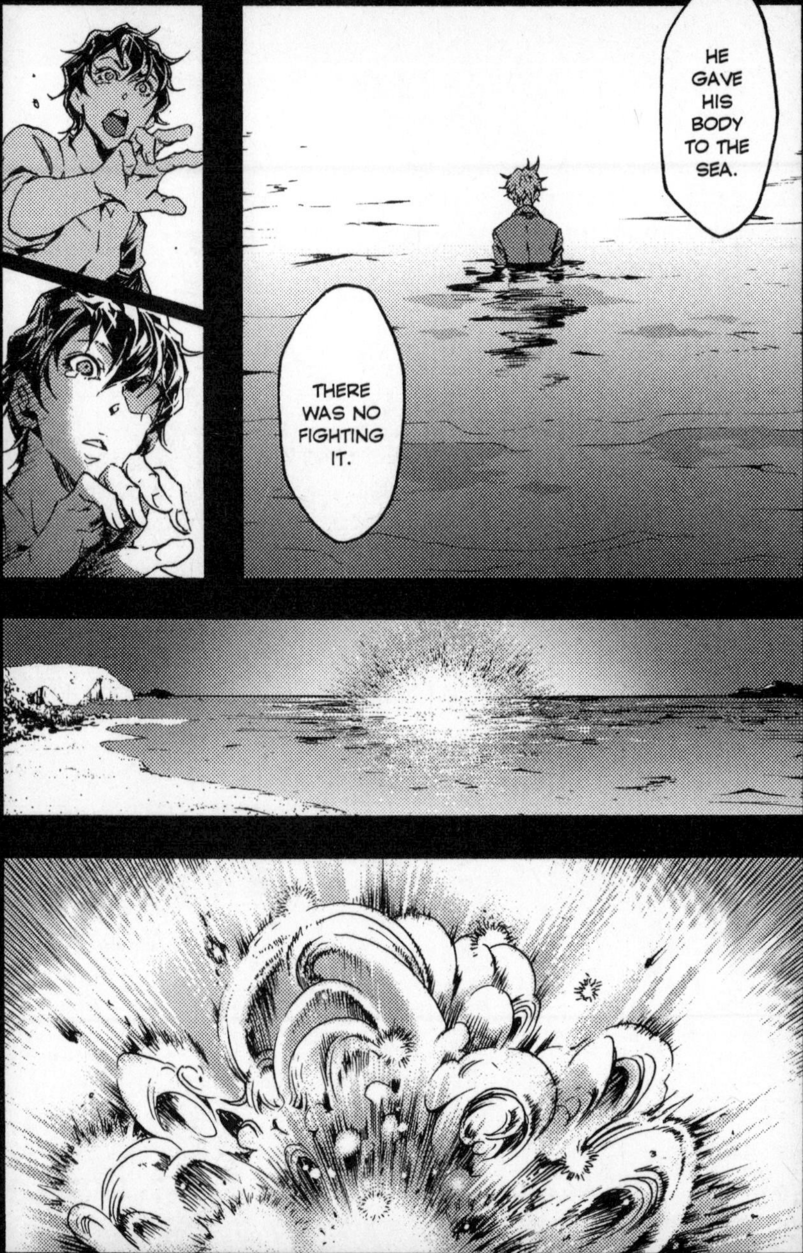
HE GAVE HIS BODY TO THE SEA.
THERE WAS NO FIGHTING IT.

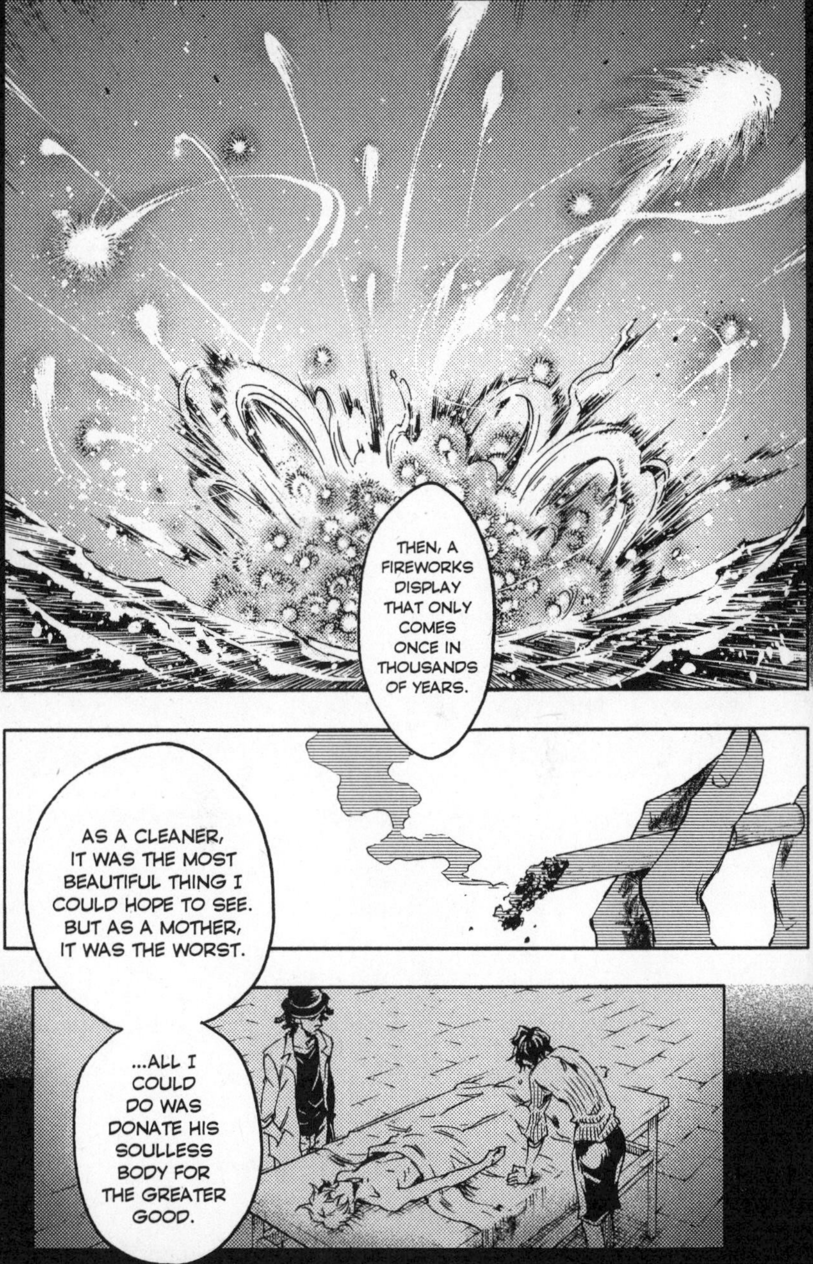
THEN, A FIREWORKS DISPLAY THAT ONLY COMES ONCE IN THOUSANDS OF YEARS.
AS A CLEANER, IT WAS THE MOST BEAUTIFUL THING I COULD HOPE TO SEE. BUT AS A MOTHER, IT WAS THE WORST.
...ALL I COULD DO WAS DONATE HIS SOULLESS BODY FOR THE GREATER GOOD.

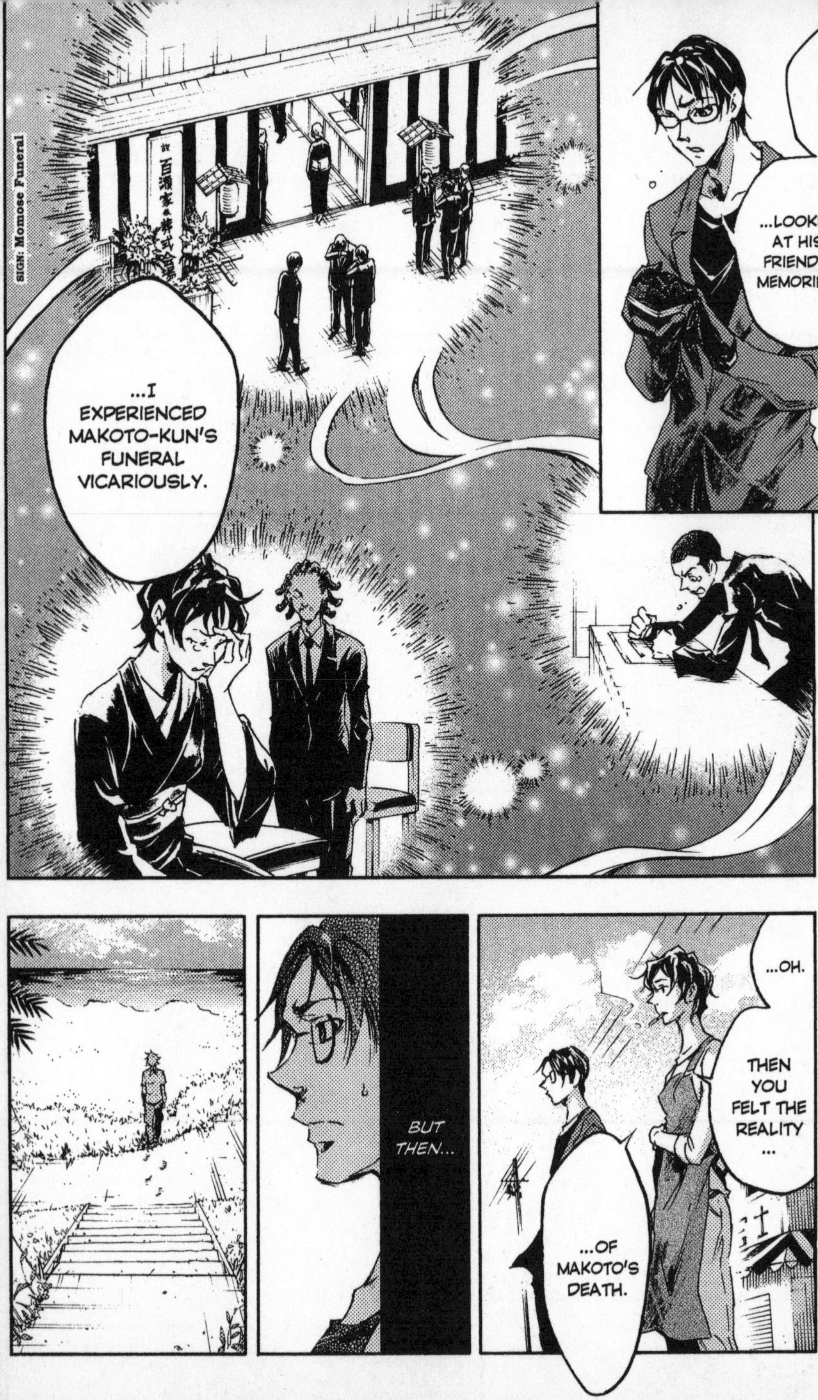
I...
...LOOKED AT HIS FRIEND'S MEMORIES.
SIGN: Momose Funeral
...I EXPERIENCED MAKOTO-KUN'S FUNERAL VICARIOUSLY.
...OH.
THEN YOU FELT THE REALITY ...
...OF MAKOTO'S DEATH.
BUT THEN...

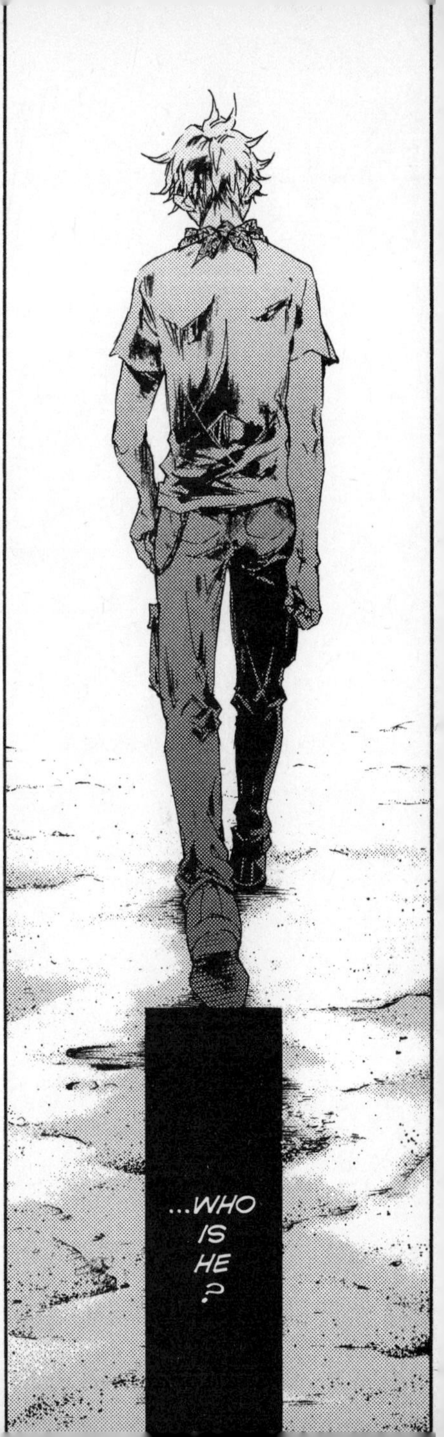
...WHO IS HE?

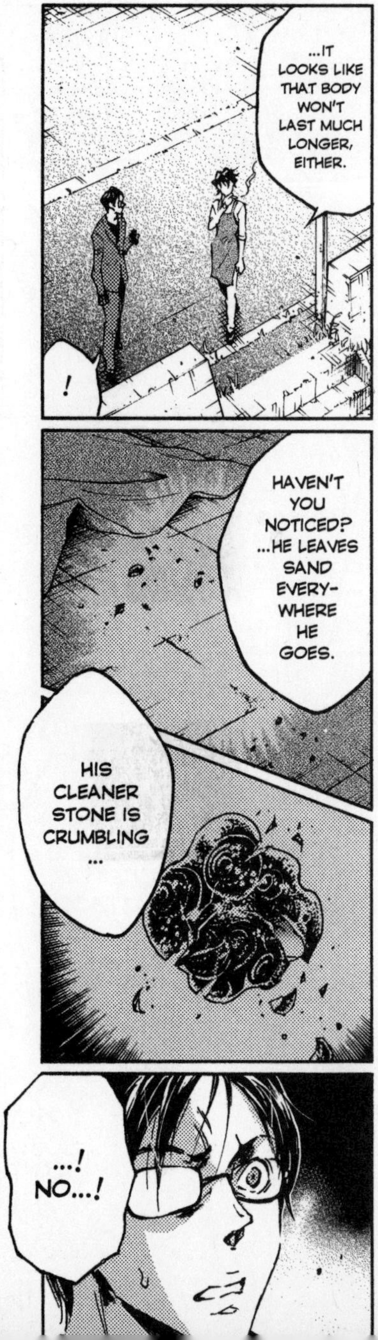
...IT LOOKS LIKE THAT BODY WON'T LAST MUCH LONGER, EITHER.
!
HAVEN'T YOU NOTICED? ...HE LEAVES SAND EVERY-WHERE HE GOES.
HIS CLEANER STONE IS CRUMBLING ...
...! NO...!

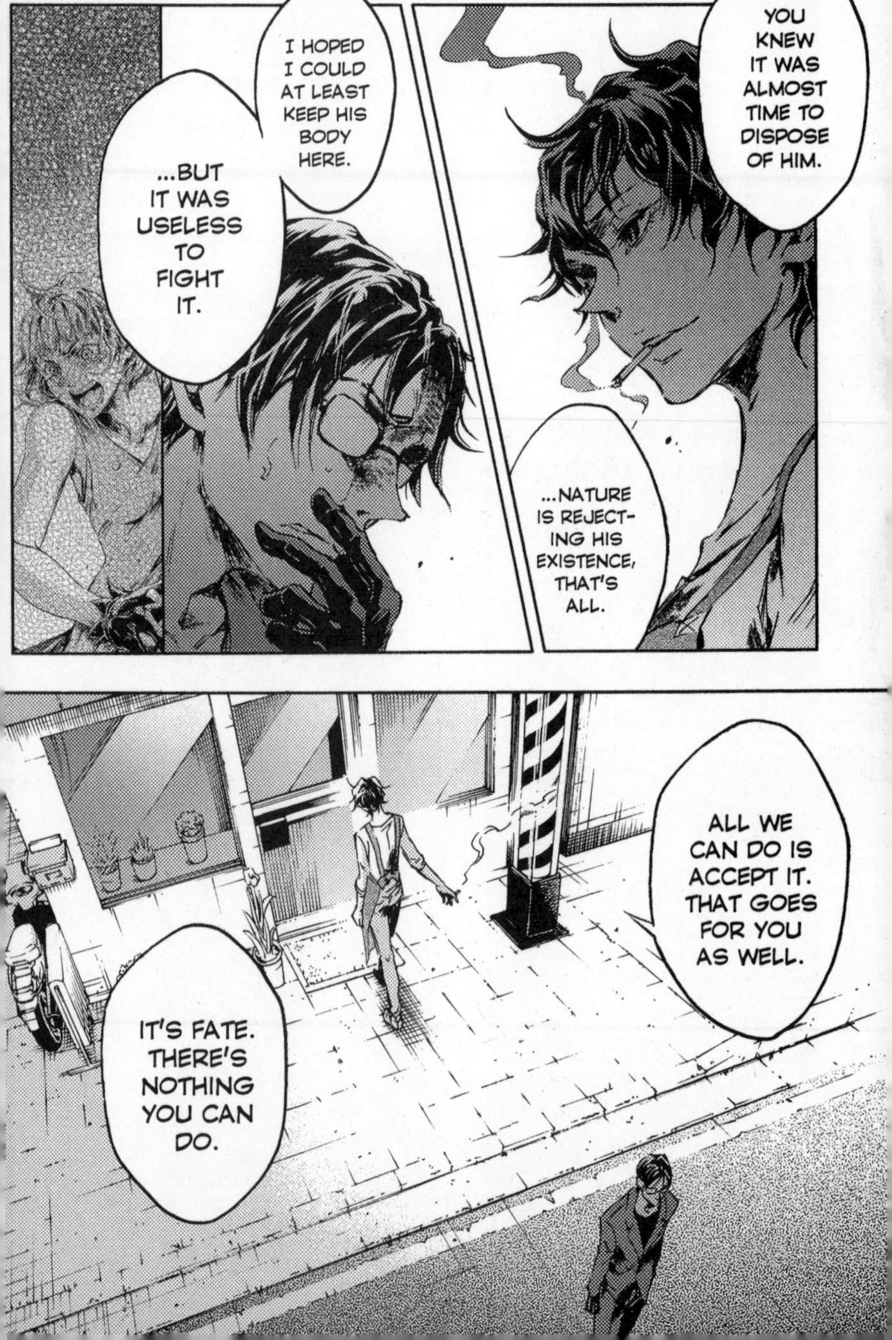
YOU KNEW IT WAS ALMOST TIME TO DISPOSE OF HIM.
...NATURE IS REJECTING HIS EXISTENCE, THAT'S ALL.
I HOPED I COULD AT LEAST KEEP HIS BODY HERE.
...BUT IT WAS USELESS TO FIGHT IT.
ALL WE CAN DO IS ACCEPT IT. THAT GOES FOR YOU AS WELL.
IT'S FATE. THERE'S NOTHING YOU CAN DO.

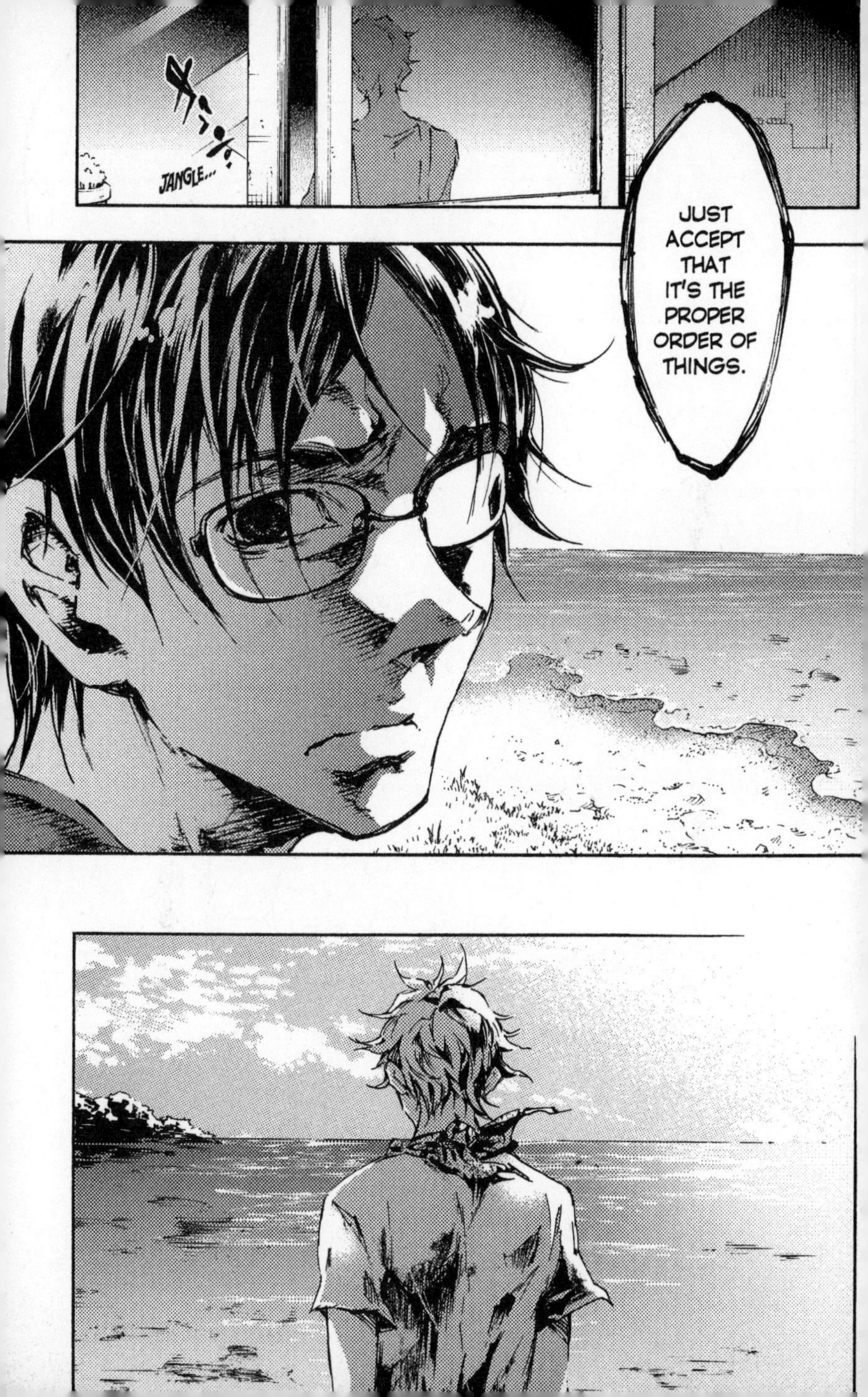
JANGLE...
JUST ACCEPT THAT IT'S THE PROPER ORDER OF THINGS.

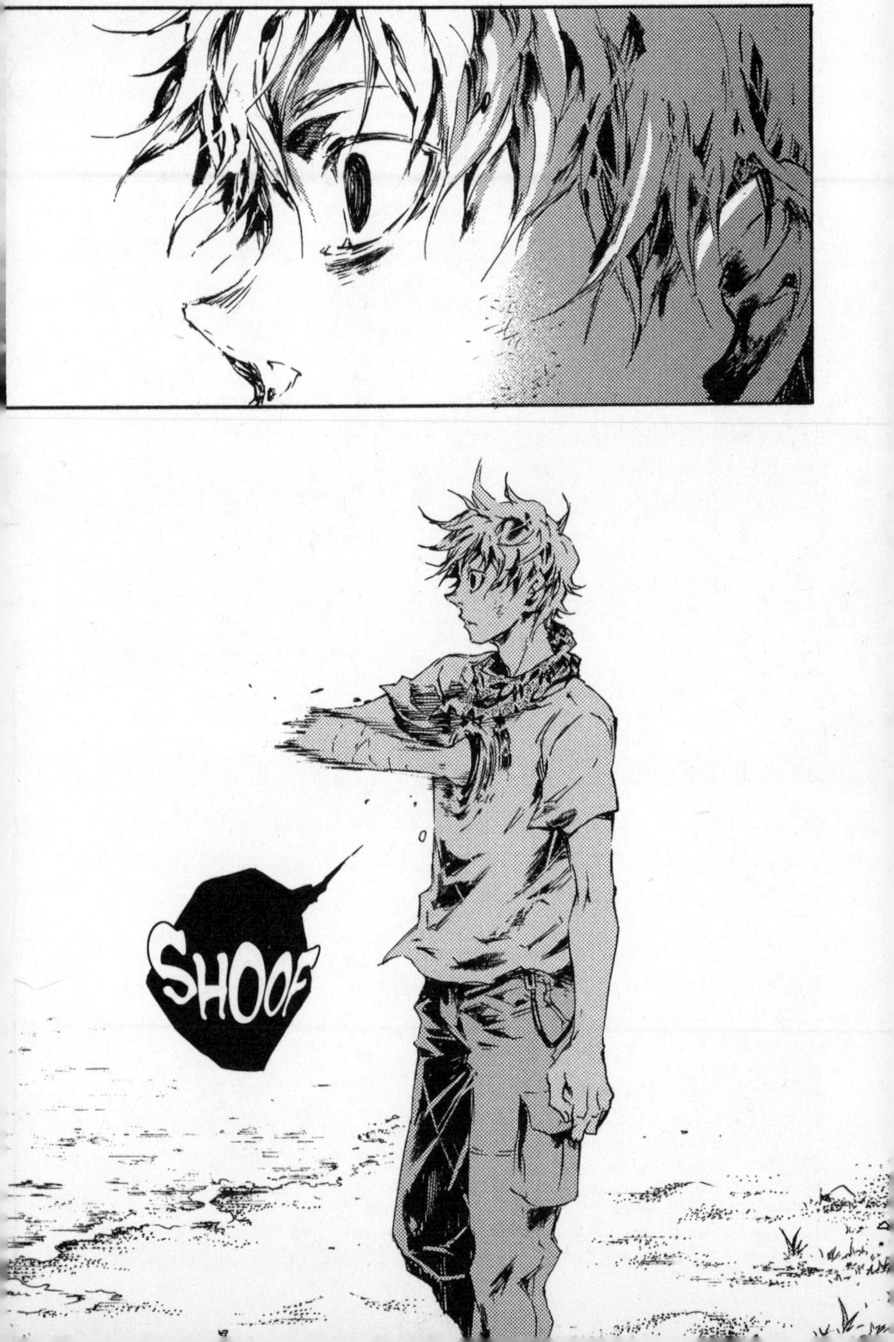
SHOOF

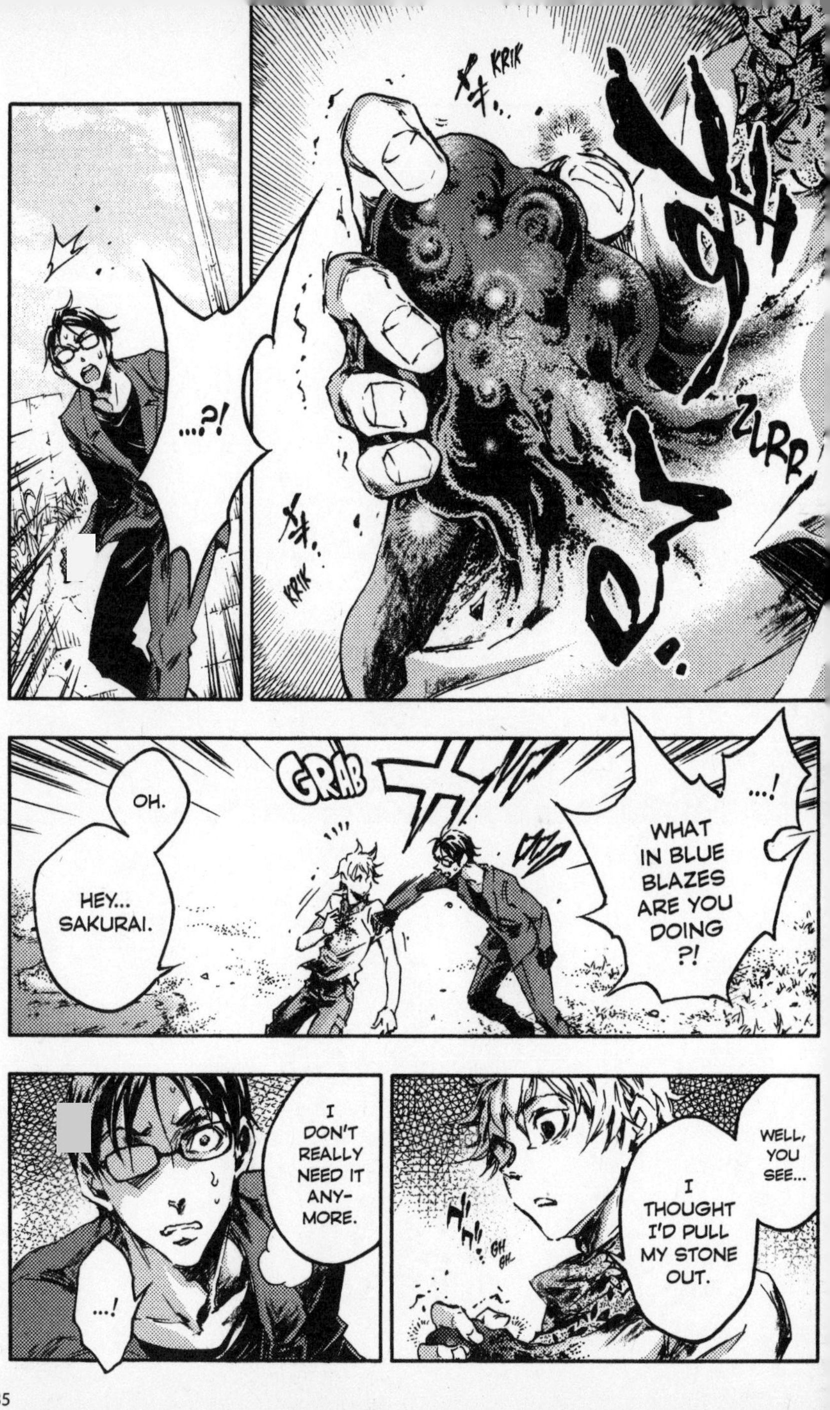
KRIK
ZLRR
KRIK
...?!
...!
WHAT IN BLUE BLAZES ARE YOU DOING ?!
GRAB
OH.
HEY... SAKURAI.
WELL, YOU SEE...
I THOUGHT I'D PULL MY STONE OUT.
GH GH.
I DON'T REALLY NEED IT ANY-MORE.
...!

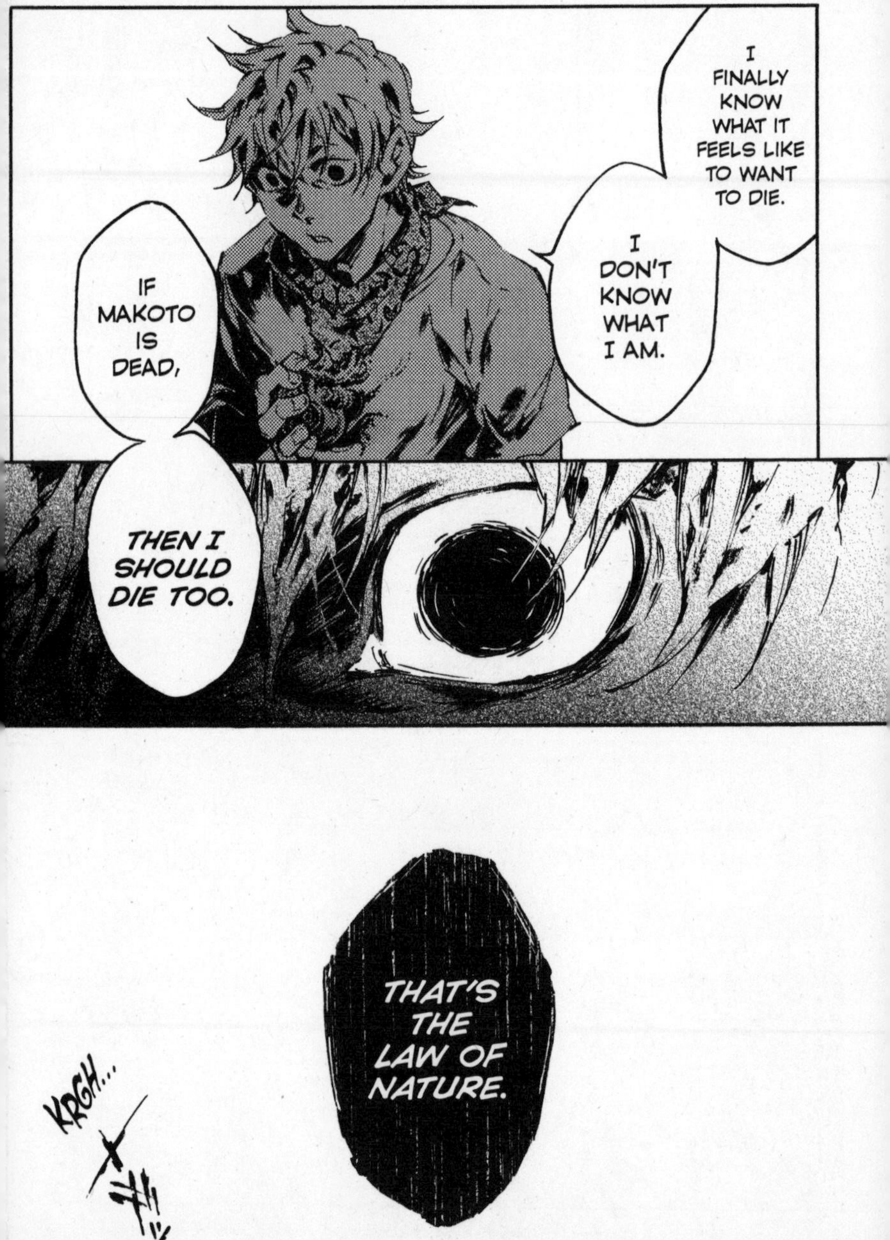
I FINALLY KNOW WHAT IT FEELS LIKE TO WANT TO DIE.
I DON'T KNOW WHAT I AM.
IF MAKOTO IS DEAD,
THEN I SHOULD DIE TOO.
THAT'S THE LAW OF NATURE.
KRGH...

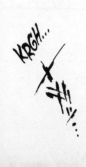

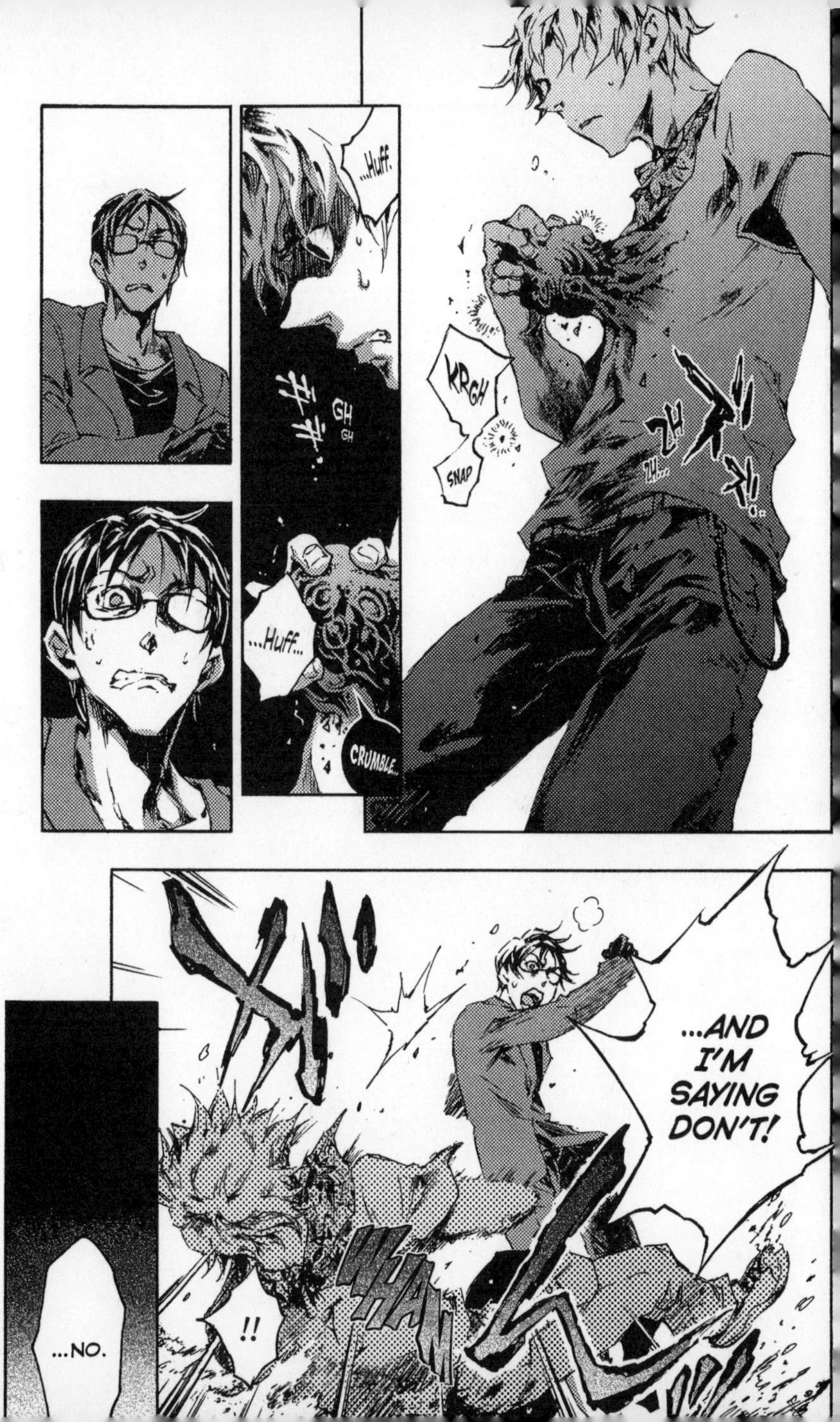
KRGH
SNAP
...Huff.
GH GH
...Huff...
CRUMBLE...
...AND I'M SAYING DON'T!
WHAM
!!
...NO.

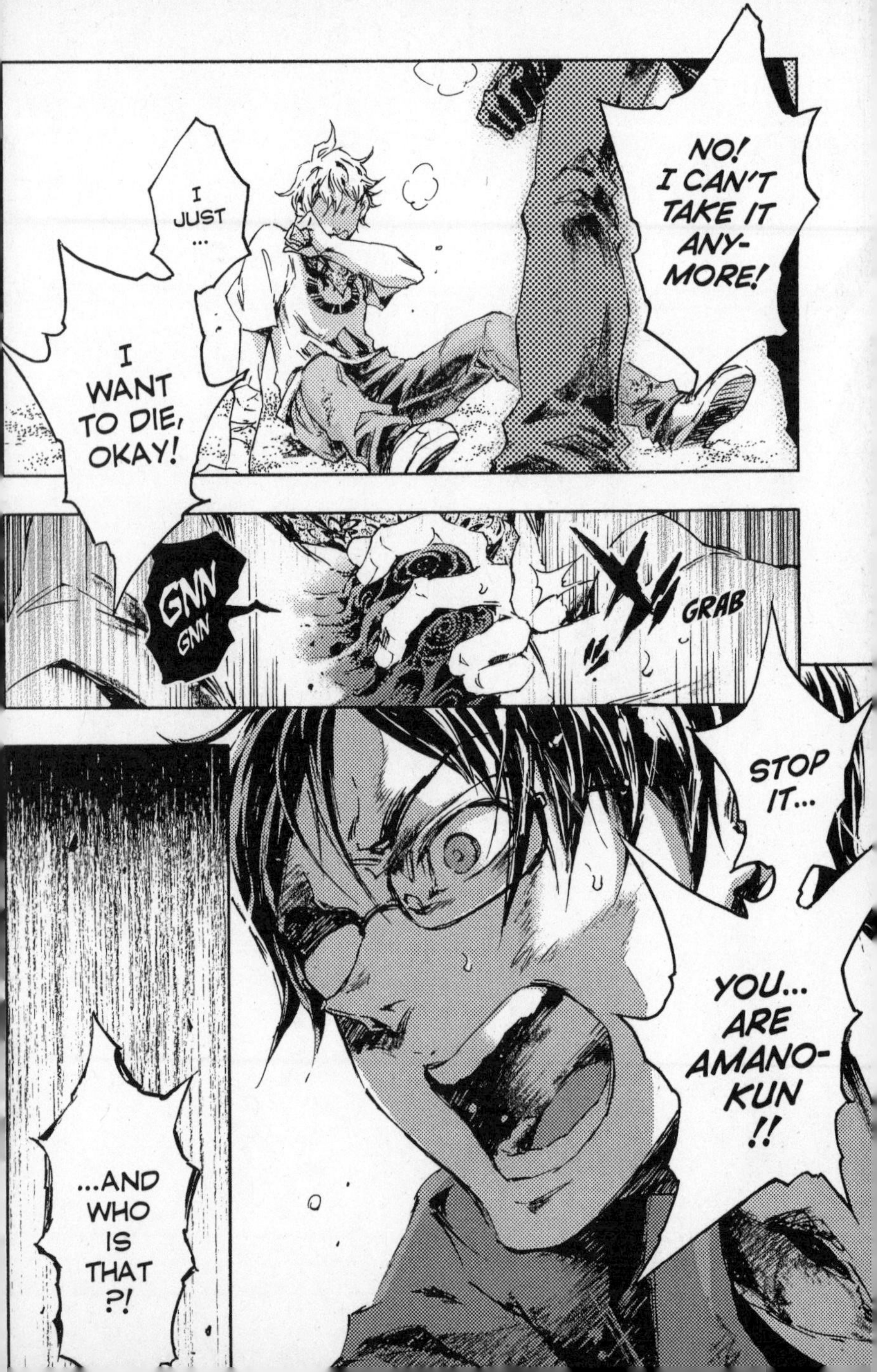
NO! I CAN'T TAKE IT ANY-MORE!
I JUST ...
I WANT TO DIE, OKAY!
GRAB
GNN GNN
STOP IT...
YOU... ARE AMANO-KUN!!
...AND WHO IS THAT?!

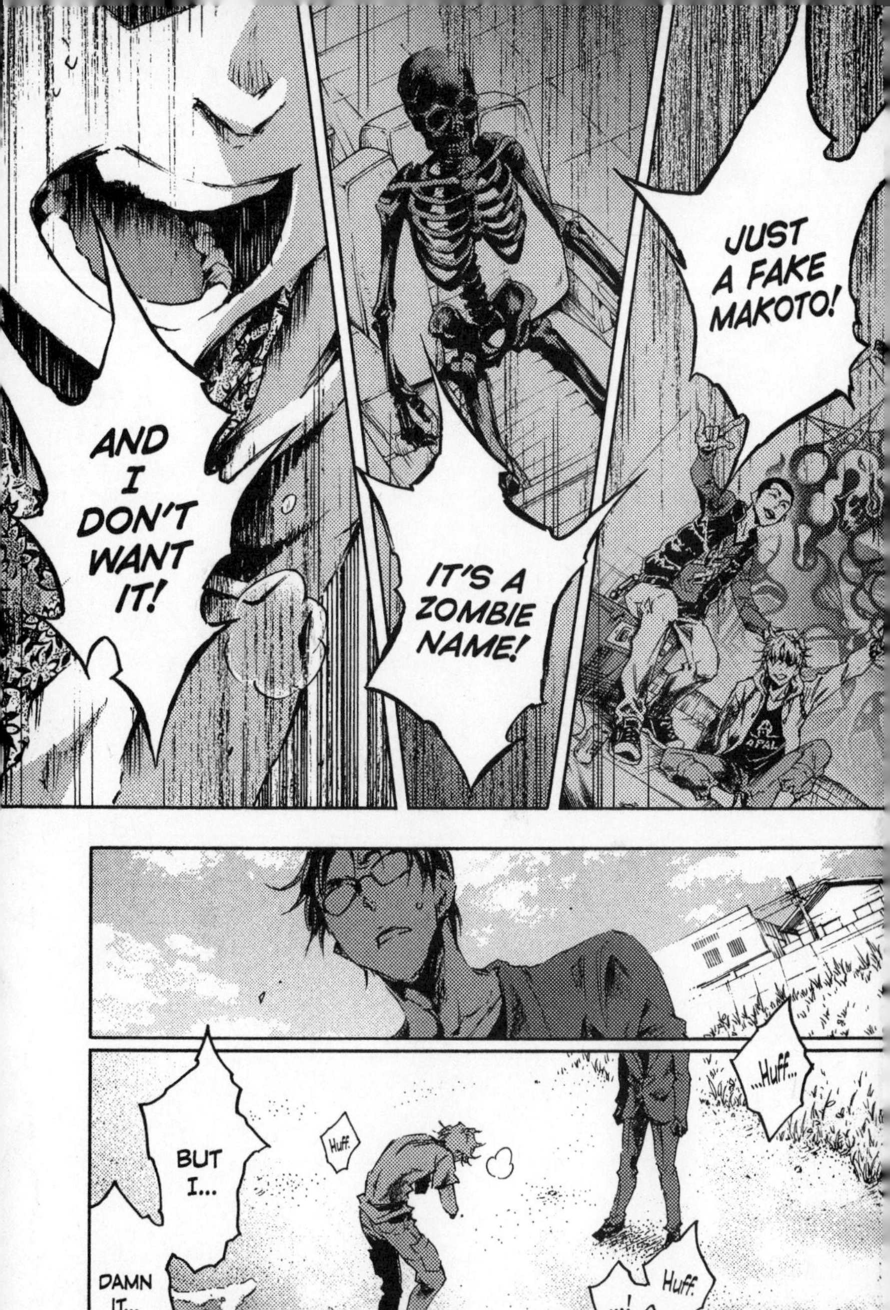
JUST A FAKE MAKOTO!
IT'S A ZOMBIE NAME!
AND I DON'T WANT IT!
...Huff...
Huff.
...!
Huff.
BUT I...
DAMN IT...

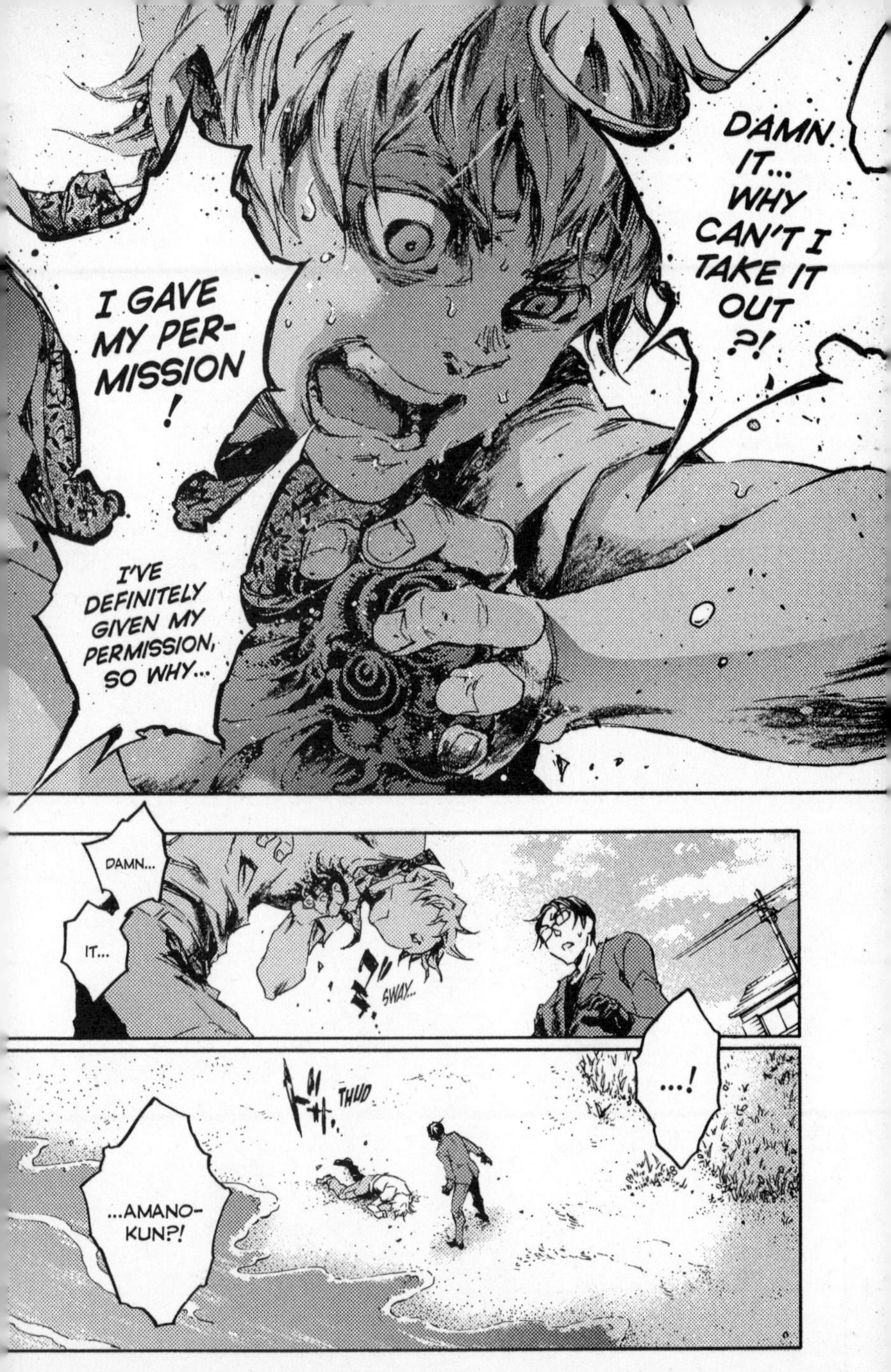
DAMN IT... WHY CAN'T I TAKE IT OUT?!
I GAVE MY PERMISSION!
I'VE DEFINITELY GIVEN MY PERMISSION, SO WHY...
DAMN...
IT...
SWAY...
...!
THUD
...AMANO-KUN?!

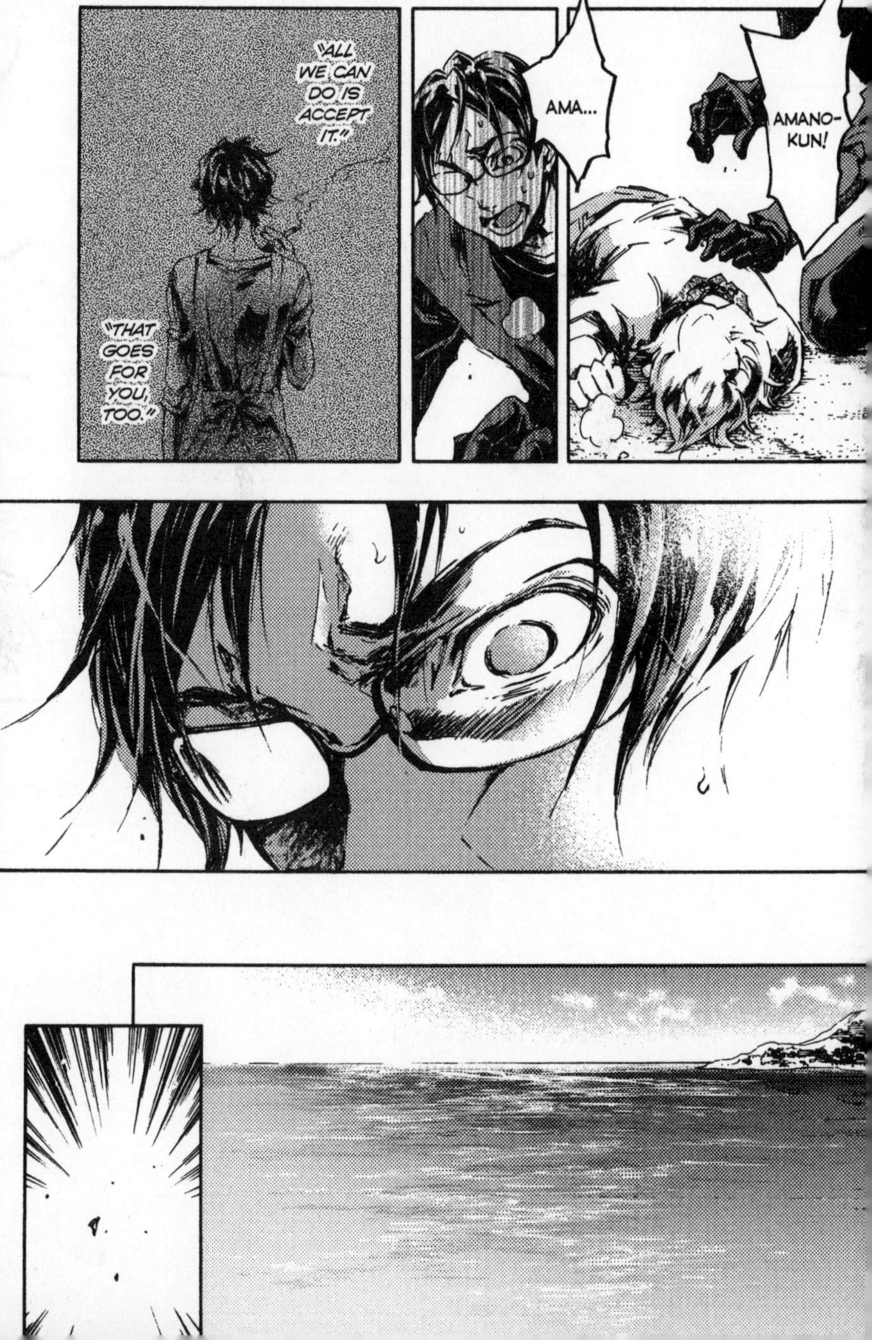
AMANO-KUN!
AMA...
"ALL WE CAN DO IS ACCEPT IT."
"THAT GOES FOR YOU, TOO."

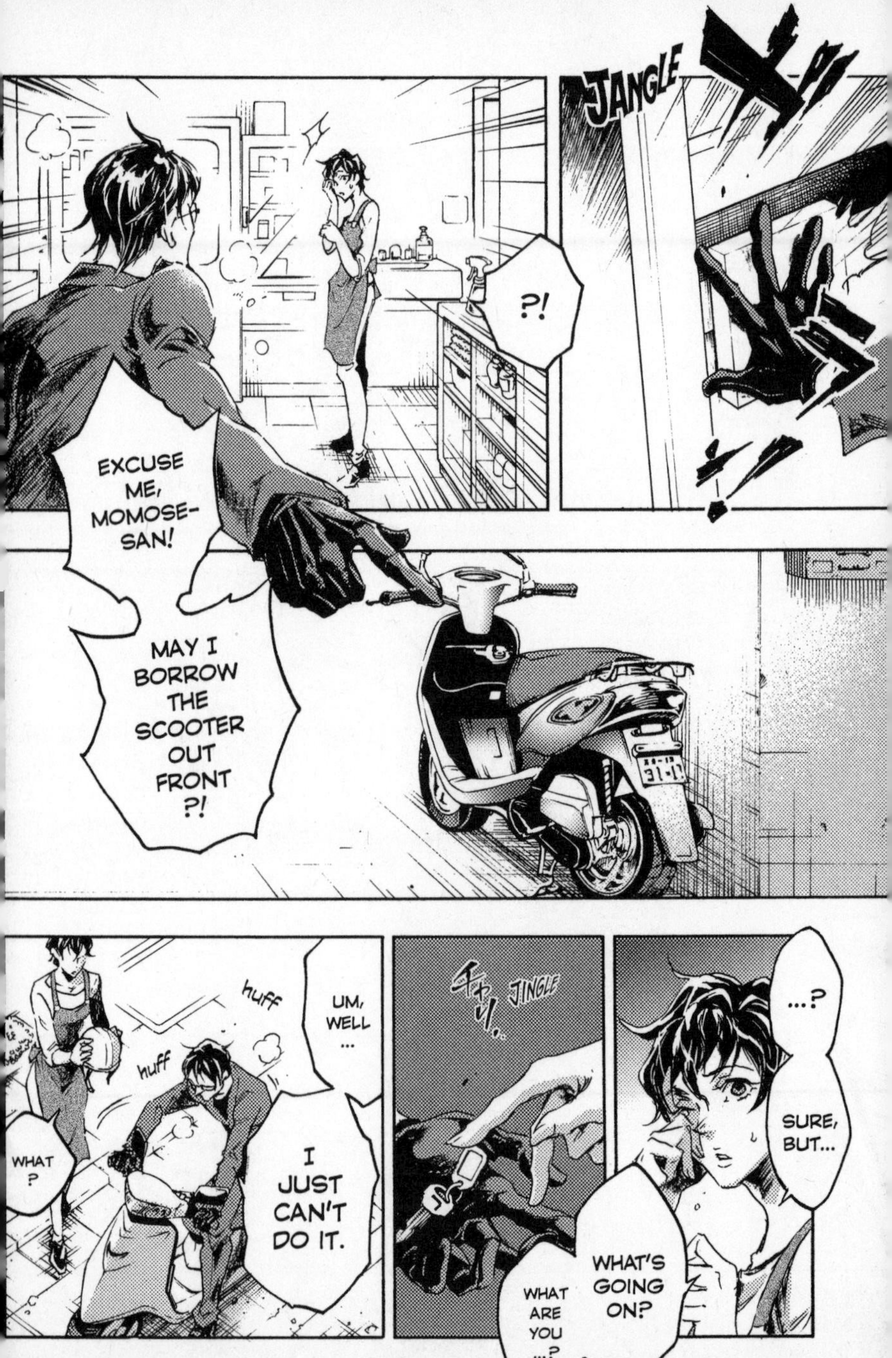
JANGLE
?!
EXCUSE ME, MOMOSE-SAN!
MAY I BORROW THE SCOOTER OUT FRONT?!
...?
SURE, BUT...
WHAT'S GOING ON?
WHAT ARE YOU ...?
JINGLE
UM, WELL ...
huff
huff
I JUST CAN'T DO IT.
WHAT ?

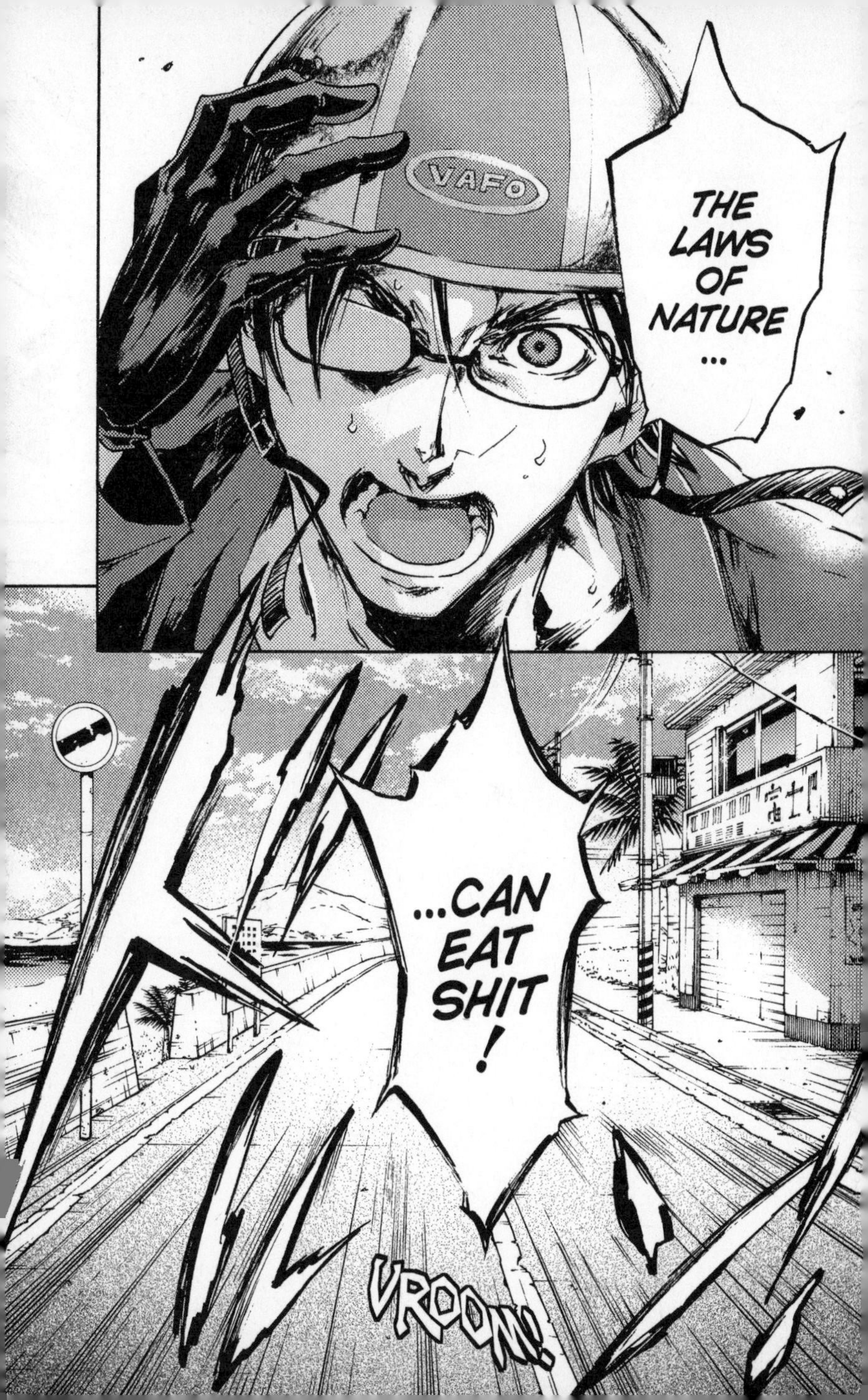
VAFO
THE LAWS OF NATURE ...
...CAN EAT SHIT!
富士門
VROOM!

Is there such a thing as a soul?

Since time immemorial, there have been countless stories about the soul. This is probably because thinking about the soul is the same as thinking about being human. In the broadest sense, all stories may be thematically divided into two categories: "what is a human?" and "what is the world?" Medical science and physics have different methods, but their goal is the same. The sciences don't use the word "soul" because they have no way to observe it, so we can't definitively state that the soul exists. Even so, reading the news about terminal care, the issue of brain death, robotic technology, AI, etc., I get the feeling that cutting-edge science is coming close to understanding that subject.

I don't think there's ever been a correct answer, now or in the past, to the question of "what is a soul?", but since I started *Livingstone* based on that theme, I think this manga should present a conclusion that makes sense for this story. I thank all you readers who have considered this question with me. Now then, where is our soulless Amano-kun headed?

Tomohiro Maekawa

From Niigata prefecture.

A writer and producer who writes slice of life stories that take place in supernatural settings. He has a wide range of work, from *Super Kabuki II* with Ennosuke Ichikawa IV, to modern theatre written in collaboration with Yukio Ninagawa.

Chairman of the Ikiume theatre troupe, his *Taiyou [The Sun]* won the grand prize in the Yomiuri Drama Awards.

Final Chapter   My Home Town

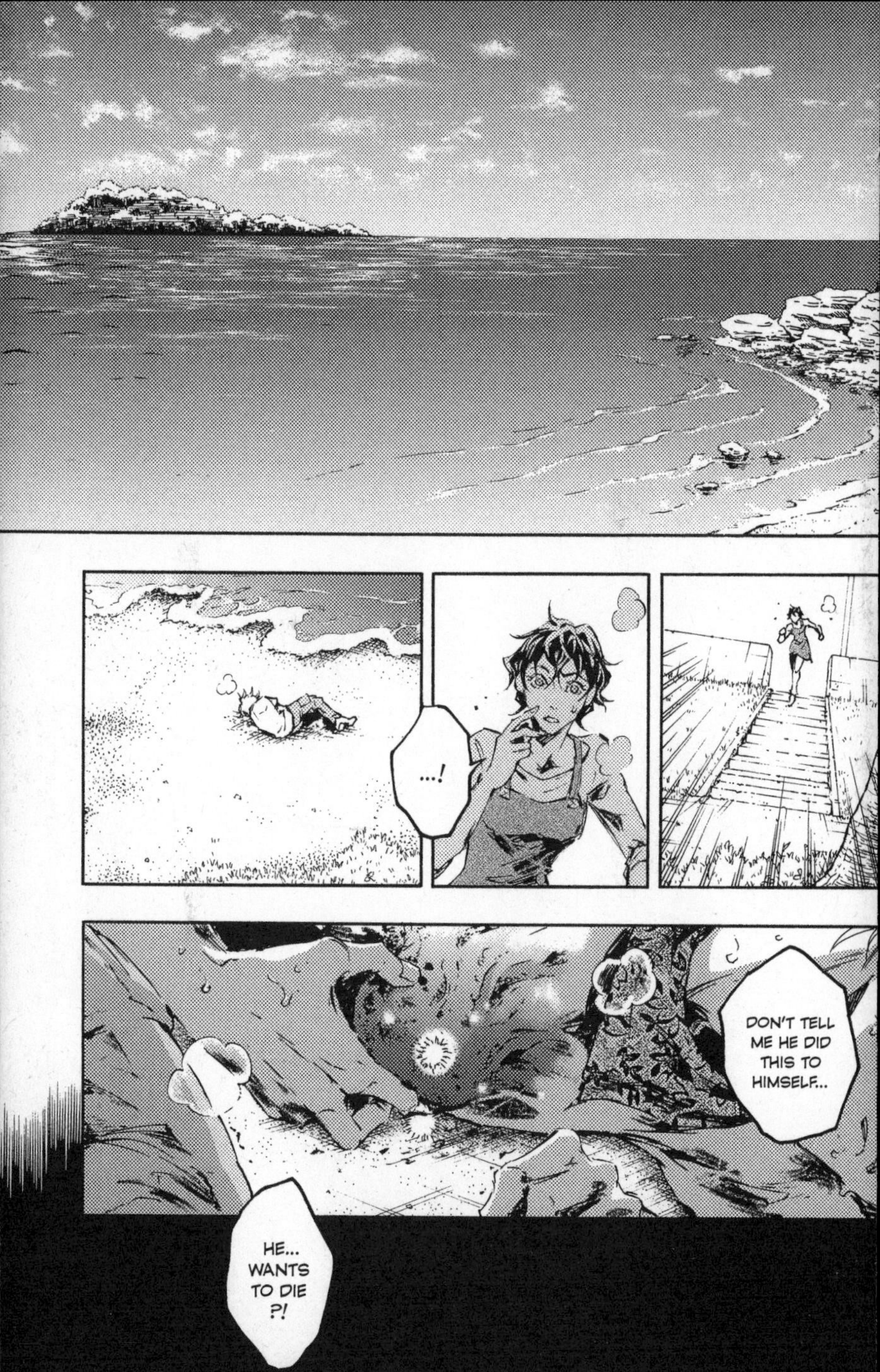
...!
DON'T TELL ME HE DID THIS TO HIMSELF...
HE... WANTS TO DIE ?!

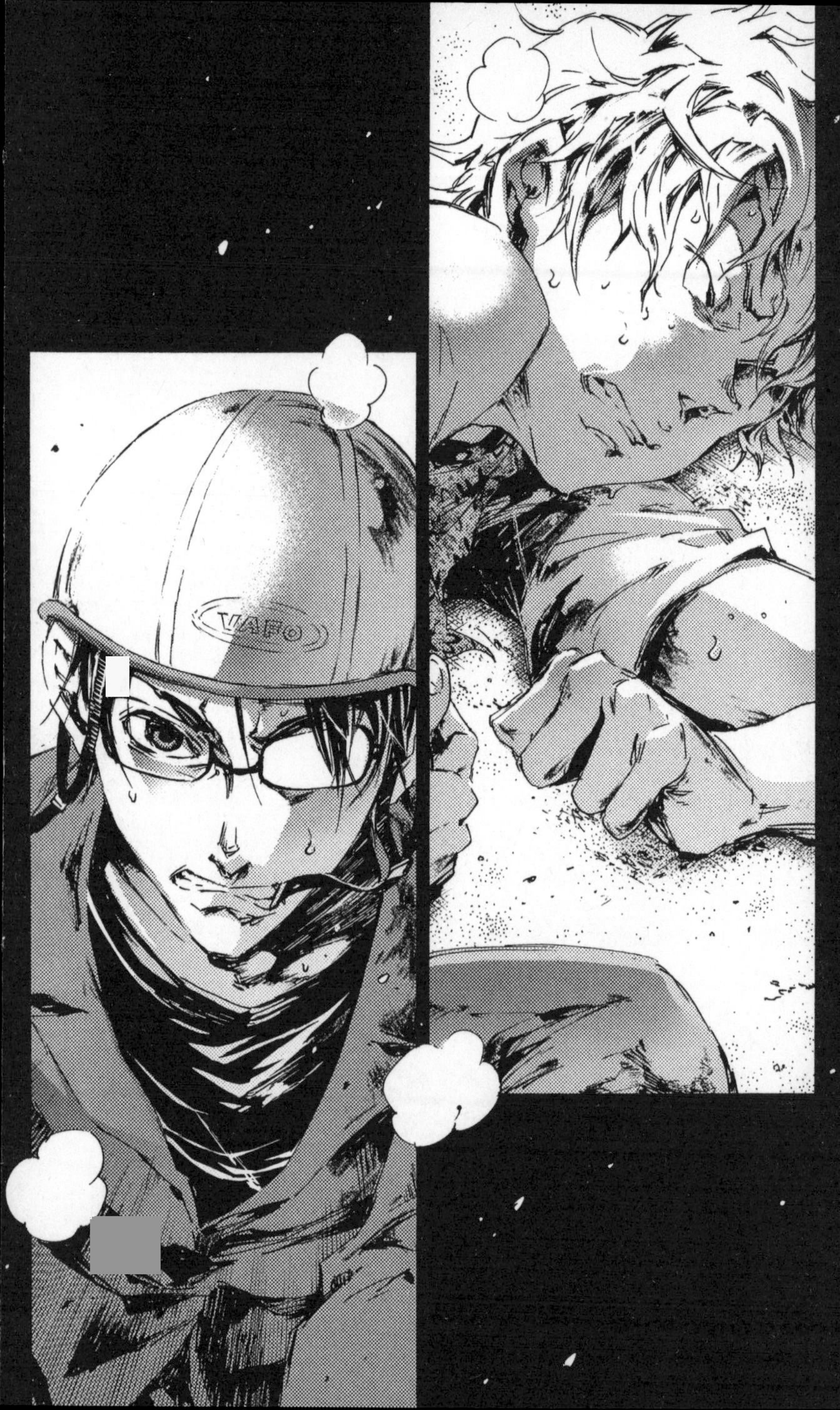

VAFO

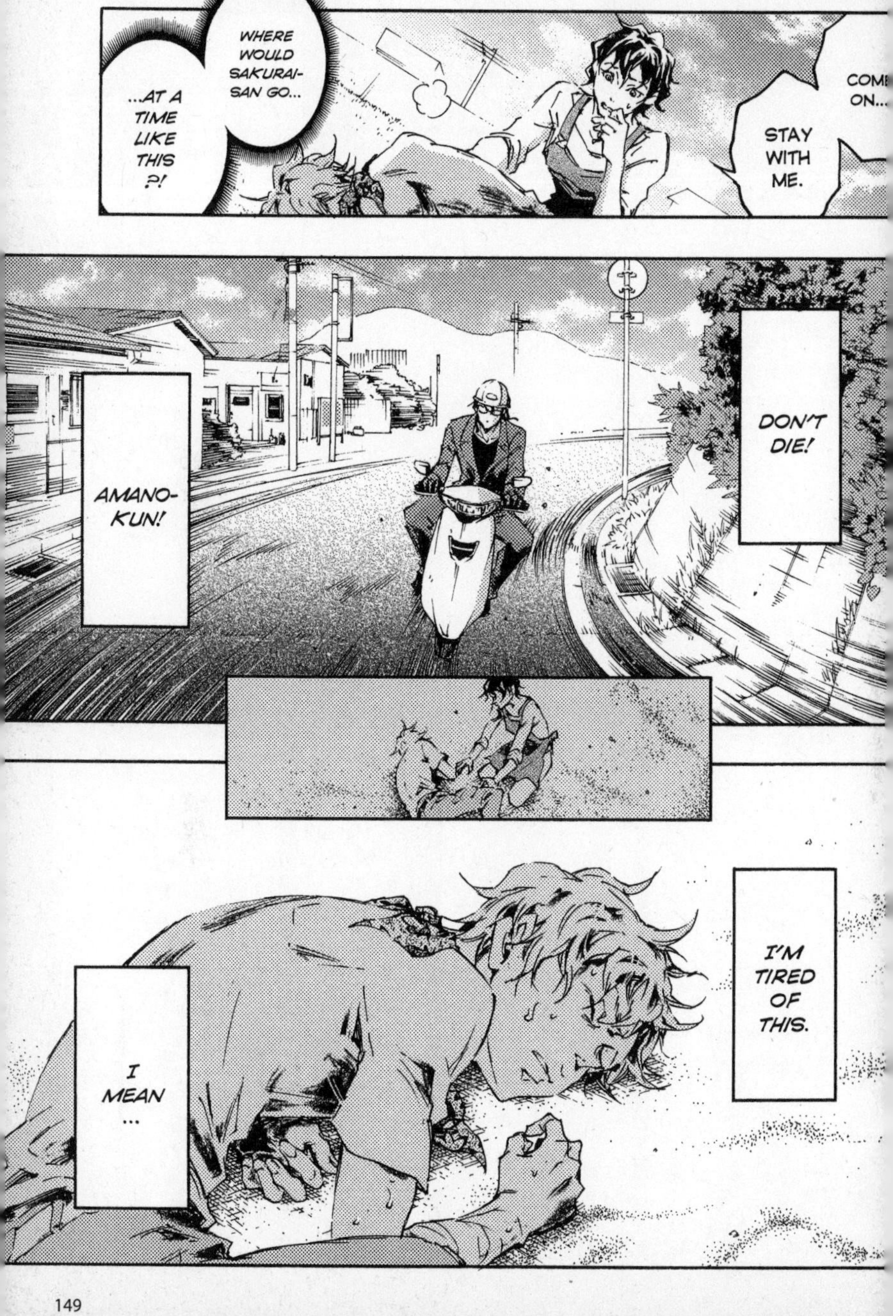
COME ON...
STAY WITH ME.
WHERE WOULD SAKURAI-SAN GO...
...AT A TIME LIKE THIS ?!
DON'T DIE!
AMANO-KUN!
I'M TIRED OF THIS.
I MEAN ...

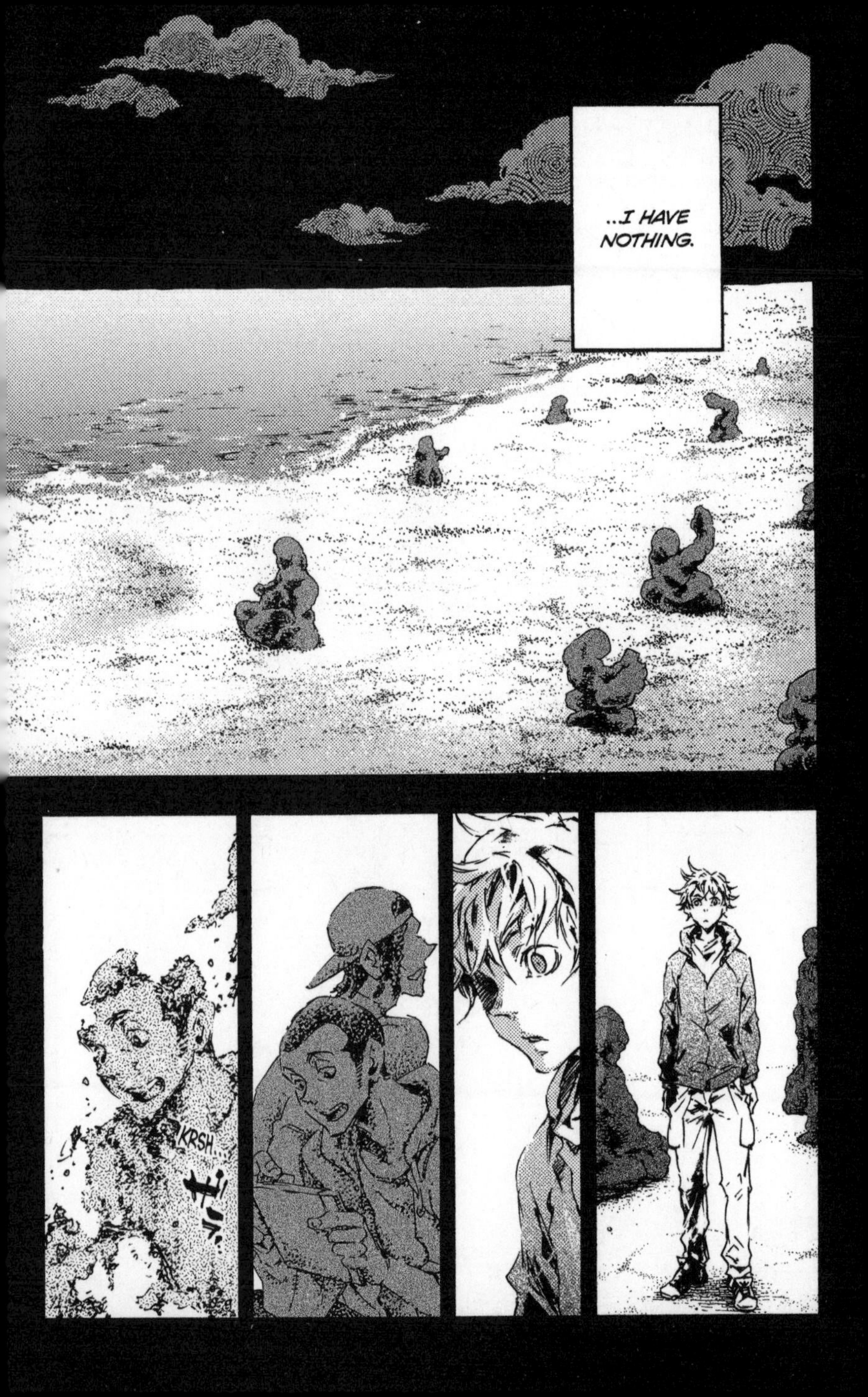
..I HAVE NOTHING.
KRSH...

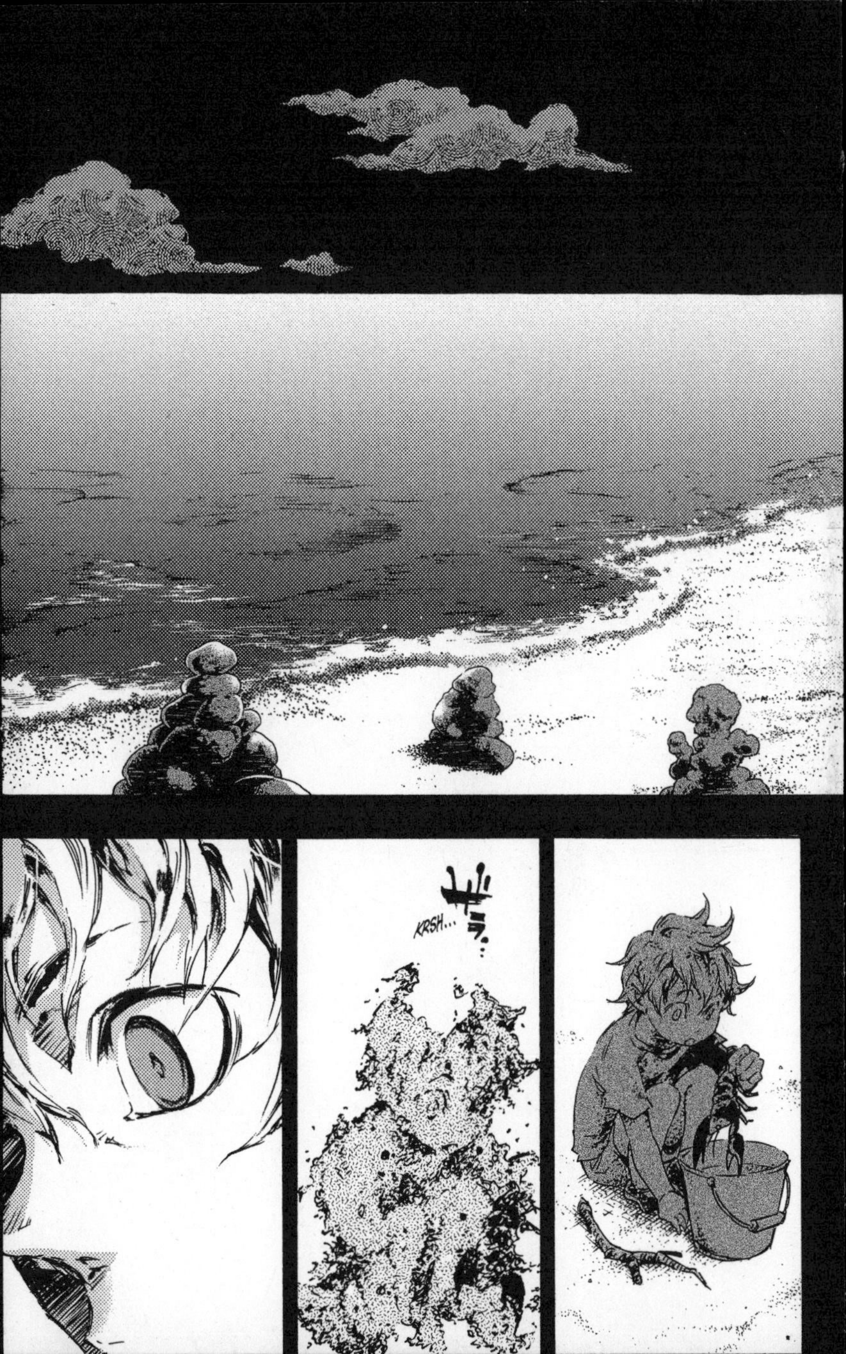
ザラ…
KRSH...

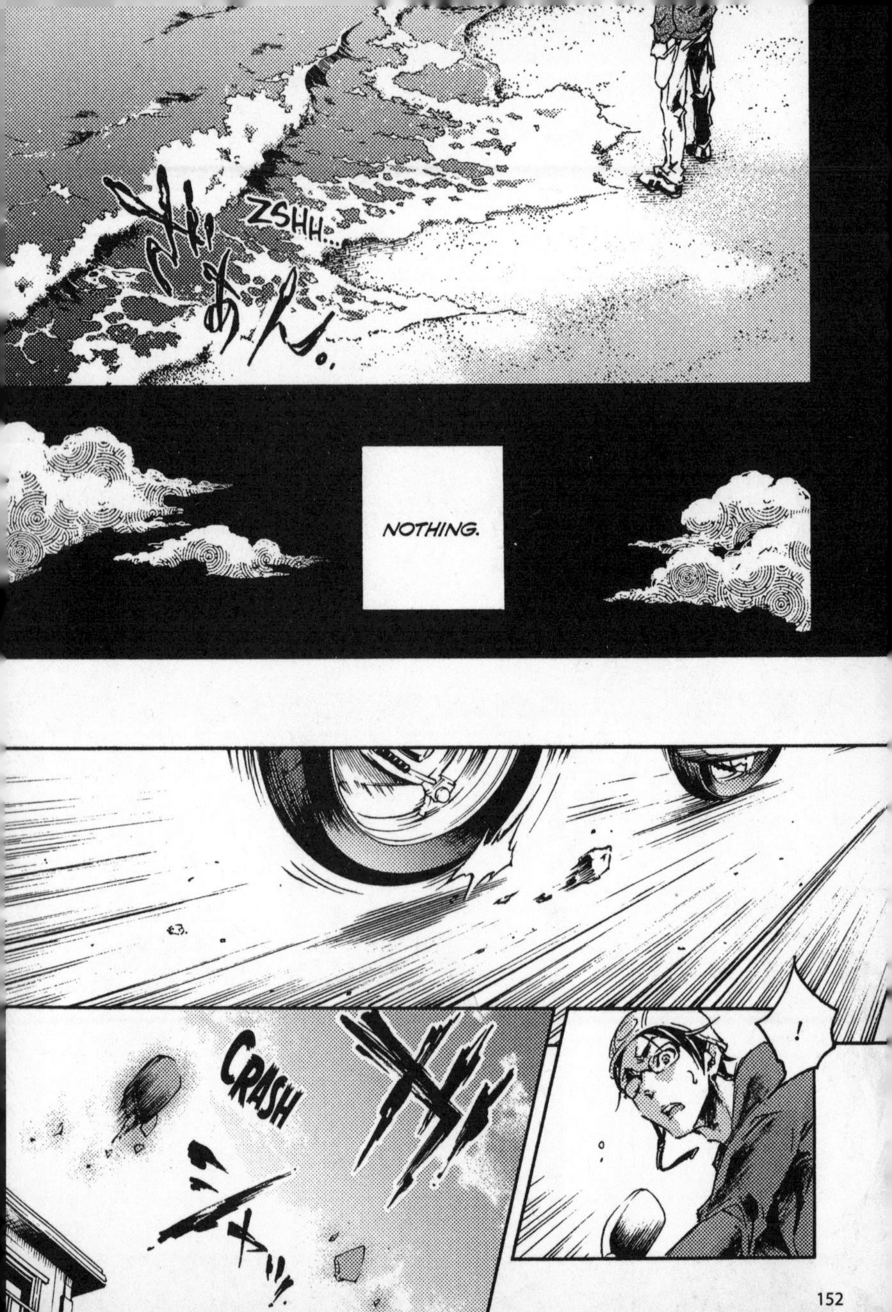
ZSHH...
NOTHING.
!
CRASH

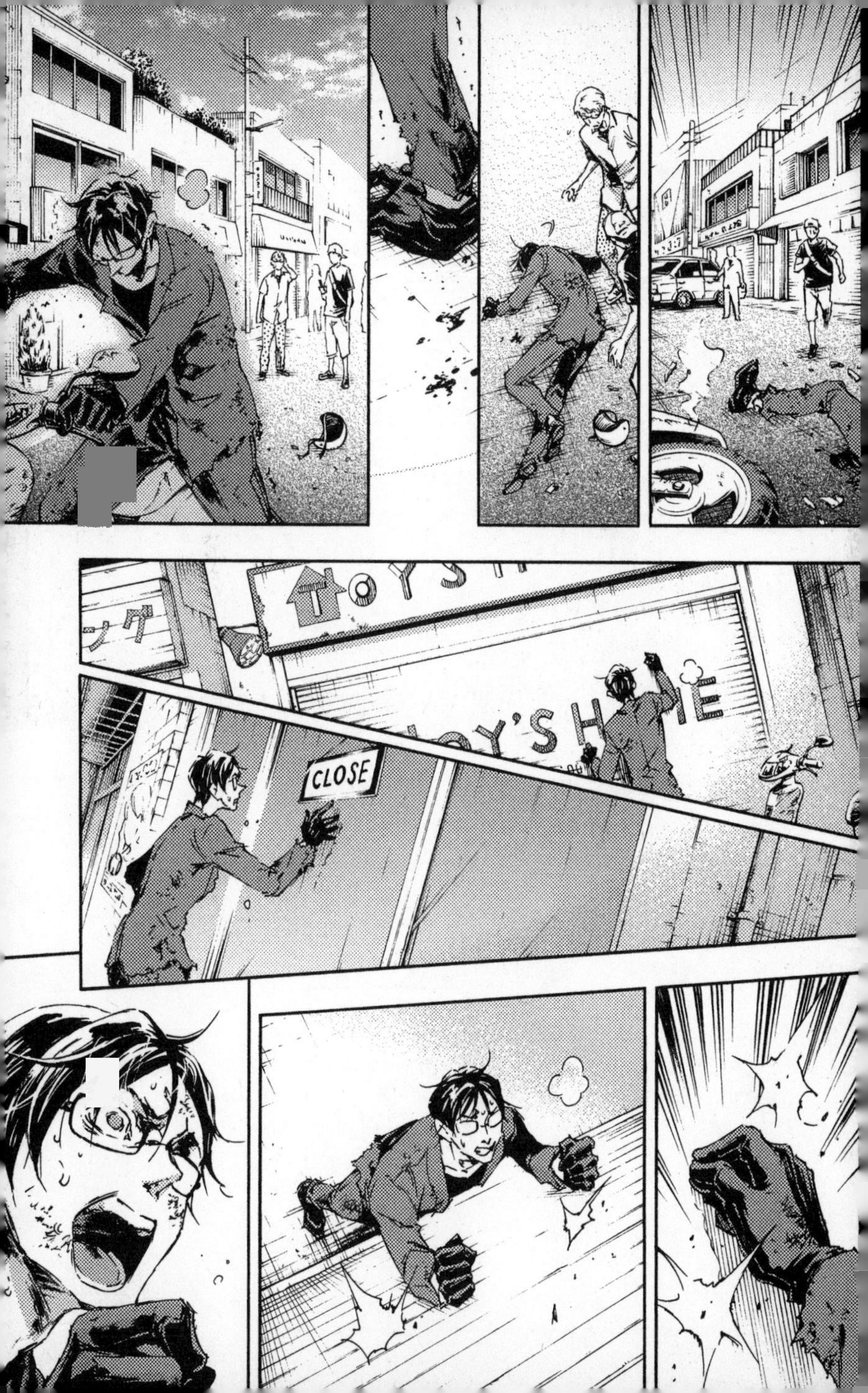
CLOSE

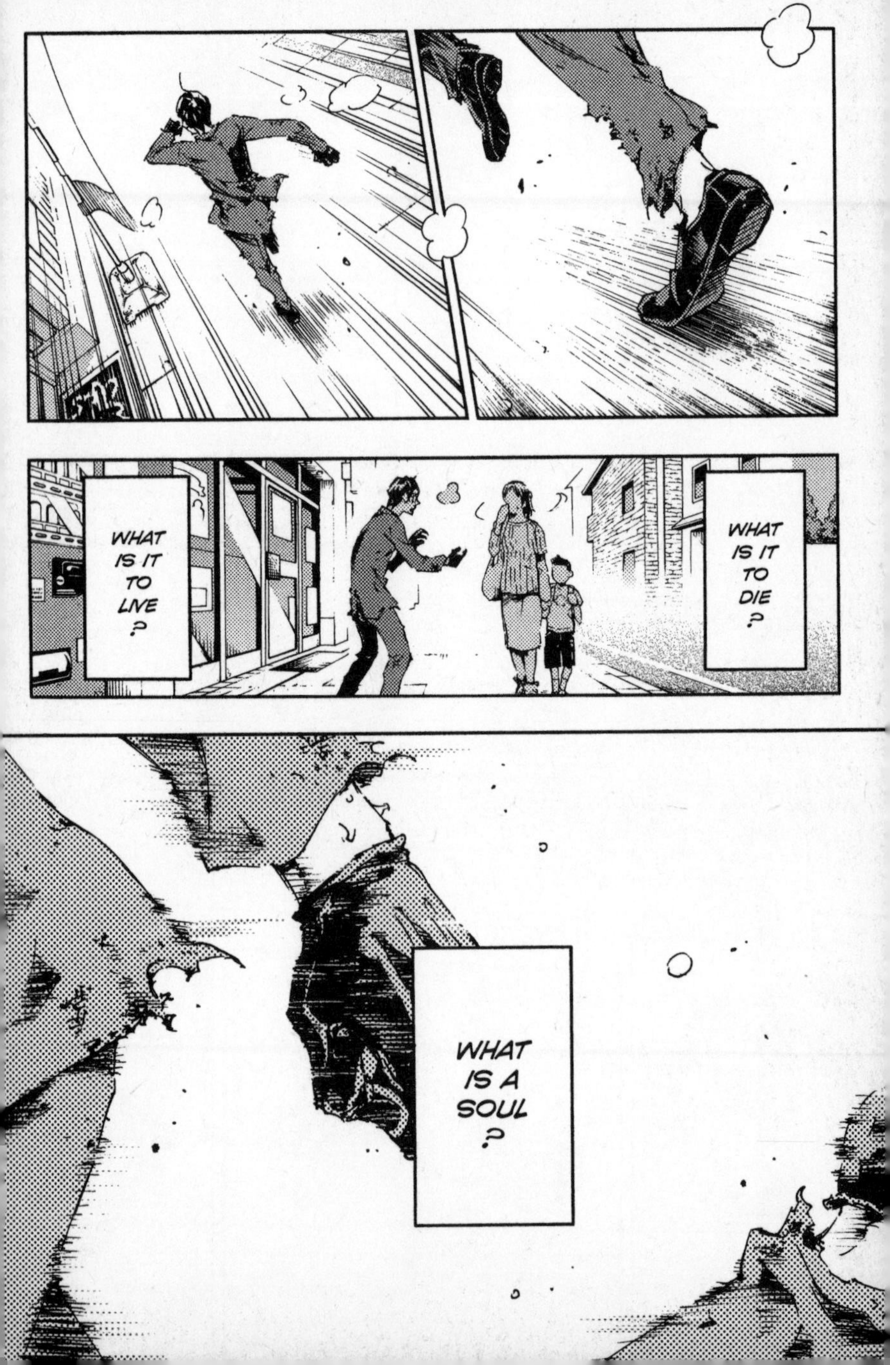
WHAT IS IT TO DIE?
WHAT IS IT TO LIVE?
WHAT IS A SOUL?

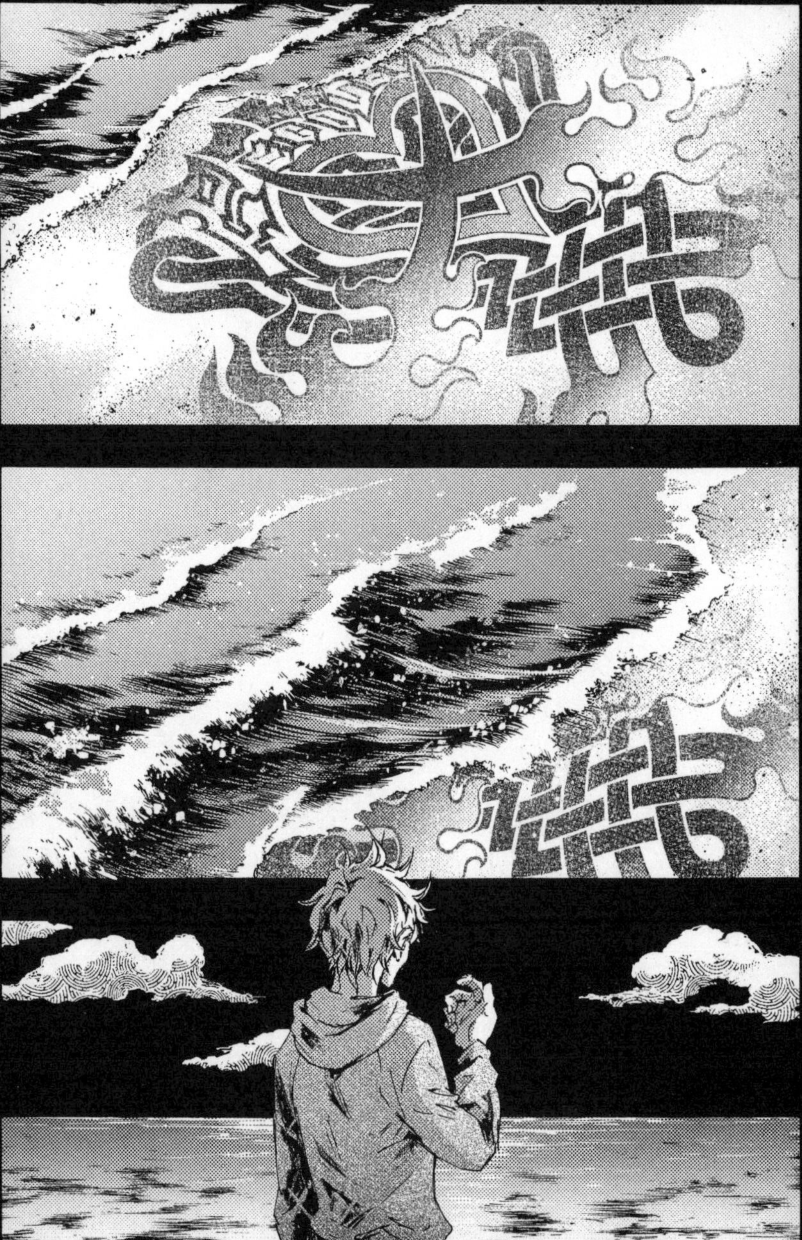

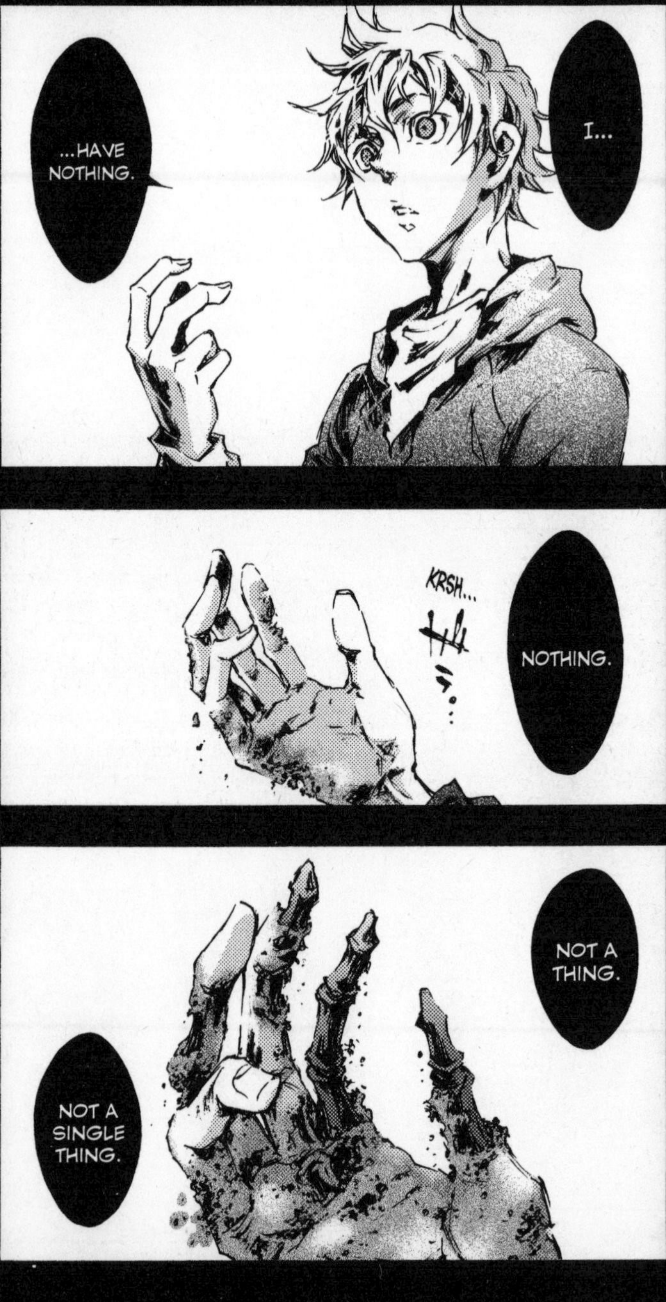
I...
...HAVE NOTHING.
NOTHING.
KRSH...
NOT A THING.
NOT A SINGLE THING.

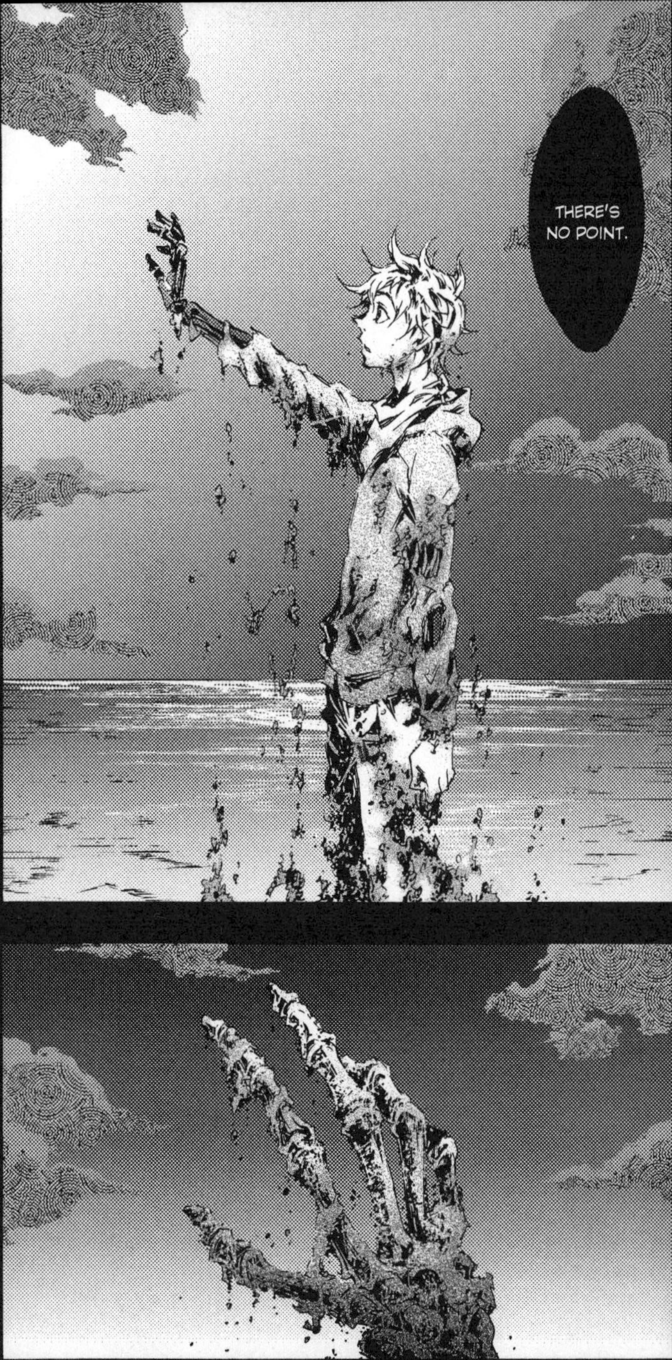
THERE'S NO POINT.

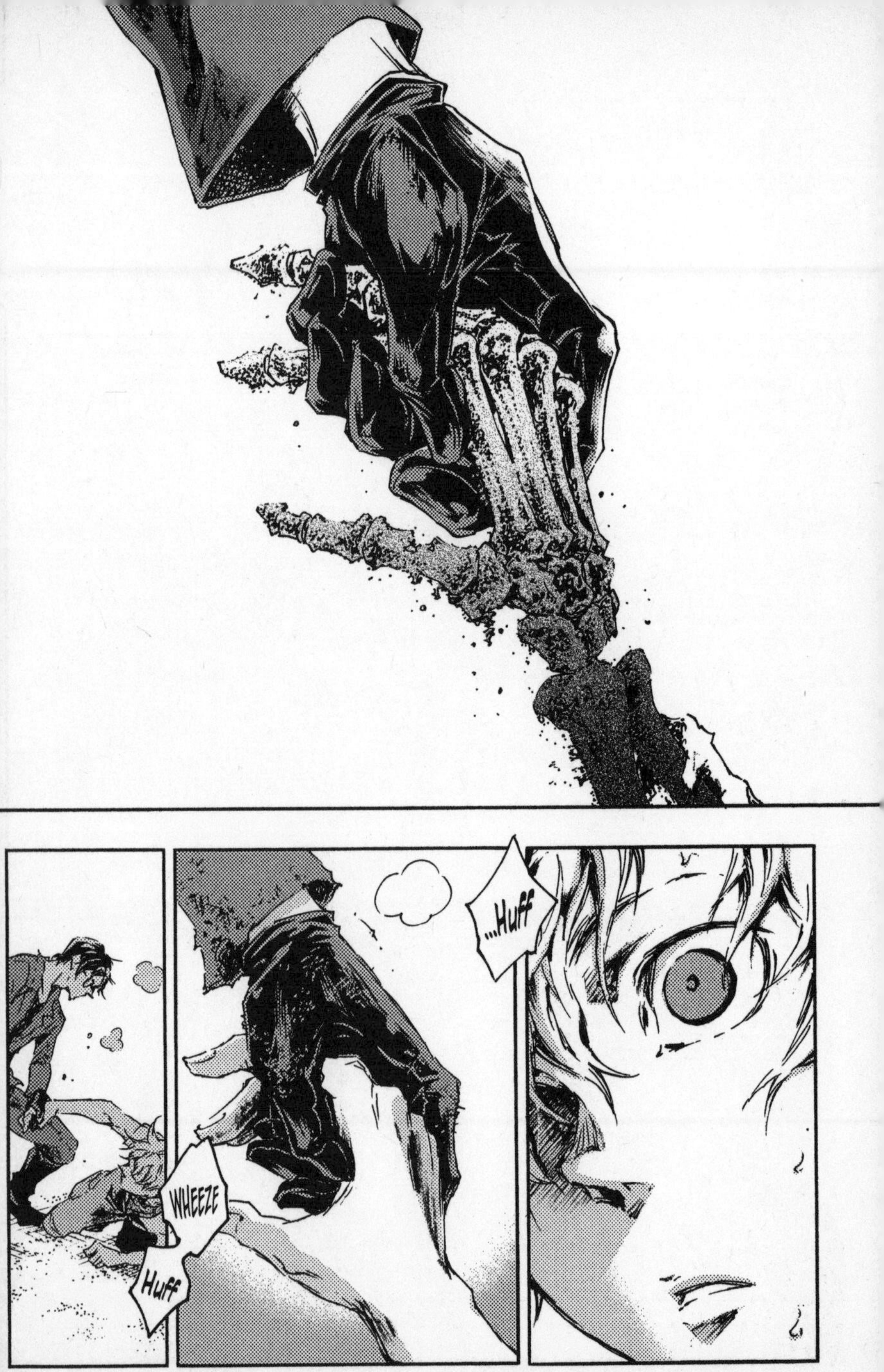
...Huff
WHEEZE
Huff

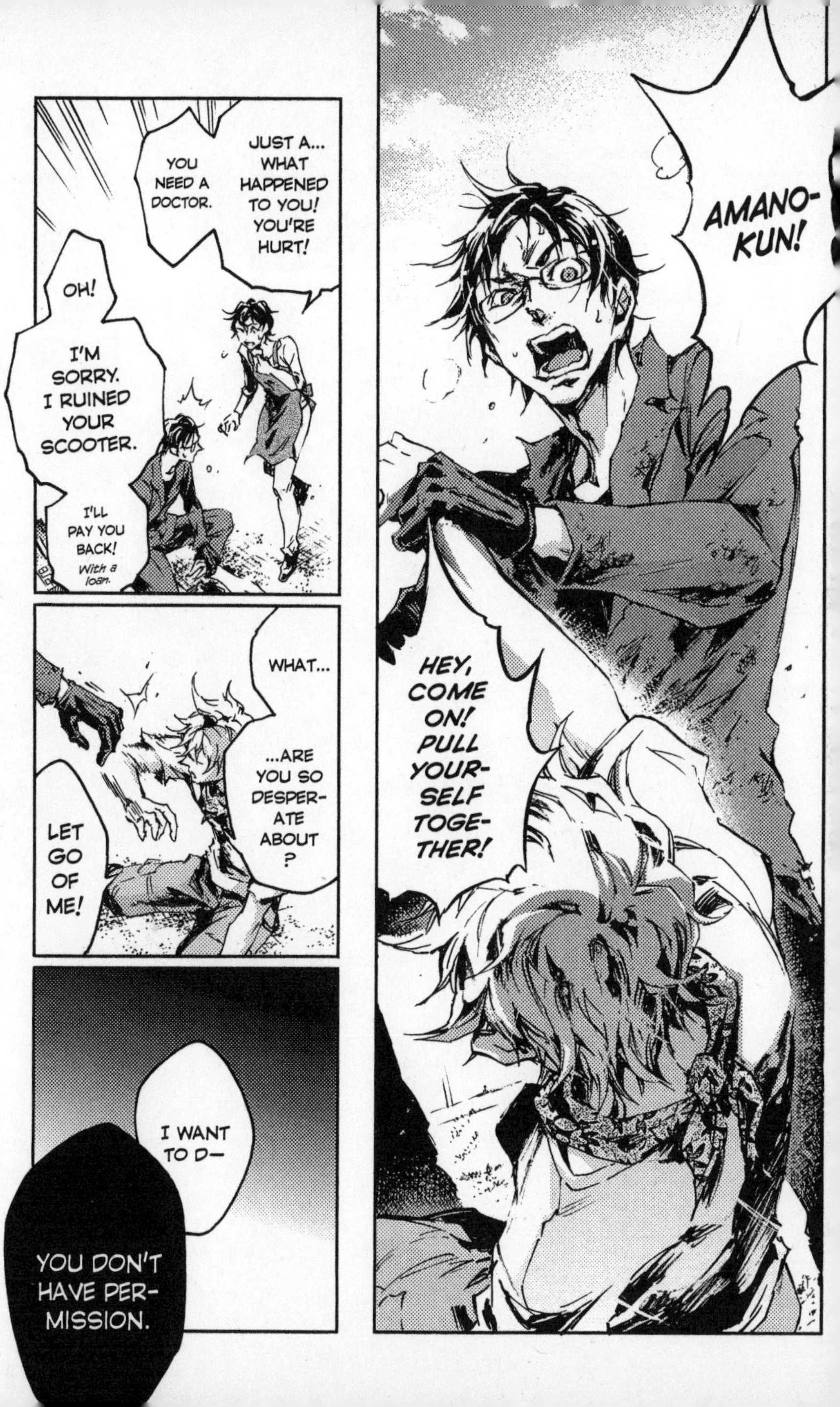
AMANO-KUN!
HEY, COME ON! PULL YOURSELF TOGETHER!
JUST A... WHAT HAPPENED TO YOU! YOU'RE HURT!
YOU NEED A DOCTOR.
OH!
I'M SORRY. I RUINED YOUR SCOOTER.
I'LL PAY YOU BACK!
With a loan.
WHAT...
...ARE YOU SO DESPERATE ABOUT?
LET GO OF ME!
I WANT TO D—
YOU DON'T HAVE PERMISSION.

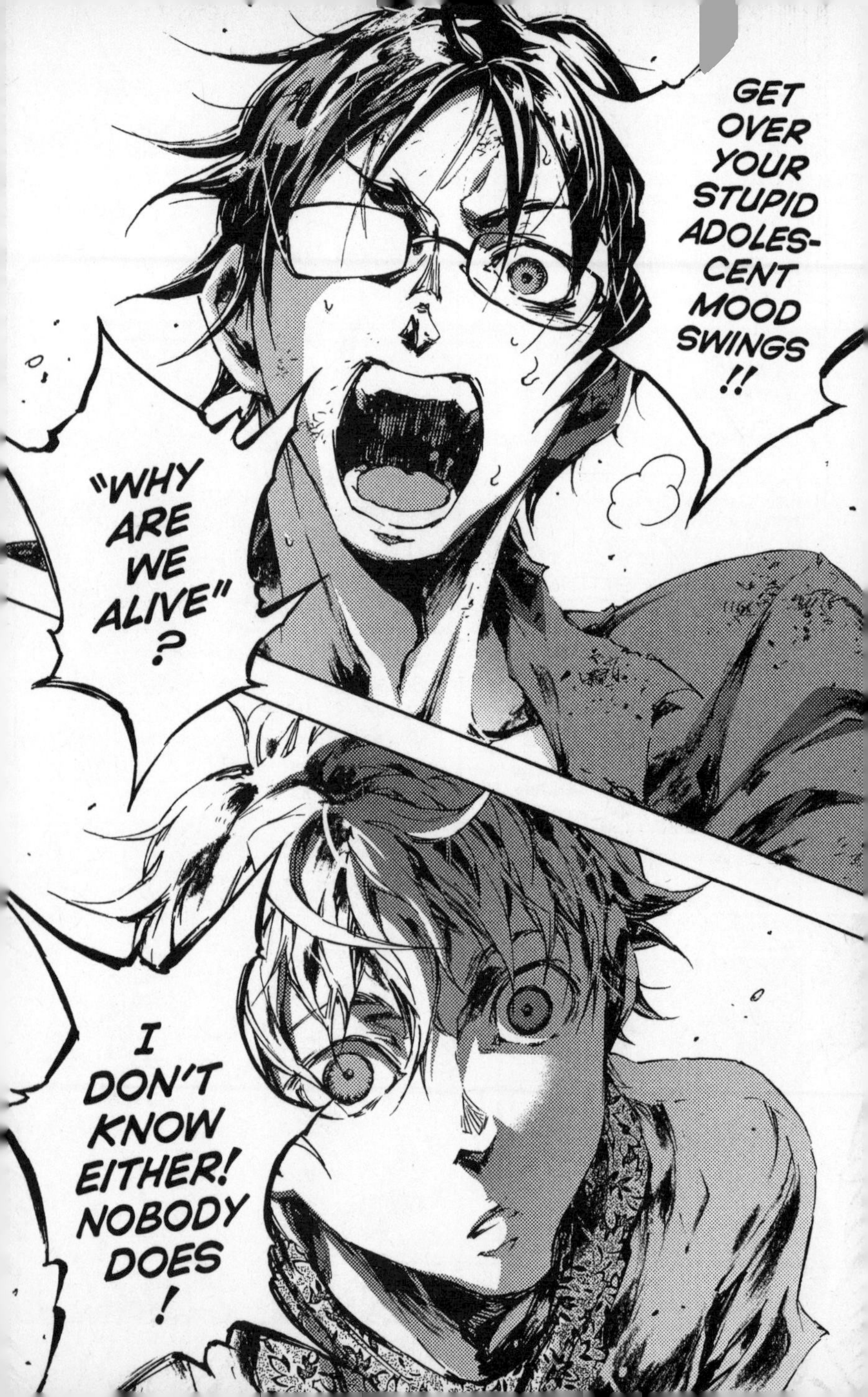
GET OVER YOUR STUPID ADOLES-CENT MOOD SWINGS!!
"WHY ARE WE ALIVE"?
I DON'T KNOW EITHER! NOBODY DOES!

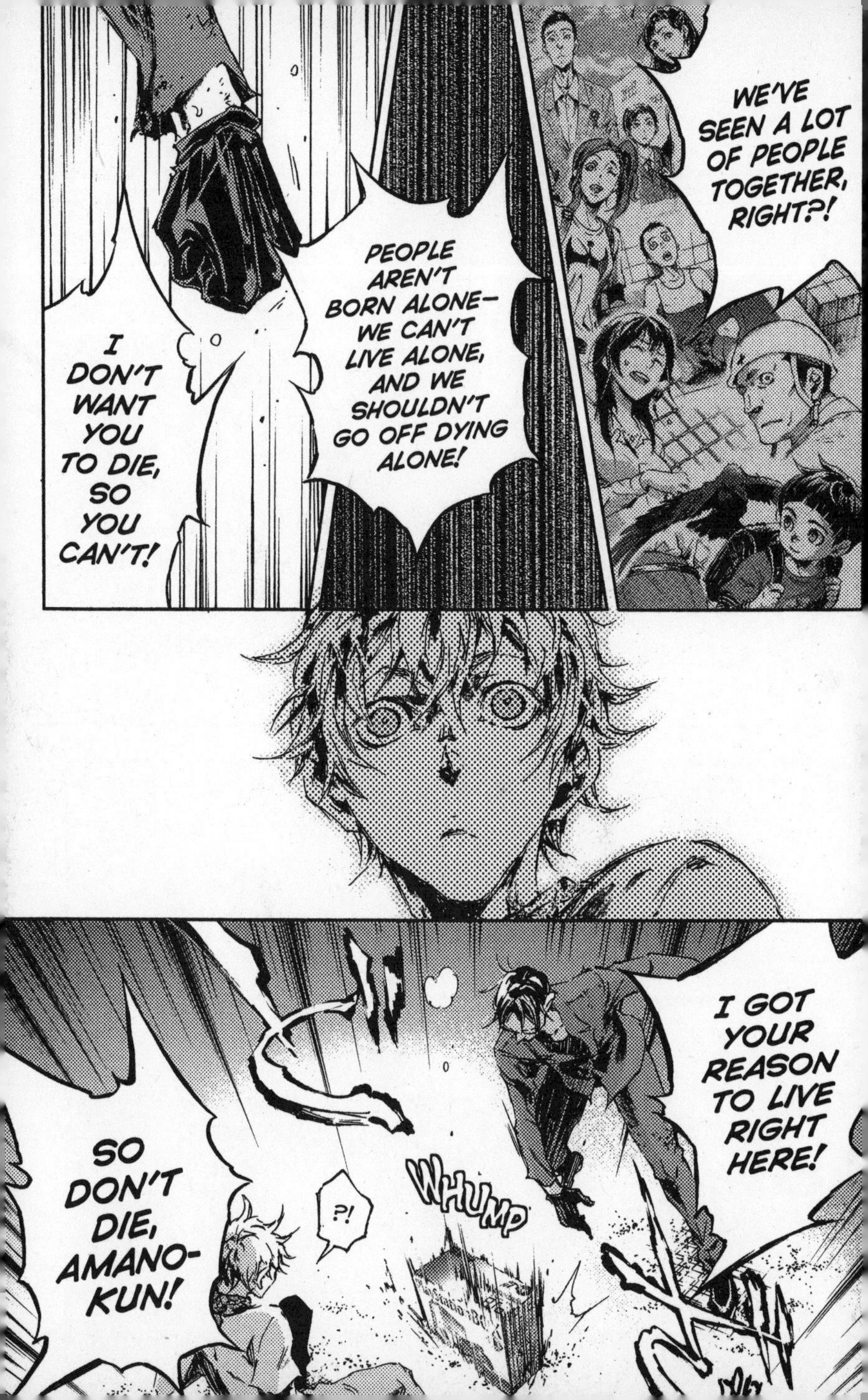
WE'VE SEEN A LOT OF PEOPLE TOGETHER, RIGHT?!
PEOPLE AREN'T BORN ALONE—WE CAN'T LIVE ALONE, AND WE SHOULDN'T GO OFF DYING ALONE!
I DON'T WANT YOU TO DIE, SO YOU CAN'T!
I GOT YOUR REASON TO LIVE RIGHT HERE!
WHUMP
?!
SO DON'T DIE, AMANO-KUN!

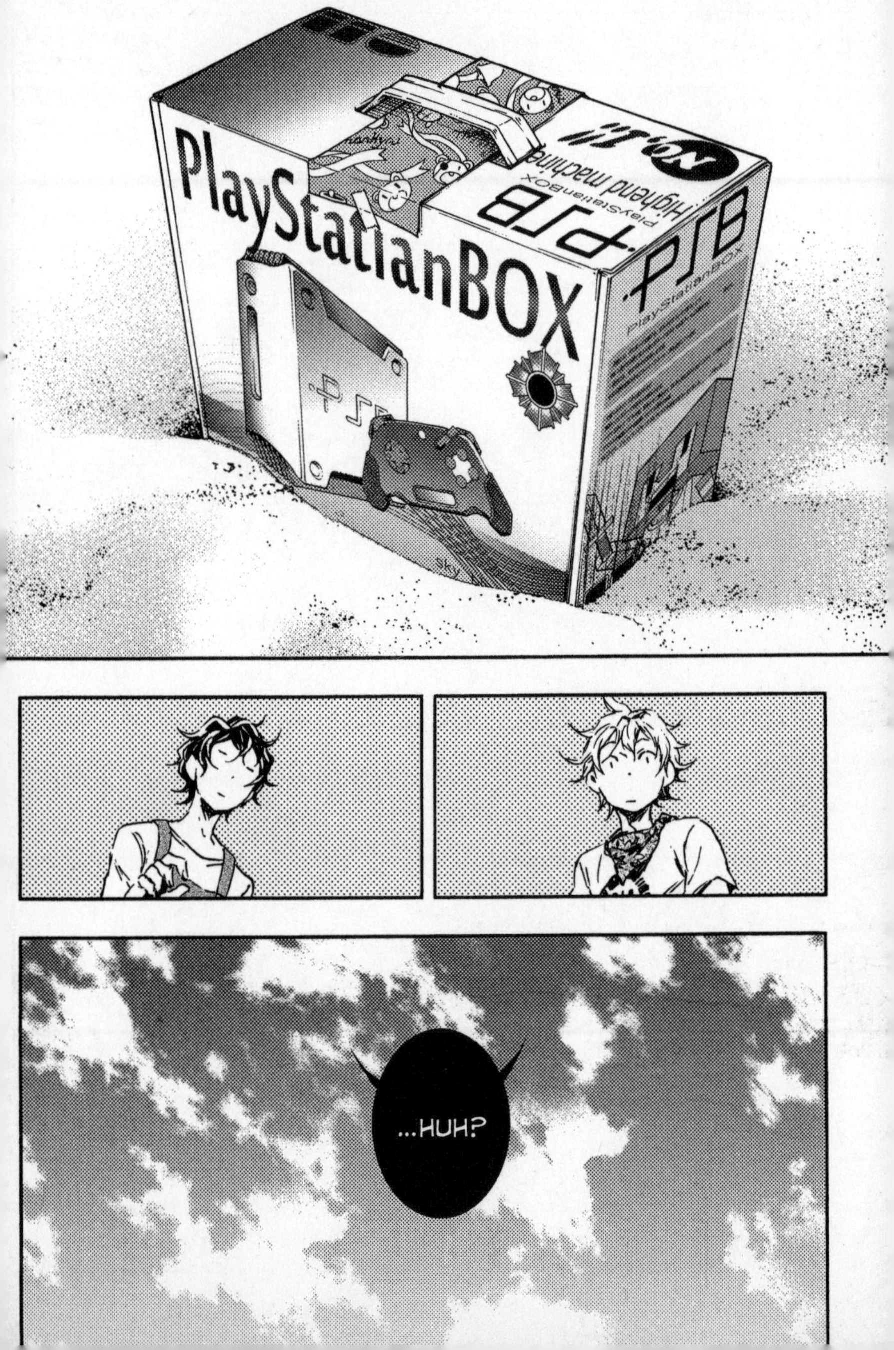
PlayStatianBOX
...HUH?

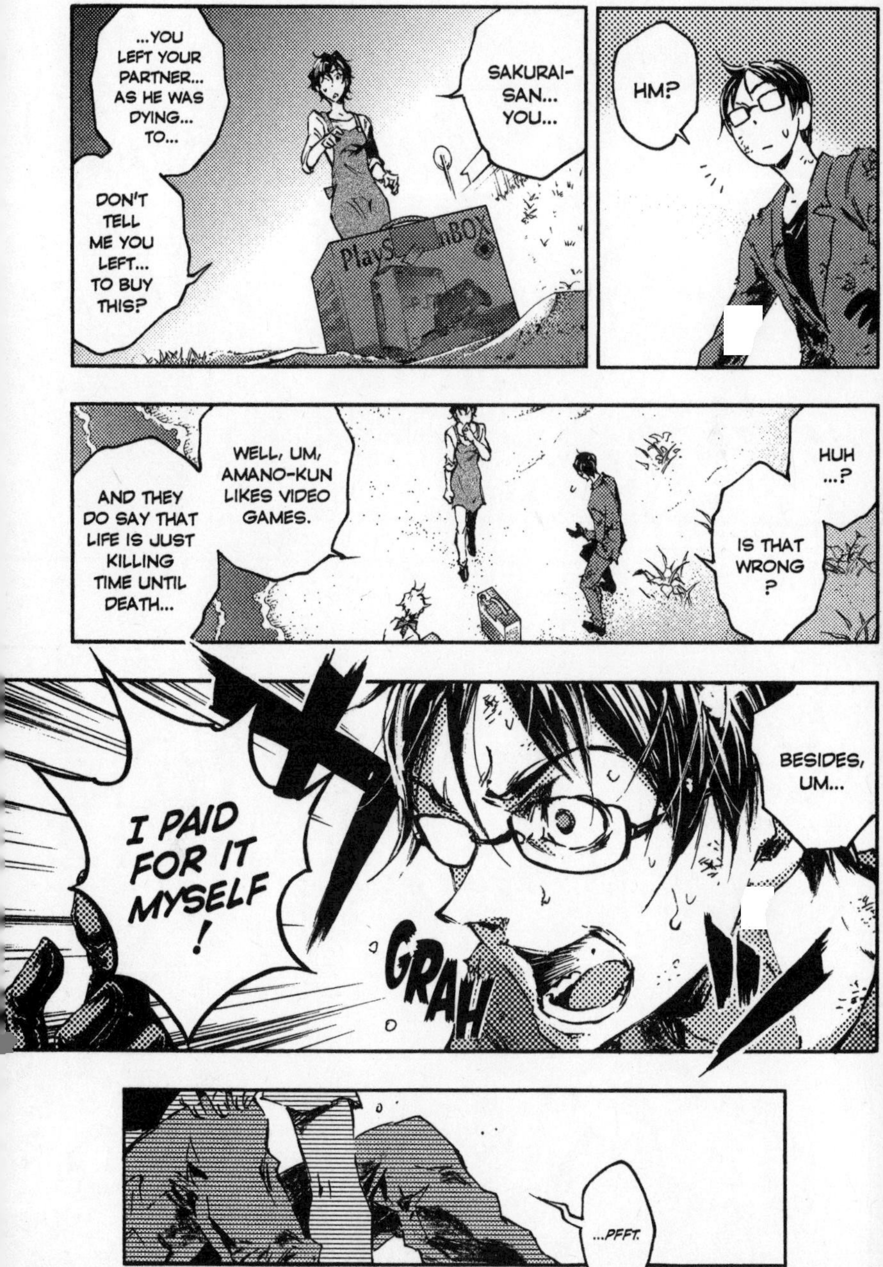
HM?
SAKURAI-SAN... YOU...
...YOU LEFT YOUR PARTNER... AS HE WAS DYING... TO...
DON'T TELL ME YOU LEFT... TO BUY THIS?
HUH ...?
IS THAT WRONG ?
WELL, UM, AMANO-KUN LIKES VIDEO GAMES.
AND THEY DO SAY THAT LIFE IS JUST KILLING TIME UNTIL DEATH...
BESIDES, UM...
GRAH
I PAID FOR IT MYSELF !
...PFFT.

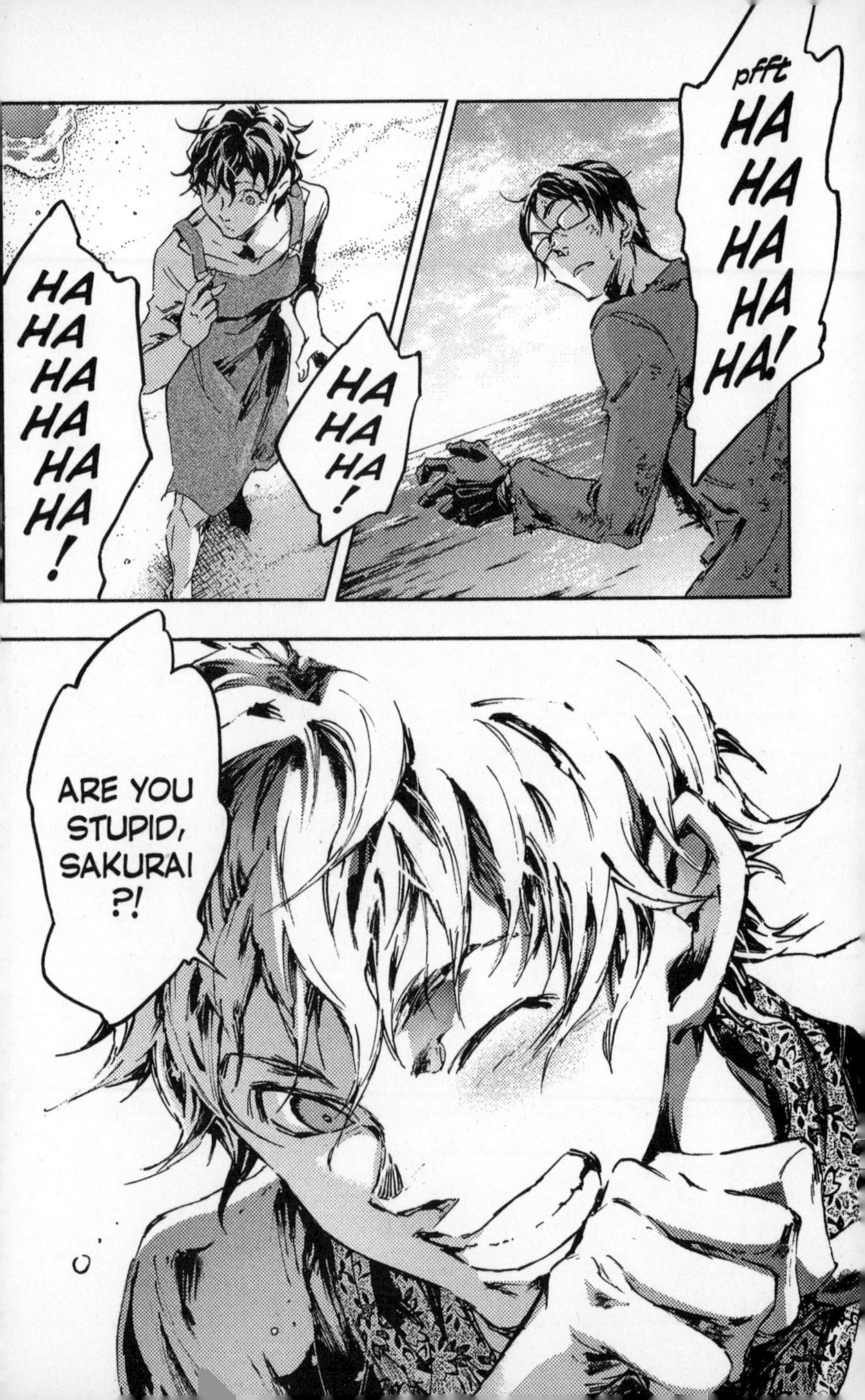
pfft
HA HA HA HA HA!
HA HA HA!
HA HA HA HA HA HA!
ARE YOU STUPID, SAKURAI ?!

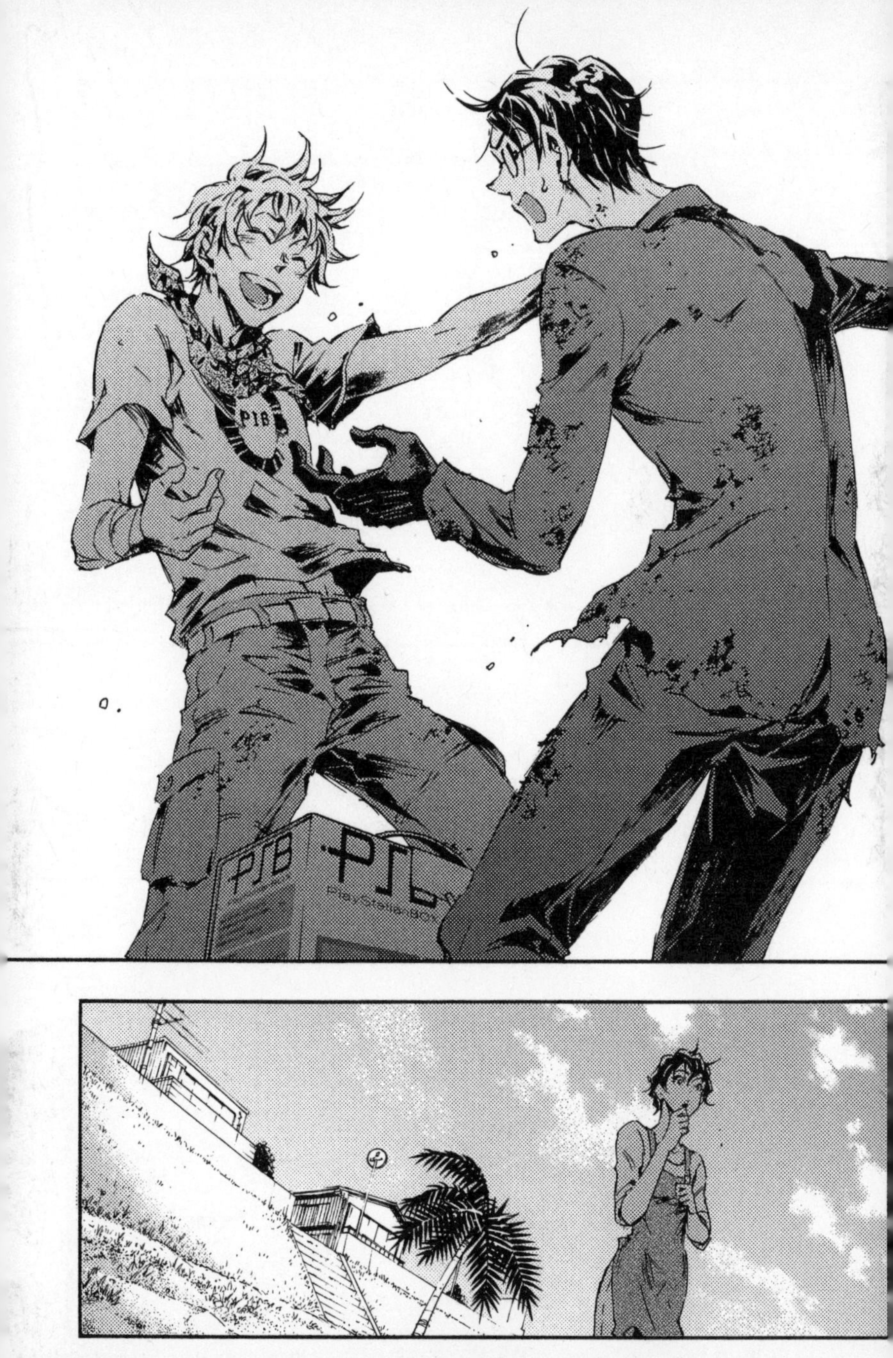
PIB
PIB

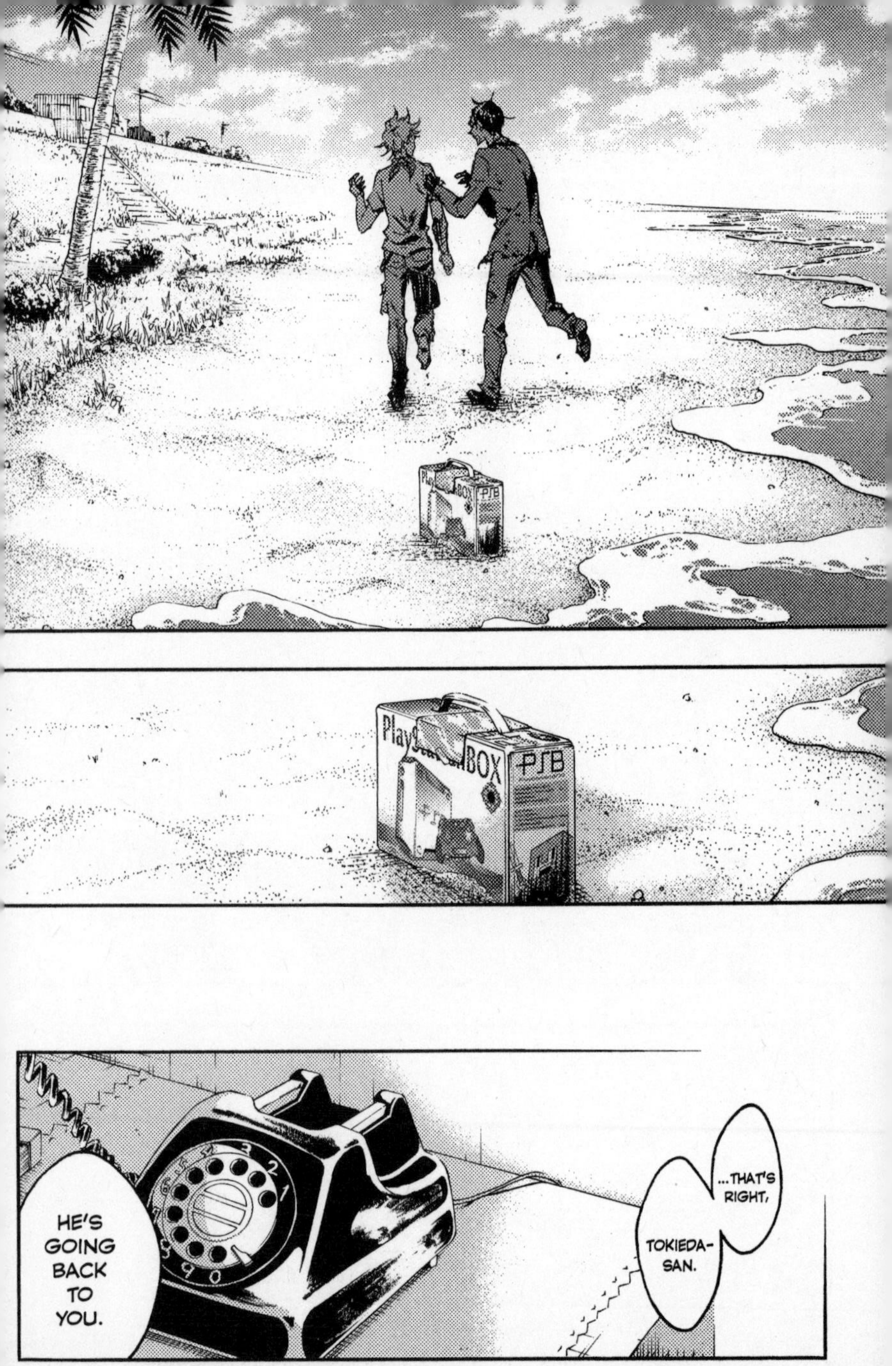
...THAT'S RIGHT, TOKIEDA-SAN.
HE'S GOING BACK TO YOU.

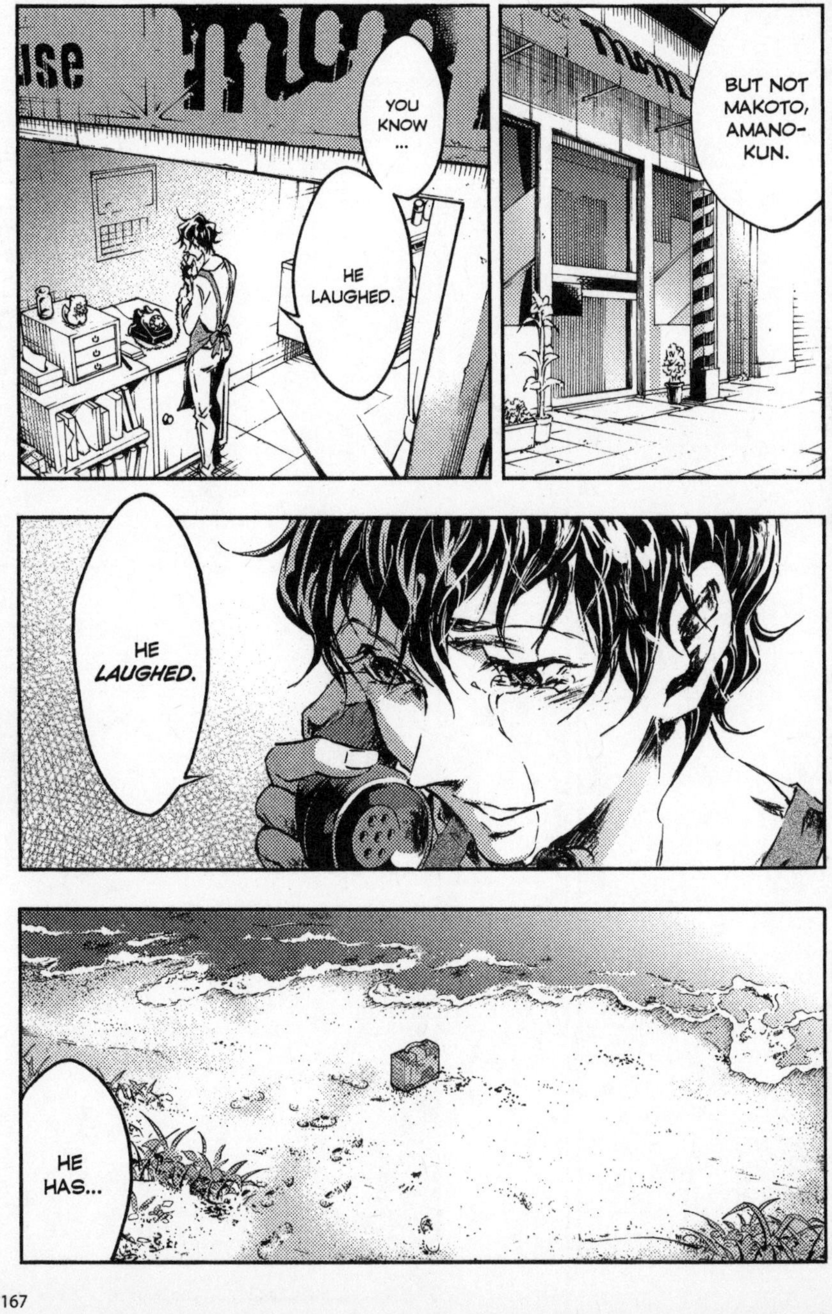
BUT NOT MAKOTO, AMANO-KUN.
YOU KNOW ...
HE LAUGHED.
HE *LAUGHED.*
HE HAS...

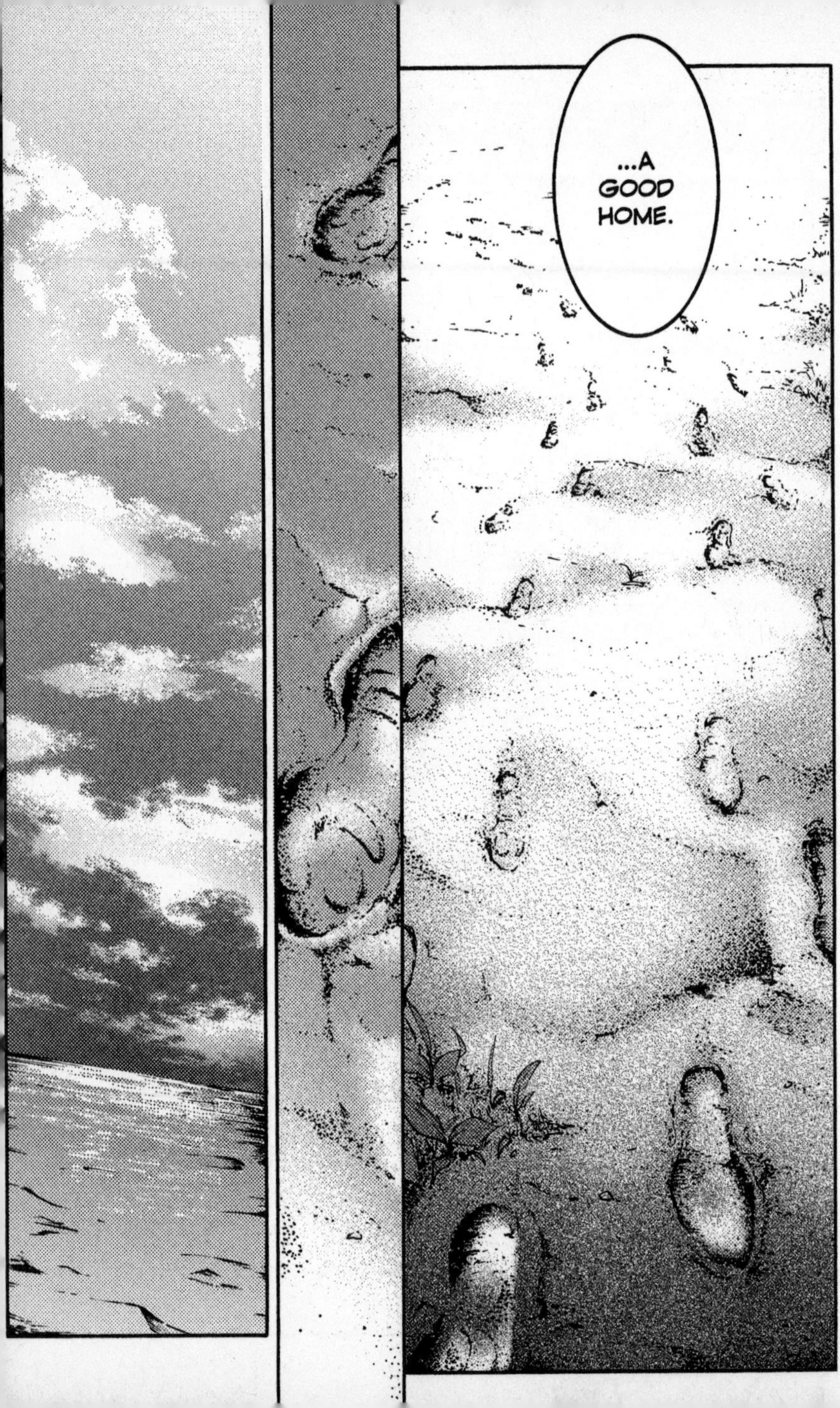
...A GOOD HOME.

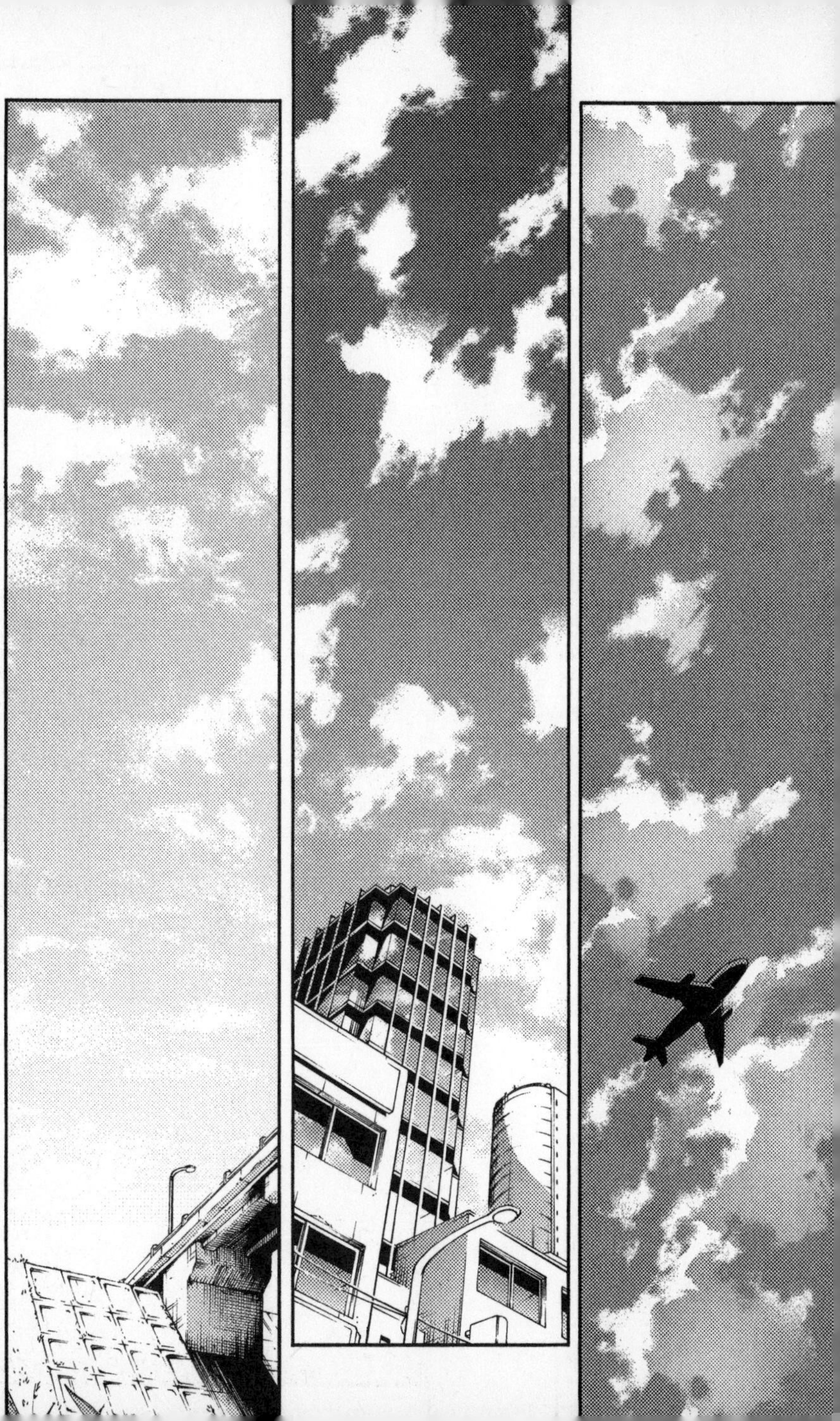

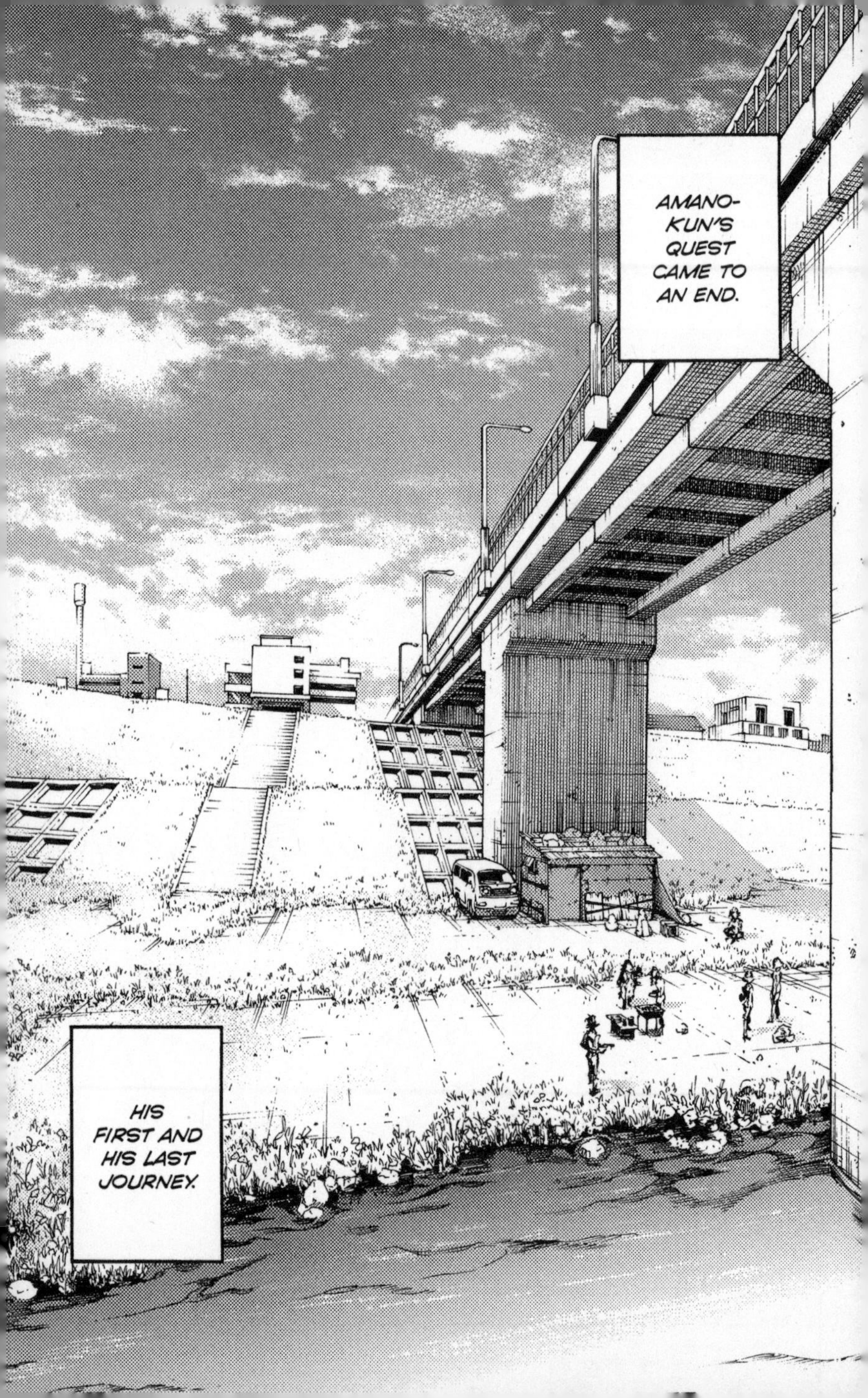
AMANO-KUN'S QUEST CAME TO AN END.
HIS FIRST AND HIS LAST JOURNEY.

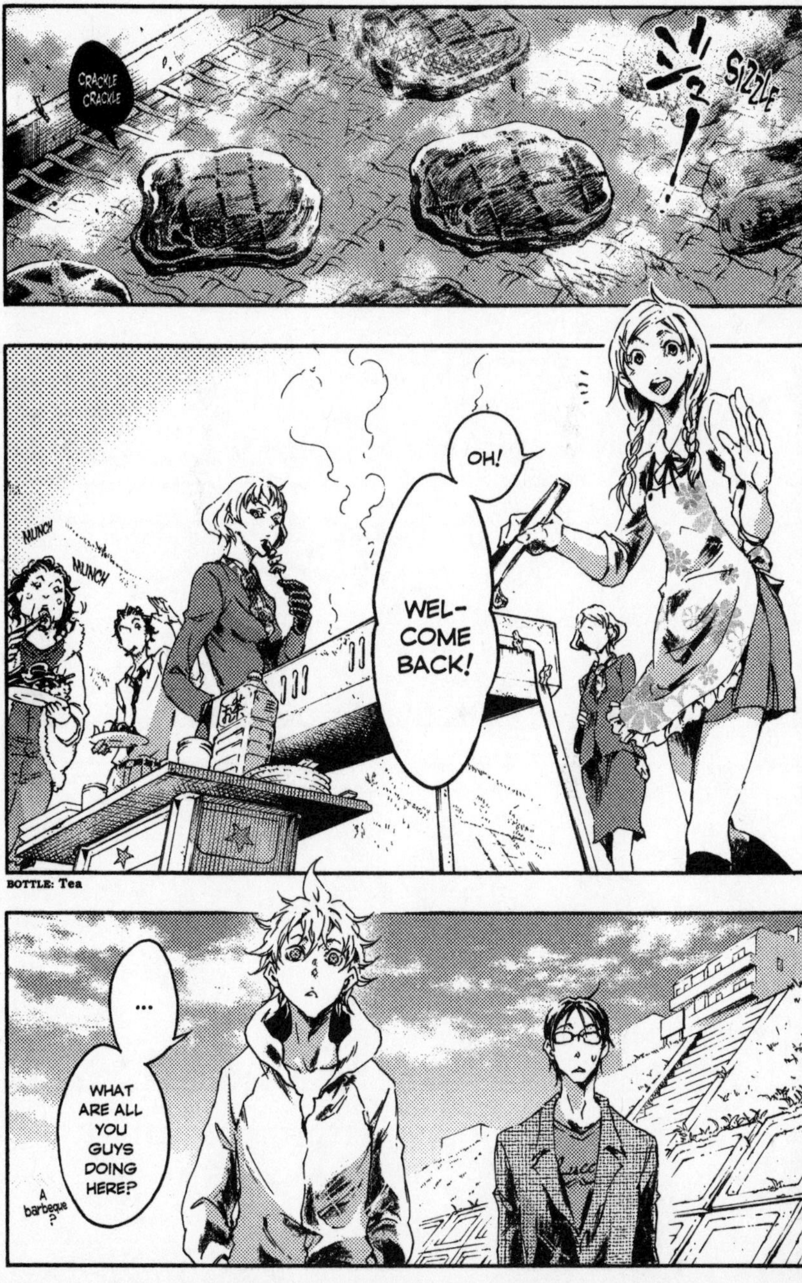
SIZZLE
CRACKLE CRACKLE
OH!
WEL-COME BACK!
MUNCH MUNCH
...
WHAT ARE ALL YOU GUYS DOING HERE?
A barbeque?

BOTTLE: Tea

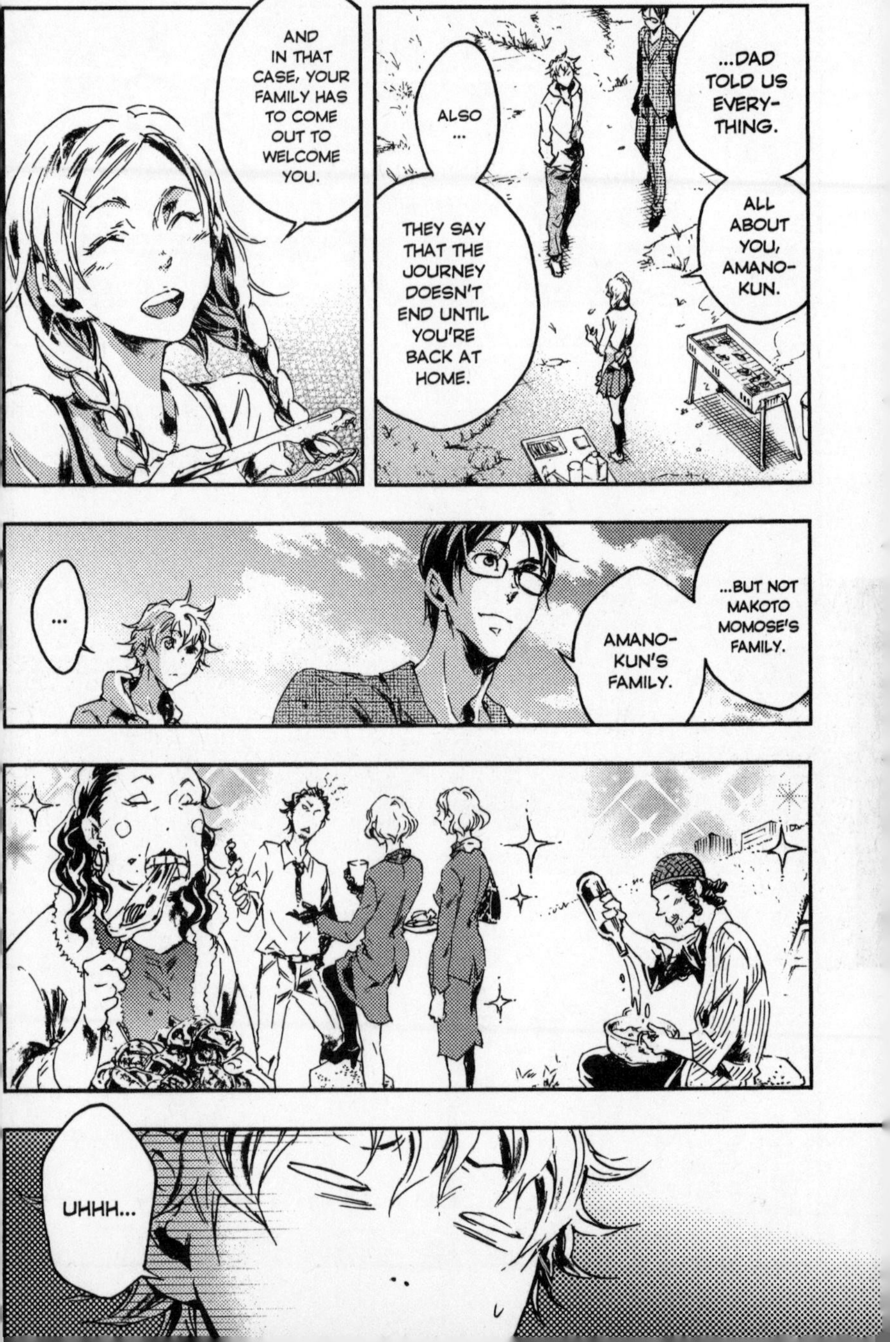
...DAD TOLD US EVERY-THING.
ALL ABOUT YOU, AMANO-KUN.
ALSO ...
THEY SAY THAT THE JOURNEY DOESN'T END UNTIL YOU'RE BACK AT HOME.
AND IN THAT CASE, YOUR FAMILY HAS TO COME OUT TO WELCOME YOU.
...BUT NOT MAKOTO MOMOSE'S FAMILY.
AMANO-KUN'S FAMILY.
...
UHHH...

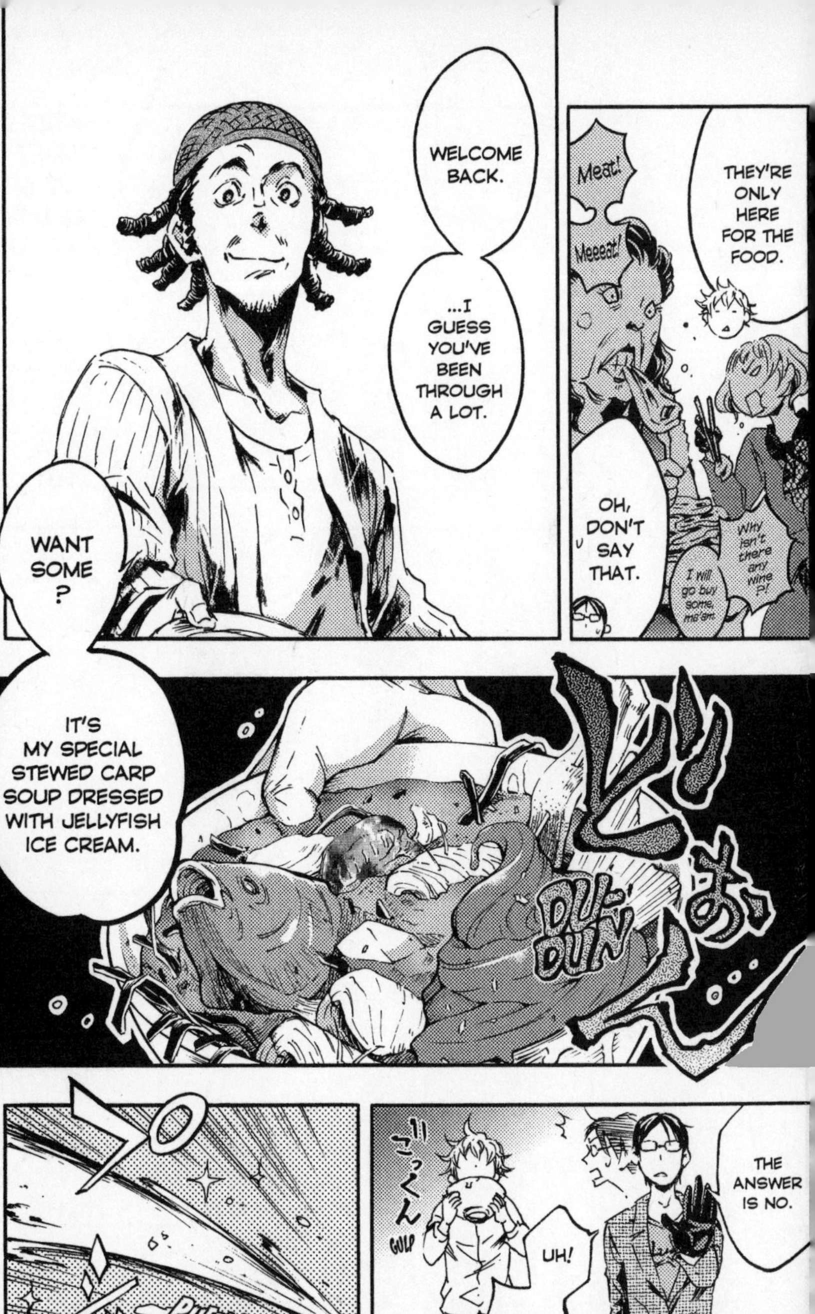
THEY'RE ONLY HERE FOR THE FOOD.
Meat!
Meeeat!
OH, DON'T SAY THAT.
Why isn't there any wine?!
I will go buy some, ma'am.
WELCOME BACK.
...I GUESS YOU'VE BEEN THROUGH A LOT.
WANT SOME?
IT'S MY SPECIAL STEWED CARP SOUP DRESSED WITH JELLYFISH ICE CREAM.
DU-DUN
THE ANSWER IS NO.
GULP
UH!
DON'T-
PHFFAUGH

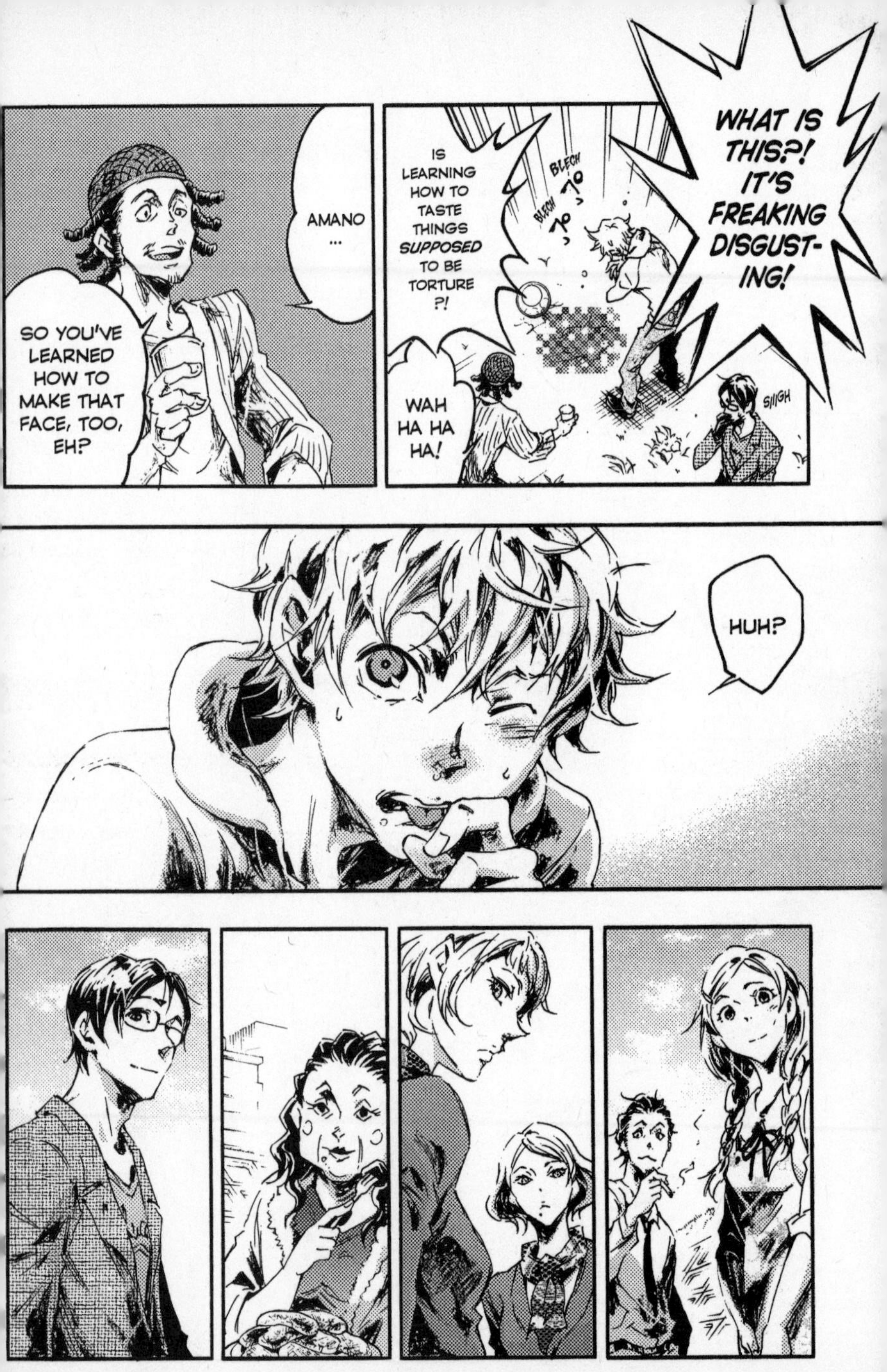
WHAT IS THIS?! IT'S FREAKING DISGUST-ING!
BLECH
BLECH
IS LEARNING HOW TO TASTE THINGS SUPPOSED TO BE TORTURE ?!
SIIGH
WAH HA HA HA!
AMANO ...
SO YOU'VE LEARNED HOW TO MAKE THAT FACE, TOO, EH?
HUH?

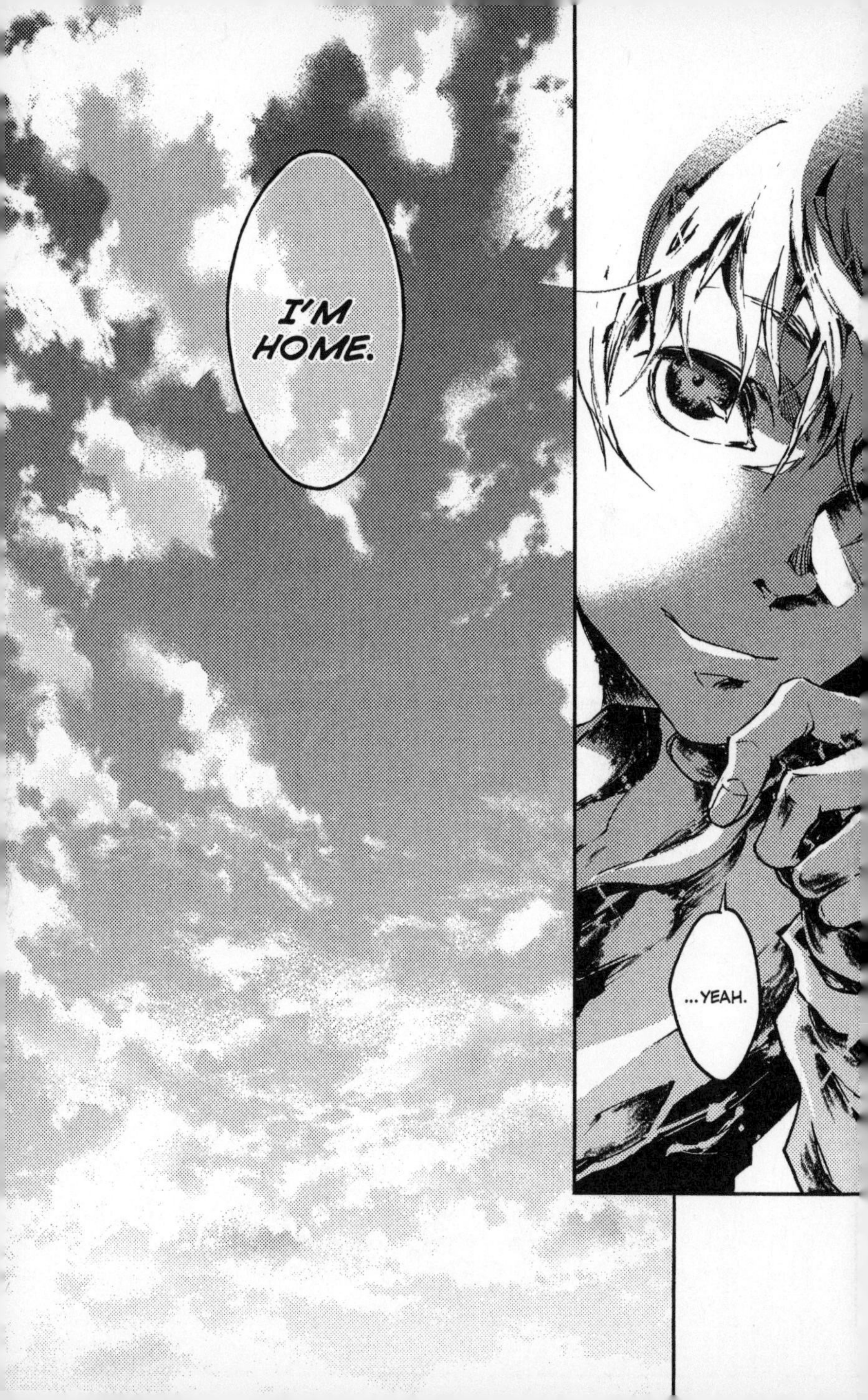
...YEAH.
I'M HOME.

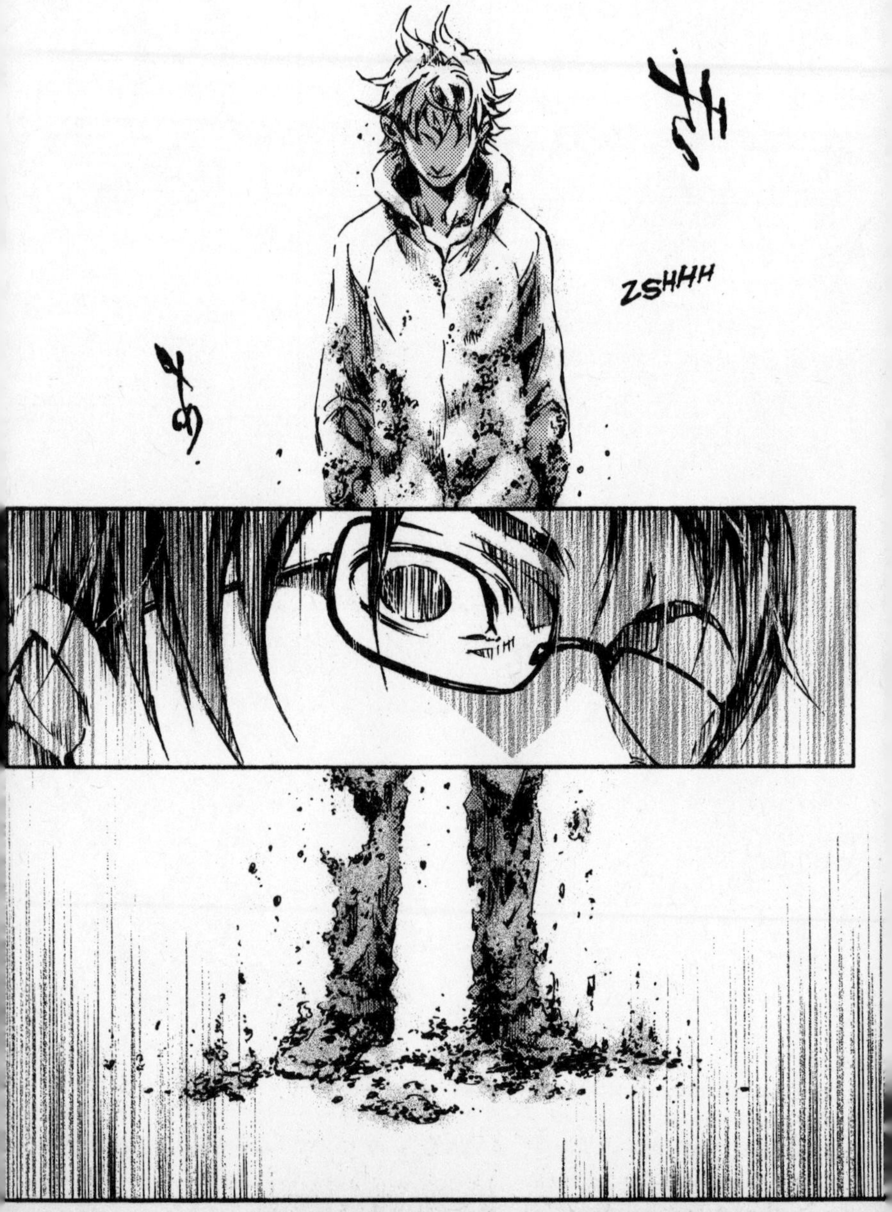
ZSHHH

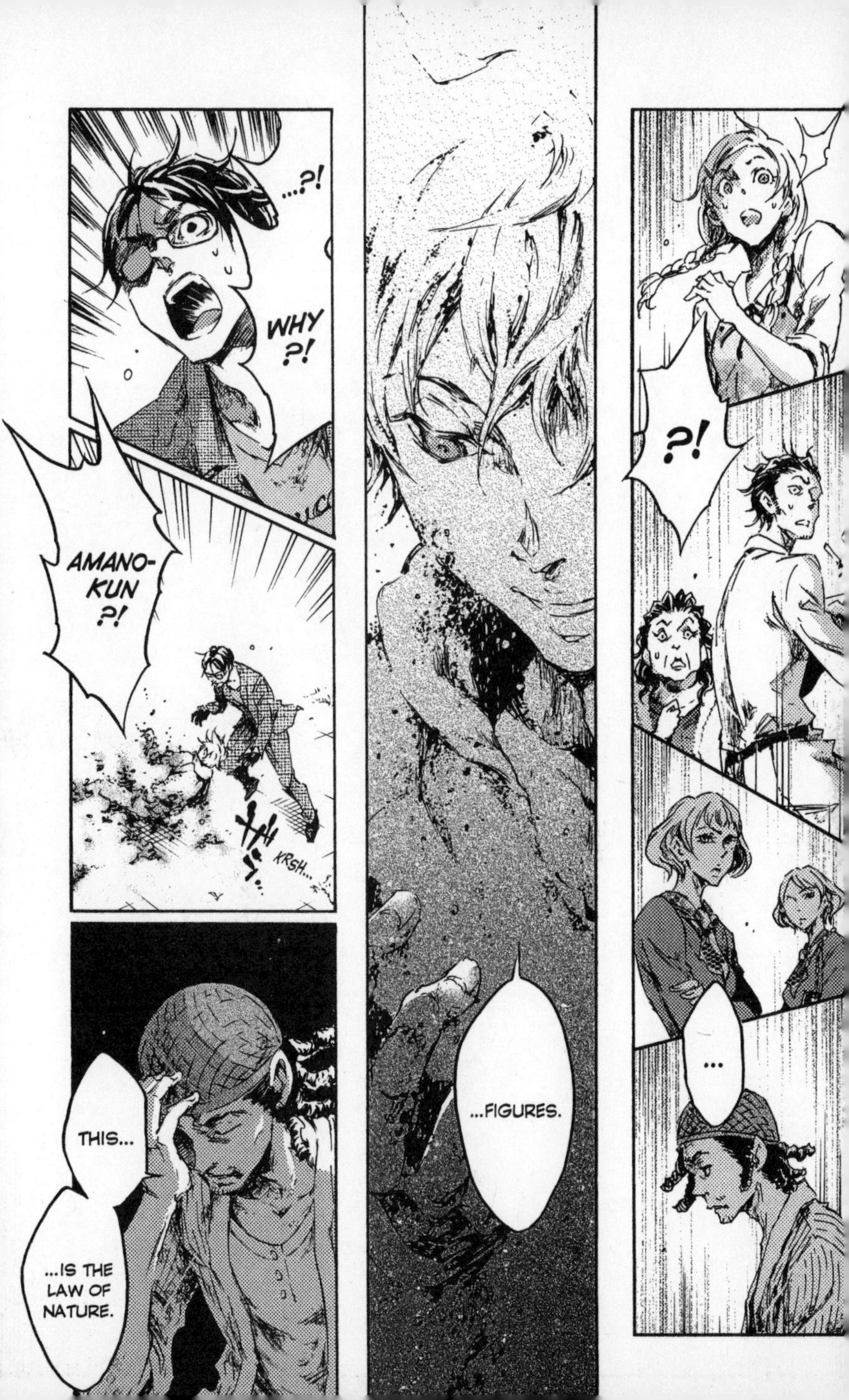
?!
...
...FIGURES.
...?!
WHY ?!
AMANO-KUN ?!
KRSH...
THIS...
...IS THE LAW OF NATURE.

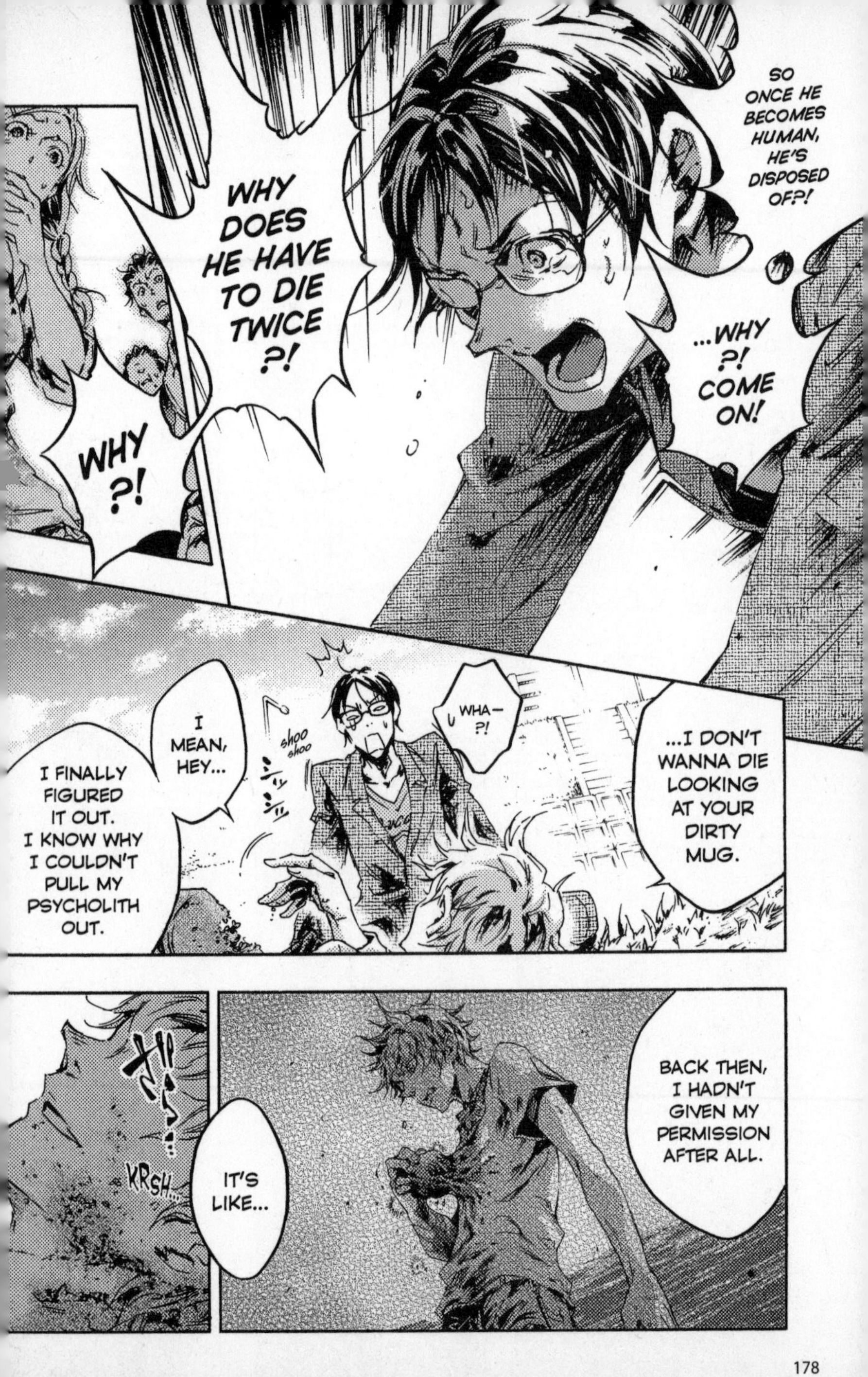
SO ONCE HE BECOMES HUMAN, HE'S DISPOSED OF?!
...WHY ?! COME ON!
WHY DOES HE HAVE TO DIE TWICE ?!
WHY ?!
...I DON'T WANNA DIE LOOKING AT YOUR DIRTY MUG.
WHA— ?!
shoo shoo
I MEAN, HEY...
I FINALLY FIGURED IT OUT. I KNOW WHY I COULDN'T PULL MY PSYCHOLITH OUT.
BACK THEN, I HADN'T GIVEN MY PERMISSION AFTER ALL.
IT'S LIKE...
KRSH...

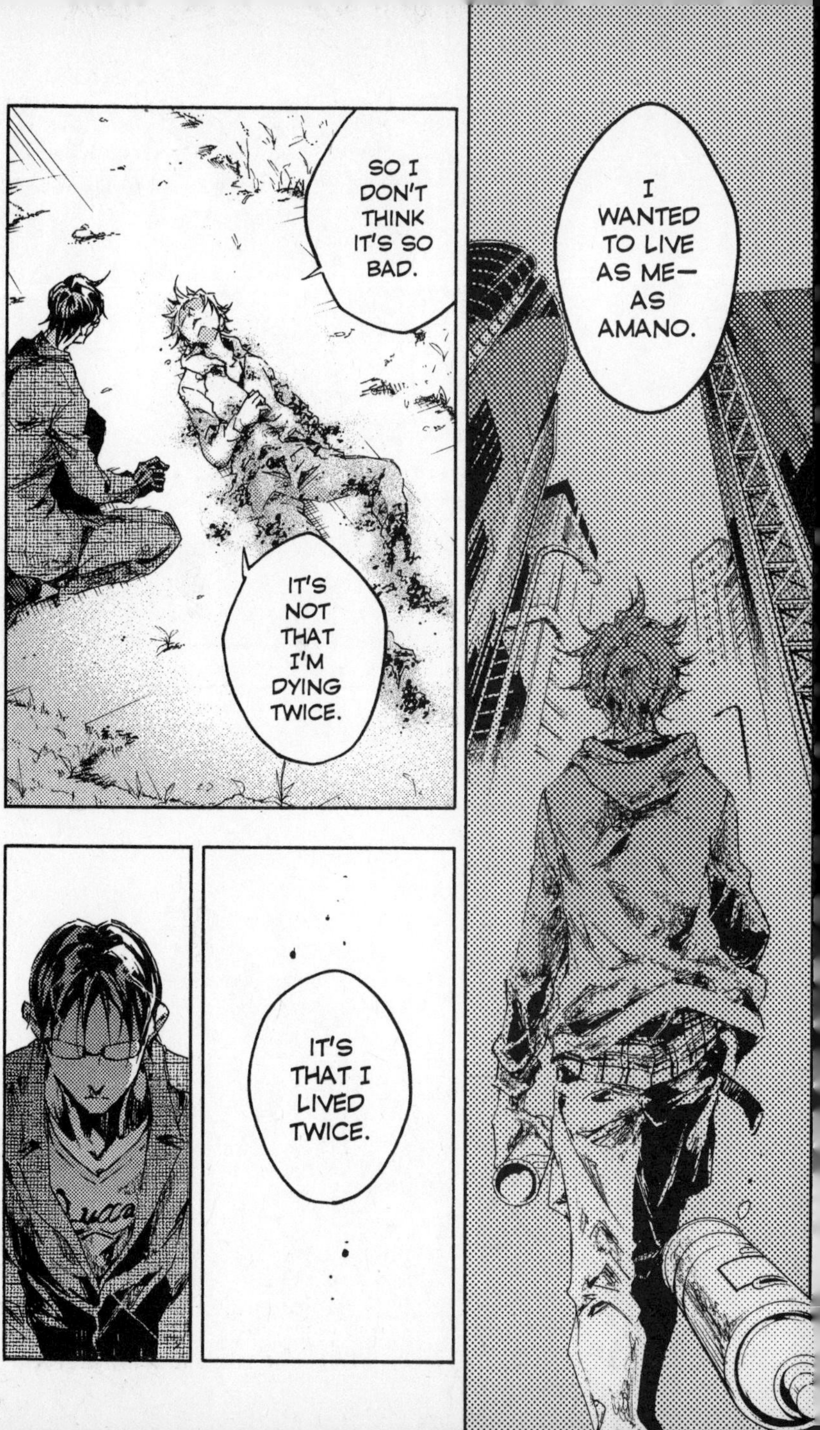
I WANTED TO LIVE AS ME— AS AMANO.
SO I DON'T THINK IT'S SO BAD.
IT'S NOT THAT I'M DYING TWICE.
IT'S THAT I LIVED TWICE.

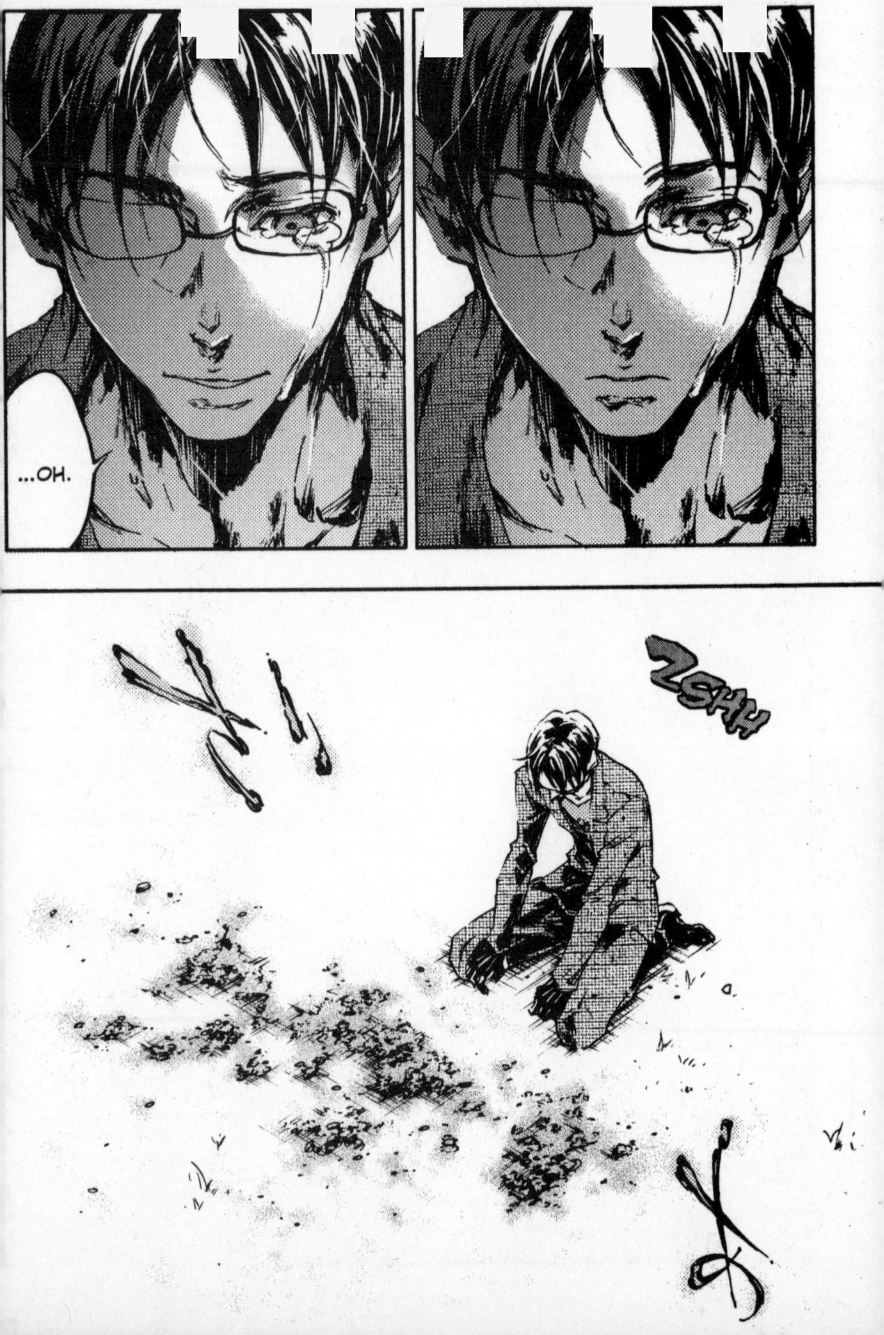
...OH.
ZSHH

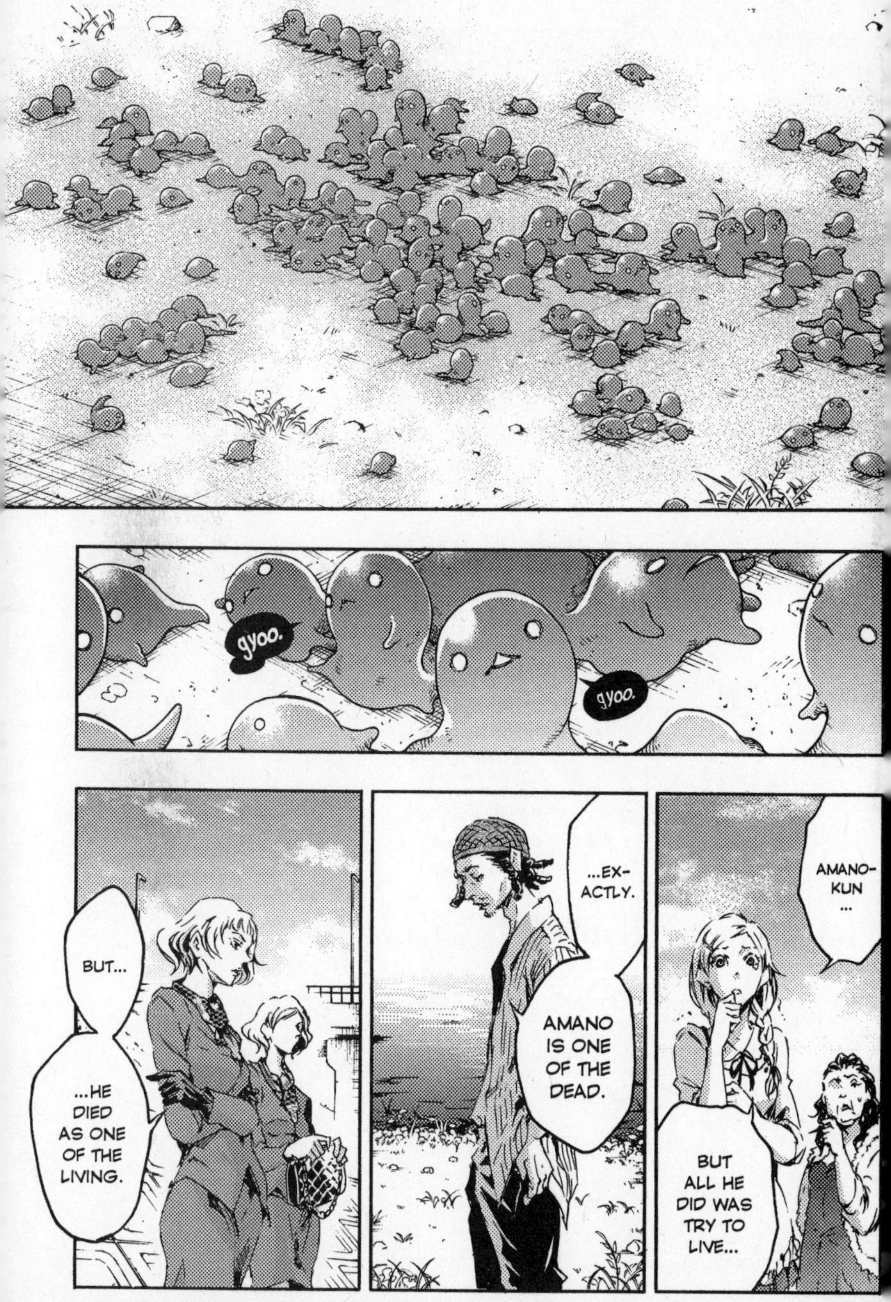
gyoo.
gyoo.
AMANO-KUN ...
BUT ALL HE DID WAS TRY TO LIVE...
...EX-ACTLY.
AMANO IS ONE OF THE DEAD.
BUT...
...HE DIED AS ONE OF THE LIVING.

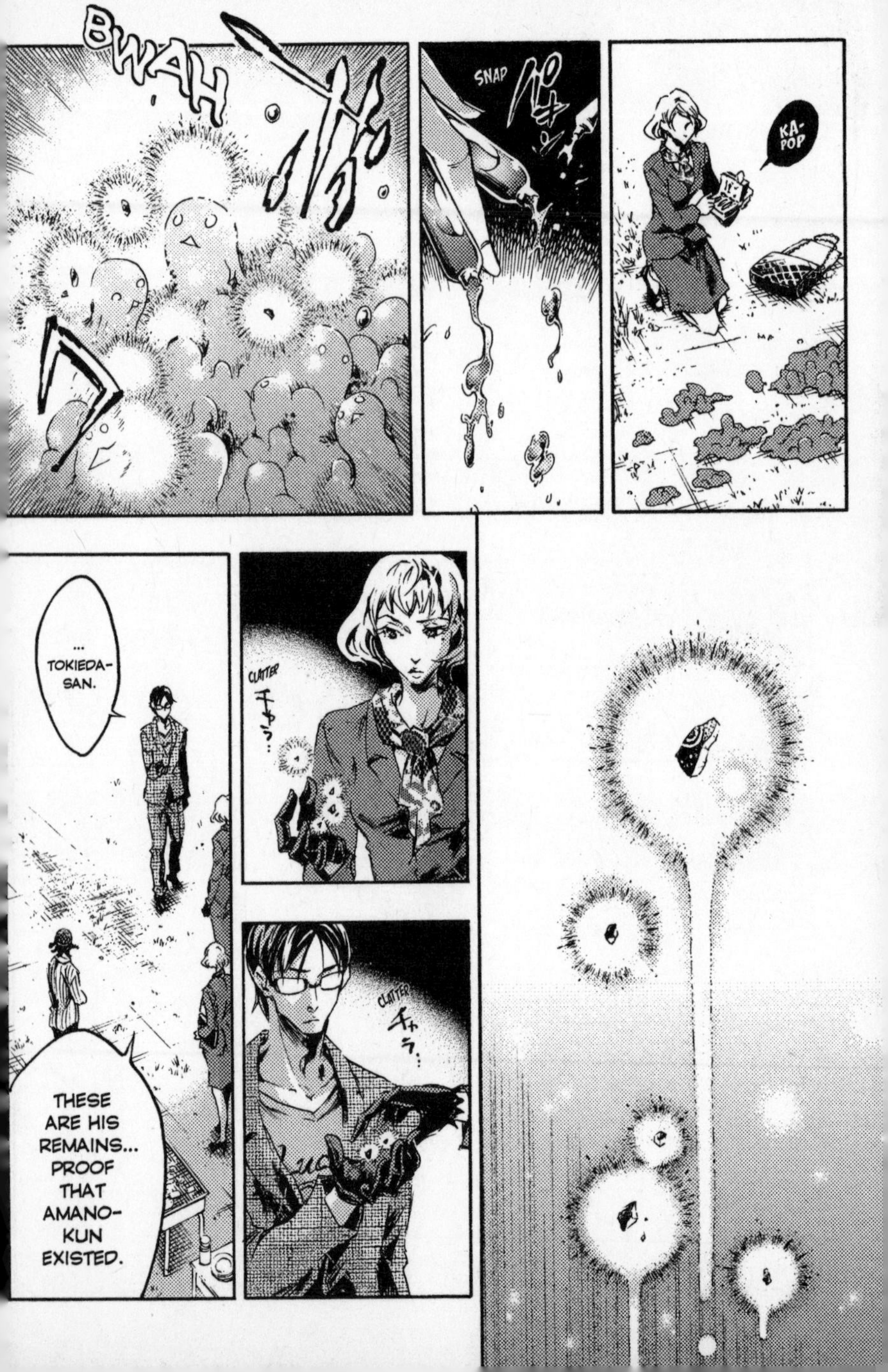
KA-POP
SNAP
BWAH
CLATTER
CLATTER
... TOKIEDA-SAN.
THESE ARE HIS REMAINS... PROOF THAT AMANO-KUN EXISTED.

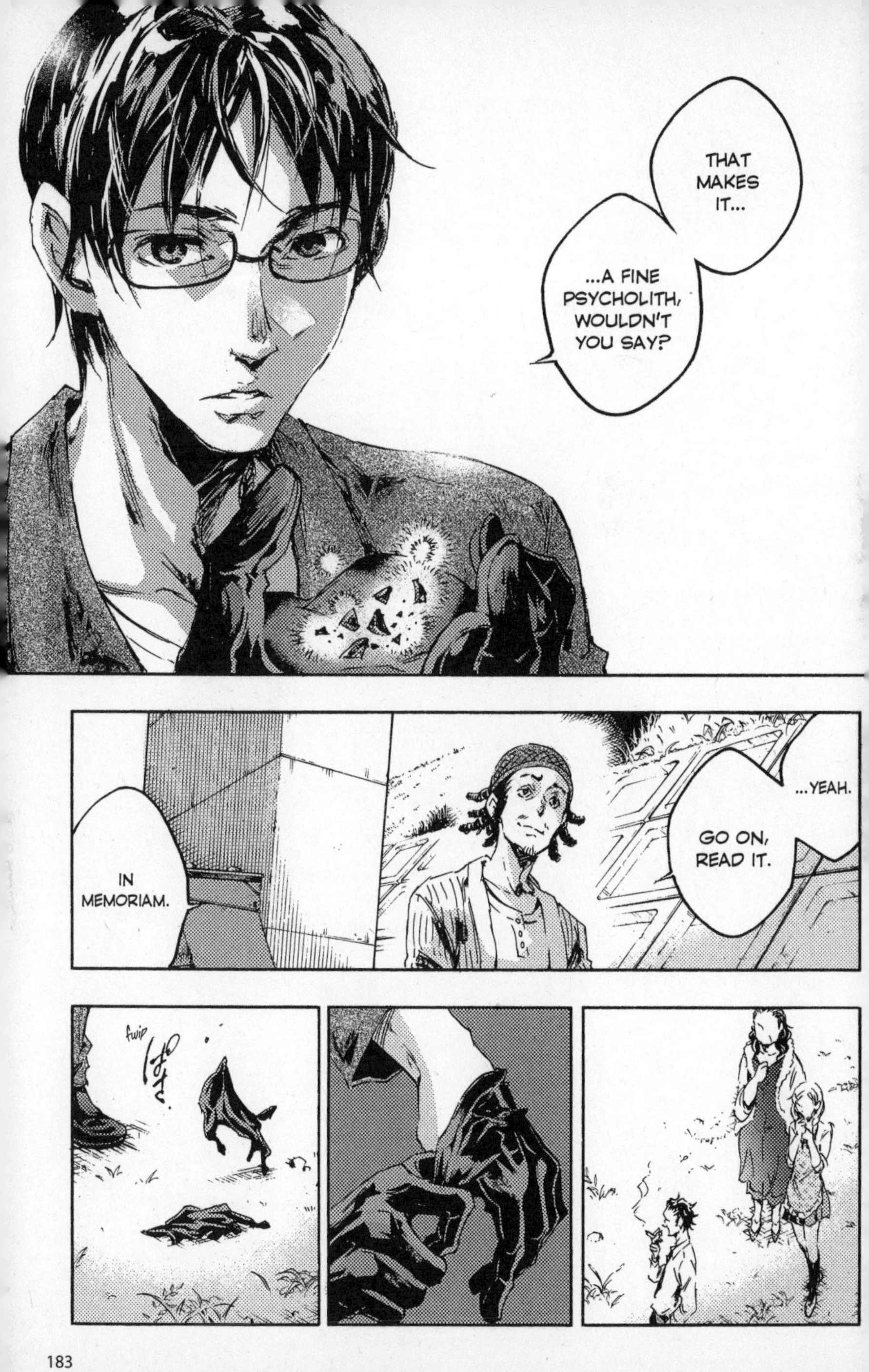
THAT MAKES IT...
...A FINE PSYCHOLITH, WOULDN'T YOU SAY?
...YEAH.
GO ON, READ IT.
IN MEMORIAM.
fwip
ぱさ

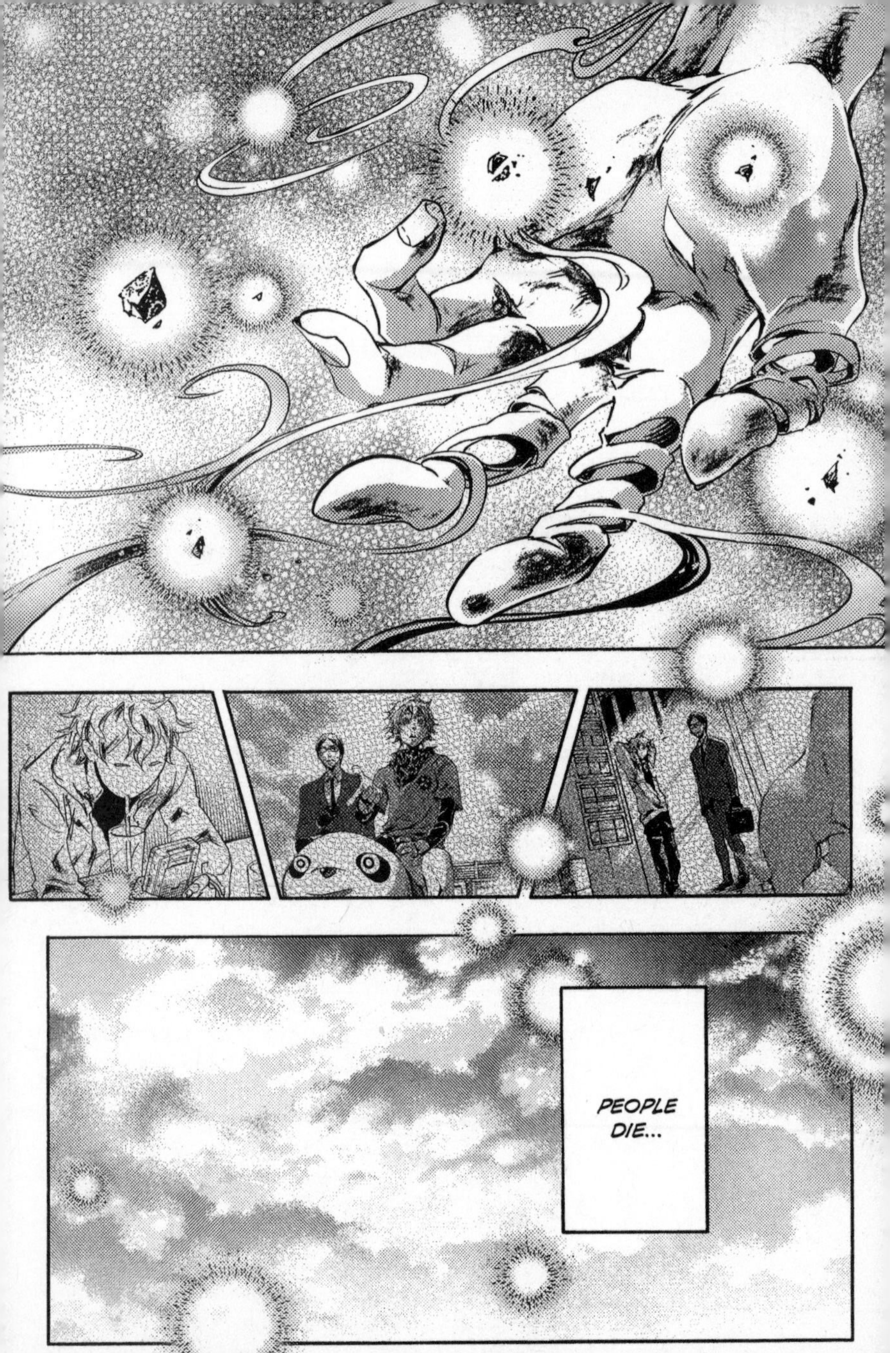
PEOPLE DIE...

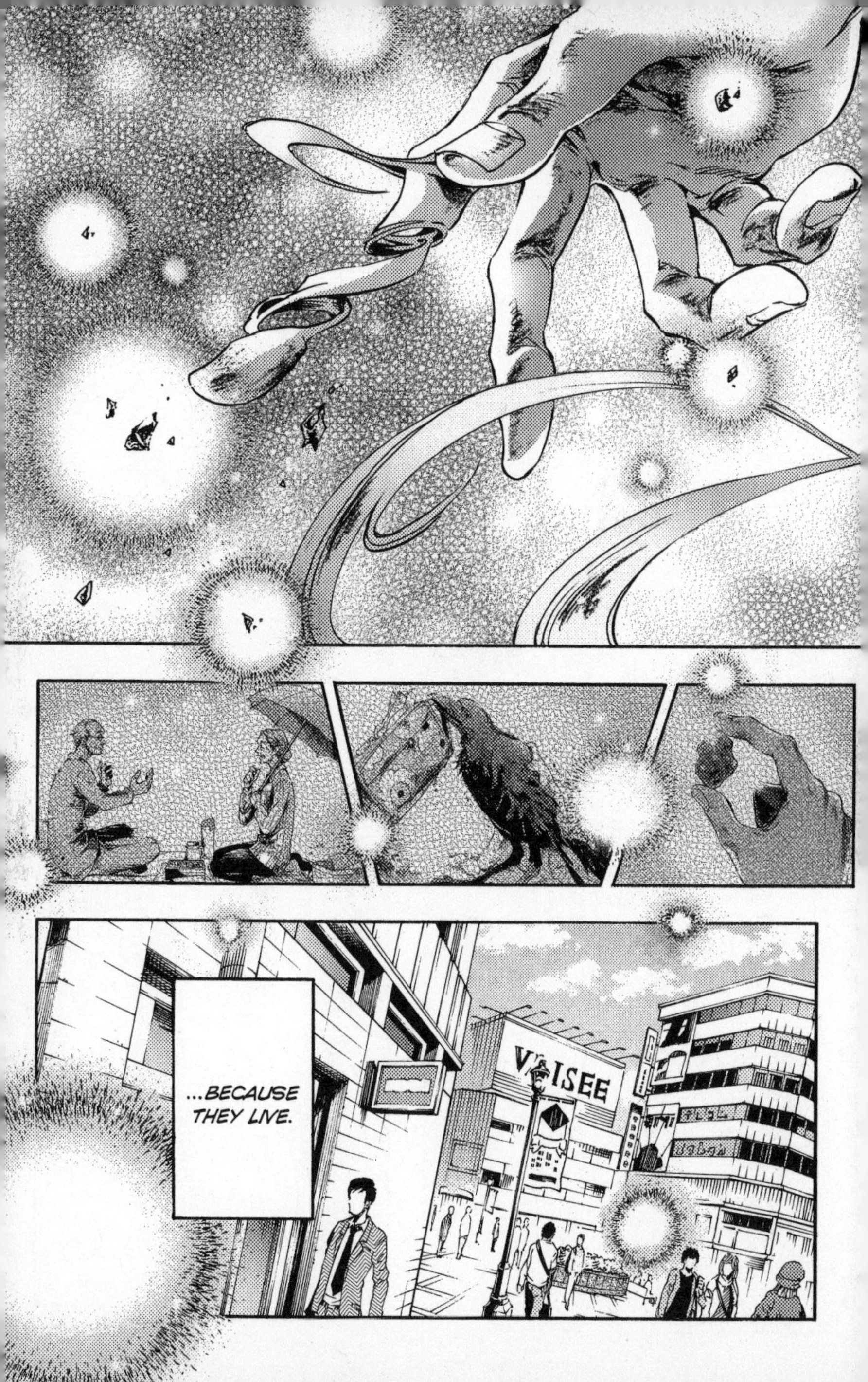
...BECAUSE THEY LIVE.

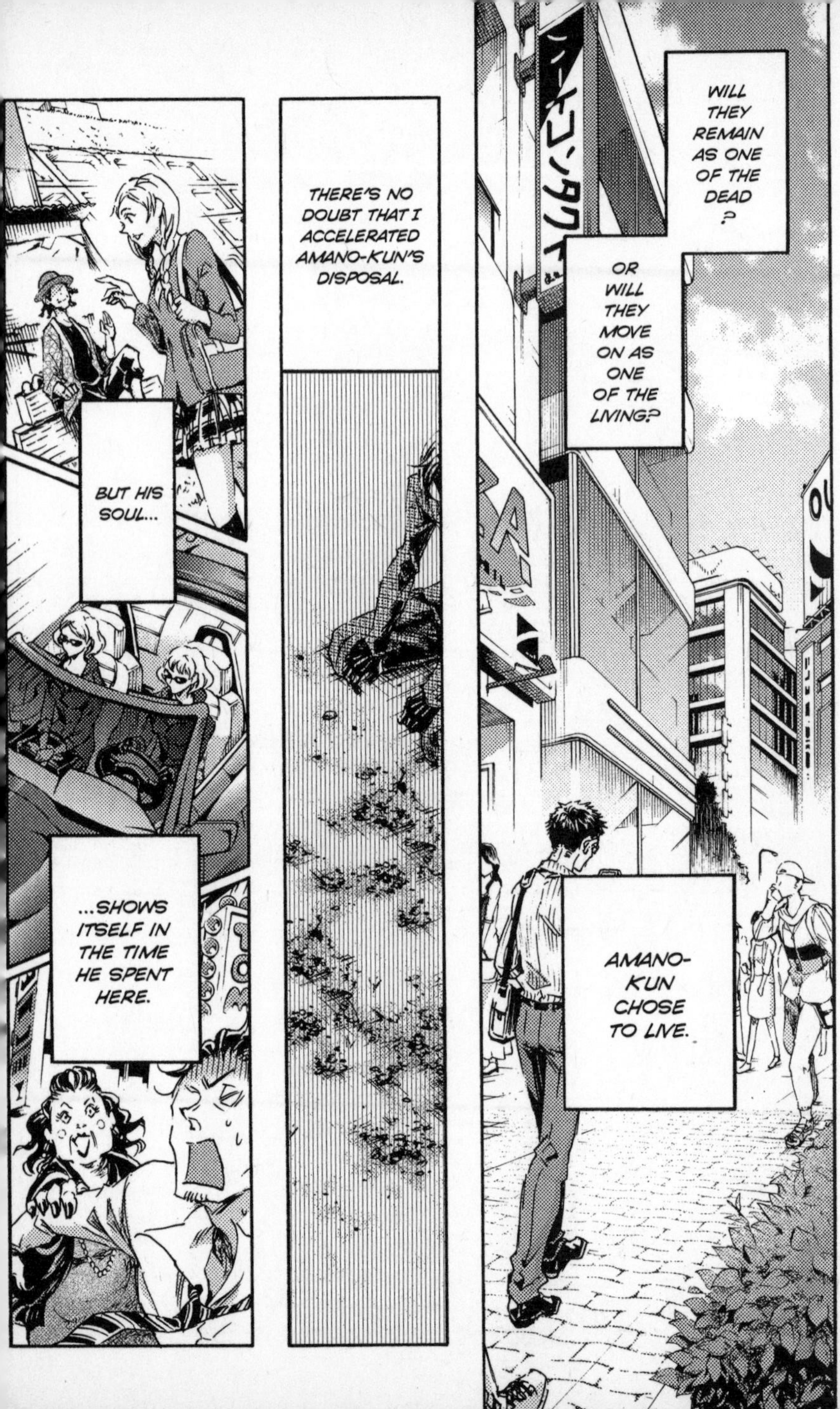
WILL THEY REMAIN AS ONE OF THE DEAD?
OR WILL THEY MOVE ON AS ONE OF THE LIVING?
AMANO-KUN CHOSE TO LIVE.
THERE'S NO DOUBT THAT I ACCELERATED AMANO-KUN'S DISPOSAL.
BUT HIS SOUL...
...SHOWS ITSELF IN THE TIME HE SPENT HERE.

SIGN: Heart Contact

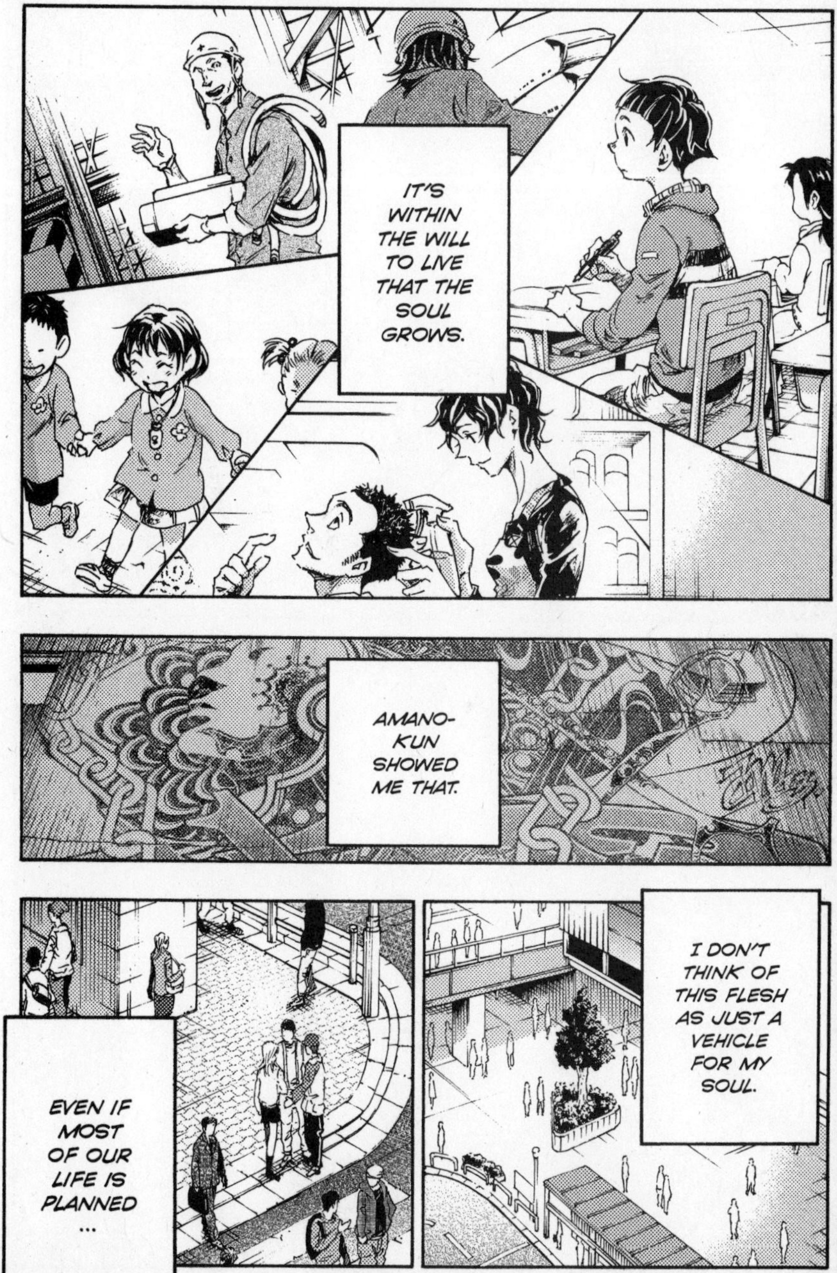
IT'S WITHIN THE WILL TO LIVE THAT THE SOUL GROWS.
AMANO-KUN SHOWED ME THAT.
I DON'T THINK OF THIS FLESH AS JUST A VEHICLE FOR MY SOUL.
EVEN IF MOST OF OUR LIFE IS PLANNED ...

188

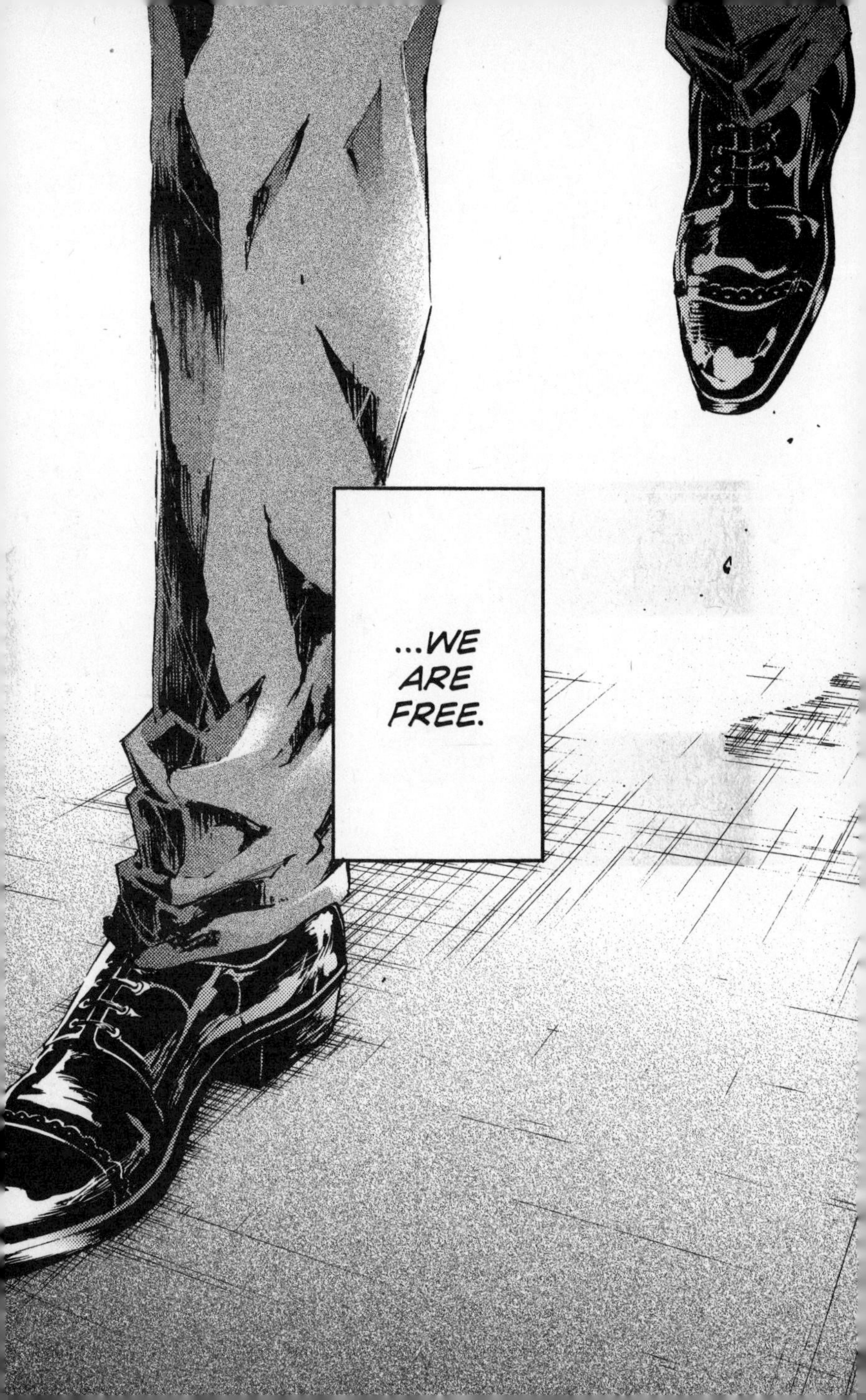
...WE ARE FREE.

gyoo.

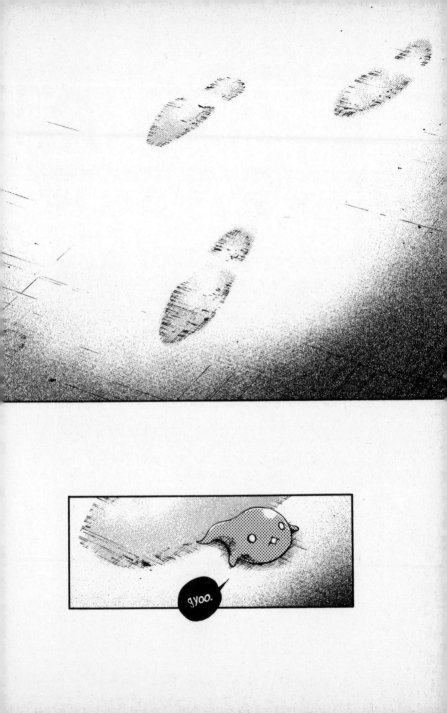

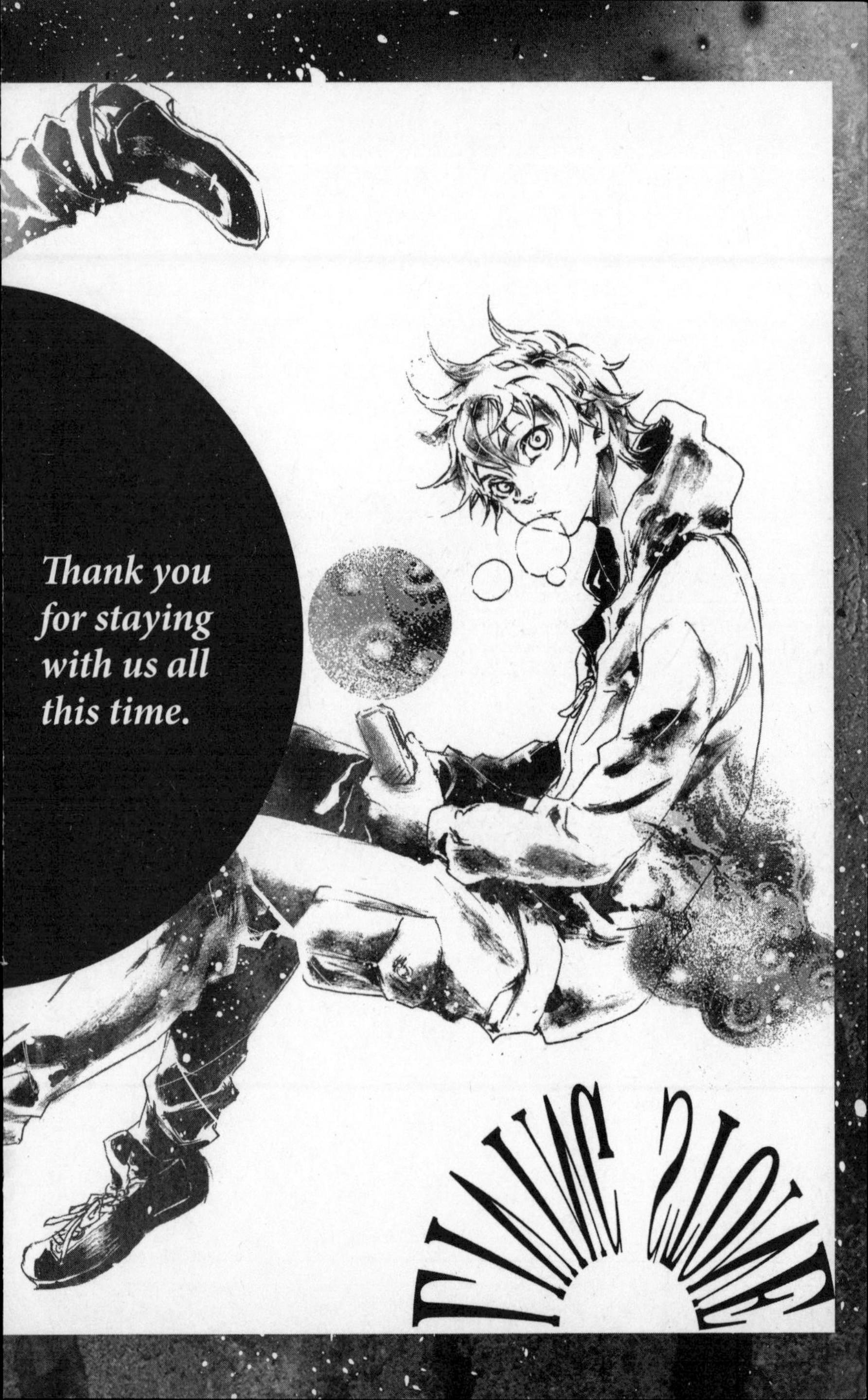
Thank you for staying with us all this time.

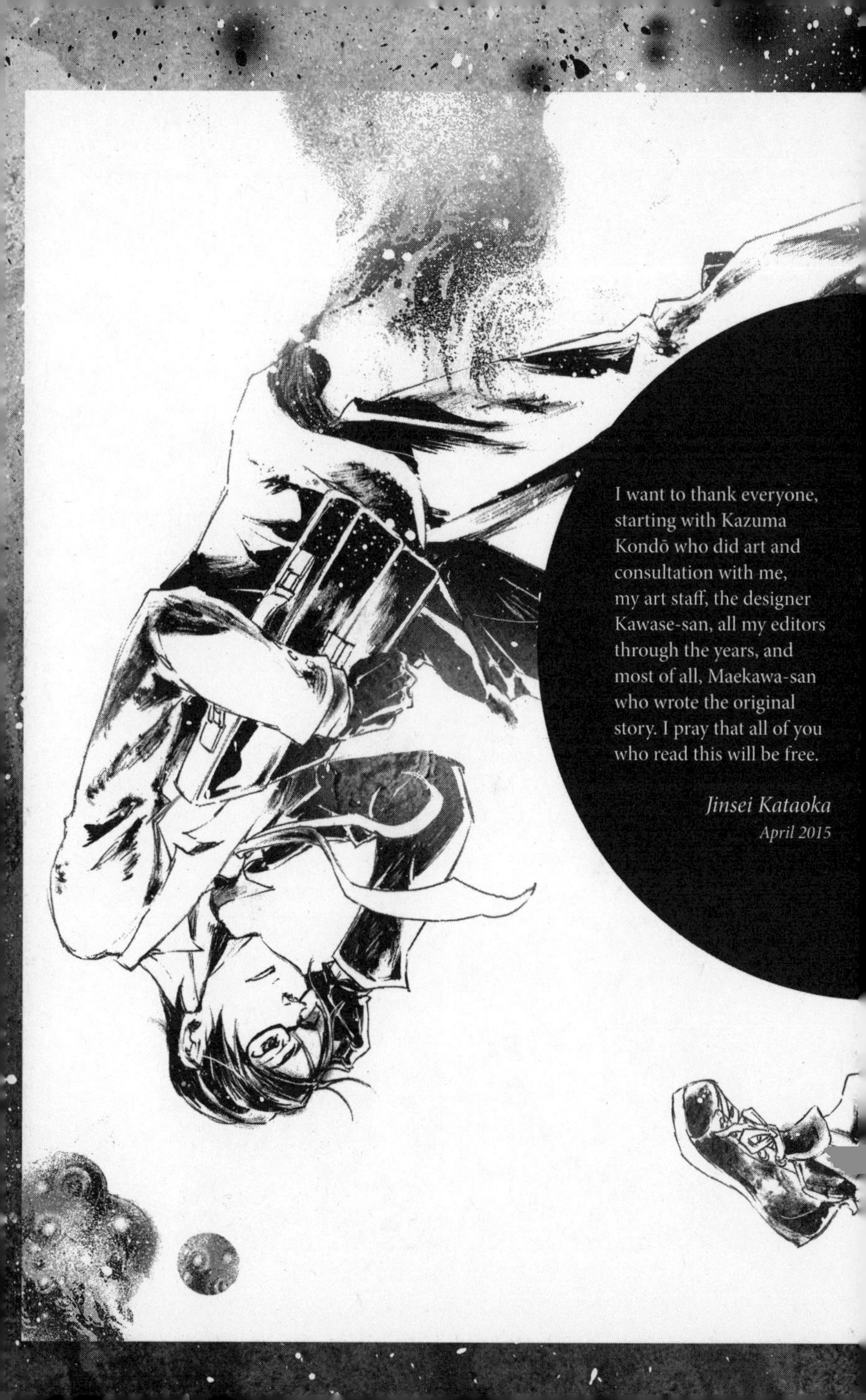

I want to thank everyone, starting with Kazuma Kondō who did art and consultation with me, my art staff, the designer Kawase-san, all my editors through the years, and most of all, Maekawa-san who wrote the original story. I pray that all of you who read this will be free.

Jinsei Kataoka
April 2015

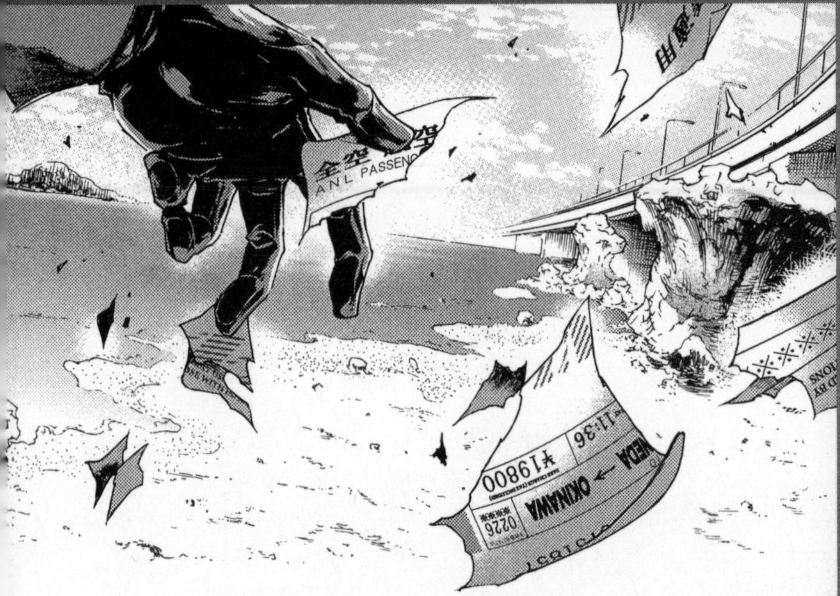
OKINAWA
¥19800
11:36
0226

TRANSLATION NOTES

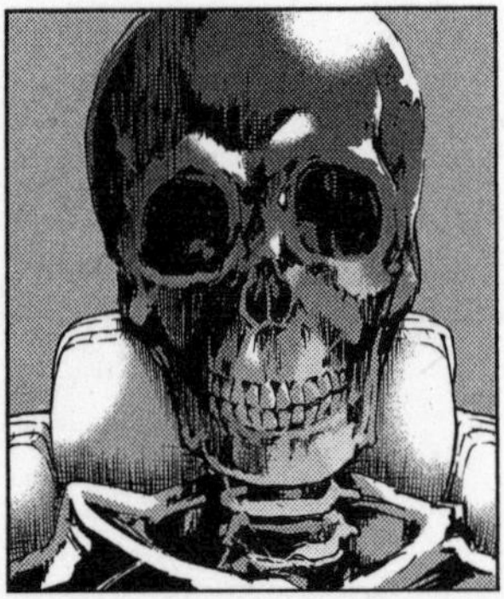

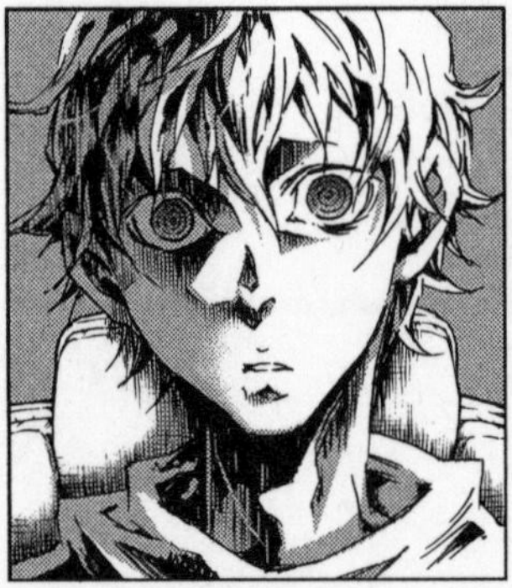

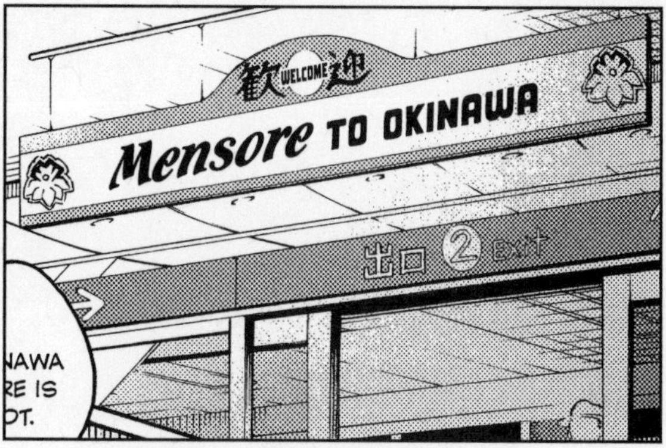
歓 WELCOME 迎
Mensore TO OKINAWA
出口 2 EXIT

MENSORE TO OKINAWA
page 10

Although Okinawa is a part of Japan now, it was originally part of the Ryukyu Kingdom and as such had its own language. Much of that language is still part of what is called the Okinawan dialect. The reader can guess from the sign that *mensore* (men-SO-ray) means "welcome".

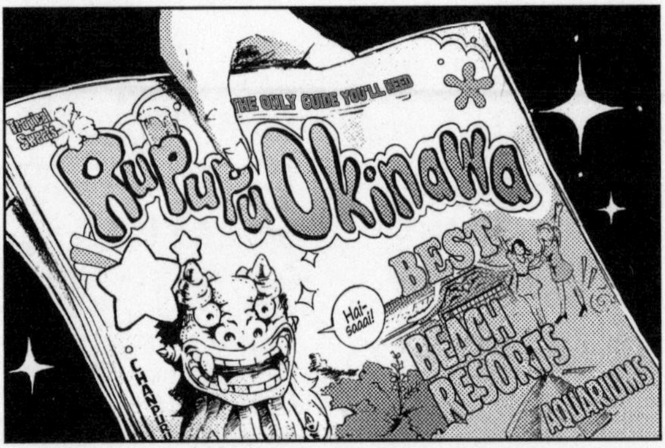
THE ONLY GUIDE YOU'LL NEED
Tropical Sweets
RuPuPu OkinaWa
Hai-saaai!
BEST
BEACH
RESORTS
AQUARIUMS

THE ULTIMATE GUIDE TO OKINAWA
page 11

This *Rurupu* travel guide is the *Livingstone* version of the *Rurubu* series of travel guides. On the cover is a creature from Okinawan folklore saying, "*hai-sai,*" which is Okinawan for, "Hey, how's it going?" "*hai-sai*" is the masculine form of the word; a woman would say, "*hai-tai.*"

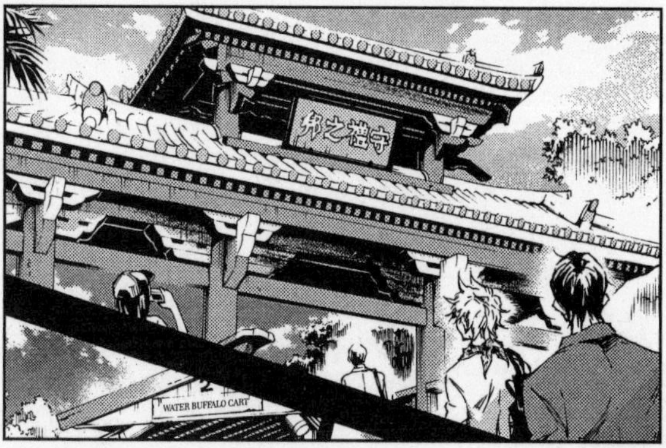
WATER BUFFALO CART

OKINAWA SIGHTSEEING TOUR

page 12

Although Tokieda specifically told Sakurai that this was not a vacation, he and Amano have become tourists, visiting famous Okinawan places in an attempt to find Amano's heritage. The first stop is Shureimon, a gate that was built nearly 500 years ago, back when Okinawa belonged to the Ryukyu Kingdom. Next, they visit the Himeyuri Monument, a tribute to the Himeyuri students, or Lily Corps, who were students and teachers from women's high schools in Okinawa that formed a nursing unit for the Japanese Army during the Battle of Okinawa. After a tour of Taketomi village via water buffalo-drawn carriage, they head off to Pineapple Park in Nago. Then it's off to the Okinawa Churaumi Aquarium, one of the largest aquariums in the world, boasting a tank that houses manta rays and whale sharks. Of course, no one can go to Okinawa without seeing plenty of *shisa*, a Ryukyuan mythological creature that wards off evil spirits, much like the gargoyles of Europe. Finally, they visited Ryukyu Mura Village, where they went to the Habu Center to see the indigenous *habu* pit vipers.

MAYBE WHAT YOU'RE GOING THROUGH IS SOMETHING LIKE AN IDENTITY CRISIS.
WE
'S
?
?

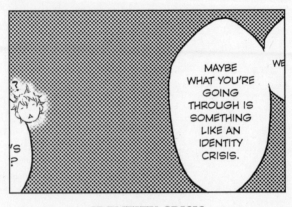

IDENTITY CRISIS

page 13

The Japanese that was used here is actually something called *chūnibyō* (literally, "second year of junior high illness"). Though a sort of identity crisis, it's better identified as the self-conscious stage of puberty, hence its name indicating an illness that takes place in the second year of junior high school (typically ages 13-14). This is not a real illness, but more of a slang term to describe a set of behaviors that occur in teenagers around this time, and in some cases, adults who act like teenagers. The main symptoms are related to delusional thoughts that make the afflicted believe that they are special in some way, such as thinking that they are an alien or have special powers. This could also lead to questions of identity and in turn, an identity crisis.

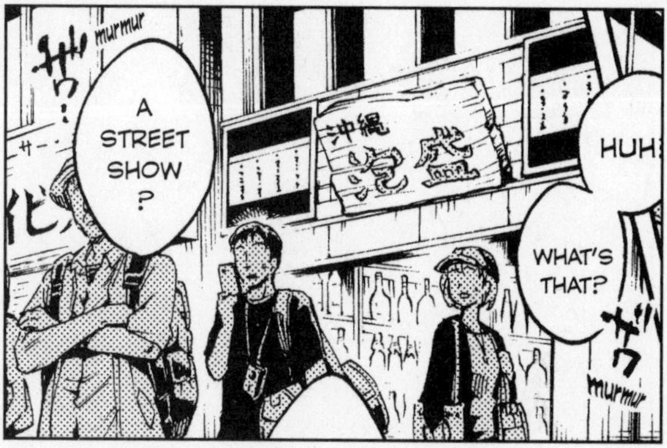
HUH
WHAT'S THAT?
murmur
murmur
A STREET SHOW?

TACO RICE AND AWAMORI

page 26

Both of these are local specialties of Okinawa. Taco rice, as one might expect, is taco-seasoned ground beef on rice, often served with such taco regulars as lettuce, tomato, and shredded cheese. *Awamori* is a distilled liquor made from long-grained Indica rice.

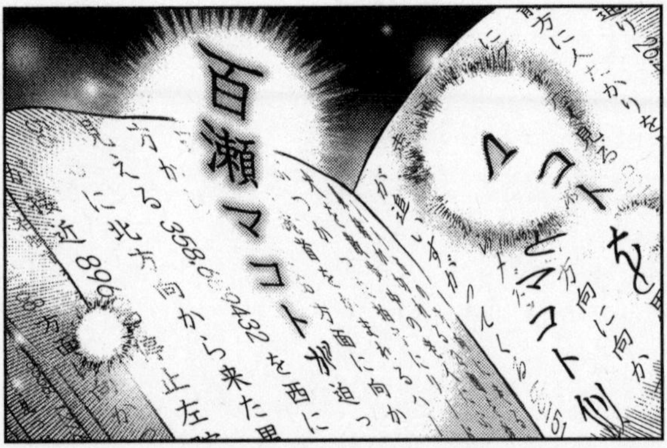
百瀬マコト
マコト

REMOVING SOUL DATA

page 55

Though Azusa later explains what's happening in this scene, some of the details may have been lost on those who are unable to read Japanese. Soga's soul has been opened up and perused like a book—a book that seemingly contains every single piece of information from his life. The Japanese text included reads like a very detailed diary with things like, "…restaurant, drinks beverage, 14-minute break, rides motorized bicycle along Route 58." And in the second panel featuring this "book" it details the scene that just happened, with things like, "…sandal strap breaks, trips into park rail, bumps into old man walking dog, causing him to let go of leash, dog bites him on wrist…"

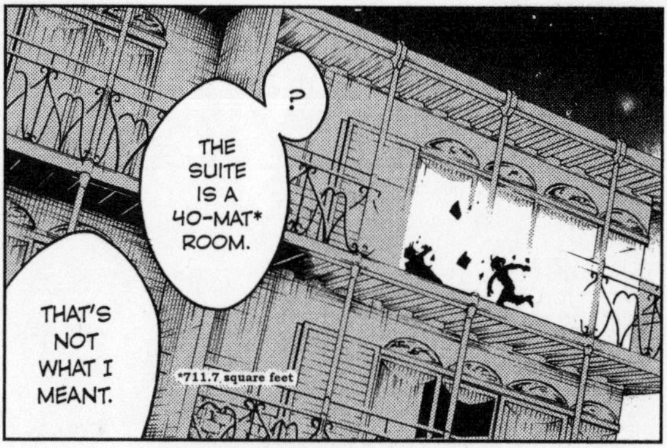
?
THE SUITE IS A 40-MAT* ROOM.
THAT'S NOT WHAT I MEANT.
*711.7 square feet

THE 40-MAT SUITE

page 73

In Japan, the standard measure of floor space is done in *tatami* mats—a type of straw mat that is the standard flooring in traditional Japanese-style rooms. It's a rectangular mat which is twice as long as it is wide, and one is about 17.8 square feet in area.

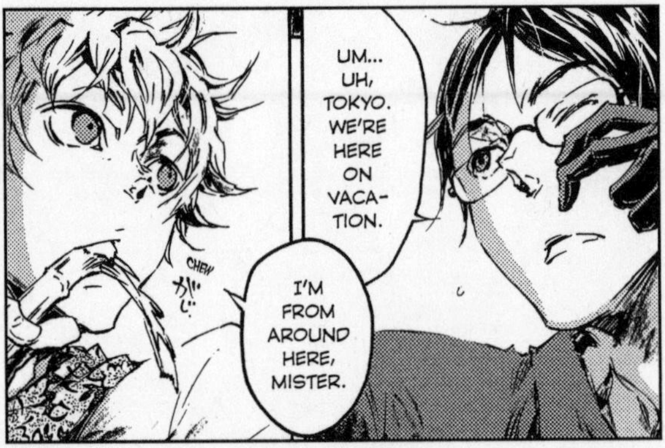
UM... UH, TOKYO. WE'RE HERE ON VACA-TION.
I'M FROM AROUND HERE, MISTER.
CHEW

“MISTER?”
page 104

As Amano and Sakurai get closer to Amano’s roots, his personality begins to change. Normally, Amano refers to himself using the first-person pronoun *ore*, which means “I” but is a very casual way to say it. But here, he uses the more polite *boku*, which also means “I.” Someone who usually uses *ore* will generally switch to *boku* if he wants to show respect to the person he is speaking to, but since Amano has never showed respect to anyone, Sakurai can’t help but wonder about the change. Since both words translate to “I,” translators have to get creative when replicating this change. In this case, it’s possible that Amano’s body remembered using *boku* as a child, so the translators chose to have him call their driver “mister,” as a childlike way of showing respect.

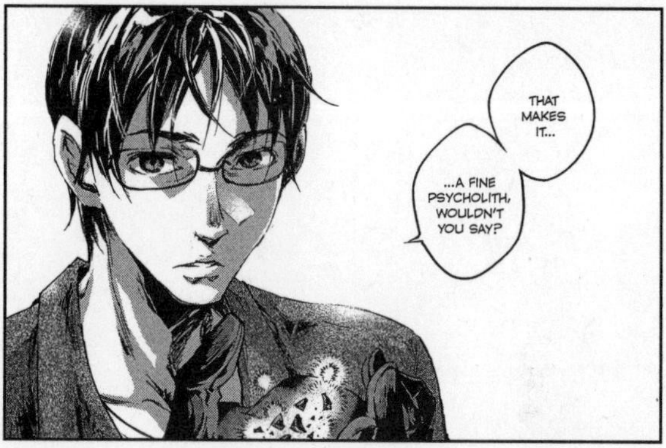
THAT MAKES IT...
...A FINE PSYCHOLITH, WOULDN'T YOU SAY?

AMANO'S PSYCHOLITH

page 183

The word that Sakurai used for "remains", which he then defined as "proof of existence," is *konseki*. Written another way, the word *konseki* is also the Japanese word for "psycholith." In other words, by being a *konseki* (remains), the proof of Amano's existence becomes his *konseki* (psycholith)—his soul.

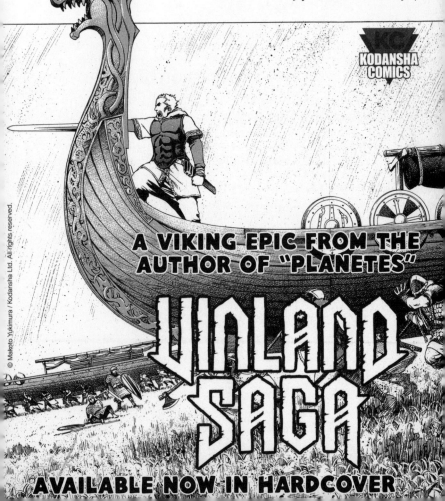

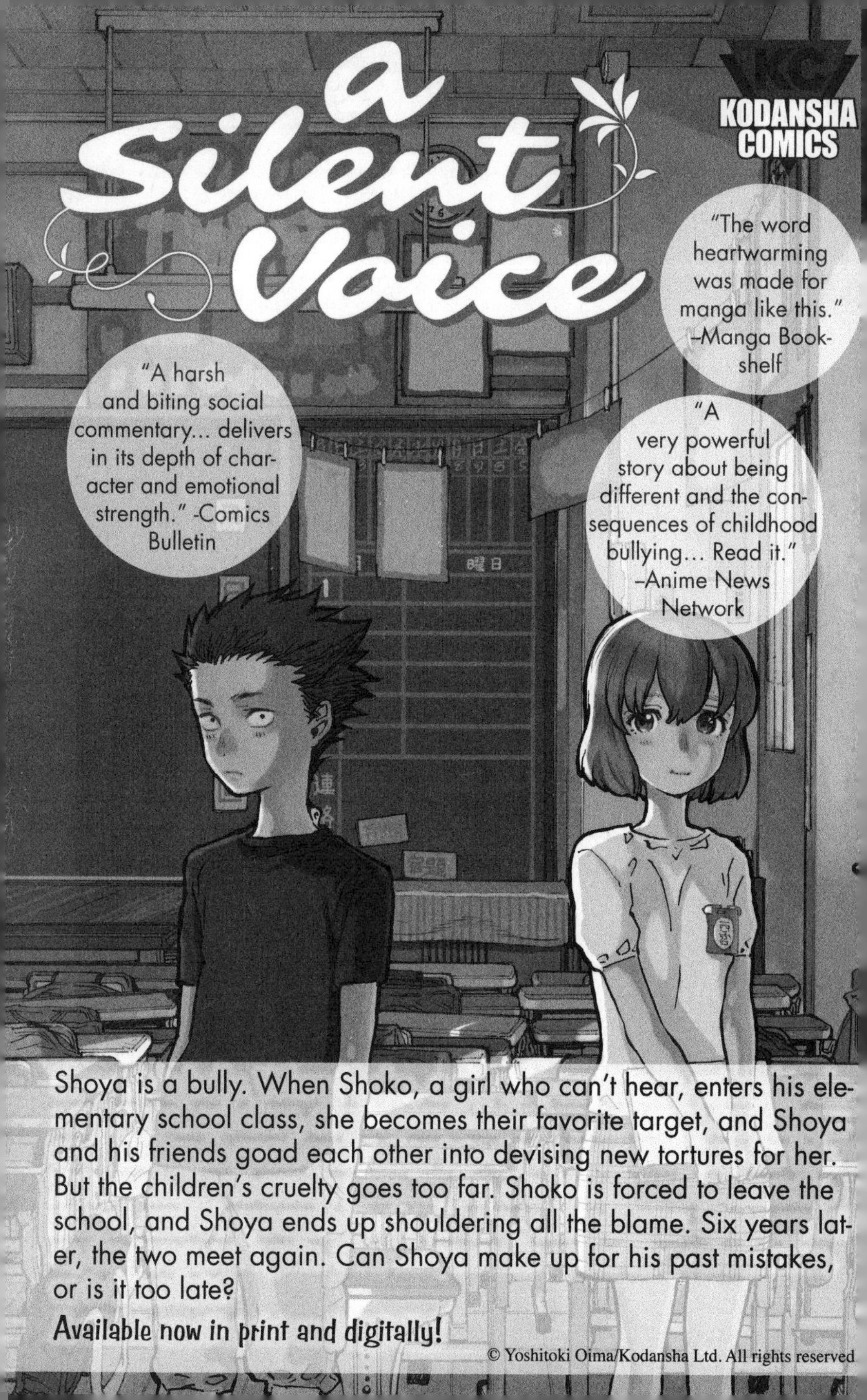
a Silent Voice
KODANSHA COMICS
"The word heartwarming was made for manga like this." –Manga Bookshelf
"A harsh and biting social commentary... delivers in its depth of character and emotional strength." -Comics Bulletin
"A very powerful story about being different and the consequences of childhood bullying... Read it." –Anime News Network
Shoya is a bully. When Shoko, a girl who can't hear, enters his elementary school class, she becomes their favorite target, and Shoya and his friends goad each other into devising new tortures for her. But the children's cruelty goes too far. Shoko is forced to leave the school, and Shoya ends up shouldering all the blame. Six years later, the two meet again. Can Shoya make up for his past mistakes, or is it too late?
Available now in print and digitally!
© Yoshitoki Oima/Kodansha Ltd. All rights reserved

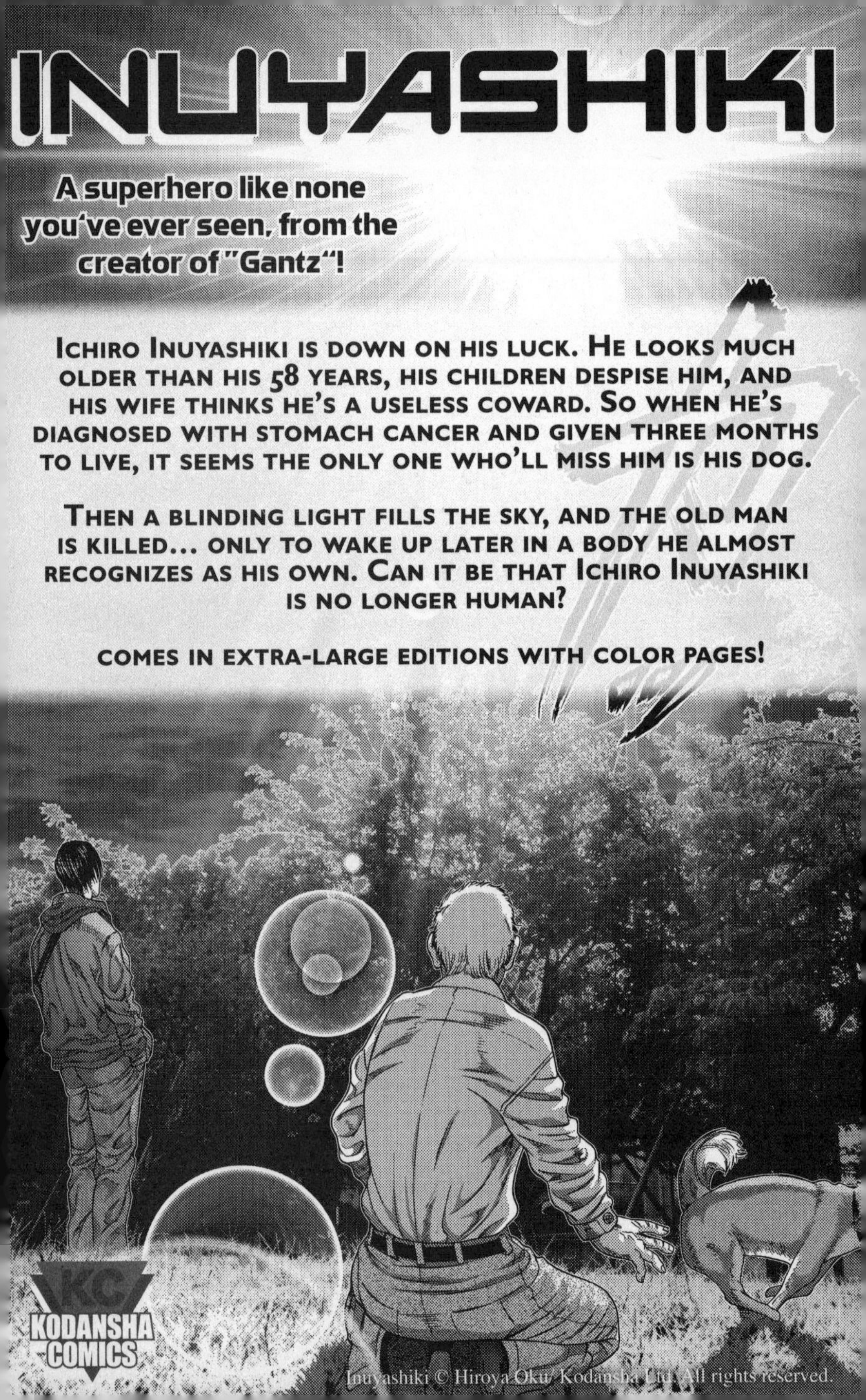
INUYASHIKI
A superhero like none you've ever seen, from the creator of "Gantz"!
Ichiro Inuyashiki is down on his luck. He looks much older than his 58 years, his children despise him, and his wife thinks he's a useless coward. So when he's diagnosed with stomach cancer and given three months to live, it seems the only one who'll miss him is his dog.
Then a blinding light fills the sky, and the old man is killed... only to wake up later in a body he almost recognizes as his own. Can it be that Ichiro Inuyashiki is no longer human?
Comes in extra-large editions with color pages!
KC
KODANSHA COMICS
Inuyashiki © Hiroya Oku/ Kodansha Ltd. All rights reserved.

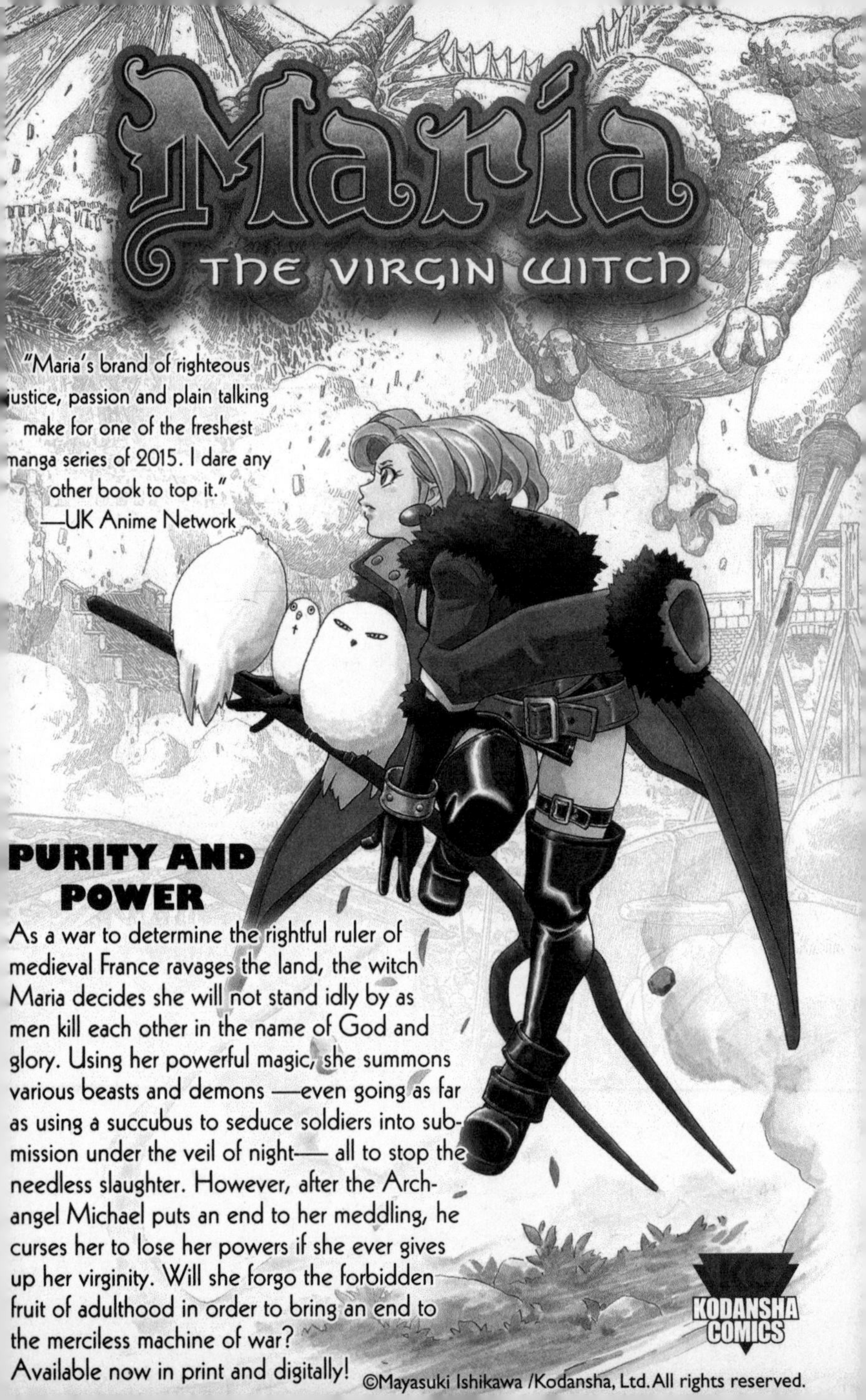
Maria
THE VIRGIN WITCH
"Maria's brand of righteous justice, passion and plain talking make for one of the freshest manga series of 2015. I dare any other book to top it."
—UK Anime Network
PURITY AND POWER
As a war to determine the rightful ruler of medieval France ravages the land, the witch Maria decides she will not stand idly by as men kill each other in the name of God and glory. Using her powerful magic, she summons various beasts and demons —even going as far as using a succubus to seduce soldiers into submission under the veil of night— all to stop the needless slaughter. However, after the Archangel Michael puts an end to her meddling, he curses her to lose her powers if she ever gives up her virginity. Will she forgo the forbidden fruit of adulthood in order to bring an end to the merciless machine of war?
Available now in print and digitally!
KODANSHA COMICS
©Mayasuki Ishikawa /Kodansha, Ltd. All rights reserved.

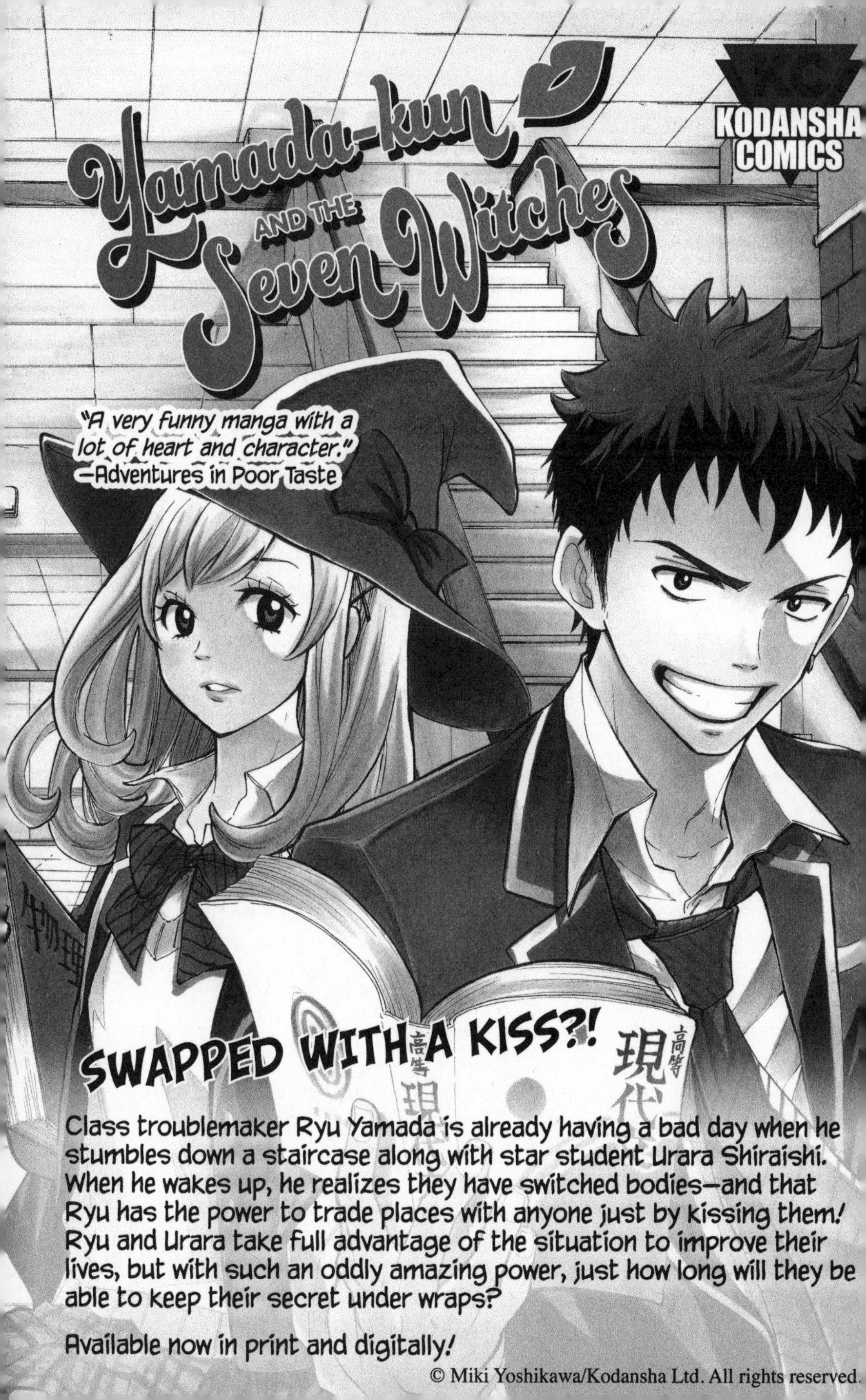
KODANSHA COMICS
Yamada-kun AND THE Seven Witches
"A very funny manga with a lot of heart and character." —Adventures in Poor Taste
SWAPPED WITH A KISS?!
Class troublemaker Ryu Yamada is already having a bad day when he stumbles down a staircase along with star student Urara Shiraishi. When he wakes up, he realizes they have switched bodies—and that Ryu has the power to trade places with anyone just by kissing them! Ryu and Urara take full advantage of the situation to improve their lives, but with such an oddly amazing power, just how long will they be able to keep their secret under wraps?
Available now in print and digitally!
© Miki Yoshikawa/Kodansha Ltd. All rights reserved

Livingstone volume 4 is a work of fiction. Names, characters, places, and incidents are the products of the author's imagination or are used fictitiously. Any resemblance to actual events, locales, or persons, living or dead, is entirely coincidental.

A Kodansha Comics Trade Paperback Original.

Published in the United States by Kodansha Comics, an imprint of Kodansha USA Publishing, LLC, New York.

Publication rights for this English edition arranged through Kodansha Ltd., Tokyo.

First published in Japan in 2015 by Kodansha Ltd., Tokyo, as *Livingstone*, volume 4.

ISBN 978-1-63236-305-3

Printed in the United States of America.

www.kodanshacomics.com

9 8 7 6 5 4 3 2 1

Translation: Alethea Nibley & Athena Nibley
Lettering: Evan Hayden
Editing: Ajani Oloye
Kodansha Comics edition cover design: Phil Balsman